TURKEY HUNTER'S DIGEST

REVISED EDITION

by
Dwain Bland

DBI BOOKS, INC.

Staff

Senior Staff Editors
Harold A. Murtz
Ray Ordorica

Production Manager
John Duoba

Editorial/Production Associate
Jamie L. Puffpaff

Editorial/Production Assistant
Holly J. Porter

Electronic Publishing Manager
Nancy J. Mellem

Electronic Publishing Associate
Robert M. Fuentes

Assistant to the Editor
Deana L. Walker

Managing Editor
Pam Johnson

Publisher
Sheldon L. Factor

About Our Covers

The cover photography used on our front and back covers was supplied by four outstanding outdoor photographers. On the front cover, the strutting gobbler was taken by Mr. Bill Kinney of Ridgeland, Wisconsin. Back cover photography was supplied by: Mr. Lloyd Hill of Heber Springs, Arkansas (fighting gobblers); Mr. Gary Griffen of Griffen Productions, Rhinebeck, New York (gobbler standing on log); and Mr. Mark Picard of Hatfield, Massachuesetts (roosting gobblers at dawn).

The views and opinions of the author expressed herein are not necessarily those of the publisher, and no responsibility for such views will be assumed.

Arms and Armour Press, London, G.B., exclusive licensees and distributor in Britain and Europe, India and Pakistan; Media House Publications, Sandton, Transvaal, exclusive distributor in South Africa and Zimbabwe. Lothian Books, Auckland, exclusive distributor in New Zealand.

ISBN 0-87349-164-5   **Library of Congress Catalog Card #85-73743**

Contents

Foreword

YEARS AGO, I met some men who were impressed (they didn't know any better) with what I knew about turkey hunting. They asked me to write an article for their publication.

"Sure," I said, "no sweat. I'll write you an article about turkey hunting." And I did, and I sent it to them.

I was mad when that thing came on the newsstand. The only thing about the article that was "me" was the photo. Those guys thought my article stunk.

I thought, "I'll show you-all. I'll learn to write."

I'm still learning.

My turkey hunting experience was why DBI asked me to do these books. They presumed that anyone who had done so much of it had surely absorbed a little something along the way. Like the typing, I am also still learning some things about turkey hunting.

During an average year, I'll hunt at least three of the five bearded and spurred wild turkeys. Some years I'll hunt all five—the Eastern, Osceola, Rio Grande, Merriam and Gould's, a mountain turkey found high in Old Mexico's Sierra Madre mountains.

These days everyone wants to be a wild turkey guide. Those words seem to have a mystique. I suppose that if a person says he is a wild turkey guide, it makes him some sort of super woodsman, world-class caller, shotgun artist and public relations executive, all rolled into one. I've been a wild turkey guide for longer'n some of you've been born, and all it's made me is tired. I still do some of it when I get to feeling foolish. One winter I'll guide for Rio Grandes and Easterns; the next spring I may take after Merriams, Osceolas and Gould's. I mention these so you can get an idea of how much hunting I do, and how different it can be, switching from one terrain to another so much. Traveling has taught me about all the kinds of people we have in this great country, what they do for a living, how they farm, cut timber, catch channel catfish out of the Mississippi, and a jillion other things. I've learned that what's considered OK insofar as hunting ethics in one section of the country may well be thought of as potshooting slaughter in another. A good guide knows all these things *before* he hunts in a new and strange area.

Throughout this book I have tried to impress on the reader the need to educate the young people about hunting. The American hunter wants to keep part of America wooded with fresh, running streams, the country alive with birds, animals and even snakes, too. The anti-hunting movement thinks we are the enemy when, in reality, we are trying to stem the losing battle of habitat loss. Unless the country changes its ways drastically, the anti-hunters will have won their fight. There won't be anything but shopping malls, interstate highways, oil wells, strip mines and clearcut forests. The hunter will be gone. And so will all that he stands for—wilderness America.

Recently I was asked, "What qualitites do you look for in a turkey hunter?" Just as different as two people's fingerprints are, no two people are alike. I like to think turkey hunters have some manners, and use them around children and women, and even among themselves. My greatest admiration is for folks who learn from what they see and hang in there when the going gets tough. I don't mind if a person has a shot of whiskey, just so they wait until after hunting time to do it.

Other qualities a person should possess for being a better-than-average turkey hunter are determination, time, patience and a knack for being in the right place at the right time. Let me explain some of these a bit further.

Turkey hunters gotta have time—an old cliche well known among older turkey hunters. It hasn't got anything to do with alarm clocks, but is just the opposite. A turkey does not wear a wristwatch and the hunter shouldn't either. Forget the time. Just hunt. You will become better for it.

Patience. Do you know what the dictionary definition of "patience" is? *The ability to wait without pain.* A doctor's patients wait with pain, but the turkey hunter must wait without it. Can you wait without pain, for an hour, as a gobbler tears down the woods with his gobbling, while

Determination, time, patience and a lot of hard work—all these are needed to become a better than average turkey hunter. And the author oughta know. He's been doing it right for more than thirty years.

mosquitoes make your face a donor to the local blood bank? The gobbler has so much patience you almost never do see him.

Patience should be lumped together with luck. I greatly admire those people who successfully play the stock market, because they must have some amount of luck. Or do they? Too often luck is nothing but hard work. Much of my good luck, or being in the right place at the right time, was nothing but my hunting hard with a good portion of patience thrown in.

A turkey hunter must have complete confidence in his abilities, because the turkey is working constantly to erode this idea, and unless a person has the confidence, there will be many days when he may as well stay at home. To get this "sure of hisself," the hunter should study the wild turkey, both through books and by getting out into the woods during the off-seasons. The hunter should practice with turkey calls, put in time on the shooting range, and compare notes with other hunters.

Being at the right place at the right time is just another term for hunting alot and hunting hard. That's what it takes. Being in the right place when it counts. I can recall times when I've traveled a strange woods, didn't know if I was even inside of a mile of a turkey, and hunted from daylight until dark, but then made a kill. I found just enough sign to tell me there could be turkeys in those woods if the birds had not wandered off some place. Having the time, I simply stuck with it until I found turkeys.

And on the other hand, there have been times when I would no more than get into an area and I'd bump into turkeys. Hunting new and strange areas can be this way. Folks who hunt the same old place day after day never face such challenges so they quit thinking. Knowing what the birds have done in the past, they fall back on that knowledge. And though each hunt and each turkey is different, hunting on the same old terrain lulls the hunter into hunting in a trance-like state. He no longer learns; he's just going through the motions.

I have tried to make this book readable to folks who have never hunted wild turkeys. It hasn't got all the "turkey talk" that us turkey hunters use.

Hope you'll have some laughs reading this. Hang tough, hunt hard, but never lose sight of having a good time. But if you like new horizons and want to put some challenge back in your turkey hunting, then traveling to hunt the various subspecies will be the medicine for you. It's your choice.

Dwain Bland

When Columbus Discovered the Turkey

HANGING ON THE WALL behind my desk is a large, elegant reproduction of an old photo of a gang of hunters from the late 1880s, at least so says the handwritten notation on the back. Truly, it's a scene from "the good old days." Meat poles are loaded down with wild turkeys, a few deer, coyotes and small game. It was taken in the region where I live, where I grew up, in northern and western Oklahoma, which was later scene to the ravages of the Dust Bowl. From all accounts, Oklahoma was the last great stronghold for the huge flocks of wild turkeys our ancestors found in this country.

Undoubtedly, Christopher Columbus' first contact was with the gorgeous Ocellated turkey, which inhabits the Yucatan Peninsula and possibly jungles of various Central American countries. It is the only bird of the genus *Agriocharis*. Anyone who studies this bird will find its name spelled one of two ways—Occelated or Ocellated—and I've seen one version just as many times as the other. The Ocellated is different from the bird many of us know as a wild turkey in that it has no beard; does not "gobble" in the sense that we characterize gobbling; nor is it as large in size as the other species. This tropical bird does, however, have very well developed spurs. My old friend, Dave Harbour, long gone now, always thought the Ocellated to be the world's most beautiful bird. Dave hunted them all and wrote about his jungle turkey hunts.

But for us dyed-in-the-wool turkey nuts, there must be a beard on a turkey, so we're mainly interested in the world's bearded and spurred wild turkeys, the birds of the genus *Meleagris gallopavo*. (It is interesting to note that many natives in the tropical rain forest of Central America, who have contact only with the Ocellated, call the bird "pavo," the last four letters of *gallopavo*, yet the bird is of the before-mentioned non-bearded genus *Agriocharis*.)

Nobody knows how the turkey came by its name. Perhaps as good a guess as any is that the explorers, upon landing on our shores, thought they found a new route to the Far East and had landed on the coast of Turkey. When they carted some birds back to Spain, some country lad said, "Hey, those are turkeys," and it stuck.

Cortez and Coronado, while seducing the lands of Mexico, found the Indians had domesticated the wild birds. You can give these two explorers credit for shipping the world's first turkeys back to Spain. These birds found their way across most of Europe and, in time, became forerunners of the turkey in France, then England, and later coming back to the North American East Coast with the pilgrims. The wild turkeys encountered here by the pilgrims were true Eastern wild turkeys; the ones they brought from England had as their ancestors the presumed-extinct species found far south in Mexico, the bird known at one time as the Mexican turkey.

The Indians of the Southwest and those inhabiting the Isthmus of Mexico found the turkey, both domestic and wild, to be a main source of food. Other North American tribes would not eat the birds due to "culture" beliefs. Some warriors thought eating turkey meat would make them run from the enemy, as they'd so often seen the birds flee from them.

Apaches were known to use the turkey's yelps and gobbles when signaling each other, whereas the Cherokee considered the gobble the death cry, used in battle only when death appeared to be the only outcome. "Cherokee Bill," an infamous renegade outlaw of the old Indian nation, in attempting to break out of jail, somehow got his hands on a revolver. Later, a lawman at the scene made the remark, "...above the din of the shooting could be heard the nerve-racking gobbling of Cherokee Bill."

(Below) Turkey hunting pictures from the good old days tell of times when turkey populations were limitless. Back then, the birds were found in great flocks, particularly across much of the Southwest, what is today parts of Texas, New Mexico, Oklahoma, Arkansas and Arizona.

(Above) Old-time accounts of hunts made back during the days when the country was unsettled tell of the vast numbers of wild turkeys found in many parts of the United States. General William Strong's vivid account in his *Canadian River Hunt* gives the reader an insight into the hunting methods used during that period—methods completely illegal today.

(Right) All turkey hunters should read the old accounts of what turkey hunting was like many years ago. You'll discover we now have turkeys in many regions where there were none before the modern trap-and-transplant programs. To many an old-time hunter, killing a wild and wary old gobbler was very close to a miracle.

(Below) The author has found many uses for both the wild turkey's beard and spurs. He is a blackpowder traditionalist, and blackpowder hunting, if done in the traditional sense, involves much decorating of both clothing and weapons.

It's said that many a settler was decoyed to his death by an Indian holding aloft a dried turkey tail from behind bushes, imitating a strutting gobbler. The Pawnee shot a settler in 1876, having mistaken him, they said, "for a big turkey."

But Indians weren't the only ones who knew about turkeys. Daniel Morgan, at the Battle of Saratoga, used a turkey call to rally his band of riflemen. Nor were the fairer sex excluded. Belle Starr, the gal outlaw, riding home one evening from the trial of one of her husband's cousins for horse stealing, which was the family business, was peeled off her horse with a "load of turkey shot" by Edgar Watson. He took her guns as she laid on the ground and shot her "til she was dead." Finished. Somewhere afterwards I read that Watson was using No. 5s. By gosh, he knew his turkeys. I've been using No. 5s on lots of stuff besides turkeys—deer, hogs, but *no women*.

During my wanderings in Old Mexico, and throughout the Southwest, I've noticed many references to the turkey in paintings on pottery, arrow fletchings, and the use of feathers in decorating Indian dress and ceremonial objects. Drawings of turkeys have been found on the walls of caves and in some cliff dwellings, and bone awls made from turkey bones have

been found. Turquoise was known among Indians as "turkey stone," because of its resemblance to the color of a turkey's head.

The Comanche used the hair of the wild turkey's beard in making the "hair roach," the scalp adornment so often seen in old photos of wild Indians and held in place by an eagle feather or a handmade silver roach pin. The one in my possession

From the number of turkeys I saw and the noise and rush of fluttering wings in the forest below us, I should estimate there were thousands...

Canadian River Hunt

was made for me by a Comanche and is from the beards of turkeys I killed with vintage muzzleloaders. Undoubtedly, I'm the only hunter today who can make such a claim.

Wild turkeys were so plentiful then that today many landmarks bear reference to wild turkey numbers. An endless variety of Turkey Creeks, Turkey Point, Turkey Feather Pass, Tur-

key Foot Ranch, Gobblers Knob, just to name a few, can be found across the country. The turkey track brand for marking cattle is undoubtedly registered in numerous western states. A foundry here in northern Oklahoma has such a moniker—The Turkey Track Foundry.

Anyone who studies western history, the cavalry, the Indian Wars and the early settlement of this country will come across many stories about huge flocks of wild turkeys and the shooting of these birds. Among my book collection is a small cased copy of a hardback reproduction, *Canadian River Hunt*, by General Wm. E. Strong, a book of notes made by Gen. Strong when he accompanied a group of military buddies on a turkey hunt into the Indian Territory. The book includes a large map encompassing Oklahoma, parts of west Texas, southern Kansas, etc. I'm told only 1000 copies were printed. Let me quote:

"Hurry up, Strong, and eat your dinner," Sheridan said, as I dismounted, "I have discovered an immense turkey roost, and will give you rare sport tonight..." The roost was an immense one. I should judge it was a quarter of a mile in width, by a mile or more in length, lying on both sides of the creek mentioned. From the number of turkeys I saw and the noise and rush of fluttering wings in the forest below us, I should estimate there were thousands...

Numerous local wild turkey sightings brought about the great many Turkey Creeks scattered across the country today. This one, which feeds into a large stream and becomes simply Turkey Creek, lies just south of the author's home in Oklahoma. Others are found within sixty miles of here.

Should you ever be hunting up along the Cimarron and bump into this guy, then, my friend, you are probably tresspassing. John Adams is the ranch boss of the Adams ranch, which straddles the Oklahoma and Kansas state lines. You won't meet a finer man if you're on friendlier terms. But like many ranchers, folks trespassing aren't welcome anywhere. There's wild turkeys the full length of the Cimarron—Merriams on its upper reaches and Rio Grandes along the rest. Down where it dumps into the Arkansas River, it's not too far to Eastern wild turkey country.

The wild turkey almost went the way of the passenger pigeon, but thankfully before it became extinct, a few states and some dedicated men decided that if something wasn't done to stop the year-round slaughter the turkey might not survive. Game departments were formed, and laws set in place, to prevent this from happening. Today, with men like Frank Huebert, a long-time veteran with the Oklahoma Game Department, we can rest assured that there will always be turkeys to hunt, so long as there remains suitable habitat for the birds.

Both Generals Sheridan and Strong were toting nine-pound 10-gauge guns, breechloaders, double-barreled, using shells containing five drams of blackpowder and 1½ ounces of No. 1 shot. (A poor choice, but they probably had very little to choose from.) Their guide, the famous Ben Clark, was carrying a Winchester rifle, with which he could supposedly blow a turkey's head off. Range was not mentioned so perhaps Clark could if the birds were near. If not, then such feats smack of what was termed back then as "gilding the lily."

The usual method of such hunting was to journey to the roosting area in the late afternoon, then after the birds had flown up into the tree and it was dark enough for the men to slip beneath them, the shooting would begin. Guns became rather hot after continued shooting, but the end of the hunt was usually due to running out of shells. Six of Strong's stalwarts bagged a total of only nineteen birds that first night, a very poor showing considering that Strong went through two boxes of shells; apparently the others were similarly prepared. The problem was that these turkeys were sitting at the top of huge old cottonwoods. Besides it was dark. The area became known as Sheridan's Roost due to his continued trips to it and

(Right) Numerous Indian tribes used the feathers of the wild turkey in their daily lives, often as decoration on clothing. Sarah Boyd, of Delaware ancestry, the author's niece, is crowned with a single tail feather. Though only ten years of age, Sarah is an accomplished dancer, taking part each summer in Oklahoma's summer pow-wows and tribal rituals.

(Left) Many Indian artifacts, like this religous piece, were adorned with the feathers of wild turkeys. Indians from the far Southwest were also known to have made blankets from turkey feathers.

"Cricket" Ward, a full-blood Comanche, wears a hair roach made from the beards of wild gobblers all bagged by the author.

Today's turkey hunter can very possibly find artifacts from long-lost generations of hunters. This small jar, from the mountains of northern Mexico, was probably made by the extinct Paquime tribe. A basic agricultural society, the Paquime may also have domesticated the wild turkeys found in those regions, the birds we know today as the Gould wild turkey. The light tan arrowhead is one the author picked up on a hunt down in the state of Durango. Who knows, perhaps the head was once mounted to a shaft that was shot at a wild gobbler.

The Gould's wild turkey inhabited what we know today as Mexico. These Mexican men shown on a hunting trip back into the Sierra Madres tell of Gould's gobblers that weighed thirty to forty pounds back in the days when the mountains were home to thousands of the birds. Sadly, all of the virgin pine forests have been completely wiped out, and today all that remains of this excellent turkey country are huge stumps and rusting ironworks from ancient sawmills.

Old Western lawman Bill Tilghman once remarked he'd seen cedar logs eight inches thick worn halfway through from turkeys stepping on them as they followed a well-used turkey trail. Can't say that this is much of a comparison, but this cedar log lies across a trail in the same region. Hopefully, years from now wild turkeys will still be passing this way.

Lennis Rose looks at a sign hanging on a gate in Texas. *Guajolote* (pronounced *wha-ho-LO-tay*) is commonly used in Old Mexico to denote turkeys. There are probably other ranches by the same name, and no doubt many that go by the name Turkey Track Ranch. I recall a ranch deep in Mexico's state of Chihuahua with a painted sign above the gate, *El Coconito*, which means *little turkey.*

you'll find it so listed along the North Canadian River in Northwest Oklahoma on today's maps. I've hunted up and down the river below this area, as well as Sheridan's Roost, having killed birds there, for years. This is along the old wagon road from Camp Supply, today known as Fort Supply, and old Fort Reno, which was a cavalry post near what today is El Reno, Oklahoma. In another incident, a company of troopers, going into bivouac for the night, suddenly found themselves

What God and Nature had taken a millenia to sculpture, mankind and civilization had wrought asunder—in a very short span of 400 years.

overrun with turkeys going to roost, so began blasting away. Suddenly one of the soldiers' horses dropped dead, felled by a rifle ball intended for a wild turkey. Such was the Old West.

With settlement of the Old West came the lawman. One famous lawman, U.S. Marshall Bill Tilghman, in his youth killed turkeys for the Ellsworth, Kansas market, selling the

birds for 75 cents each. At Fort Cobb, in the 1800s, the Indians could trade a wild turkey for a pound of flour or salt. However, birds on the Chicago market, far away from any sizable turkey population, might bring as much as $5. But, like the passenger pigeon and the buffalo, the wild turkey was on the road to doom. Market hunting took its toll—the huge flocks disappeared and the long strands of woods fell silent. Birds were killed by the wagonload. And so what if they spoiled before getting to market; there were more where those came from. Bill Tilghman once made the observation that he'd seen cedar logs eight inches wide lying across turkey paths that were worn halfway through from so many birds feet having passed over them. (If you know anything about the iron-like toughness of a dead cedar log, you know this meant one heckuva lot of turkeys over several centuries.)

Thankfully, wild turkeys never were completely wiped out—stragglers held on in wild hard-to-reach areas. At long last we came to the realization that if the country didn't legislate game laws, and back them up with the firm hand of a game warden, America's hunting was going to be a thing of the past.

What God and Nature had taken a millenia to sculpture, mankind and civilization had wrought asunder—in a very short span of 400 years.

But turkeys are tough.

Under the Stars and Stripes flying from our camp flagpole, Lennis Rose admires a young Merriam bagged in the old-time fashion, with a long smokepole caplock rifle. Lennis often hunts in old-time clothing and is usually toting a side-by-side flintlock shotgun. To many of us who hunt in this fashion, turkey hunting has taken on a new reverence, carrying us back in time to the days when all hunters lugged heavy longrifles or scatterguns through the woods. Camouflage clothing hadn't even been thought of, much less the word.

Turkey numbers are up to a point that hunting them is allowed all across the United States. There are open seasons in all of the forty-eight contiguous states plus Hawaii. Many of us older hunters can easily recall when half of the country didn't allow turkey hunting.

(Above and right) The American Indian used both the iron trade point, ordinarily made from the rim of a wagon wheel, and the traditional flint arrowpoint for hunting turkeys. Many Indians had no access to flint, so they had to trade for it. The author has only hunted turkeys a few times with a bow, killing one bird with each style of point. Tied with sinew, the flint-pointed arrows were made by Comanches from stone supplied by the author. The bow used is a short Indian-style made from *bois d'arc* (pronounced *bow dark*). This is the same tree also known as Osage orange or hedgeapple.

2

The Big Four—
the United States' Wild
and Bearded Turkeys

YOU'LL FIND FOUR kinds of wild turkeys in the U.S.—the Eastern, Osceola, Rio Grande, and the Merriam. These four birds make up the so-called Grand Slam of turkey hunting.

Now, anyone who hasn't hunted wild turkeys, or even hunters who have never hunted but one subspecie, would probably take a look at any or all of these birds, if each were placed side-by-side, and think there isn't any difference in them. They all look alike. And, to an unpracticed eye they do.

But, physically each subspecie differs from the others. Over the centuries each specie has adapted to its terrain and as a result its physical characteristics have altered to allow it to live more easily in that environment. For example, the plumage has evolved into hues that allow the bird to better fit into its surroundings and camouflages it from the eyes of its natural enemies.

Let's look at each specie—beginning with the subspecie which inhabits the least amount of range, the Osceola wild turkey.

The Osceola Wild Turkey

This bird was named after the great chief of the Seminoles, Osceola. If a hunter wants to pursue a pure-blood Osceola, then I'd suggest staying south of a line drawn east-to-west across south Florida at Orlando. Birds found north of this line may be pure Osceola blood, but often as not they may have a bit of Eastern blood, the Easterns inhabiting all the country to the north. Just because the bird has less barring in the wings, doesn't mean it's a pure blood Osceola. I've bagged some birds as far northwest as Copiah County, Mississippi, over

near the Mississippi River that showed the distinct lesser primary wing feather barring associated with the Osceola. And, I'm talking more and more with other hunters throughout the South who have made the same observation. This is disturbing, as this cross-breeding seems to be spreading and overlapping the ranges of all the various wild turkey subspecies. I ponder whether in a couple decades that there will be any of the four pure strains left. Trapping and transplanting of wild turkeys across statelines has set up this situation, and although this has helped to open up the sport of wild turkey hunting in all of the "old 48," it's also brought about the intermixing of the subspecies.

Anyhow, if the desire is a pure Osceola, then hunt southern Florida. The Osceola is a gorgeous bird. Lots of gold and greenish hues with very little white on its wings distinguish this breed as well as a long tail to help them steer well when flying through thick creek swamp or oak hummocks. No other of the subspecies has such well-formed spurs, often very long and needle sharp on the older gobblers. Long legs enable the bird to utilize its watery habitat, and if you're lucky enough to spend lots of time with the Osceolas, you'll see them wade into water all the way up to the lower leg feathering.

One of my greatest memories centers on cranking up an old bird one morning that took to gobbling like crazy at my pleadings. But, as a huge pond laid across the pasture toward the hummocks where he was standing, I truthfully just cranked him up to hear him gobble. Wasn't any way he'd come over to where I was, too much water, and besides I assumed there were plenty of hens over there, too. I'd dealt

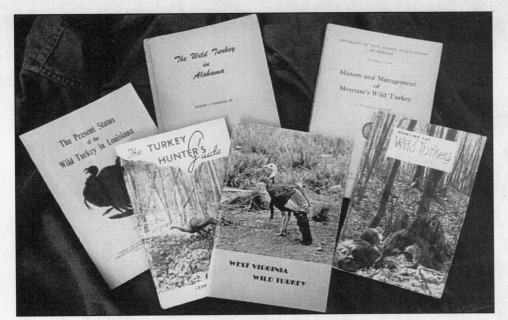

There has been a great deal written about the various wild turkey subspecies by both hunters and biologists. The bulk of the biological data is free upon request. For the serious turkey hunter, both kinds of reading will make for much more successful hunting.

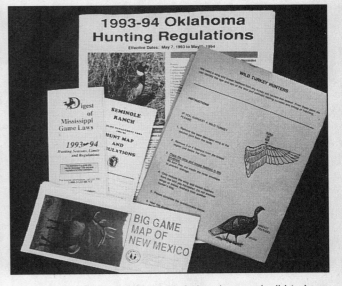

The serious turkey hunter studies any and all kinds of fauna in the various regions where he intends to hunt. Not only will this increase a person's enjoyment of an area, but it also helps identify sources of food and cover.

with a passle of turkeys and water through the years, so I knew what my chances were. Oh, once in a while turkeys will cross water to calling. I've called complete droves over water, but I've also had birds hang up on the other side of tiny streams which they could have jumped, or rivers with open banks or high banks over which they could easily have flown. Nonetheless, they'd just remain on the opposite side of the water and holler their heads off, yelping, gobbling or what-have-you.

That old Osceola at last came into view, then began wading toward me, sloshing along like some kid tromping through mud puddles on his way to school. Luckily I was hiding in a hole I'd cut into a palmetto clump so I just sat there and took it all in.

That gobbler came across a good hundred and fifty yards of

If you want to hunt all of the bearded and spurred wild turkeys, you'll have to hunt in many places. Good luck. I don't think I need to tell you to "have a good time." Of course, it's all the "gooder" if you get an old boss gobbler in your sights.

shallow water, some of it up near his knees. For all his troubles I nailed him when he stepped out on dry land near my hide. Turkeys are crazy sometimes.

Due to the tall legs, I've always thought Osceola gobblers strutted "tall," at least the birds appear to have more clearance between the ground and their wing tips (when strutting) than do the other breeds. Primary feather brooming on the tips is excellent, and can be severe, which I attribute to the bird's standing a bit taller so the angle of drag is oblique.

Osceola hens are a beautiful burnished light-brown, to me the prettiest of all the turkey hens. And, unlike the Merriam, a hunter will see numerous hens during a spring hunt. I've called bunches of up to fifteen hens during March hunts, and lagging behind, hustling to keep up the pace would be an old gobbler. Hunters like myself, who have spent days and sea-

Turkey hunters pause at a quail feeder in a south Florida turkey woods with their swamp buggy ready to haul them safely from place to place. Bobwhite hunting is excellent on improved tracts of saw palmetto where it has been bushhogged to open up lanes. South Florida's large ranches also offer excellent Osceola wild turkey hunting.

Comparing the primary feathers from the wing of an Osceola and Gould's wild turkey show us how easy it is to tell these two apart. The Osceola is the only sub-species with so little white barring on the large primary flight feathers. The larger primary can only come from the wing of a mountain-killed Gould gobbler, whose overall measurements easily exceed that of any wild turkey found in the United States.

sons hunting Merriams throughout the bird's historic habitat find this interesting because so often Merriam gobblers will be alone, or in company with another gobbler or two. Very rarely will I observe hens during spring hunts into Arizona, New Mexico, or Colorado.

Folks who hunt rough country will think, "boy, this place is flatter'n a pancake," the first time they set foot on Osceola ground. High ground in Osceola country will be the banks of a canal being dug, or a dredged drainage ditch so runoff can escape.

Water, water everywhere and not a drop to drink. That's it in Florida as the stuff isn't safe. It stands everywhere you look—ponds, mudholes, swamps in cypress strands, creeks, rivers, rainwater flats. Except when they have a truly dry year, you will find water to be your main obstacle in trying to get to where turkeys are located or in hoping to call one across the stuff to you. Much of it is less than chest deep so unless you are spooked by alligators and leeches and cottonmouths then a hunter can get across to where birds are. I've done this a number of times. Only once did I have to turn back and that was due to the water getting up under my chin. I simply couldn't hold the old muzzleloader any higher. With a modern cartridge shooter I may have gotten across.

The best of Osceola country will be dotted with huge clumps of saw palmetto, small open areas of pasture, cypress strands or heads, creek swamps, and oak hummocks with their tangles of Spanish moss and cabbage palm. The cabbage palm

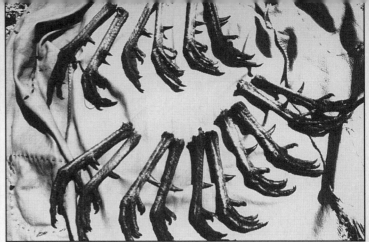

Part of a spring kill by the author, these legs are from all four of the subspecies found within the United States' lower 48. Very seldom will a spring hunt result in the bagging of so many gobblers with sharp-pointed spurs.

Turkey feet are not immune to deformity, as is evident from a gobbler killed by the author and held aloft by his brother, Dick. For some reason, the toenail on one foot kinda took off on its own, probably due to a fungus. Many turkeys have foot deformities, from missing toes to clubfeet.

John L. Rogers, whose family owns the "7 Lazy 11" ranch in south Florida, is an avid hunter. The excellent quail management program he's undertaken on the ranch—pasture management, pasture rotation and improved pastures—has also resulted in increased quail and turkey numbers.

and saw palmetto are the greatest thing to happen to turkey hunting since Gibson & Boddie began selling box calls back in the 1800s. There's no finer cover from which to hunt turkeys on this earth. Birds can be easily stalked, bushwhacked, still-hunted, called, driven, even dry gulched. The fact is, the rankest of callers has a chance to bring a turkey into gunshot in saw palmetto as the birds simply cannot see through the clumps so they have to go look. Called birds can get too close, inside the shot spread of an ideal shotgun pattern, so try to locate when you have a visible shot out to thirty yards. Of course, the best hunting is outside the thicker hummocks, along open pasture edges, there the hunter can hunker inside the saw palmetto edge or, with a good sharp knife, can cut a few fronds and throw together a sightproof blind in a few moments.

The worst problem for a non-resident hunter in Florida is finding a quality place to hunt. There are a number of public management areas but these are heavily hunted except for those with permit drawings. Anyone interested in these must apply well in advance. So a person wanting to hunt Florida needs to get a copy of the game regulations and study them a year or so before the planned hunt. Most of Florida belongs to large ranch holdings, and if you get an invite you are a lucky bugger. I've hunted a number of the larger spreads in south Florida and have yet to find one of these large cattle operations short on turkeys.

Saw palmetto takes over the land if unchecked so many of

the ranches have an annual burning program. This tends to keep the junk in check and helps control rattlesnakes, too, as numbers of them are fried in the burning. Osceolas head for these recently burned areas to seek out foodstuffs and new grasses. But the birds are darned hard to see on the stuff at a distance and binoculars are a "must" for this old boy when he heads for Florida.

Osceolas roost in three areas, oak hummocks, cypress heads, strands or swamps, and in creek swamps. Now, in oak hummocks the birds may roost in the oaks or in pine trees

Folks who hunt rough country will think, "boy, this place is flatter'n a pancake."

within the oak clump. Creek swamp turkeys roost in any of the larger trees, some of which can attain a huge size. Creek swamps are dark foreboding places but turkeys do use them.

Snakes are plentiful throughout Florida, so if you have a dread of snakes, you're going to have an uneasy time hunting those woods. You just have to remember that a snake hates seeing you just as much as you do him, and given any kind of chance to wiggle away from you, the little beast is going to do so. If you see one, just steer clear. After all, it's not going to jump up and chase you down through the palmettos.

Around water, which is a foot deep or deeper, you may find

Talk to locals. They can tell you more in ten minutes than you can learn in a week about where to find turkeys. Most farm folks like to talk, but you will have to learn to relax and forget those city schedules. If you do, you'll make many new friends.

alligators. They'll scram, too, on sight of a human. The only time one may charge is if a hunter happens to walk between it (probably dozing) and its home, the water, or comes upon one migrating from a waterhole that is drying up. Of course, getting between a mommy and its babies is bad news. If you happen on a pool with a passle of small foot-long black and yellow gators paddling around, just remember, momma's nearby. Take heed. Binoculars come in handy for seeing those sunning gators up close, the big ones, and for looking at wild hogs, or

studying the endless bird life or the far sides of any pasture, nook, and cove where an old Osceola might be strutting.

Osceolas eat a variety of plants (grass seeds, stems, wax myrtle fruits, huckleberries, etc.) and insects (mainly various kinds of butterflies, beetles, moths, crickets, etc.), acorns and mast. I've always been surprised at the diversity of food stuffs found in turkey crops. I'd advise any hunter new to an area to open the craw or crop of a late morning kill, even more so if the turkey is taken before dusk, and spread out the contents on

Florida is where a person can find huge groves of orange and grapefruit trees. What's better than fresh oranges and gobbling turkeys? From the look on David Jackman's face—nothing. David and his wife, Sally, are long-time hunting partners of the author. They are old hands in the Turkey Wars.

The Osceola wild turkey prefers live oak and saw palmetto, plus stands of cabbage palm, cypress, bay and other trees and undergrowth found throughout the creek swamps, oak hummocks and cypress strands which make up what's considered good turkey country in far south Florida. Some open pasture is a must. Any time you find a large cattle ranch in Florida, you invariably find Osceolas in the pastures also.

the bare ground. You'll not only be amazed and amused at what these birds will gulp down, but this will tell you where to hunt. Find food, and you'll find turkeys.

The two principal roosting trees found in Osceola country are the live oak and the bald cypress. If the landscape is dotted with tall straight trees standing in water, trees with a lacy-like foliage, these are cypress. The large trees may be used as roosts. Those forming a line along a water course are known as "strands," while smaller round clumps standing in around a pond are "heads." If it's been dry, the water may be gone, but it's easy to tell it once stood among the trees. Throughout Osceola terrain will be huge expanses of swamp and sloughs, where stands of cypress will be found. Gobblers roost out in

If you happen on a pool with a passel of small foot-long black and yellow gators paddling around, just remember, momma's nearby.

these as do the hens. Osceolas have a great fondness for roosting over water.

Southern Florida also has a great number of magnolia, bay, sweet gum, and other trees, as well as the live oaks, laurel and myrtle being the principal ones. Oak hummocks are often dark inside the grove, the trees sprawling three or four feet at the base of the trunk and the huge limbs curled out like gigantic arms, draped with Spanish moss like tattered clothes hanging on a scarecrow.

Wild hogs root up the cool sands, pockmarking the landscape with hollows resembling the bombed bunkers of Guadalcanal. Fascinating places to sit, a hunter can watch for wild hogs, armadillos, whitetails, swallowtailed kites, cracaras, snakes, sometimes an eagle or two, all the while listening to

the distant cry of sandhill cranes or the faroff drone of airboats.

Fall hunting for Osceolas is just as sporting as the spring hunts. They seem to be a prolific turkey, as I've found plenty of birds during the fall hunts. They're easily scattered because of thick cover which allows a close approach to a drove. Once scattered, the birds call considerably, and come to a call readily. There isn't much of that old "get together on sight" business which is found so often in Rio Grande and Merriam country, and sometimes in Eastern wild turkey habitat.

Just as with other turkeys, it is possible to hear an old gobbler sound off on a winter morning, and with luck, the hunter can stalk the bird. Old birds can be called if a bunch of them is scattered—I've had them come on the dead run and on the wing. Osceola country and its grand turkey is fascinating.

The Eastern Turkey

Day-in and day-out, the Eastern wild turkey is the largest of the subspecies found in this country. Perhaps anywhere, at least weight-wise. And, it is the most hunted, inhabiting the largest range.

Easterns get big, an old gobbler weighing upwards of 30 pounds, and standing 30 inches tall. Such a bird can be 48 inches long, have a 12-inch beard with legs sporting 1^1/$_2$-inch spurs. The average bird will weigh near 16 or 17 pounds, with the hens tipping the scales from 6 to 8 pounds.

At a distance in the woods Easterns will appear black. The tail is a gorgeous combination of blacks and chestnuts with the large wing primaries distinctly barred black and white. Perhaps I'm wrong, but I think that the overall beard development and spur growth of the Eastern is second only to Osceola. These "woodland" turkeys have long tails for keener flight control through heavy woods, slightly shorter legs than the Osceola, thinner toes and feet than the Rio Grande, and none of the white found on the Merriam or Gould's wild turkeys.

While we've all heard and read of huge bodied "wild" gobblers of late, I, as well as many wild turkey biologists and others, consider big birds to be "tainted" with domestic turkey blood. Pure-strain, old historic terrain turkeys simply don't exist. Wild turkeys have been hunted for decades across the Deep South, and those who have hunted these states for years have never seen a gobbler weighing 25 pounds, an unheard-of weight for a true wild gobbler.

The Eastern wild turkey's old historic range began in Pennsylvania, Vermont and ran eastward through part of New York, followed the East Coast south to northern Florida, encompassed the states of the Deep South, Kentucky, Ohio, the Virginias, the Carolinas, Georgia, Tennessee, Arkansas, Missouri, Louisiana, east Texas and the eastern portions of Kansas, Nebraska and Oklahoma. Of course, now that the Eastern turkey has been introduced into states like Michigan, Minnesota, even Canada, it has as they say, "come a long way, baby."

Deciduous trees are found in all these areas. So to hunt Easterns, one needs to hunt where the trees lose their leaves each fall. The soil throughout this range will usually be dark, and what's often called "tight" in consistency. There's an abundance of swift flowing streams due to rough topography, rocks, rocky gravel-laden soils, a great abundance of underbrush and trees, vines, and wide deep rivers. Some of the Eastern range is flat, particularly along and inside the levees of the Mississippi River. Overall the habitat is rough, rolling, even mountainous. This brings with it a diversified range of weather, from hot, humid areas in the south to regions of severe cold during winter months in places like Vermont and New York. The consummate Eastern hunter can choose late March Easterns in Dixie, where short sleeves would be the number one clothing choice if it weren't for the hordes of mosquitoes, and

A turkey will eat anything which hasn't eaten him first.

then later in May find himself hunting a gobbler in a late season snow storm in New York. You might find yourself taking off your clothes in one place and putting 'em back on in the other.

And, the trees are as varying as is the weather. Throughout the Ozarks the hunter will find post oaks, blackjack and white oaks, a scattering of pines, sycamore, elm, ash, to name just a few of the principal overstory. Climax vegetation in Vermont or New York would be sugar maples, black cherry, conifers such as hemlock, spruce and white pine, white oaks, perhaps even some beech. Pecan, ash and tupelo are found in much of the Eastern's range. Down South I'll hunt among all sorts of oaks—water oak, red and white oak, overcup, burr, blackjack oak, plus pines like the longleaf and shortleaf, slash pine, along with loblolly pine. Again, beeches and pecans help fill in part of the food chain. Acorns are an important part of the Eastern wild turkey's habitat. Seems like anywhere I've hunted this grand turkey bird, I've always busted acorns underfoot.

The author's long rifle lies across the blind overlooking a stand of tall pines and mixed oaks with just a hint of snow coating the fallen pine needles and brown leaves. This ridge trail overlooks excellent Eastern turkey woods in Dixie.

It seems Easterns prefer big mature pines for roosting or at least that's where they are often found. And, if we take a hard look at a big pine, we can understand why. The tree grows straight and tall, a mature pine having no boughs near the ground. The tree is nothing but a heavy group of large horizontal branches at the top of a long pole. Many of the older pines just above the roof of the surrounding forest and any turkey perched on this branch-studded treehouse can see all around its domain. Predators such as wildcats will not tackle such a tree in hopes of acquiring the groceries in its top.

A turkey will eat anything which hasn't eaten him first. That about says it for this turkey's dietary habits. Acorns are a mainstay, but I've found countless grasshoppers, beetles, walking-sticks, dogwood berries, stink bugs, grass stems and leaves, ragweed seeds, sumac berries—the list is endless. Like all wild turkeys, the birds love cultivated row crops like milo, millets, soybeans, mungbeans, and of course, corn. Once any of these crops have matured and begin to shatter, turkeys will make a beeline for them. All of us who've for decades hunted Easterns have lain and watched them spend hours scratching under oak trees, pecking at this and that, seemingly not locating any acorns. But when examined, the craws of such birds will be filled with small bits and pieces of acorn mast. During fall hunts I've bagged old gobblers that had been feeding on the huge burr oak acorns, acorns that are as large as the end of a man's index finger. I've also bagged old birds that had spent hours filling up on ragweed or crabgrass seeds. Nothing is sacred. You'll observe these old geezers stripping the grass heads of Indian bahia or bluestem grass. Many years ago when it was legal to bag two turkeys on the same day, I bellycrawled a couple hundred yards just so's I could ease the gun out through some weeds and cut down on a small gang of old gobblers that had been feeding, and were still feeding, on a patch of ragweed not thirty yards across. Got one on the ground, another on the fly. The worst part of the whole thing hit me

(Left) Pennsylvania has many excellent wildlife programs to benefit not only the turkey addict, but all hunters. Probably no other state has so many varied areas open to hunting. Parking areas dot the roadsides, and signs posted in these areas advise hunters about what is offered and the rules governing the area.

(Right) Wherever you find wild turkeys, you can bet your last dollar that there are acorns in the area. Turkeys spend many hours either where those trees are located or in traveling to them. Surely, there's not a more universal food sought by turkeys.

(Above) Turkey droppings can tell a hunter a number of things. This round dropping found in Eastern turkey country indicates it was made by a hen and is very recent due to soft, wet condition. This means the bird is probably still nearby. Gobbler droppings are more apt to be straight, measure an inch to an inch and a half in length, and as large around as a pencil.

A turkey camp in the Northeast is surrounded by excellent Eastern wild turkey habitat consisting of small ridges covered with hardwoods, conifers, rhododendren, and numerous berry-producing bushes and trees. Wild turkeys in such habitat often come close to the house.

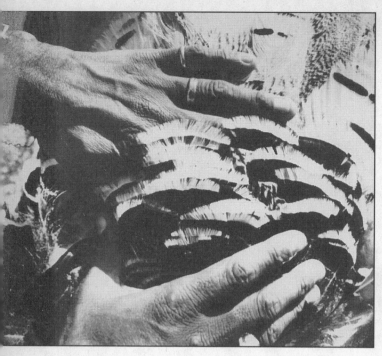

The beautiful white-tipped lower rump feathers of this turkey mark it as coming from either the Rockies in this country or the Sierra Madre Mountains (Mother of Mountains) in Mexico. Both the Gould's and Merriam turkeys have white-tipped feathers.

Here, side-by-side, are a young gobbler (left) and a legal bearded hen. Though both are short-bearded birds, they are easily recognized because of the gobbler's black-tipped belly feathers; the hen's feathers are tipped a light buff color. Body size is also a giveaway, as is head size. There's no excuse for shooting the wrong bird, if the turkeys are within easy shotgun range.

when I had to lug them back through a canyon which was a cousin to the one out in Arizona, the one more popularly called the Grand.

Eastern turkey range has many things going for the hunter. Extensive acreage in all sorts of programs gives a hunter access to good turkey hunting cover. National forests are the large part, but there's countless state-run management areas. Large paper and timber companies, along with other wood product manufacturers oftimes allow hunters access, some for a small fee; others require a hunter to purchase a yearly permit. Many allow free hunting.

States like Pennsylvania have a number of lease programs for hunter use. Often when driving the backroads or highways in the Keystone state, signs at parking areas list the rules and seasons open to hunting. States like Pennsylvania are proof that good hunting in populated areas can be made available to the hunter, if the hunter and the state work together toward this end. If there's another state with a finer hunter education program, I hope somebody will tell me; I certainly admire the game folks of Pennsylvania for the grand job they've done.

Shooting wild turkeys from out of a tree is pretty well frowned on if it's very early in the norning, or toward dusk when the birds have flown up for the night. But, I've never felt guilty about nailing a turkey up high in a tree if it's full daylight, and I saw the bird fly to its perch because some other hunter scared it there. I was hunting in southern Pennsylvania one day and a couple hours past first day, I heard and then watched, a bird fly toward me, alighting way up on the crown of a big oak. Luckily, when I eased down to the ground as the turkey settled in, I saw my salvation smack in front of me. Now, very seldom does a turkey hunter feel fortunate to find a

rhododendron thicket. Ordinarily these "Hells" are to be avoided. That's what you'll hear 'em called back East in Pennsy, the Virginias, anywhere the stuff grows. And Hell is what it is if you have to crawl through one. You can't walk through.

Turkeys will use these for "escape" cover, if the birds are pursued relentlessly. I've found that hard pressed wild turkeys will go into canebrakes, willowbrakes, cedarbrakes, huckleberry tangles, smilax tangles, rank stands of switch willows,

---

Luckily, when I eased down to the ground as the turkey settled in, I saw my salvation smack in front of me.

---

plum thickets, and remain there until well after all sign of danger is gone.

But it was easy to slip into the edge of that rhododendron thicket, work along it until I had a clear shot at the spooked turkey, then ease up the old sootblower and cut the bird outta the big oak. Still remember thinking I made a heckuva lot of noise but the bird probably thought it was deer or some other critter.

Today Eastern wild turkeys are hunted in all the states east of the Mississippi River, along with a few west of it. No other subspecie is hunted so much by so many. Yet, the birds continue increasing. It just shows what a truly tough adversary you're hunting. My advise to those who've never hunted Easterns, sometimes called woodland turkeys, ridgerunners, swamp turkeys, Ozark gobblers, mountaineers or piney woods

gobblers is that they haven't really hunted turkeys until they get after one of these old cusses; particularly a well-experienced veteran gobbler of the deep woods that has heard a good many turkey calls.

Now we are talking some kind of turkey hunting.

The Rio Grande

Let's discuss the Rio Grande wild turkey, the bird found in much of west Texas, western Oklahoma, Kansas, and parts of other lower midwestern states.

The Rio Grande differs from the Eastern and Osceola in that the bird has buff-tipped tail and lower rump feathers to better camouflage it in the sandy, lighter-colored surroundings. All turkeys have black breast feathering, which definitely helps to screen them from being seen in the dark woods, where turkeys like to scatter to when danger threatens. Cloudy days, or dark shadows, make the task of locating dark birds in the dark woods even more difficult. Rio Grandes, therefore, appear lighter in coloration if walking away from the observer and, if standing still, blend into the terrain so well they may not be seen.

The Rio Grande hen's coppery sheen makes the bird entirely invisible when on a nest in light grasses. I've all but stepped on nesting hens. Eastern and Merriam hens, being darker, prefer to nest nearer tree trunks or in areas where the dark plummage blends with the dark background and makes them all but impossible to see.

All hens will remain on the nest until a hunter is very close. So if you scare a bird from her eggs, don't touch them, don't ever stick around. Get away from there quick, with as little disturbance as possible, and she'll invariably return.

Not many places have signs such as this one located on the outskirts of a wonderful town called Coleman, Texas. Coleman is in the heart of excellent Rio Grande wild turkey country, not to mention the fine hunting of wild hogs, bobwhites and whitetails.

Live oak thickets are where a hunter will often find Rio Grande turkeys in south Texas. These thickets are often large, covering several acres, and flow on into the next, with open pasture areas mixed throughout.

Raymond Adams, cattleman-owner of the largest ranch in Kansas, pauses at a rattlesnake den, where spent 410 shotgun casings tell of snake kills made by some of his ranch hands. All of his cowboys tote 410 pistols simply for snake killing. All of Rio Grande turkey country is home to numerous kinds of rattlers, but predominantly the big western diamondback and little prairie sidewinder.

Ken Warner, well-known editor of *Gun Digest*, hefts a large Rio Grande gobbler, killed while hunting with the author. The average spring-killed Rio gobbler will weigh around 17 to 18 pounds. This old bird tipped the scales just 2 ounces short of 23 pounds. And, yes, Ken killed the bird with that little Italian-made 20-gauge.

Beard development is good on Rios, but the spurs aren't on par with Easterns or Osceolas. Many Rio Grande hens sport beards so it's not unusual to see five to six in a huge wintering flock of say a couple hundred birds. The legs of a Rio are slightly shorter than those of the Osceola, and the feet larger than an Eastern's with thicker toes for walking in sandy-type soils. Anyone who has hunted Rio Grandes in Oklahoma and Texas will find that these southern-most birds have, on the average, sharper spurs, much like those of some Easterns and most Osceolas.

Folks who journey to Rio Grande terrain notice two things—the dry terrain, and the wide open expanses. Often, "you can see for miles." Water, or the lack of it, is a serious limiting factor in this habitat. There are many thousands of acres which would support flocks of Rio Grandes if there were only a permanent source of water. Creeks, windmills, pasture ponds, scooped out waterholes (what us westerners call "tanks," and rivers dot Rio Grande range. And the Rio Grande is like all turkeys, where there is no water, there are no turkeys. Easterners will be amazed at seeing so many rivers on the western plains, for instance the old South Canadian, which many of us think of as "a mile wide, and a half inch deep." But they flow only if there's been a very recent down pour; much of the time they're bone-dry. Us guys who've hunted the upper reaches of the Cimarron are durned well aware that just because the river is dry at a certain bridge doesn't mean it's all dry, as there are isolated waterholes all up and down the river.

An old gobbler might have a hundred or two hundred hoppers in its craw.

Up along the Kansas-Oklahoma-Colorado lines it is not unusual to hunt on one ranch where the cattle are watering out of the river, then go downstream the next day thirty miles, maybe only ten, and find the beeves heading to the windmills cause that same river is dry sand. It's gone underground, and probably upstream the riverbed is dry, too. If only all windmills were left running year around. But, anyone who's spent a

The makeup of ideal turkey country calls for rough, hilly country terrain; a good number of varying kinds of brush, vines, trees, grasses and small open areas of pasture; and an abundance of larger trees for roosting. Throw in a mountain brook here and there, and if the place doesn't have any turkey population, then it should.

Wild turkeys are often found near old corrals, regardless of the subspecies. The birds have learned that free groceries can sometimes be found at these locations. This knowledge is passed on by the hen to her young, so generation after generation will pass by such cattle feeding places in search of grain.

lifetime fooling with such conglomerations has put in his time fixing leathers, greasing the cussed things, and all the other contrary gimmicks a windmill can come up with. So cowboys shut the things down after the cattle have been moved to another pasture.

Rio Grandes are found where there are several kinds of oak, shinnoak, burr oak, blackjack, live oak and post oak, along with cottonwoods, sycamore, some pecan, hackberry, chittum berry, walnut, willow and ash. Chinaberry groves are seen in many areas, along with hedgeapple (bois d'arc or osage orange), hickory, locust and elm. Underbrush can be mesquite, catclaw, sumac, sand sagebrush, salt cedar and buck brush. I've hunted around lots of skunk brush and some areas even have plenty of cactus. A hunt down on the big King ranch in Texas, near the coast, will be through sprawling thickets of live oaks. Hunters from forested regions will wonder where the birds roost, as none of the trees are of any height compared to the tall trees found along streams in the East. A big old Southern pine would tower above the roost trees used by Rio Grandes in south Texas.

The diet of the Rio Grande is similar to the other species. The birds eat a tremendous variety of foods, but mainly grasses, bugs, beetles, acorns, hackberries, chittum berries, ragweed seeds, dove weed, to name just a few. They will return day after day to standing or cattle-grazed crops of milo, millet, oats, wheat or soybeans. They like green grasses in the spring and have to be the world's best grasshopper chasers. An old gobbler might have a hundred or two hundred hoppers in its craw. Cold weather slows down the hoppers, but by then the birds have eaten so many they've tired of the diet. So in late fall or early winter they'll turn to berries and the falling crop of acorns.

Very often Rio Grande hunters are faced with a great deal of wide open country. Places like west Texas and Oklahoma or western Kansas also have lots of wind; some of it so bad it'll "pile up the barbs on the fences agin the posts." Well, it's not *that bad*, but there'll be times when the wind will blow hard for day after day. Hunting turkeys in these blows are kinda like the old boy who thinks it's time to head for the house when he's out fishing and a rain sets in. Hell the fish are wet anyhow. Go on fishing.

You can't mistake the black and white of a huge old Merriam gobbler. Shooting an old vintage muzzleloader made it even more challenging.

The same is true of the Rio Grande on the high prairie. The bird has lived his life in such conditions, and the wind is part of it. Many's the time I've heard an old bird gobble so close that all I needed to do was cock the hammers and shoot. But, then, the wind would begin to howl like a banshee and drown out the bird to the point it sounded like it was over in the next county. Old gobblers coming to a call on a bad, windy day will fool many a hunter. Worse yet, the bird may be coming through a maze of sandsage, bluestem, or mesquite clumps, even salt cedar if very near a river, so it's not uncommon for

Old gobblers coming to a call on a bad, windy day will fool many a hunter.

the bird to get inside easy shooting distance, perhaps ten or fifteen yards before the hunter sees him.

Of course, anyone hunting Rio Grandes definitely needs to carry binoculars. I said, carry them. Don't leave them at camp or in the pickup. And use them. Rio Grandes like to head for open areas just after flydown, both in the fall and the spring, they can often be easily picked up with a good set of binoculars and studied to see which hunting method might work best.

Large flocks of Rio Grandes, when scattered during the fall, often get together by sight, so calling can be useless. On the other hand, if a person hasn't got any hangups about getting down on hands and knees, maybe even his belly, and making long sneaks, many Rio Grandes can be easily stalked into easy

range. This calls for heavily padded hands and knees so wear gloves and maybe slip a pair of old pants over the ones you usually wear. Much Rio Grande country has no end of sandburrs, goathead stickers, cactus, stuff which makes crawling not the easiest thing, but I've never let little things like these keep me out of range of a wild turkey. Watch out for rattlers if the day is warm; you may belly up face-to-face with one of these. The large western diamondback is the most aggressive of all the rattlesnakes so give him room. Ordinarily, they have a banded black and buff tail, much like a raccoon. Throughout the West they're called "coontails."

Rio Grande country is also home to blue kites, (Mississippi kites to confirmed birders), shrikes, sparrow hawks, scissortails, prairie chickens, coyotes, bobcats, prairie dogs, bobwhite and scaled quail, and roadrunners. If a hunter's never chased Rios out on the open prairie, he'd best get his affairs in order and head west. Who knows, the wind may change direction overnight, and blow all those barbs back down the fence t'other direction.

The Merriam Wild Turkey

Merriams, the Rocky Mountain turkey, is a big, black and white bird from the ponderosa country. The mention of Merriams makes me think of towering pines, Gambel's oak thickets, snow, rugged mountainous terrain, pinyons, junipers, and brawling mountain streams. The bird's old historic range included areas in Arizona, New Mexico, the far west end of the Oklahoma Panhandle, Colorado, and perhaps a bird or two in the far southwestern corner of Kansas. Today, with restocking, the Merriam is found all across the northwest, from

Merriam turkey country can be intimidating to many hunters, due to the vast size of the mountains and the ruggedness of the slopes. Any mountain can be cut down to size with just a little walking.

(Left) Wild turkey beards can be displayed in any number of ways; this Rio Grande jake bird (left) is simply glued in a 12-gauge shell casing, while the narrow Eastern turkey hen's beard is inserted and glued into a short section of bone from the bird's wing. The large Merriam beard is also inserted into an old 12-gauge paper shell casing. All are easy to hang by the small brass cup hook glued into the end. The cartridge casings are minus the fired primer.

(Right) Notice the differences on wild turkey primary wing feathers. Both are from a Merriam gobbler. The one all-gray feather stuck out like a sore thumb among the other standard barred feathers. Such melanistic-type feathers are very unusual among wild turkeys.

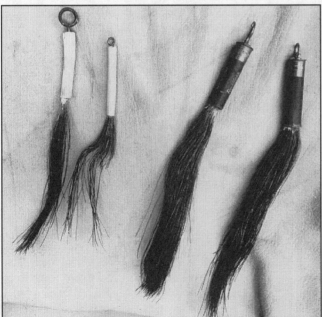

Wild turkey beards vary tremendously. The two small beards on the left are from bearded hens, the others from old adult gobblers. Nearly all hen beards are very slender, with only a few hairs making up the beard. Very few bearded hens are found in the Osceola subspecies, and not many are seen on Merriams. But there are numerous Eastern bearded hens and even more among the Rio Grandes.

The hunter should study not only the subspecies to be hunted, but also inquire as to where hunting is allowed, taking a good long look at the hunting regulations. Shown here is just a beginning of what's needed for hunting Merriam wild turkeys in Arizona. After a quick look at the state's rules, the hunter will realize he must first apply for the permit if he wants to hunt a spring gobbler because all permits are by draw. He can forget the San Juan forest map because it doesn't extend into Arizona, but the Apache-Sitgreaves National Forest is an excellent place to find Merriam gobblers.

Nebraska to Washington state. The Merriam has been around man for centuries. Probably the bones found in caves throughout what is now Arizona and New Mexico are his ancestors. Indian tribes living in those areas back when Coronado and Cortez were searching for the Seven Cities of Gold had a great many domestic and penned turkeys. Dried turkey carcasses, and hundreds of bones found in cliff dwellings indicate the birds were hand fed. Most likely the Indians caught young birds, penning them, and perhaps breeding them in confinement.

The predominant coloration of the Merriam is black and white. The tips of the tail and the lower rump feathers are snow white and the wing barring whiter than that of the other three subspecies. Weight and spur development are on par with the Rio Grande, but beard growth seems a little slower. Few Merriam gobblers attain 10-inch beard lengths which is not uncommon in the other three subspecies.

Merriams eat all sorts of foods too; muhly grasses, beetles, grasshoppers, sumac, rosehips, dandelions, pani grasses, along with small snails and frogs the birds catch along tiny mountain meadow brooks, seeps and springs. Of course, these birds spend a great part of their lives among the Gambel's oaks if these are present. This tree is similar to the thicket oaks, known as the shinnoak, found across some Rio Grande country. Such clumps of oaks in Texas and Oklahoma are referred to as "shinnery clumps." Gambel oak clumps are much the same with the trees ordinarily under twenty feet in height and the isolated clumps anywhere from half-an-acre to several acres in size. Much of the time the clump is surrounded by open pasture or grasslands. Blowing sand often builds up the elevation of the clump, so turkeys have an excellent observation point from within. Shinnoaks and Gambel's oak are both prolific trees, bearing each year a crop of small acorns about the size of a large pea or small marble.

Merriams can be hunted in fifteen or sixteen states today, most having both spring and fall seasons. Probably more Merriam turkeys are bagged with rifles than shotguns since turkey season and big game season overlap.

I must warn the Merriam hunter that these birds are known to migrate long distances between wintering range and breeding grounds, perhaps forty or fifty miles. Much of their historic range is acutely elevated. When the snows get too deep, the birds move down to lower elevations but may migrate back to the higher ground when the snow melts. And, don't get the idea that they'll wait until it's all melted off. Some will go back up as soon as open patches of ground begin to show. What this means is that gobblers found one day may be miles from there the next if they happen to be "on the move."

Certainly, there's no greater thrill than hearing an old boss Merriam cut loose far above on a Rocky Mountain pinnacle with one of those gobbles that'll change the stripes on your overalls. Then the first thing that comes to mind is, "Boy, I got to get above that turkey, or at the very least on his level."

And, it's not only *all uphill*, it's *steep, too*. And it's hard to breathe up there in the thin air. But, just remember, it's all downhill coming back when you're carrying that big Merriam gobbler back to camp.

Fall Turkey Season Dates

Check with state game department for correct regulations and dates before you hunt. Dates and prices subject to change.

Alabama (Nov. 19-Jan. 1, 1995) One gobbler per day, five combined fall and spring, Eastern subspecies. Daylight hours. Annual license, $175; 7-day trip, $50; issuance fee, $2. AL Dept. of Conservation and Natural Resources, Accounting Section, 64 N. Union St., Montgomery, AL 36130; 205-242-3486.

Arizona (Oct. 7-13, gun; Aug. 19-Sept. 8, archery) One turkey per year, Merriam's subspecies. Daylight hours. License, $85.50; turkey tag, $52.50. AZ Game & Fish Dept., 2221 W. Greenway Rd., Phoenix, AZ 85023; 602-942-3000.

Arkansas (Oct. 8-16, gun; Oct. 1-Feb. 28, 1995, archery) One bird either sex, Eastern subspecies. One-half hour before sunrise to sunset. Annual all-game license, $185; five-day all-game, $125; three-day all-game, $95. AR Game & Fish Commission, #2 Natural Resources Dr., Little Rock AR 72205; 501-223-6300.

California (Nov. 12-Dec. 11; fall season closed in San Diego county) One turkey either sex per day, one in possession, Rio Grande, Merriam's, Eastern, Eastern/Rio Grande hybrid, Merriam's/Rio Grande hybrid, California hybrid subspecies. 8 a.m. to sunset. Hunting license, $86.90; upland game bird stamp, $5.25 or $5.50. CA Dept. of Fish and Game, License and Revenue Branch, 3211 S. Street, Sacramento, CA 95816; 916-227-2244.

Colorado (Sept. 1-Oct. 2) One turkey either sex, provided no more than two harvested in spring, Merriam's and Rio Grande subspecies. Most hunting of Rio Grandes is by permit only for which the application deadline was Aug. 2. One-half hour before sunrise to sunset. Hunting license, $75.25. CO Division of Wildlife, Dept. of Natural Resources, 6060 Broadway, Denver, CO 80216; 303-297-1192.

Connecticut (Oct. 15-29, shotgun in northwest zones; Sept. 15-Nov. 19 and Dec. 26-31, archery statewide.) One bird either sex, Eastern subspecies. One-half hour before sunrise until sunset. Fall small game firearms license, $42; turkey permit, $10; archery small game and deer permit, $44; turkey permit. $10. CT Dept. of Environmental Protection, License and Revenue, 79 Elm St., Hartford, CT 06106; 203-424-3105.

Delaware (No fall season)

Florida (Nov. 12-Jan. 8, 1995, south zone; Nov. 12-

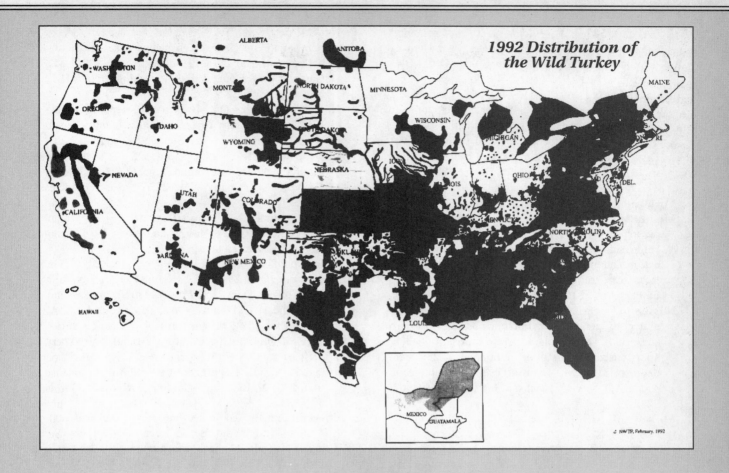

1992 Distribution of the Wild Turkey

Jan. 8, 1995, central zone; Nov. 24-27 and Dec. 10-Jan. 15, 1995, northwest zone) One bearded turkey or gobbler per day, two per season, Eastern and Florida subspecies. One-half hour before sunrise to $1/2$-hour after sunset. Annual hunting (except AL residents), $150; annual hunting (AL residents only), $100; ten-day hunting (except GA residents), $25; ten-day hunting (GA residents only), $121; turkey stamp, $5. FL Game & Fresh Water Fish Commission, 620 S. Meridian St., Tallahassee, FL 32399-1600; 904-488-4676.

Georgia (No fall season)

Hawaii (Varies Nov. 5-Jan. 10, 1995.) One bird, Rio Grande subspecies. One-half hour before sunrise to $1/2$-hour after sunset. Hunting license, $20. DLNR, Division of Conservation Resources, Enforcement, 1151 Punchbowl St., Honolulu, HA 96813; 808-587-0077.

Idaho (No fall season)

Illinois (Oct. 15-23, shotgun; Oct. 1-Jan. 12, 1995, archery) One either sex, Eastern subspecies. One-half hour before sunrise until sunset, gun; $1/2$-hour before sunrise to $1/2$-hour after sunset, archery. Hunting permit, $75 for first and $25 for second if available;

archery permit, $75. IL Dept. of Conservation, Permit Office, P.O. Box 19446, Springfield, IL 62794-9446; 217-782-7305.

Indiana (No fall season)

Iowa (Oct. 10-Nov. 30, shotgun/bow conbination; Oct. 1-Dec. 2 and Dec. 19-Jan. 10, 1995, archery only) Iowa residents only.

Kansas (Oct. 1-Nov. 29, Dec. 12-31, archery only for nonresidents) One turkey either sex, Eastern and Rio Grande subspecies. One-half hour before sunrise to sunset. Hunting license, $60.50; plus turkey permit, $30.50. KS Dept. of Wildlife & Parks, 512 SE 25th Ave., Pratt, KS 67124; 316-672-5911.

Kentucky (Oct. 1-31, archery only) One turkey either sex, Eastern subspecies. Daylight hours only. Annual hunting license, $95; turkey permit, $17.50. KY Dept. of Fish & Wildlife Resources, #1 Game Farm Rd., Frankfort, KY 40601; 502-564-3400.

Louisiana (No fall season)

Maine (No fall season)

Maryland (Nov. 5-10 Washington, Allegany and Garrett counties only) One turkey either sex, Eastern subspecies. One-half hour before sunrise to $1/2$-hour after sunset. Hunting license, $120.50; DE and PA residents, $83; VA residents, $120; WV residents, $85. MD Dept. of Natural Resources, Fish, Heritage & Wildlife Administration, Tawes State Office Bld., Annapolis, MD 21401; 301-974-3195.

Massachusetts (Nov. 14-19) One turkey either sex, Eastern subspecies. One-half hour before sunrise to $1/2$-hour after sunset. Big game license, $48.50; turkey permit, $5; mandatory land stamp, $5. MA Division of Fisheries & Wildlife, Leverette Saltonstall Blvd., 100 Cambridge St., Boston, MA 02202; 617-727-3151.

Michigan (No fall season, a change from fall, 1993)

Minnessota (Oct. 12-16, 19-23). One turkey either sex per lottery permit, Eastern subspecies. One-half hour before sunrise to sunset. Hunting license, $56. Application deadline was July 1. MN Dept. of Natural Resources, Information Center, 500 LaFayette Rd., St. Paul, MN 55155-4040; 612-296-6157.

Mississippi (Varies Nov. 5-13 and Dec. 3-11) Two either sex per fall season (four possible), Eastern subspecies. One-half hour before sunrise to $1/2$-hour after sunset. Annual all-game hunting, $225; three-day trip, $105. MS Dept. of Wildlife, Fisheries & parks, P.O. Box 451, Jackson, MS 39205; 601-362-9212.

Missouri (Oct. 17-30, firearms; Oct. 1-Nov. 11 and Nov. 21-Dec. 31, archery) One turkey either sex each week of season (two maximum); same for archers except only one for first season, Eastern subspecies. One-half hour before sunrise to $1/2$-hour after sunset for archers. Fall firearms license, $75; archery, $75. MO Dept. of Conservation, Permit Office, P.O. Box 180, Jefferson City, MO 65102-0180; 314-751-4115, ext. 335.

Montana (Sept. 1-Dec. 15) One wild turkey, Merriam's subspecies. One-half hour before sunrise to $1/2$-hour after sunset. Upland game bird license, $55; hunting license, $13; conservation license, $5. MT Dept. of Fish, Wildlife & Parks, 1420 E. Sixth, Helena, MT 59620; 406-444-2535.

Nebraska (Oct. 22-TBD) One turkey either sex, Merriam's and hybrid subspecies. One-half hour before sunrise to sunset. Hunting license, $50; habitat stamp, $10. NE Game & Parks Commission, Permits Division, P.O. Box 30370, Lincoln, NE 68503-0370; 402-471-0641.

Nevada (Oct. 22-Nov. 4) Nevada residents only.

New Hampshire (Sept. 15-Dec. 15, archery only) One turkey either sex, Eastern subspecies. One-half hour before sunrise to $1/2$-hour after sunset. Archery license, $36.50; turkey tag, $6. NH Fish and Game Dept., 2 Hazen Dr., Concord, NH 03301; 603-271-3421.

New Jersey (No fall season)

New Mexico (Sept. 19-25) One turkey either sex, Merriam's and Rio Grande subspecies. One-half hour before sunrise to sunset. Hunting license. $79. NM Game & Fish Dept., Villagra Building, Santa Fe, NM 87503; 505-827-7885.

New York (Varies Oct. 10-Nov. 20, depending on WMU) One per day (two per season in southeastern, NY), Eastern subspecies. Sunrise to sunset. Small game license, $50; turkey permit, $25. NYS Dept. of Environmental Conservation, License Sales Office, 50 Wolf Rd., Albany, NY 12233-4790; 518-457-3521.

North Carolina (No fall season)

North Dakota (Oct. 8-Nov. 6 and Nov. 7-Dec. 4.) North Dakota residents only.

Ohio (No fall season)

Oklahoma (Oct. 29-Nov. 18, gun; Oct. 1-Nov. 13 and Nov. 28-Dec. 31, archery) No fall gun season in southeast Oklahoma. One turkey (one tom or one either sex), Eastern and Rio Grande subspecies. One-half hour before official sunrise to official sunset. Hunting license, $74.50; turkey tag, $7.75. OK Department of Wildlife Conservation, 1801 N. Lincoln, Oklahoma, OK 73105; 405-521-3855.

Oregon (Tentative controlled hunt in two southeastern counties) Hunting license, $53; controlled fall turkey tag, $44. Call for more information. OR Dept. of Fish & Wildlife, P.O. Box 59, Portland, OR 97207; 503-229-5400.

Pennsylvania (Oct. 29-Nov. 5 or Nov. 12, depending on zone; zones 1 and 9 closed) One bird either sex, Eastern subspecies. One-half hour before sunrise to sunset. Hunting license, $80.75 for adults and $40.75 for ages 12-16. PA Game Commission, 2001 Elmerton Ave., Harrisburg, PA 17110-9797; 717-787-4250.

Rhode Island (No fall season)

South Carolina (No fall season)

South Dakota (Oct. 1-Dec. 18 in Prairie units; Oct. 8-14 in Black Hills unit) One per license (some two-tag licenses are offered where allowed), Merriam's subspecies. One-half hour before sunrise to sunset. Hunting license, $40. SD Game, Fish and Parks, Information Office, 523 E. Capitol, Pierre, SD 57501; 605-773-3485.

Tennessee (Sept. 24-Oct. 20, Oct. 25-Nov. 10, Nov. 15-24, Nov. 29-Dec. 31, archery only on LBL only) One either sex, Eastern subspecies. One-half hour before sunrise to sunset. LBL hunter use permit, $15; plus, depending on the state in which you are hunting, either TN annual hunting license, $156, or seven-day trip, $105.50; or KY annual hunting license, $95, and turkey permit, $17.50.

**Spring Turkey Seasons
(Approx. Dates)**

WA
April 15-May 10

MT
April 11-May 10

ND *
Opening April 18

MN
April 15-May 19

VT
May 1-31

ME
May 4-30

NH
May 4-31

OR
April 15-May 24

ID
Varies
April 13-May 10

SD
April 11-May 17

WI
Varies
April 15-May 17

MI
April 20-May 24

NY
May 1-31

MA
May 4-23

RI
April 29-May 17

CT
Varies May 6-26

WY
April 4-May 3

NE
Varies
April 1-May 15

IA
Varies
April 13-May 10

PA
May 2-30

NJ
Varies
April 22-May 22

NV *
Varies
March 28-May 10

IL
April 13-May 6

IN
April 22-May 10

OH
April 27-May 16

WV
April 27-May 23

VA
April 18-May 23

DE
Varies April 21-May 11

MD
April 18-May 16

UT
April 11-26,
May 1-24

CO
April 11-May 24

KS
April 15-May 10

MO
April 20-May 3

KY
Varies April 8-25

NC
April 11-May 9

CA
March 26-May 3

AZ
April 24-May 17

NM
April 18-May 10

OK
April 6-May 6

AR
April 6-30

TN
April 4-May 7

SC
April 1-May 1

MS
March 21-May 1

AL
Varies
March 20-April 30

GA
March 21-May 15

FL
March 21-April 26

TX
Varies
April 4-May 3

LA
Varies
March 21-April 26

HI
March 7-27

*Residents only

Check state seasons and regulations before you hunt. Dates subject to change.

TN Valley Authority, Land Between the Lakes, 100 Van Morgan Dr., Golden Pond, TN 42211; 502-924-5602.

Texas (Nov. 5-Jan. 1, 1995, northern Texas; Nov. 12-Jan. 8, 1995, southern Texas; Nov. 12-Jan. 15, 1995, in ten select southern counties; Oct. 1-31, archery.) Four Rio Grande birds per license year. One-half hour before sunrise to $1/2$-hour after sunset. General hunting license, $200; turkey stamp, $5. TX Parks & Wildlife, 4200 Smith School Rd., Austin, TX 78744; 512-389-4800.

Utah (No fall season)

Vermont (Oct. 1-21, archery only; tentative Oct. 22-28, shotgun or archery) Tentative one turkey either sex per pserson for all fall seasons combined, Eastern subspecies. Sunrise to sunset. Hunting license, $75 (except non-residents under 18, $25); turkey stamp, $15. VT Fish & Wildlife Dept. 103 S. Main, Waterbury, VT 05676; 802-244-7331.

Virginia (Varies by county, Nov. 7-Jan. 7, 1995.) One either sex per day, Eastern subspecies. One-half hour before sunrise to $1/2$-hour after sunset. Hunting license, $60; required big game license, $50; National Forest permit, $3, if you hunt on National Forest lands. VA Dept. of Game & Inland Fisheries, P.O. Box Box 11104, Richmond, VA 23230-1104; 804-367-1000.

Washington (Nov. 18-22 in specific counties) One either sex, per day. Only one each subspecies per calendar year, Eastern, Merriam's and Rio Grande subspecies. One-half hour before sunrise to $1/2$-hour after sunset. Hunting license, $150; $60 turkey tag. WA Dept. of Wildlife, 600 Capitol Way N., Olympia, WA 98501-1091; 206-753-5700.

West Virginia (Oct. 22-Nov. 12) One turkey either sex, Eastern subspecies. Dawn to dusk. Hunting license, $85 for all states except KY, OH and PA; KY, $90, OH and PA, $95; plus National Forest stamp, $2, if you hunt on National Forest lands. WV Dept. of Natural Resources, License Section, 1900 Kanawah Blvd. East, Charleston, WV 25305; 304-558-2758

Wisconsin (Varies Oct. 6-Nov. 10) One turkey either sex, Eastern subspecies. One-half hour before sunrise to 15 minutes after sunset. Application fee, $3; hunting license, $50; turkey stamp, $5.25. Information Desk, WI Dept. of Natural Resources, P.O. Box 7921, Madison, WI 53707; 608-226-1877.

Wyoming (Varies Oct. 1-Nov. 30) One turkey per season, Merriam's subspecies. Daylight to dark. Fall hunting license, $40. WY Game & Fish Dept., Information Section, 5400 Bishop Blvd., Cheyenne, WY 82002; 307-777-4601.

Ontario, Canada (No fall season)

Anyone looking for fresh signs of turkey is always watching for the tell-tale scratched out dishes where the birds have been feeding. These are usually located among the leaves under the overhanging branches of mast trees, like oak, hickory or dogwood.

Knowing something about the life of a wild turkey is definitely an aid in understanding something about the methods of hunting these birds.

Wild turkeys are a ground nesting bird, and like I mentioned earlier, if you stumble across a nest, leave it be, and leave the area. Lots of critters break up turkey nests, coons, opossums, foxes, coyotes, snakes, crows, free-ranging dogs, and probably cattle step on some. Wild hogs will eat whatever they can get, hens, eggs, the young.

Turkeys begin laying in late March in the Deep South, but as a person moves north this falls back in time. Birds in the northern states lay in May and perhaps early June. Once a "clutch" is laid, which may be from five to sixteen eggs, the hen then begins "setting" the nest, and she'll incubate the eggs for about four weeks. Although it took perhaps two or three weeks for the hen to lay her bunch of eggs, Old Mother Nature treats her as she does all birds; all of the eggs will hatch within a period of hours.

The hen quickly leaves the nest area once the tiny poults have hatched, as the little birds can walk at birth. They may travel a half-mile that first day, and from then on throughout the spring and summer, the hen and her brood will spend all day eating, dusting, watering, chasing bugs, and being hassled by all the varmints found in whatever woods possible. Probably coyotes, bobcats and foxes are the worst culprits, though there are many others—domestic cats and dogs, hawks, man, to name a few.

Throughout these escapades, the old hen will teach the poults to "freeze" when danger is around. If you blunder into

Doyle Whitfield points out some gobbler tracks. All subspecies of wild turkeys must have water, just how much or how often is debatable. While many folks think the birds must drink every day, it's the author's opinion that many do not. Nevertheless, we all agree that where there is no water, there are no turkeys.

an area where a turkey hen begins flopping like she's hurt, or staying very close but chirping alot, take care where you step. Tiny turkeys when "froze" blend into the ground clutter like another clod or rock; it's easy to step on one.

Young turkeys can fly up into small trees and large bushes by the time they are a couple weeks of age. From then on they become strong fliers, and by the fall can fly up into large trees.

In September the old hen may cross paths with another hen with young, and the two will begin spending all their days together. This process continues throughout the fall and winter months, and by December, but more likely in January,

If you're gonna stay in the kitchen, you gotta learn how to cook.

there may be flocks of a hundred or two hundred turkeys gathered together in what's known as the "wintering" flock. All of the fall hunting methods are based on the makeup of the turkey flocks. Most early fall flocks consist of a single adult hen, and what's left of her brood. I say, "what's left" because there's probably never been a wild turkey hen which by September had the same number of poults as she had eggs in the nest.

Early fall droves may number four birds or fifteen. Later on, as the hens and young band together, a November drove might contain fifteen birds, or fifty. One fall I busted up a little band of only three young birds, bagged two through calling and could have killed the third but didn't because I hoped to locate an older bird for my third tag.

The flock bands can vary in makeup. One drove may be nothing but hens, another nothing but young gobblers, a third only old gobblers, a fourth any combination of these. I killed an old gobbler just this past winter on Dirk Ross' Ranch Rio Bonita down near Junction, Texas. That old long beard was in the company of about twenty-five hens and one jake. Two days later I was holed up, hoping a big black boar hog would come along, and watched five old gobblers walk past me. Should'a shot one of the gobblers as the hog never showed.

Drove makeup is tremendously varied. This is why a fall hunter must make every effort to determine what kinds of turkeys make up any drove he suddenly comes upon. Watch these birds as they scramble and fly off. Are they old gobblers? Are they young birds and mother hens? Are they jakes, or a mixed bunch? Having this information will give you a clue how to hunt them. We'll go into that in Chapter 6, the fall hunting chapter.

Perhaps you stumble onto a lone turkey, but you stare at his beard as he makes his way off through the woods. You mutter, "Whoo-ee, wish I could nail that old critter." More'n likely you've crossed paths with what's called a "hermit" gobbler, an old male who has taken to traveling by himself and shuns the company of other turkeys. He's tougher'n nails to get into killing distance. You just missed out on your best chance to shoot him, and that's cause you weren't ready when he boomed skywards. If you're gonna stay in the kitchen, you gotta learn how to cook.

Many a hunter has been intimidated by such country as this. These hunters are studying a tiny bit of Arizona's Tonto Basin. It's no different than other places where you'll find wild turkeys, but it is big. And if you've not been in such country before, you'll truly need to obtain a map of the area, study it thoroughly before you hike into it, and then carry the map with you as you hunt. Do not forget your compass, some wooden matches and a good sharp knife.

Wild turkey country in the Rockies—huge flowing slopes dotted with juniper on the lower reaches, giving way to countless Gambel oak thickets at higher elevations, and creeping upward to Ponderosa pines on which many Merriam turkeys roost. This scene is near the Twin Peaks area on the Colorado-New Mexico border.

Big, wide open woods—a great place to find turkeys, but very often not the greatest place to have to shoot one. Too often a hunter located in such stuff can be seen by any approaching turkey, even more so if the hunter is calling, which pinpoints the turkey's keen eye to the hunter's exact location. Far better is to call from cover, which requires the turkey to come into shooting range before the bird can see where the call is coming from. Hunting and calling from a location out in the open woods is what causes most of those circling turkeys you're always hearing hunters talk about.

As winter fades into spring, the older gobblers begin gobbling each morning. They begin strutting and fights take place quite often. Then the winter flocks begin breaking apart into small groups. An old gobbler or two, accompanied by a few hens scatter over the range. This is the time of year when wild turkeys can and are observed in areas where they've never been seen, or at best since last spring. Throughout Rio Grande and Merriam habitat there are numerous places where turkeys can be found each spring, year after year, but in the fall disappear completely. Those folks who hunt the spring birds will never have a turkey to hunt during the fall seasons. This is because the birds have migrated back to the the winter flock grounds.

But this can be reversed also. I know of ranches with huge wintering flocks that after the spring breakup are devoid of turkeys. For years I loved to hunt fall birds on a spread not many miles from Sheridan's Roost, but I never bagged a spring turkey on that ranch. Didn't hunt it. Wasn't any use as the turkeys skedaddled outta there during March and April like the woods were on fire.

So, spring hunting methods are built on the gobblers' mating instincts. We hope to call an old he-turkey to us by making the mating call of the hen. And, the truth is, the killing of wild gobblers during a spring hunt is considerably easier than calling one to the gun during fall and winter hunting.

3

Have You Forgotten Any Gear?

TODAY'S AVERAGE AMERICAN seems to have a love affair with gadgets. If you don't believe me, just drive down a residential street, and notice what's stacked inside most garages. On the floor, on shelves, hanging from nails or hooks, gadgets are everywhere to the point there often isn't any room left for the family auto. Civilization advancements in these United States are about to run a person out of house and garage.

This has lapped over into hunting, fishing, camping, hiking, all the outdoor pastimes. Recently, I happened to walk into a large store in a big city. The store's principal merchandise was hiking, climbing, and camping gear. I was stunned at the collection of small stoves, pitons, climbing gear, shoes, boots, axes, hammers, ropes, tents, the list goes on and on, not to mention all the packaged foods for such jaunts on mountain faces, or rock walls.

Fishing. I've been with guys who had almost no room left in the car because of all the tackle boxes—one for each type of lure, I swear. Being an old catfisherman, my handful of hooks and a gunney sack of crawpaps doesn't seem like much compared to those guys. Of course, pound for pound I'll put those guys in the shade any day of the week—my catch will be better eating too.

But let's not forget turkey hunters. Certainly there's plenty for them to lug off into the woods, and one day you may run onto some guy who's toting fifty pounds of junk, from range finders to solar blankets. He's got problems if he happens to kill a turkey. Other guys won't have anything but a call, a few shells, and a shotgun.

What a hunter wears and carries has lots of bearing on the outcome of the hunt.

On some hunts I'll be wearing one of these "new" type vests. These really aren't new anymore, but to many of us who hunted for years before these came on the market, such things are new. They have several pockets for calls, and a big pouch on the back which will hold a full grown gobbler. These things are great. But, don't put so much in one that you leave tracks an inch deep in bedrock.

Every now and then I dump all my vest's contents to cull out stuff I know I won't use that particular day. Then, I pack just what I think I'll need. If I'm hunting someplace where I'll want to build a hide, I stick in a bow saw or a small folding saw, and maybe a set of tree pruners. Invariably I'll have hunks of heavy cord (for blind building), a sling shot and ammo (this is for chasing off cattle, deer, crows, anything I deem detrimental to hunting success), a water bottle, the makings for reloading whatever muzzleloader I'm carrying, a small set of binoculars, perhaps a small compact camera, a few paper towels, and maybe a snack. This could be a candy bar, a sandwich, cookies, whatever. Many, many days I don't come in at noon, hunt all day (or until successful), so go prepared for such a stay. Very few hunters do, this but among those of us who do, we've killed lots of turkeys during the middle of the day, spring, fall, winter, regardless of the season.

You may ponder my carrying a slingshot—let me say a few things about what can happen if you don't. Let's presume you are hunting where cattle are present. It's very easy for an old cow to walk smack between you and a turkey just when you're about ready to open the ball. If you hunt around cattle long enough it will happen. Many range cattle are very curious about turkey noises coming from a bush. Calves are even worse.

Whitetails can also be bad medicine. Spooking the heck out of a deer just when a big gobbler is getting near, guarantees there's a good chance the tom will get the idea that perhaps he too shall make for yonder mountain. Ranches that stock exotic game animals have so many they become a nuisance. I may be the only guy who's laid a stone on an aoudad with a slingshot,

Many hunts back into rugged mountain terrain means camping out, and that means toting along stuff to eat. The Indians used to gorge themselves before going on a raid. They said it was easier to carry it in their belly than lug it along on a horse. However, I've found my stomach isn't that big so I have to carry along the makin's.

but I don't want the critters around when I'm dealing with a gobbler. And though the beasts don't seem to pay a hunter much mind, when a big old grandaddy turkey walks into sight, the darned animal snorts and carries on, and runs off the bird. Nope, one smack on the rear with the slingshot will prevent such shenanigans. I nailed a wild hog in the backside one hot evening too, and you should have seen him light out. Seemed like I could hear him breaking brush for a half mile. Anyhow, what a hunter wears and carries has lots of bearing on the outcome of the hunt, whether it be for personal comfort, or scragging a turkey.

Footwear

Let's take a look at what a turkey hunter should wear from the ground and work our way up. What about feet? Footwear will vary with time of year and terrain. For example, a spring hunt to Florida calls for lightweight boots, preferably ones made of canvas. The hunter after Osceola turkeys oftentimes finds it necessary to wade water, and the feet could be wet for

A camp in backwoods Florida means a tent, ice chests, and if you like to really be comfortable, some lawnchairs. Ed LeForce (left), Lennis Rose (center) and Phil Conrady, loaf around camp during the afternoon, since Florida doesn't allow afternoon hunting for turkeys.

hours. 'Nam boots, those Army brogans of black leather made famous by United States soldiers during the Vietnam War, are often seen in Florida swamps. I wade around in the creek swamps and cypress strands in plain old Redwing work shoes. They dry out quickly, keep their shape drying on my feet, and are light. I don't wear any socks when I'm planning on doing some wading.

The Rocky Mountain springtime hunter, hoping to put his sights on a Merriam wild turkey will probably be wearing 8-inch, or ankletop, lugged-sole mountain boots. Feet need the protection from rocks and the traction that the lugs provide. In most instances, these boots will also do the trick for the fall turkey hunter with perhaps the addition of heavier socks or a second pair. I know hunters who wear nothing but shoepacs for fall and winter hunts, as the lower waterproof portion keeps the feet dry in water and snow. Too, shoepacs ordinarily have good tread-like soles which give excellent traction on damp terrain. The famous L.L. Bean boot with its rope tread design is a favorite because it keeps feet dry, is light in weight,

The author's high-top Bean boots come in handy especially when hunting much of the Deep South's swamp country where so many cagey old Eastern gobblers hang out. Deep snow, sandburrs, brush, heavy dew, a pair of 16-inch topped Bean boots will protect you and keep you dry.

35

and the shallow tread does not allow a buildup of several pounds of clinging mud. My 14-inch pair of Bean boots have seen me across many streams, swamp ponds, and what have you without my feet getting wet. Even when the water is above the tops, I won't take on much water if the boots are laced tight and I wade across hurriedly.

Hightop boots also offer some protection against snakes. For those hunters who fear snakebite, 14- and 16-inch hightop boots made of heavy leather will turn a snakebite. I have a pair of Gokey Bullhides that a rattler tried his teeth on some years back, and he bounced off them like hail off a tin roof. Snake leggings made of lightweight plastic also work. Many folks scoff at talk about snakebite, but don't be misled. There are few pains that compare to the pain immediately after a rattlesnake has sunk in his fangs. But whatever you wear, have shoes that fit and feel comfortable. I've been in camps where street shoes, work shoes, all sorts of hightopped boots, and cowboy boots were worn. Tennis shoes, too. More than anything else though, the wearer felt good in them.

A springtime hunter seeking Eastern wild turkeys can wear most lightweight 8-inch boots or hightop work shoes. I've noticed hunters in everything from jogging shoes to shotgun top Wellingtons. Lightweight socks fill out the bill.

Hunting turkeys farther west, late in April, calls for footwear very light in weight, and if possible, a boot or shoe that allows the foot to breathe. It is often hot when you are hunting Rio Grandes in Texas and Oklahoma, and your feet will perspire considerably. Blow sand, sometimes encountered in this terrain, calls for a boot with traction, but not the heavy lugged variety; they are a turkey hunter killer in such stuff. Loose sand can sap the strength from legs quicker than any other ground cover. Weed seeds and sand burrs are also problems in Rio Grande country. The best footwear here are 8-inch boots with canvas or light leather tops and a treaded sole. Keep these as light as possible.

In Nicaragua, I wore a pair of old canvas wading shoes, my favorites for wading swamps while limb-lining for catfish. A perfect choice for the jungle terrain as I was in and out of water. And they were very light while climbing volcanoes. A month later hunting the outback of old Mexico's Sierra

Part of any traveling hunter's equipment must be maps and hunting regulations. You can't hunt if you don't know where you are or where you're going; and you darned sure better keep the gun cased if you don't know what the rule book says.

Madres vast mountain range, I wore my old work shoes. They are also lightweight, and weight's critical when climbing steep mountains where each step isn't measured by the ground gained, but by how much weight is being carried uphill. Choose footwear that fits the area to be hunted. Anyone who's

I have a pair of Gokey Bullhides that a rattler tried his teeth on some years back, and he bounced off them like hail off a tin roof.

hunted much of south Texas, places like the King ranch, are aware that canvas shoes are a bad choice there due to cactus spines. Cactus is tough and folks who've never been around them have no idea how quickly these can penetrate.

Clothing

Pants and shirts? Most of today's hunters wear varying weights of camouflage clothing. Heavy or lightweight under-wear will make up for what the outer garments lack, and the heavy outer garments can be peeled off as needed. What most hunters fail to take into consideration is what they will be doing while hunting. If you plan on considerable walking, you won't need so many clothes and should always leave camp feeling a little cool. The hunter who sits and calls for much of the day will need heavier clothing, since he will chill during the early morning and late afternoon hours. During mid-day, though, he may need to remove garments so it's smart to wear a fanny pack, or a small daypack, to carry excess clothing. Chances are, sometime during the day he will be calling from a stand for some time and may need to put some of that clothing back on.

I hunt often in Old Mexico, back high in the Sierra Madres. Camp is usually at a lower altitude than where the Gould's wild turkey is found. Therefore, the first order of the day upon leaving camp is a long hard climb. Before this climb has ended, I am soaked with sweat. But it is cold high up in the Sierras, so once I am up there, I get chilled, as my "longhandles" are wet. But, I carry my coat and heavy over-shirt tied to my

I don't go anywhere without a well-stocked First-aid chest. Cough drops, aspirin, prescription pain killers, flu tablets, eye and ear drops, bandages of all sorts, even a device for opening up an air-way in the throat.

belt, directly along my backbone and out of the way while climbing and put them on to warm me up. Often I am cold while climbing, but it is better then than later.

The number of camouflage patterns on the market have finally come to the ridiculous stage—there're so many, making a choice becomes confusing. All-Purpose Realtree, Universal Trebark, Mossey Oak Tree Stand, Woodland, take your pick, all are good in the proper surroundings. You'll bump into hunters wearing several different patterns in the same hunk of woods, some far more suited for the area than others. I have clients who come outfitted in camos that in no way blend to the terrain. Two guys came draped in duck marsh stuff; that shows up like a hog at a lawn party when I try to hide them in dark green foliage. Just makes my job all the tougher. Far the best place for them is in sight-proof blinds. There's only one excellent camo for dark green foliage and that is the dark version of the old woodland pattern. The darker the better.

Trebark is excellent out in sagebrush country, and equally at home in big woods, particularly big pines or against cottonwood bark. The All-Purpose stuff is just that, and fits many different terrains. I like Universal Trebark, and Mossey Oak too. Actually all of them are fine, but a hunter should try to look at his camo of choice in the woods, and objectively. Lay them against the surroundings, hang 'em in a tree, across a bush, or have a buddy sit against a tree or two to see how he fades in with the trees and the surroundings.

All sorts of wearing apparel is made in camo material—gloves, face masks, caps—you can even get belts, billfolds, underwear, handkerchiefs, and heck knows what else. (Who'd be crazy enough to want a billfold made in camo?)

Ed LeForce, a hunting buddy of mine, always had his favorite turkey gun covered with camo tape, but he took the stuff off. Said as it got older (or he did) he couldn't find the barrel when he raised the gun. The camo faded it right into the landscape. I heard hunters say they laid the gun down then had to look for it. Can you imagine camo toilet paper? *Hey, they have such stuff, really!*

Rain gear comes in all sorts of camouflage material. Be aware though that rainwear does not "breathe," and after you've worn it awhile, you may be as wet as if you'd been out in the rain. Perspiration can't escape. The more you move around, the worse it'll get.

One critical piece of clothing or camouflage not often worn by turkey hunters is the face mask, or face paint. Out in turkey country their smiling kissers loom up like a searchlight in a fog. Wild turkeys aren't blind. And while these folks might get by in areas where the birds are seldom hunted, it's a dead cinch they'll go home empty-handed in areas where the birds are heavily hunted. A true wild turkey, one of those woods stalking critters with a binocular stuck on each side of his head, will lock on a hunter's white face at sixty or seventy yards every time. Numerous areas in the country have been restocked with birds I refer to as "tame turkeys" because these birds aren't very difficult to hunt. In fact, often the hardest part is getting permission to hunt on private land. But don't confuse these turkeys with the real thing.

If the hunter isn't dressed for the hunt, he may not enjoy it as he'd hoped. These two men are outfitted for mountain hunting, both wearing sturdy boots and coveralls.

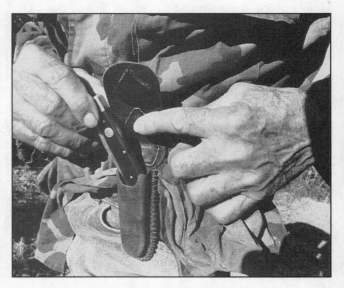

When you purchase a knife, whether it's a belt model, or pocket model, you'll always be smart to buy the very best you can afford. I tote a Boker pocketknife in a belt sheath. If there's a finer steel for staying sharp, I've yet to find it.

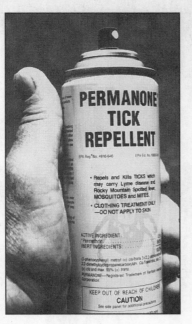

Ticks and Lyme disease—the very mention makes folks shudder. Only this past spring I hunted some areas simply crawling with the little beasts. Chiggers too. All of them will play havoc with a good time. I haven't found a spray repellent that keeps every last one from hiking up your pant leg, but this new Premanone comes pretty close.

When hunting big country, like the Rocky Mountains or Sierra Madres range in Mexico, I carry two knives, a belt knife and a pocketknife. With a compass and a safety box of matches, I can spend the night out if I get lost.

When I switched over to muzzle-loading shotguns years ago, I decided to hunt the way my grandad did, and his grandad before him. They had no camouflage clothing or other such stuff and I decided I wouldn't use it either. So I began hunting without camos. And facepaint. Boy, the first turkey I called in made me feel like one of those naked jaybirds we've always heard about. Over the years, I've lost a number of chances simply because I was detected before the bird got into range. And, range with an old muzzleloader isn't forty or fifty yards. At least not to me, it's inside thirty, best if within twenty-five. But, all this did is make a better hunter of me. I learned how to utilize terrain and cover probably to a finer degree than many Indians had. Today I have to laugh when some so-called expert gives a seminar on the fine points of shooting turkeys, and then tells his audience he uses a 3½-inch Extra Full choke 10-gauge, loaded with shells to match. Usually his listeners never grasp the fact that the expert hasn't yet learned the true meaning of the words "good hunter." Long-range blasting with a big-bore gun is the mark of a man with no confidence in his abilities to draw the game into close range.

When buying rainwear, it is wise to "listen" to it. Depending on the material, rainwear will make all sorts of sounds when worn through brushy country. A turkey will hear the coat coming well in advance of the hunter's footsteps. Slip it on in the store, brush your hands across it, brush it against other clothing, making note of the noise it will make in a silent woods once the rain has ceased. You will be able to walk ever so quietly on the soaked leaves, but will your clothes give you away?

If you hunt areas where insects are a serious problem, you'd be smart to get a headnet. I have a camo jacket, very lightweight, which has a complete full-size headnet. This thing rests on my hat, gives me good vision, but keeps out everything. Tight cuffs around wrists and a tight waistband won't let in bugs. Dog ear gnats, Buffalo gnats, no-see'ums, blue-tailed flies, mosquitoes, and in some regions, sweat bees are all out there just waiting to make your hunt uncomfortable.

The first turkey I called in made me feel like one of those naked jaybirds we've always heard about.

Of course, there're a jillion kinds of bug sprays available, all of which are simply repellents. Some repel better than others, but none makes the little critters stiff-legged-stone-dead, which is what we wish it would do. A couple years back I found a new brand of tick spray, advertised as *the best*. I used up one whole can on a short Texas hunt. Obviously the maker had never tried it on a tough Texas hill country tick. They drank up the stuff, waded through beach-heads of it, never slowing down, but attacked me like I was meat on the table. Chiggers too. Darned near each day, smack in the middle of hunting, I'd have to peel off clothes to ferret out some of the little beasts which I could feel clambering about my body.

I usually carry with me in my hunting vest: water bottle, knife, compass, crow call, turkey call, notebook and pen, small saw (or pruners), and a slingshot with a bunch of .40 balls. There will also be a few short hunks of heavy cord, small slips of sandpaper, and some chalk, the last two for use on the box call, or on a slate if I'm using it. Invariably I take two or three small plastic Zip-Loc bags, two or three paper towels, and a small camera.

Other Essentials

I never hunt without a bandana. It can be used as a bandage, a washcloth, a gun cleaning rag, or left tied to a tree telling friends the direction I've gone. I've toted no telling how many gobblers from the woods with one, using it to tie the legs together.

I never leave camp without toilet tissue folded into a tiny packet and secured with a rubber band. Nor would I be caught in the woods without a knife. What style of knife is strictly a personal choice. Ordinarily, I pack a belt knife if I know I'll be away from the pickup for several hours, or hunting two or more days on end. You won't catch me hunting strange country, places new to me, without a belt knife. A good knife is one of the best friends you'll have if you get lost. What I like about a belt knife is that it doesn't take up room in a pocket. Many Westerners tote large folding knives in a belt-worn button-down sheaths. I often use a belt knife for spreading butter on bread, maybe to cut a chunk of venison, spear a pickle, or smear applesauce on a tortilla. When it isn't being used for

You've heard the credit card ad, "Don't leave home without one." Well, if you are heading out to find some gobbler back in the high lonesome, I'd suggest you never leave camp without a good compass.

those tasks, or cutting small branches to open up a shooting lane, I can always cut a toothpick with it, and then lean back and whittle.

Turkey hunting usually begins in the dark hours just before dawn. You may need a flashlight. These are plentiful today, in all sizes and colors. Though I seldom carry one in the field, I never leave home without one stuck in the duffel bag. My

A *good knife is one of the best friends you'll have if you get lost.*

favorite is an old Army surplus, olive drab two-cell with a short cord tied to it. After I no longer need it, I tie it to my belt near my back where it is out of my way. I have another flashlight which works well; it uses a tiny lithium battery and drops into a pants pocket.

Another handy light for the early morning turkey hunter is the headlamp mounted on an elastic band used by fishermen for years. This leaves hands free and the band can also be tied around a belt loop when not in use. The batteries are small and fit in a hip pocket. Head lamps put out a stronger beam than an ordinary flashlight. Invariably, I'll carry an extra light in case someone forgets his, or his batteries are dead. A hunter travel-

ing back into areas as remote as Mexico's high Sierras should always pack spare batteries. Check them to be certain they work, are fresh and fully charged.

Matches? Some folks need them for smoking. Or if it is chilly while you are standing there waiting for the eastern sky to begin streaking light, you may want to build a fire to warm up. Many mornings I've arrived in some far neck-of-the-woods too early and, while waiting for an old bird to gobble, have used my matches to build a tiny fire. Feels good if you are hunting Rocky Mountain Merriam turkeys up on the high mountains where springtime mornings can be quite cold. Keep the fire small, and the turkeys will pay no mind whatsoever. Make certain you *do not set the woods afire. Make certain that you put the fire out thoroughly.*

I carry my matches in a small tin matchsafe. These are ordinary kitchen matches, wrapped in wax paper, tied in tiny separate bundles, and placed in the matchsafe so each bundle can be removed without bothering others. You may have cold wet hands when you need matches, and they will be more easily handled if wrapped. The small fold of wax paper can also be utilized with wood punk or grass to get a fire blazing. I replace them at least twice a year to keep them fresh and usable. If you get lost always remember that dry wood can often be found on the underside of small trees that have fallen over and hung up

I always carry two flashlights with me and some extra batteries and bulbs, too.

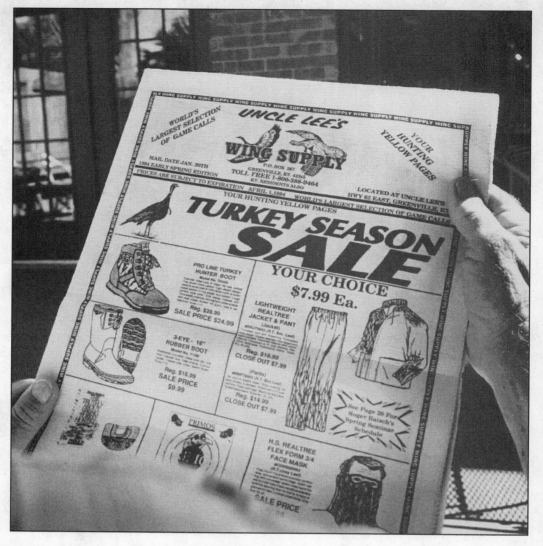

Wing Supply is a supply house in Kentucky that has everything a turkey hunter could want but the turkey. And, my money says they'll find you one of those if you'll lay enough greenbacks on the counter.

on another tree. Fallen logs can often be kicked apart, revealing dry punky wood inside. If you are hunting piney woods, a pine knot kicked free from a downed tree makes a good fire starter. The knot contains pitch which lights easily. Whittle a pile of bark and slivers from dead saplings or branches for a little kindling to get the fire going. Throw your cap over your kindling to keep it dry.

Very often I will have a section of map in a pocket. I won't need the complete map, as I'll only be able to hunt a tiny portion of it, but I'll study the area as a whole, then cut out the area I plan to hunt. Topographical maps are excellent for this purpose, as they give elevations, creeks, trails, plus a jillion other landmarks which can be used as reference points for the wandering hunter. Ordinary national forest maps will quite often do, but once again, these are very large, and it is best to cut out the portion needed. The turkey hunter who studies maps becomes acquainted with turkey habitat requirements for the various subspecies and can then apply this knowledge to locate areas which could be very productive. In addition, the person who has done his homework, will be able to give all his concentration to hunting turkeys if he is reasonably sure of not becoming lost.

My advice to anyone who suddenly gets disoriented in the wilderness is to quietly sit down and study his moves up until the present time. Go over your route as best as you can recall. You may be able to untangle your confusion before it becomes a reality. Study your surroundings. In your mind's eye, picture yourself as you traveled the last few hours. What direction were you headed when you left the vehicle? Did you study the area map before you took off on your hunt?

Probably a great number of turkey hunters have become lost, at least for a short time, after chasing a gobbling turkey. On one occasion, I was thoroughly confused for a couple of hours after I'd chased a piney woods turkey around and over some up-and-down hills in the Deep South. I was sure of my directions when I first heard him gobbling, but by the time it was over, the wind had quit, and the sky had clouded over. I no longer knew north from "sic 'em." What's worse, I didn't get the turkey. After coming to the conclusion that I was walking in circles, I began striking a straight line (by keeping trees lined up as far ahead as I could see) and soon broke out on a road. Since that day years ago, I have been turned around a number of times. In every instance, it was because I concentrated more on the kill than where I was; I was no longer paying strict attention to my whereabouts, noting landmarks, the

No, I'm not a cook so don't bring your knife and fork to my place. But, there are times a person has to make do and this was one of them. So I won't forget anything, I have a master list of camping gear.

distance traveled, and all the things I would have noticed had my mind been free. I have never spent the night in the woods as a result of being lost, because I have always studied maps of all the areas I've hunted, and by taking a compass reading, and then striking a general line, have been able to walk out.

Nobody has a greater respect for the elements than I. I search out backcountry since I prefer the extra miles it takes to get back to where there are fewer hunters. Therefore, getting truly lost could have its setbacks. Traveling to many places far from roads and trails in Arizona, New Mexico, and in particu-

Probably a great number of turkey hunters have become lost, at least for a short time, after chasing a gobbling turkey.

lar, far back in Mexico's Sierra Madre Mountains, I plan on hunting hard, intent on bagging turkeys. So I prepare before I go, and when I get there, I tote along the few items which could mean the difference between walking out, or *staying there for good!* Don't forget to keep your compass a few feet

away from a metal magnetic source because it will upset its field. *Have faith in your compass!* If you hunt enough in back out-of-the-way places, the time will come when you need the instrument only to feel that it is wrong. Compasses don't lie. The needle will point to magnetic north. It will be up to you to decide the direction you should walk.

As for extra items you may want to tote—a camera is nice to have along. Looking at color photos will bring back all the fond memories of a hunt that otherwise might be soon forgotten. Others will bring a burst of laughter and a longing to go back to a place you grew fond of in just a few short hours. You don't need to be weighed down these days carrying a camera. There are a number of compact full-frame 35mms the size of a package of cigarettes on today's market. I bought an Olympus a couple of years ago which weighs only a few ounces, and I carry it everywhere I go.

Binoculars fall into the same class. They aren't something you must have, but there is nothing handier. Few people carry them, but those who do will observe wildlife that is not often seen. Except when I am hunting areas I am familiar with, I am seldom without field glasses. Binoculars should be light in weight, compact in size, and for turkey hunting, have a wide field of view. Do not skimp when buying field glasses; cheap binoculars often will not focus properly. Take the time to read the brochure included with the binocular *before purchasing*. If the glass cannot be focused properly in the store, it won't work any better in the field and my advice is not to buy it. Take the time to find a good glass and spend a bit more money than

Do not skimp when buying field glasses; cheap binoculars often will not focus properly.

you'd originally budgeted to get the best you can afford. You won't regret it.

Too many folks treat binoculars the same as they do a camera. When they need it, it's back in the truck or at home. I agree, binoculars are just another something to pack around, but when a priority is placed on what to carry while afield, and what not to carry, then these items should be measured in terms of their ability to make the hunt a success. Time after time, while hunting Gould turkeys in Mexico, or Rio Grandes on the vast shinnoak prairies of the Southwest, or Merriams among the Rocky Mountains, or Osceolas in the sprawling palmetto burns on vast Florida ranches, even Eastern turkeys in various places, you wouldn't catch me leaving the truck

without them. Field glasses fall into the same category as the shotgun, shells, calls and pocketknife.

Today's market offers a tremendous selection of binocular sizes, powers, styles of construction and some even come with camouflage finishes. The bulk will have a strap for carrying them about the neck. Binoculars should be carried high. Shortening the strap brings them to mid-chest. And, since a binocular bounces as the hunter walks or runs, a strap arrangement, known commercially as a Cuban hitch, is needed to keep the glasses snug against the body. I invariably slip my binocs inside my shirt or jacket to prevent this bouncing.

If you don't sleep like a log, because your buddies snore like a bunch of fat hogs all through the night, you owe it to yourself to go to the drugstore and buy a couple pairs of ear plugs. I never leave home without them. The noise stoppers I use are made of a soft plastic-like material, which form-fits the wearer when inserted into the ear. I can still hear the alarm clock if I set it near the head of my sleeping bag. These soft ear plugs are cheap, disposable, clean and easy to carry. If you sleep like a log, pack an alarm clock, or buy yourself a wristwatch with an alarm.

Drinking water! Are you going to drink from the streams or take it with you? Time was when I drank from streams all across the country. Nowadays, I'm leary of doing this, mostly due to all the hoopla about pollution. About the only water I'll

Your vehicle may resemble those of the Okies leaving Oklahoma for California back during the '30s by the time you get everything loaded into, and onto, it.

Don't forget the bedroll, your alarm clock and your gun.

For the hunter planning on being away from vehicle or camp from pre-dawn to dusk, I would suggest a small rucksack, fanny pack, or back-slung daypack for toting a lunch and a bottle of water. Fanny packs have become quite popular, because these belt-slung bags are easy to get into, regardless of the layers of clothing the hunter may be wearing. My first one was made of green canvas and sewn to my specifications by the local canvas company. Fanny packs were not even a foggy idea back in those days. Today, they can be bought with zippered pockets, padded waistbands in contour design, and the whole thing made of rain resistant camo material.

Daypacks fit over the shoulders, ordinarily have a back pocket plus side pockets, and come with, or without, internal framing. The old models had wooden frames. These will tote a canteen, spare jacket, rain gear, and lunch, with room left over for other small items.

From daypacks, the choice grows ultimately to the Alpine pack in which a small spike camp can be carried. It is possible to still-hunt while shouldering a large backpack, though if done often, the hunter should buy a model with a narrow frame to allow slightly better gun movement. Whatever pack a hunter chooses, he should strive to buy one of tough, durable material, as backpacks snag on branches, and one with shoulder pads if the wearer is not accustomed to wearing a pack.

A hunter packing far into the back country, where he will be out of touch for a few days, should stick a new compact first-aid kit in his pack, along with a small book on first-aid treatments. Special items may be added, such as cough drops, cold tablets, or any special medications needed. A hunter with pre-existing physical problems—for example, a heart condition—should make this known to others in his party, plus give them instructions as to the location of emergency medications, and how to administer them. The medicine containers should have the instructions clearly marked for easy reading and, if the medication is taken aboard airliners, or across borders into other countries, it is wise to tape the prescription to the outside of the container.

People who wear eye glasses should pack an extra pair if they are seriously handicapped without them. I have a friend who had one set of prescription lenses mounted in a set of frames to which a camo headnet is glued. Works like a charm.

Because I call with a trumpet caller so much of the time, you'll often find a roll or two of Life Saver mints in my pockets. These can be quickly popped into the mouth to prevent "dry mouth," which is so common when using trumpet calls. The excitement of listening to an old gobbler sound off, or hearing the whistling of scattered young birds, causes the hunter to suddenly suffer "dry mouth," and not be able to make a decent note on the call. Mints or coughdrops will ease this quickly.

Hunting from horseback offers a wider selection of what can be taken along for a day's hunt. The essential gear is the same, though a spike camp including a lightweight tent, sleeping bag, coffee pot, and other such stuff can be stuffed in saddlebags or packbox. A rain slicker can be tied on the saddle.

drink today is when I can see the source, be it melting snow, a spring, or an artesian well. And, the stream must be small in size. In many areas of the West, streams will go underground for long distances, surfacing well filtered. In Mexico it is not uncommon to find a stream bed that runs a foot deep immediately after a heavy mountain shower, but downstream a few miles where it has not rained, is dry, the water having gone underground. There are also a great many additives on today's market which make water safe to drink. A tiny bottle plus a cup to mix it with water is all that's required. The directions are on the bottle. Another device which will purify water is a long plastic straw-like tube through which water is drawn, straight from the creek into the hunter's mouth. It is as much trouble to carry as a fountain pen and gives the user the option of drinking as much as he pleases. These little devices make drinking time-consuming, but if a person is thirsty, the time is well spent.

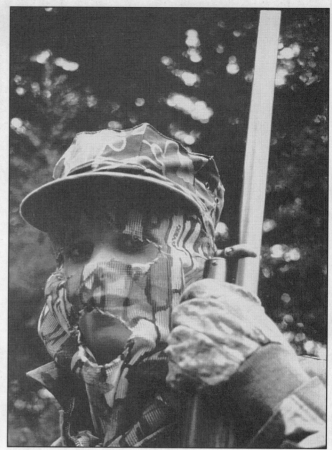

This is what camouflage will do for a pretty girl. My grandaughter, Chantell Preston, shows how a facemask, gloves and cap can hide a person's face and hands from the binocular-like vision of a wild turkey.

Few outfitters furnish scabbards for shotguns, so the shotgun hunter, should fit his gun with a sling, or carry along his personal shotgun scabbard. I advise the latter because hunting from horseback involves moving among trees, and without a scabbard, tree branches will catch on it continually. In packing saddlebags, packboxes, or backpacks, remember to pack the items you'll use throughout the day in side pockets, or on top, where these can be easily retrieved.

I am never without a full set of hand tools, from hammer to nails, wire, pump pliers and lineman pliers.

The close-to-home hunter will undoubtedly be driving a vehicle. Like so many of today's hunters, he will want to drive the car just as near to where he hunts as possible, which is often too near, but he will do this anyhow. Since he will run the risk of getting stuck in mud, sand, or perhaps snow, he should keep a shovel, crosscut tree saw, a length of chain, a few 4x6 wooden blocks, and a couple 8x10 sheets of heavy-duty plastic in the vehicle at all times. The chain is for pulling the truck out, providing someone can be found to give him a pull. The wooden blocks are used in stabilizing the jack should

the vehicle need to be jacked off the ground in unstable soils. The plastic sheets are used when it is necessary to lie in mud or snow in order to perform tasks on a broken down vehicle. I am never without a full set of hand tools, from hammer to nails, wire, pump pliers, lineman pliers, socket wrenches, spare fanbelts, jumper cables, a spare tire, and the jack. In the kit bag with all these are extra fuses for the truck, and spare light bulbs.

I'm also never without a water can, or a grub box with eating utensils and some cans of food. Wooden matches, a can of insect spray and spare mantles for the gasoline lantern can be found in the grub box, too. Paper towels and a couple of complete changes of dry clothing, including socks, are always in my pickup, and there have been a number of times when I, or a buddy, have been darned glad these were along. A well-supplied first-aid kit remains in a compartment in the vehicle, as do two fire extinguishers, one in the cab, the other in the pickup's camper shell.

The average hunter traveling by air will need to scale down the hunting items he carries. This is not due to the restrictions airlines place on numbers of pounds allowed per passenger, but in being aware that the hunter will be digging through luggage each time he needs the tiniest article. So the fewer bags he has along, the less digging.

No knife at all is better than a dull one. This little brass knife sharpener comes with a belt holster, is easy to use, doesn't weigh much and will turn a dull blade into a sharp one pretty quick.

I take two pair of footwear, wearing one, stowing the other in the baggage. I'll bring a set of clothes for eating out, if such an occasion arises. When hunting backcountry, I'll hang my good clothes on a nail, leaving them there until ready to head for home. Often I've worn or carried a coat on board an airliner, lessening the baggage weight. I'll pack one set of hunting clothes, whereas at home I would have two in the truck. I'll count the days I'm to be gone, then throw in socks and underwear for each, plus one. Very often I'll leave the shaving gear at home and worry about that when I get back. I do pack a large towel and washcloth. I put in a small flashlight; it could come in handy on the hunt or when searching my luggage for something. The alarm clock? If I know a buddy will have one, I leave it at home. I carry a camera and hope it doesn't get busted plus an extra roll or two of film. Last, but very important, *two or three heavy-duty large plastic trash bags,* folded compactly, and tied with a short wire.

Aside from a billfold, or whatever it is you wish to carry your hunting license in, plus a turkey call or two, all else you should need are a few shotgun shells. A few, I said, not half a box.

Talking about traveling to hunt turkeys makes me think about hunting Florida one spring with Mike Monier and Ed Norwood. I'd flown in from Oklahoma, Ed from ole Miss., and Mike from upper New Jersey. We camped out back toward a swamp that was labeled Gator Slew, and of all things had rented a small red hatchback when we left the air terminal.

Anyhow, one morning while trying to raise a gobbler we spied a wild boar, a really good one. Mike said he'd like to take the critter if we could slip into near gunshot. The only thing we had for hogs were several 00 buckshot. Telling Mike to stick to me like glue, I began a long stalk, which ended up out in very short cover where the hog stood facing us. Hogs are ugly, but it seemed this one just made a point of it. His attitude needed adjusting real bad. With a faceoff at what turned out to be near sixteen yards, I advised Mike he'd best lay the gun across my back (we were bellycrawling) and fire when ready. The quicker the better.

I said, "Shoot 'em in the face."

Mike shot.

Here comes His Majesty Hog full tilt, all out, the pedal to the metal.

"Shoot, shoot, shoot," I was pleading by then as old Bad Breath was closing like a freight train in open pasture.

Mike's shooting had no effect. But, luckily just as the big hog was at arm's length, he canted off to the left, made a big circle, and gave up the ship. His tusks, "tushes" we always called them on the farm, looked a whole bunch bigger now that he was laid out. It was some three miles back to camp, so I told my buddies to drag the critter over in the shade and gut him while I went to get our vehicle. Trotting back towards camp, that is when I wasn't walking, I made note of all the swamp holes along the trail. Not much of a trail for a small hatchback, made strictly for good old pavement. Mike and Ed were stunned to see us coming, me and the car. They couldn't understand how I'd gotten there but we propped Mr. Pig in the

My only regret was that there was no turkey hunter standing along that trail that day.

back seat, loaded ourselves in what was left, and with nary a *"Hi-ho Silver,"* lifted off.

You've heard of cars planing—the only times we planed were when the wheels came back to earth. It was then that my friends learned how I got that little semblance of an automobile three miles back into a swamp. My only regret was that there was no turkey hunter standing along that trail that day.

Can you imagine what he'd have thought? A wild man at the wheel. And a hog yelling instructions from the back seat. That'd make anyone give up chasing turkeys.

Until that day, I'd searched after turkeys in boats, all sorts of trucks, cars, horses, three-wheelers, big airplanes and small airplanes, (bad airplanes, but that's another story), but my finest hour was driving a little hatchback to Gator Slew.

Gear for Hunting in Far-Off Places

A hunter wanting to kill a Gould's or the small Ocellated turkey will have to leave the United States, so let's talk seriously a moment about such a project. First, you can't locate a guide after you get to your destination. At least I'd certainly not plan on such foolishness. You'll need to make those kind of arrangements well in advance of your departure and then with that person's help make your plans. Supposedly there are guides and outfitters who take hunters after Gould's turkeys in Mexico. A guy who claims to do just that has called me a few times and though I've never hunted with him, I understand he's telling prospective clients that I've booked hunts with him. I have never booked a hunt in Mexico with *anyone* so this guy's stories are just that, *stories*.

How best to take advantage of camouflage clothing is shown here. Hunters in rock strewn country have a great ally in these rock piles. With such protection at his back, nobody can shoot him from behind.

Those of us who fly across country to hunt the various subspecies of wild turkeys transport our gun in a hard case, usually one made of high impact plastic. Don't forget to pack your regular gun case, as you'll need it once you've begun your hunt. George Stover, a hunting buddy of the author's, removes his gun from a camo case.

Plastic throwaway soda bottles make excellent water bottles or canteens. The author always carries a few in the truck for emergencies.

Be aware that in addition to Gould's turkeys, Mexico also has Rio Grandes in some areas. So, if your hunt is not back in the high mountains, you may be hunting Rio Grandes instead of Gould's. You want to get this straight with your guide. *All* of my hunting for the Gould has been back in the high Sierra Madres range, which runs north and south toward the west side of the country. It's simply a continuation of what we know in the U.S. as the Continental Divide.

Your whole trip will be easier if you get a passport before you go. This costs $50, is good for ten years, and can be applied for at your local post office. It can take several weeks to get one so start early. If you don't get a passport, you'll have to fill out a Visa. I also carry along a letter from my police chief attesting to my character, and a copy of my birth certificate, just in case I ever need them.

There are few modern conveniences back in Mexico's mountains; sometimes you'll have trouble finding a bar of soap and a pan of water. And, with bad water, there's always a chance you'll come down with some alien bug. Your family doctor can give you prescriptions for those emergencies, and you should discuss with him where you're going in case he has other suggestions in terms of immunization shots for cholera, yellow fever, malaria, etc. Don't forget a booster shot for tetanus. Doctors and hospitals are scarce in Mexico. Don't think that back in Mexico's mountains you can just go to a doctor's office, or a hospital if you suddenly need it. If you're far in the outback where you're most likely to find Gould's wild turkeys, you won't even find a house or two; the nearest hospital is probably the one you left back home.

If you're touchy about what you eat or drink then either carry all your food and water with you from this side of the border or stay home. Mexico may not be for you.

You must definitely take with you all your personal medical aids, clothing, sleeping bag, etc., so the better your communication with the guide, the better your chances for knowing what to take. Iron out with him the purchase of your license, whether he's the one arranging it or you. Also find out from him what you'll need in order to get one. Ask your outfitter to send you the small booklet published each year in Mexico showing the season dates. This can vary from state to state. No longer is there a fall hunt for turkeys in Mexico, which is sad.

Ask your outfitter about guns—will he want you to bring yours, or is he going to furnish you with a gun? I never take one; it's so much easier to shoot whatever my host has. But, some hunters insist they can't use a "strange gun." I've yet to understand how such folks get along in the Army.

You will need a gun permit and the further you get from civilization the more you'll need one. If you should be halted by the Federales, the first thing they'll want to see is your gun permit. If you've mislaid it, then you'll get a chance to try and recall exactly where while you lie in jail. Good luck, amigos.

You'll not find nicer people anywhere than in Mexico, but for too many years they've been treated badly by some gringo Americans. It's kinda hard for them to forget such stuff so keep your mouth shut except when spoken to, follow their lead, be a good guest, and you'll get along fine. I eat their food, drink their water, sleep where they have made arrangements, and have never had a better time.

Below is a master list of the items I always carry along on my Mexican hunts. You may wish to revise it and include your items of choice. I'd advise keeping such a list, and every time you head out for something more than an overnight hunt, go over the list before you leave. It will help prevent you from forgetting anything.

Camping Gear

Tent
Sleeping bag (with foam mattress and ground cover)
Pillow (optional)
Short broom
Shovel
Axe
Bow saw (chain saw optional)
Folding stove, fuel and lantern
Box of wooden matches
Large First-aid chest, fully stocked
Weed cutter
Fifty feet of small rope and clothes pins
Plastic Bags
Black plastic tape and duct tape
Soap, towel, washcloth, bucket
Wet wipes
Paper plates, cups, metal forks, spoons and knives
Several rolls paper towels
Toilet paper
Collapsible water cans (plastic)
Small mirror
Flashlight and spare batteries
Heavy-duty pliers and wire cutters, needle nose pliers, construction wire, sack of several sizes of nails, hammer, hatchet, screwdrivers, channel lock pliers.
Small tarp
Lawn chairs (folding)
Folding table
Heavy-duty portable campfire grate

Personal Items

Long johns, socks, shorts, pants, boots
Heavy coats
Rain gear
Gloves
Camos
Fanny pack and/or backpack
Compass, camera, extra film
Battery razor, toothbrush and toothpaste
Match safe
Personal medications
Ear plugs
Cough drops
Canteen
Needle and thread (large eye needle, simulated sinew)
Eye glasses
Coffee cups

Face masks are almost a must for light-skinned hunters. If you don't have a mask, try to keep in the shade or deep shadows. Face paint or smearing your face with charcoal from a dead fire will work just as well.

For the likes of a trip into Mexico I'd go through both lists, then cull out what I deemed "musts" after finding out what the mode of transportation is. Where I'll be staying, what to expect in terms of the weather.

Of course, food is personal preference. Some hunts back in the Sierra Madres we've lived on only one or two kinds of food, mainly tortillas and tamales, but both were darned good. I never seem to get tired of either so no sweat. Some folks would have a problem with such goings-on, but then they've been living too good here in the States all their lives. A week or so on water (no ice) and tortillas and tamales never hurt anybody. Mix in some Gould's turkey and what better meals could you ask for.

I've been on other hunts which should have been great but weren't, even though we took everything including the kitchen sink.

Being prepared can make or break a hunt. I've been on great hunts where we've forgotten some of the stuff on the list, yet got by, killed turkeys, had a grand time. I've been on other hunts which should have been great but weren't, even though we took everything including the kitchen sink. Killed turkeys too. Usually the weather messes things up, but rain's never kept me from hunting and killing turkeys. However, wet boots and soggy clothes, day after day, while slipping and sliding through the countryside, with rain and snow getting down your neck, can get pretty discouraging and disgusting. Without a good camp, such conditions can simply ruin a trip.

Planning, being ready, is what makes a hunt a fond memory. Every day living has enough of the bad times. Turkey hunting is all good ones. Or can be.

Oh, by the way, did I mention you ought to always pack along a few large plastic bags. Yeah, guess I did. You won't need them if you don't kill a turkey.

A Turkey Call Is What You Make It

Ed Norwood, one of the author's few close hunting buddies, makes turkey talk with a section of an old musical instrument. I was surprised at how good the yelps Ed tooted forth were on this thing.

TURKEY CALLS haven't always been easy to come by. It was danged nigh to impossible to buy one only twenty-five years ago. Today, who knows how many are made and sold each year. Just recently, I tried counting what was offered in Wing Supply's catalog, but I gave up after getting up toward a couple hundred. And, there're a jillion companies that don't advertise, so outsiders aren't even aware of them.

Heck knows how or when turkey calling came into being. Facts indicate that numerous Indian tribes became adept at luring wild turkeys to their deaths, so when the settlers, mountainmen, and pioneers began invading turkey country, these folk picked up the technique from the Indians. Most Indians called turkeys using only their mouths, but there are recorded instances of the Indians using calls made from bone, calls completely unlike what we know today as wingbone calls.

The Cherokees were especially adept at making gobbles due to their use of the gobble as a "death wish." When it became obvious that death was imminent because of overwhelming odds, the Indian warrior began chanting this death cry. In one book, *Outlaws On Horseback,* by Drago, he recounts the tale of a bad Indian's jailbreak, "above the din of

Droves of wild turkeys can be called to the hunter in the early fall with a wingbone-type call, or peg'n'slate.

the shooting rose 'Cherokee Bill's' nerve-wracking gobbling." Cherokee Bill, realizing death was near and being a true Cherokee warrior, gobbled, telling all around him that he was facing death as a great warrior.

Turkey calls were probably available locally back during the late 1800s, but the first nationally advertised calls were the famous Gibson box. Olt came along later. The modern-day turkey call had its beginning with names like Turpin, Lynch, and Gaskins.

All of today's turkey calls owe thanks to those few men whose basic call types set the pattern for what has followed. Turkey hunting had all but become a thing of the past when guys like Gibson, and later Turpin and Gaskins, kept plugging their turkey calls. They never had an inkling that some day turkey hunting would be as popular as it is today, or that turkey calls would be sold all across the United States.

To help preserve the past came Henry Davis' grand book about turkey hunting, *The American Wild Turkey,* with drawings and instructions for making a number of turkey calls. No, don't be fooled that some latecomer had any influence on today's turkey call industry. That kind of bunk is from the mouths of people who are completely ignorant of the history and growth of the calling industry.

Not too long ago, the sport of turkey hunting suffered because of a few individuals who told tall tales, outright lies actually, as to how many hundreds of the birds their

Calling in old gobblers is what most hunters think calling is all about. Add some muck and swamp to it, throw in a few leeches, sort out the cottonmouths, and if there's anything that beats nailing a big old Osceola in far south Florida, then it's nailing some other old he-turkey wherever he is.

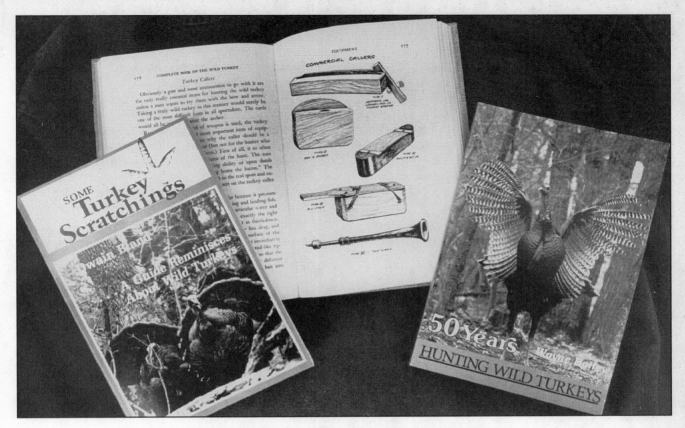

Learning to call wild turkeys isn't something you'll learn overnight, any more than learning to hunt the birds in a few short courses. Reading books on hunting and listening to the calls of hunters who have had decades of experience will help. These men can give the neophyte an insight into what kind of calls to make for different situations.

calls had bagged. Sadly, many hunters were duped by such trash talk. Thankfully, today, the turkey calling industry is largely made up of men and companies who have brought respectability not only to themselves, but to the sport we know as turkey hunting. I'm speaking of men like Frank Piper of Penn's Woods; Dick Kirby who made Quaker

Today's turkey calls owe thanks to those few men whose basic call types set the pattern for what has followed.

Boy; Allen Jenkins who carries on the M.L. Lynch tradition; Wil Primos whose company bears his name; the Haydels, Rod and Eli; David Hale and Harold Knight who own Knight & Hale Game Calls; and Jim Clay of Perfection Turkey Calls. These are the men who've not only stuck through during thick and thin (very thin, and lots of it), but have tried to maintain quality products and refuse to glorify their company name with exaggerated claims of their hunting abilities.

Other smaller operations also strive to retain the respectability we want in our sport. I only wish I had a call made by each of them, or even knew who they are and where they are. Guess

I'm like darned near every other crazy turkey hunter in this land; I never seem to have enough calls. Maybe when I write the next book I'll have the address of every turkey call maker in these old United States.

Box Calls

Box calls date back to the last century. The Gibson turkey call, made and sold by Gibson & Boddie of Dardenelle, Arkansas, is marked in black paint, "Patented Jan. 5th, 1897." This large box, with a "shuffling" lid or paddle, appears to be made of poplar or willow, the best woods available for these calls. Well-known old-timey turkey hunters Tom Turpin and Henry E. Davis hunted turkeys with them and, in fact, *The American Wild Turkey* describes this call in great detail. Roger Latham's fine book, *The Complete Book Of The Wild Turkey,* has a line-drawing plan of the Gibson box call, along with instructions for making one.

One problem with carrying a Gibson-type call is its tendency to make noises, or squawk, while the hunter is walking or moving. Obviously, this could spook a bird within hearing range. A simple remedy is to either place a heavy rubber band around the call to keep the paddle in place, or fasten a cloth or leather strap to the box and wrap this around the open box, allowing the paddle to close on the cloth. All of my boxes are muffled in this manner, have been for years, and can be brought into use almost instantly. The strap arrangement serves as a confining strap when I want to "gobble" the box and, unlike rubber bands, won't rot from heat.

Tuning a box call is a must. If the thing does not have the true ring of a wild turkey's voice, it won't be effective. Tuning requires sanding the lid and sounding edge with lightweight sandpaper. Sand lengthways on both and try to keep a rounded edge on the box; a flat edge can cause squeaks. Once sanded, both should be chalked. Chalking must be done again after several series of calls are made, or when slick places begin showing up on the paddle's rubbing surfaces.

If you have no ear for how a wild turkey sounds, I would recommend having a veteran hunter listen to your box or buy recordings of live turkeys. I don't recommend listening to the recordings of calling champions, as these are not true turkey notes, but rather imitations.

Anyone who seeks the help of a veteran hunter should also be certain that he has a turkey hunting past which ensures he knows what he is doing. The woods and roadside cafes are loaded with turkey hunters who are experts, but a great majority are more expert with the MOUTH than gun and call.

Few calls can outdo a well-tuned box call. Once the hunter has become thoroughly acquainted with an individual call,

Peg'n'slate calls are perhaps the easiest for the beginner. Extremely simple to operate, even the first-time hunter can make passable yelps after only a few minutes of practice. Keep the calling surface sanded and dry and keep your eyes on the call as you make the notes.

Turkey calls are what you make them. Darned near anything that will make turkey sounds, from high-pitched keys to low-range deep clucks, can be used to call a turkey into within shooting distance, if the hunter uses the correct cadence. The very best call isn't worth a hoot if it's not used properly.

Quality turkey calls can be purchased by today's hunter from a number of firms, Haydel's of Bossier City, Louisiana, being among the best. Like several other manufacturers, Haydel's offers a variety of calls—push button, slate, box and mouth calls.

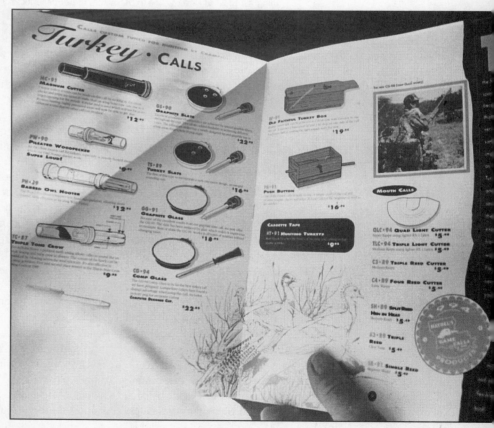

and therefore familiar with the required location of the paddle on the sounding edge for various turkey notes, this call can be used to imitate all of the yelps of both young and old turkeys. Properly operated, either with a restraining strap, or as the Lynch-type call is used with rubber bands, a box call will make a reasonably good gobble. Very definitely, this gobble will become better as the hunter practices making it. Gobbles are excellent early morning locating calls when hunting springtime gobblers, and also will bring a drove to life on some fall mornings. A large Gibson-style box, chalked and sanded, has no equal for locating adult gobblers at long ranges. The well-practiced hunter will know where and how hard to strike the paddle against the sounding edge

Dick Bland shows the proper angle between slate and peg on a slate call made by Ike Ashby of Houston, Missouri. This particular slate has an excellent design which allows more volume than the average slate. Peg'n'slate calls, in the hands of a practiced hunter, make for excellent turkey talk.

to make a note (hen yelp) that will carry beyond a mile. I've located Merriam gobblers all over Arizona's Rocky Mountains, along with a greater number in New Mexico, using a big poplar-wood box call. Some of the birds have been more than a mile from me.

A big box call can do many chores for the turkey hunter, in addition to making excellent yelps. I have heard clucks, purts, whines, and purrs made on box calls that would do justice to many wild turkeys. But, like all calls, to make these sounds with equally good quality, time after time, the hunter must *practice, practice, practice*. Few hunters do this. Unfortunately, the average turkey hunting enthusiast doesn't bother to work with "Ole Reliable" until perhaps the night before the season opener. Therefore, none of the notes have a likeness, nor a turkey-like cadence.

Buying a box call is easier said than done. Perhaps I should clarify this statement by saying to buy a *good* box call is easier said than done. There are a jillion box calls for sale, in many sizes and made of various woods. The maker of each will say flat out that his call is the best there is, with endorsements by this turkey hunter or that. Most would be best used for kindling wood. Sadly, most calls are nowadays packaged so the hunter can't try a few notes in the store before buying one. So, unless the clerk will allow the call to be removed from its wrapping, the hunter will have to buy it untested. Lately, I've received a good number of calls, many of them the box variety. None are now here, because none were of good quality. Long ago I learned that I would do best to stick with the old reliables when buying hunting gear, and that goes for buying calls, too.

As late as the 1930s, about the only turkey call advertised in hunting and fishing magazines was made by the P.S. Olt Com-

---

Gobbles are excellent early morning locating calls when hunting springtime gobblers, and also will bring a drove to life on some fall mornings.

---

pany; the same company many of us associate with duck and goose calls over the years. Though Olt began making game calls in 1904, they didn't bring out a turkey call until 1931. I have one of these early cedar models. It is about 5 inches long, close to an inch square and, like many of these small boxes, has no paddle, but is, instead, rubbed on a chalked surface, including a gunstock. Unlike the large Gibson box, they can be carried in a shirt pocket. Delicate to handle, this little Olt call could be easily broken. P.S. Olt makes and distributes fine game calls to this day, enjoying the oldest continuous name in the game call business. Such a reputation is built on but one thing—quality.

Many claim that large box calls are a nuisance to carry. However, there are any number of cloth and leather bags of the belt-loop variety available which make toting them very convenient. I've seen pouches with a separate small pocket

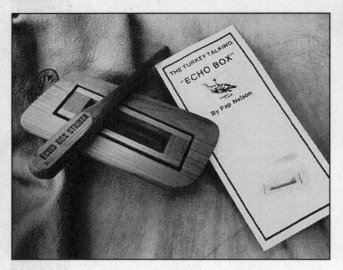

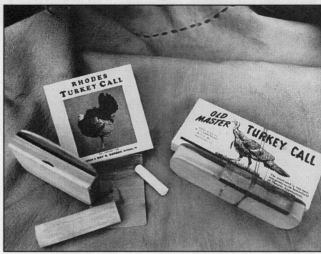

Trough calls are rare among turkey hunters, more so if they have a floating trough, as is the case with this elaborate call. Like all calls, this box will make good turkey talk, but lots of practice is the key to success.

A number of the country's older turkey hunters made turkey calls—these two by Roy O. Rhodes from Pennsylvania and Frank Hanenkrat from Virginia. Both have been retired to the author's collection, but each saw time with me in the woods before it went on the shelf.

for holding the chalk and sandpaper, as well as light skeletal frame packs which hold only the box. And many of today's hunting pants have roomy cargo pockets to hold a box call.

Years back, a man became famous in small towns throughout the South by holding demonstrations on street corners and peddling his homemade turkey calls. He offered a shuffling box call, a peg'n'slate call, a squirrel call, and a book describing their use and how to hunt the birds. The man's name was M.L. Lynch; the box call would become the now-famous Lynch's World Champion Turkey Caller. The squirrel call was known as Lynch's World Champion Chatter Box. Lynch dubbed the peg'n'slate call Lynch's Big Chief Turkey Call, maintaining he got the idea from the Indians' use of slate rubbed with a narrow pine lighter stick inserted into a corncob.

Many companies have copied Lynch calls, but only a true Lynch can carry this famous name. I wish I had a nickel for every turkey that has been called to a hunter's gun with a walnut and mahogany Lynch's World Champion Turkey Caller.

One advantage of the Lynch-style boxes is their size. They aren't as large as a Gibson, so are more apt to be stuck in a pants or coat pocket. The notes will not carry as far as those made with a Gibson shuffling box, but the tone has a slightly higher pitch. Many have a rubber band arrangement, allowing them to be held by the end of the box to make a gobble. Other models have just one sounding edge, for tapping the lid against the blank side to make clucks.

Up near Appomattox, Virginia, lives a man by the name of Frank Hanenkrat who hand-makes a small, unusually shaped box call. Frank is another old-time turkey hunter, so his calls have that built-in tone which a good call must possess. Frank's calls are hand-tuned, and though I don't know if he still does so, he used to mark the exact location the striker should be rubbed on the call's sounding edge. His fine book, *The Education Of A Turkey Hunter,* is guaranteed good reading on those long winter evenings when you want spring to bring you a gobbling turkey. An instruction sheet on hunting turkeys is included with each call. The wood Hanenkrat uses was grown on the Appomattox battlefield. Like many boxes of this style, it will drop into any shirt pocket. Amazingly, all of these little calls have excellent carrying ranges. Like any call, the hunter must be thoroughly acquainted with it to use it properly, which means handling it by the hour and learning where each note can be reproduced on the sounding edge. No two calls sound alike, even though they may be built exactly to the same dimensions.

John Grayson, of Bristol, Virginia, has been putting his feet down in turkey woods for nigh onto 50 years and sells his well-known "Lost John" box from that town in the southwest part of the state. This long, narrow box is patterned after an old one his granddaddy carried back before the Civil War. The original was "rived" from a hunk of old cedar fence post. Cedar is an excellent wood for calls because it withstands wear, does not sand off excessively fast, and will take considerable abuse. Properly tuned, cedar has the clear resonant tones of the wild turkey. John Grayson hand-makes his "Lost John" boxes and also individually tunes them. Fifty years of

The Apaches were known to use the gobble of the mountain turkey as a signal to each other when on warring raids.

listening to wild turkeys has given Grayson the ear for what a turkey call should sound like.

Down in Florida is a man whose calls have made a huge dent in the Osceola turkey numbers. This man is Tom Gask-

The author using a box call to lure birds into camera range. The electronic release for the camera is in his right hand, near the gun's forend. Calling and, at the same time, taking photos of approaching turkeys is often a time-consuming and exasperating sport.

ins. I've talked to many a Florida "cracker" who was toting one of Gaskins' little boxes. His shop is located near the town of Palmdale, but it is easily found if you follow his unique signs along the highway.

Some of the small gunstock box calls will make kee runs if the hunter will take the time to find where to make them on the call. The easiest method is to begin with yelps on the center of the box, then work out toward the end, particularly the end held by the other hand. By exerting pressure on the sides of the box with the holding hand, the yelp can be made higher on the musical scale. I have never found a large shuffling box which will make kee runs, as the amplifying chamber is not conducive to creating high-pitched notes.

Wingbone Calls

The call we know today as a wingbone call is an offshoot of the bone whistle used by the Indians. The Apaches were known to use the gobble of the mountain turkey as a signal to each other when on warring raids and when engaged with white soldiers. The owl hoot we so commonly hear used in cowboy and Indian movies is a fallacy. I haven't found any mention of this in historic accounts. And since the owl was considered an omen of death, I doubt that Indians imitated its mournful wailing.

I have hunted among Apaches a few times and have never known one who could call a wild turkey with his voice. I do have a quaint box call made by an Apache. It's made of mountain mahogany and has such an unusual opening it must have evolved somewhere in tribal history. The notes are made by chalking a spot on a gunstock and drawing the sounding edge lightly across this.

It seems ironic that the bones from a turkey's wing can be used for the undoing of others of its kind. This goes one step further in that the wingbones from a young gobbler are best suited for calling young gobblers, and the bones of a hen will make excellent notes of the hen turkey, and so on.

Making a wingbone call is not difficult, though it does take time and patience. Far the best bones to use are the two small ones found in the second or middle section of a mature hen turkey's wing. These should be laid aside after the bird has been cooked and eaten, and then boiled in a shallow pan for a few minutes, with just a few drops of liquid dishwashing soap added to the water. The soap will make the call taste better when it's finished.

After the wingbones have cooled, cut off the knob-like ends with a fine-toothed hacksaw blade. Using a long pipe cleaner, clean the bone marrow from inside the bones. The bones should telescope together and fit closely enough that the two sections can be glued, but only after they have dried for a couple of days. Once glued, I always make a

cork mouth-stopper and glue it onto the call so my mouth will butt up against it in exactly the same position each time. This is made from a simple bottle cork whittled to the size desired with a sharp pocketknife. Don't glue the cork stopper until you've moved it back and forth along the mouthpiece and found the spot that results in the best notes possible. The notes are made by sucking or pulling air quickly through the call. Clucks are made with a kissing action. Yelps are made by using the throat muscles, best described as a gulping action. It takes a lot of time and practice to master any of the trumpet or wingbone-type turkey calls; this is why you won't see many in use. Lots of hunters carry them, but few can actually call turkeys with them.

Wingbones have a tremendous carrying range and can be heard at great distances, so it's easy to call too loudly. Yelps

Many of the large box calls are best carried with a side holster, as is this one of the author's. Moulded from cowhide, it's very durable, keeps its shape whether the box is in it or not, and keeps it handy, but not in the way.

Veteran turkey hunter Diane Melillo, who calls home Holmdel, New Jersey, uses both a box call and a wingbone. Seems to me she once told me she also toted a slate at times. Diane hunts both the spring and the fall seasons with Pennsylvania and New York her favorite stomping grounds.

are not easily made, and this swallowing, drawing in air through the yelper takes time to master. These notes can often sound too quick, and more like a bark than a yelp. Too many yelps in a series often result in a call that doesn't come close to resembling a turkey.

Making a wingbone call is not difficult; though it does take time and patience.

Excellent kee runs can be made on a wingbone, but must be practiced over and over to be anywhere near authentic. The kee is made by sucking air through the call with a greater intensity than is done with a yelp. This causes the note to break much higher on the musical scale. This call is part of the

lost young turkey's vocabulary and the notes must be quick, with all the pleading in them that is possible.

Thin river cane can be used in much the same manner, but the reeds must be small in diameter and the hold the same size as that of a turkey wingbone. Several times I have come across small stands of cane and cut a section between the nodes to make a call. After running a weed stem through the center, I could make turkey notes that sound no different than those made with a store-bought Turpin yelper. The hole, whether through a cane or turkey's wingbone, must be near $3/32$-inch in diameter if you want to use it for calling turkeys.

You can't use a wingbone call with a dry mouth. I often carry mints or cough drops just for this purpose. I have cut short sections of sassafras branches and chewed on these, or willow, locust, elm, hickory, and manzanita. Placing a small rock under the tongue will also induce salivation. Wetting the

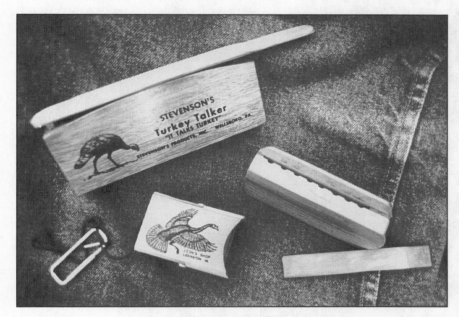

Other collector calls. At top, a Lou Stevenson box, very small and slender, sold with an instruction sheet and small vial of rosin. The call at bottom left utilizes a mouthpiece of rubber latex. The box on the far right is made from chestnut and utilizes a hunk of slate, on which its sounding edge is rubbed.

Many hunters collect calls, and, of course, the older ones are the most sought after. These two boxes came from the shop of Tom Turpin and were found in a box of things which were sold out of his shop after his death. The one at top was an experimental model, since it has a large round hole through the bottom, not visible in this photo. The author has used both boxes.

The old favorite for an army of turkey hunters, the Lynch box has tolled many hundreds of thousands, maybe millions, of wild turkeys into shooting range.

mouthpiece by simply licking it will also help. If there is dew on the grass, rub the tip of the call in this, but make sure it is thoroughly moistened.

The commercial version of the wingbone is known as a trumpet call. It isn't blown into as a trumpet is, but rather used with the same kissing, sucking, smacking actions mentioned earlier. Trumpet calls are often referred to as Turpin yelpers, named after Tom Turpin, a turkey hunter who made them well known in his writings about hunting wild turkeys. He also made and sold these calls commercially.

Wingbones or trumpet calls—either is capable of making the clucking and yelping notes of a hen turkey as well as any turkey. The springtime turkey hunter would do well to keep one of these hung about his neck. Use it sparingly, but with full concentration. In time, the hunter will master its use.

How to Use a Call

Acquiring an "ear" for wild turkey sounds is best done through years and years of hunting and listening to the birds in their natural habitat. This is where the makers of numerous calls have fallen short. They haven't heard enough turkeys to know when a call sounds like a turkey and when it is off key a note or two. An older, more experienced caller can make up

for what a call lacks by knowing when and how much to call, and how to cover any bad notes with those that follow. The novice turkey hunter is unable to do this though, so a bad call in his hands just sounds bad.

Cadence, and knowing when and where to call from, have more bearing on successful calling than do the notes themselves. Too many of today's novice turkey addicts try to learn turkey hunting and calling by listening to tapes of calling experts, or by attending turkey calling seminars and contests. No one has put this more aptly than my great friend, John Lowther, in his book, *Spring Gobblers*. Let me quote him: "Most beginners are geared to hearing the beautiful sounds that emanate from turkey calling contests. They go hunting and listen for this uniform flow of perfect yelps and clucks. I'll say this, if one would put a real turkey in a contest, it wouldn't get 10 points."

John has chased ridge-running old gobblers over enough of West Virginia's mountains to know exactly what I am talking about when I say that a wild turkey can ofttimes be a very poor caller. However, not many hunters can imitate this poor calling. For those who can master the imperfections, their calling becomes far deadlier than that of the average turkey caller. Knowing when to answer a yelp with a quick cluck or two, or

To prevent my box calls from squawking when they're not supposed to, I attach a stiffler string to the box, which is nothing more than a long hunk of heavy cord, or a coarse material, screw an eye into the box and tie the string to it.

When you want to use it, unwind the string, make your calls, and then wrap the stiffler around the box before you stick it in your pocket. No hassle and no loud squawks when you don't want them.

when to make a soft purr in thick cover, is often the difference between going home with something to pluck and just going home. And, although John Lowther and I and some other old boys I know could write 10 million words on how to call, or how to hunt turkeys, the bulk of learning boils down to learning the hard way. It harkens to the Smith-Barney ad so often seen on television, which goes, "We make money the old-fashioned way—we earn it."

K*nowing when to answer a yelp is often the difference between going home with something to pluck and just going home.*

The fast-paced living we do in America too often leaves little time for lollygagging about in some far-from-town woods, hoping a drove of turkeys will talk it up, just so he can hear them. Wild turkeys have never had a reputation for doing anything on cue, so a hunter can spend lots of time in good turkey country, often days, and not hear a single cluck.

Numerous recordings of wild turkeys can be bought by mail-order. Playing the tapes over and over will hopefully imprint the sounds into the hunter's memory so that when he attempts to make the notes with a call, he'll know what it is he is mimicking. For many, remembering the mating yelp of the hen is easy, but the kee run is hard. So, before the fall season, a hunter should listen to the kees of real wild turkeys which have been scattered practice. If he can do this every evening prior to the season, his confidence will increase, and as it does, he'll become a better turkey hunter.

Lots has been written about how to make the notes of wild turkeys, enough to fill two or three small libraries, with a bunch of my past writings thrown in for good measure. But, the truth is, telling someone about it, and doing it, are two different things. Nobody can tell someone else exactly how to call a turkey, how a call is used, how it should sound, all about the proper cadence, when to make a note and where to sit while doing all this. These things best come from hard-earned experience. So, while you're reading what I say about these things, keep this in mind.

Let's discuss the best time of the day to use a call. One thing is certain: turkeys are most vocal during the early morning hours. This often begins with a very soft yelp, pert, or clucking note. That can't be heard, even on a quiet morning, for more than 100 or 200 yards, usually less. The notes are made singly, usually with a few seconds between them. They are ofttimes referred to as "head-in-the-barrel" notes because they sound muffled, like the turkey has its head in a barrel. These are the wake-up notes the birds make back and forth to each other just as day begins to break. A hand-muffled mouth call, or a wingbone, is best for mimicking these tree calls, and the hunter should practice them as he walks toward the roosting area, making adjustments in volume as he goes along. No two mornings are alike insofar as how sounds will carry, particularly if the hunter has been hunting one terrain, and then switches to another.

When I'm hunting fall and winter turkeys, and think I'm near an ideal roosting area, or even when simply walking unfamiliar woods, I'll make these tree calls as I go, hoping to make contact with an awakening drove, or just a bird or two. This technique will work for only a short time, because as soon as the sky brightens, the birds will stand erect on the roost branches and change from the faint tree calls to yelps and clucks. Tree calls are usually made when the birds are hunkered down on the branch, head drawn in on the shoulders. Hunters use the tree call for no other purpose than in trying to locate treed turkeys. It has no use in calling them to the hunter.

The yelps, kees, and clucks, which will follow, are used to bring in the bird. If a hunter hasn't heard these sounds *many* times over, the best thing he can do is listen to the birds and try to copy the calls. I often do this when calling them from the tree if I think there are but a few, or if the birds' calls indicate they will be, or are, flying down before I can get close to them. Very often an undisturbed drove will make lots of racket while in the trees, with mixed in kee runs, whistles, yelps, clucks, perts; sometimes a young gobbler will try to gobble.

No two mornings are alike insofar as how sounds will carry, particularly if the hunter has been hunting one terrain, and then switches.

My main pre-season concern is to imprint the calls of the birds on my memory, particularly the kees and yelps of young gobblers, and, if I am carrying a call, to learn how these notes are made on that particular call. With practice, most boxes, whether gunstock or shuffling style, will imitate these coarse young gobbler yelps. The slower yelps can be made on a trum-

Lennis Rose is an expert with a slate call. This is because he spends many, many hours hunting and has a good ear for recalling what a wild turkey sounds like. Anyone who's interested in becoming a truly good caller should purchase recordings of live turkeys and listen to them each day.

pet call, but are more easily duplicated with mouth calls. Because of its versatility, the mouth call can duplicate the hoarse, drawn-out yelp, or the raspy, barking yelp of a jake gobbler.

The birds will continue to call once they leave the trees, but after a short time they will be grouped, and the drove will then wander off in search of food or water. Very often the talk will be over for the day, all the more so if the drove is small. Large droves of twenty birds or more will yelp back and forth as they walk along, but as the day progresses this will lessen. I cover lots of ground at first day, simply because I want to hear birds and attempt to make a kill, or scatter them, before they all go silent. It is no different than when hunting a gobbling bird during the springtime—I want to get near him while he is gobbling, as this tells me exactly where the bird is located. The kees and yelps tell me where the drove is, and with a little luck

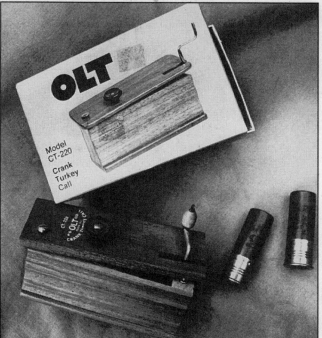

Though it never became popular, the crank call made and sold by P.S. Olt is surely the easiest of all to use. And, it makes excellent yelps, or at least the one the author has in his collection does.

For an easy-to-use quick change-off call the author would recommend a peg'n'slate. It has excellent tones if made properly, and if the user will only practice a little each day, it can call wild turkeys into easy shooting distance.

perhaps I can run among them and make a kill. One trick that shouldn't be overlooked while hunting a bunch of well-scattered turkeys is that they call back and forth to each other, and are apt to go to each other's calling. If possible, get between two of them and chances are good a kill can be made. The main problem, of course, is doing this without spooking the birds. Very often they will keep to high ground when going to each other. The cover certainly need not be wide open, as some people think. Scattered young turkeys will often walk through thick cover to reach each other. When trying to flush them out, I have had to walk into stuff so thick I couldn't shoot one in it.

Scattered turkeys can be called at any time of the day, though those separated by the hunter just before sundown often will not respond as well. They will, however, usually come to the call the next morning at dawn. Many late afternoon flushes will result in birds alighting in trees, and though they may fly to other trees before dark, very often they will stay "up" for the evening. If the hunter is a good stalker and has an eye for locating turkeys perched high among tree crowns, it isn't difficult to walk within good shooting distance of one.

A hunter's calls must sound like a turkey...regardless of how good the hunter sounds to himself, his calls may not sound so hot to a turkey.

The fall hunter should remember that turkeys will sometimes fly to calling, alighting in a tree over the caller's head. This is an easy shot, certainly not to be confused with roost shooting. This seems to unnerve some hunters, who then simply throw the gun to cheek and fire. Treat these chances just as you would an approaching turkey on foot—bring the gun up smoothly, take careful aim at the bird's neck or head, and then squeeze the trigger.

Many times a hunter will hear several turkeys calling, and then realize the birds have grouped nearby. This situation is bad for the hunter, as this bunch will call others to it, so the hunter's only choice is to attempt to scatter them once again. This is best done by running toward them as fast as possible. I don't recommend shooting over them. Some birds have already been separated once, and too much excitement could result in their not gathering for days. Simply run toward them and watch to see if they fly off in different directions. Then, take up a calling stand between the scattered birds, wait until one calls, and begin calling. There will be less calling on this second scatter so your calling must match theirs.

Whatever the season, a hunter's calls must sound like a turkey. And, regardless of how good the hunter sounds to himself, his calls may not sound so hot to a turkey. Therefore, it is very important for someone who has heard and hunted lots of turkeys to listen to another's calling, and be frank enough to tell him if it sounds good or bad. Choose a friend who will be honest, but will listen objectively. It

Tiny box calls at first may seem too small to actually call birds in. But, don't be fooled. These little boxes are deadly in the hands of hunters who know how to use them. Many places in the turkey woods are made for calls that don't need a loud voice.

won't do any good if you're told your calling sounds fine even if it doesn't. In fact, you'll just keep on getting worse. Do this in hunting terrain, and at varying distances, to soften the notes at near ranges, and maybe at longer distances, too. Sounds vary according to humidity, denseness of low ground cover, and slope of terrain. Wind has a tremendous effect, and wind intensity usually picks up after sun up.

The all-day hunter must realize that turkeys are most vocal at dawn, and with each moment of passing daylight, the calling lessens. Too much calling later in the day is apt to alert turkeys, make them spooky, and after much of this, make them call-shy at all hours.

This tiny old-time penny whistle the author found in a small box of junk at a farm auction many years ago is just the ticket for making the fine whistle of the young fall turkey. When the author doesn't have this call with him, and needs to make this whistle, he can just as easily do it with his mouth.

The quick yelps of a wild turkey hen using a wingbone call are very easy to learn and simple to make. The plaintive crying kee run of young turkeys takes much more time; many hunters never master it.

After opening day, particularly in country infested with lots of hunters, we can expect to find numerous turkeys already separated, feeding and roosting alone. These birds will readily regroup. However, one bird may answer a hunter's call, but another will completely disregard it, and yet another may not answer, but will come to the call silently. Each year there are countless numbers of these silent turkeys that come to a call but are never seen because the birds eyeball the hunter during the approach. Complete camo, plus the ability to sit quietly for long periods of time, will put many of these birds in the oven. Hand movements while manipulating a box, slate, or trumpet call must be kept to a minimum, and a sharp lookout maintained for any turkey walking into view. I've killed several

turkeys after waking from a nap deep in the woods, birds I perhaps would not have bagged had I been awake and making movements, no matter how slight. Lying there sprawled out, sound asleep, the bird has seen no movement and has no fear. All of these birds have awakened me with alarm clucks, but as the birds have been within yards, I have had time to come up shooting.

Probably others have eyed my dozing form, or heard my snoring, and made their escape silently. A hunter who is "calling blind" as he travels through turkey woods should make only an occasional yelp, kee, or cluck, and then call to any responding bird with a like number of notes. Very often, a hunter hears an answering yelp or cluck and in his surprise just sits or stands there for a moment trying to decide what to do next. This is exactly what he should do, but he should do his thinking after he gives an instant comeback to the turkey. If at all possible, the hunter should cluck back to a bird two or three times the second he hears the bird. Turkeys that are separated over a period of time return calls quickly as if to say, "Boy, am I glad to hear you. I've sure been lonely." Frequently, his instant response will result in the bird flying or running to the hunter. Remember, if you are hunting birds that have been scattered for some time, or you suspect the area has been hard hunted, call very sparingly as you ease through the woods. If a bird answers your call, *cluck, cluck* back to it as quickly as possible, one right after the other, just loud enough for the bird to hear, and with all the reassurance in them that you can muster. Don't make clucks which are sharp, loud, and spaced apart.

What kinds of notes to make while calling fall turkeys depends on what notes the birds are using in talking to each other. The older the birds, the more this is true, whether within a season, or not. Older turkeys do less calling, except during mating season, and turkeys several years old will probably go for days without making any sounds. I have been near groups of older gobblers during fall and winter hunts that have never made a sound, day after day. I presume they must talk to each other with extremely soft purrs and clucks that cannot be heard except at very close range.

Older turkeys do less calling and will probably go for days without making any sounds.

Older turkeys that have been scattered often respond to calling, but are not seen by the hunter because they approach silently. They are more wary than a young turkey, so will come in head high and on the lookout. The caller who is poorly located will surely be seen due to insufficient screening foliage or movement when making a call. A solid blind works best when dealing with these older turkeys, but this is often impossible to build, or would not be feasible. Choosing a calling location that older, hard-hunted turkeys will approach is quite different from choosing a setup for

Calling wild turkeys to a mounted camera takes no end of patience—all the time that's required to turn wood into solid rock—and all kinds of knowledge about turkeys. The author also thinks it takes somebody who is half crazy. All photos containing both turkeys and a hunter were taken by the author using a camera with electronic release.

young birds. The surrounding cover must be less dense, offering better visibility. Yet, if the hunter locates out on an open flat, the older bird will often "hang up," failing to go near the call because it can't see the calling bird. Regardless of season, the best calling place is rolling, uneven ground dotted with low bushes or hanging tree branches. Such terrain gives the spooked turkey, or even a springtime love-struck gobbler, sufficient visibility to allay its fears about hidden predators. It forces the birds to approach within easy gunshot range, but not close enough to actually see the spot the call is coming from. I prefer a place that, once I am seated, allows me to see over nearby humps in the terrain, but is not visible to the turkey until it has approached quite near. This type of cover can be found anywhere that wild turkeys are encountered, though it may vary from having to hunker on a sagebrush hill to hiding in a downed treetop on a mountain ridge. *Never* do I attempt to call turkeys while located on large open hunks of flat terrain. Even if ground clutter is present, I will make every possible effort to remain low to the ground, particularly while actually calling. The turkey *must come looking for the caller;*

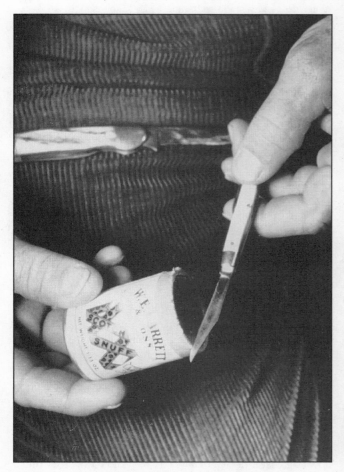

Anything that can be rubbed together may make sounds of turkeys. Sucking soda straws, smacking on a smoking pipe stem, or even rubbing a knife blade across the edge of a snuff box, all could, and probably have, been used to call turkeys.

and it is preferable that the bird not see the calling location until well within gun range.

This is comparable to hunting geese. When a hunter sees jillions of them flying about a wildlife refuge, he can't shoot any until they fly into range. A turkey, standing alert a hundred yards out on an open flat is nice to look at, but the bird would look a darned sight better at 20 yards, just above your shotgun's bead. Like the geese, the turkey can be called into range, but without a whole drove of decoys, your chances of doing so are best if you can keep it from seeing the calling location.

Whichever call a person chooses to use, most will make a number of notes that will bring turkeys to the hunter, provided the hunter is well located, the notes and the rhythm of the call sound like another turkey, and there is a reason why the bird should go to the call. A hunter can make very nice sounding yelps during the spring season, but if the listening gobbler is already with hens, chances are a hundred to one the bird will stay with his group of hens. A lost young turkey on a ridge will call its head off, but if the hunter's call is not coming from where the scattered drove has flown, the bird probably won't go to the call. What it boils down to is knowing a great deal about a turkey's lifestyle, from when it was a small poult until adulthood. Turkeys are birds of habit—flying down, feeding, watering, loafing, feeding, loafing, flying up, day after day. These habits change slowly as the weather cycles, as food availability causes them to move to other areas, and as their bodies develop. Calling to each other is a result of this lifestyle and a response to threats from predators.

The person new to calling should spend as much time as possible in close contact with the birds, listening to them as they go through each day, day after day, making every effort to learn what makes them tick, or in this case, yelp. This will reveal to the would-be hunter the whys and why-nots of calling. If he becomes a student of animal behavior, the reasons why a wild turkey will do this or that become apparent.

I always thought the best calls a hunter could make would be with his mouth. Then you'd always have it along, you wouldn't have to stew about chalk or sandpaper, or if the rubber is worn out if it's a horseshoe mouth call.

My old buddy, Lennis Rose, over in Missouri, is one of those folks who can call with his mouth. Lennis is darned good. He can call fall turkeys just as good as he can spring gobblers. Like lots of folks who use their mouths, Lennis can't call loud, but for much of the hunting he does in those Ozark hills, his mouth calling is just fine. You don't need any volume in such cover.

I haven't heard him for years, but Jack Dudley, down in Mississippi, was a darned good natural mouth caller. And, if he's still hunting turkeys, he's probably still using the call he's always got with him. I never did work at it long enough to try to ascertain whether I could use my mouth. Lots of hunters could if they'd set their minds to it.

And, lots of hunters could make their own calls if they would. Wingbones are very easy to make if a person has the wing bones. That'd be the hardest part for many hunters,

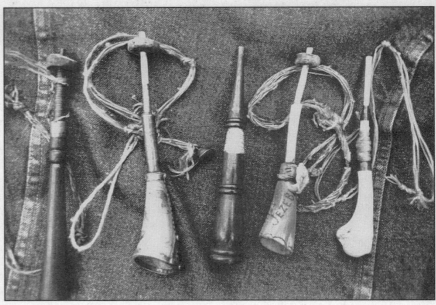

Jose Llama practices calling with a Haydel peg'n'slate given to him by the author. Jose's new to turkey hunting, but with this call could soon become good enough to woo a turkey into killing range.

Trumpet-type calls come in all shapes, including the wingbone call. Far left is a very early Penn's Woods call with solid brass ferrule. Next is a wingbone made by the author's scrimshawed and partially encased in silver. The silver work was done by a Sioux Indian friend now deceased. The mouthpiece is a sanded down hunk of hairpipe from an Indian bone breastplate. The center call is one made years ago by V.O. Johnson, in Arkansas, also now deceased. The second from right is a favorite old wingbone made by the author, Miss Jezebel, and the call on the far right a wingbone utilizing all sections of the turkey's wing, including the large single bone next to the bird's body.

getting the bones. Slate calls can be made from a small hunk of thin slate and a peg of some sort to rub against it. Even a rusty nail. Yes, I know, it's crazy to make a call when so many are for sale. But, it helps to be crazy when hunting turkeys because turkeys will do many things which seem crazy to human beings, and how they respond to a call is part of it. My advice to the beginner is to *practice, practice, practice.* Talk to other hunters about their calling, if you want; read what others have to say about it, but just remember, nobody—me, your best friend, or a hundred of the best callers in this country—can truly tell you how to call a wild turkey into shooting range. It must be learned while hunting

A great many hunters think a call guarantees them a turkey if the call is used properly.

the real thing. Nor will you get good at it overnight. There's not a turkey in this country which, at one time or another, will not come to a call, no matter what kind of call is being used. Most of the time it's a case of being at the right place at the right time, which puts turkey calling on par with other hunting methods—the more time spent at it, the better the results. This is all too obvious on many a spring morning, when a hunter tags along after a gobbling bird, hoping to lure it to him, but fails because he gives up too soon. The old rascal he is chasing is keeping company with a lady turkey, so is not about to leave her for some skirt making sweet talk off in the bushes. Two hours later, the hunter says to heck with it and goes home. About the same time, the old

gobbler's lady friend gives him the slip, so now he's got a wandering eye and a listening ear. Make one call and here he comes.

One May morning I chased a Merriam gobbler all over half the Rocky Mountains. We must've covered a good three miles in our travels, him walking and gobbling, me trying to keep up. If I'd have heard just one other gobble that morning, from any other bird, I'd have forgotten him, but he was all there seemed to be, so I stuck along.

What's worse, I am certain he didn't have a hen with him. I never did get him in sight, but I crossed places where his tracks were very clear, and they indicated he was all alone. Try as I might, I simply couldn't get him into bushwack position; he moved too fast. I didn't want to spook him because he might shut up for the rest of the day, and there I'd be up the creek without a turkey, so to speak.

At long last I followed the bird down into the basin, along a tiny brook. The terrain was some open pasture and meadows, with Gambel oak thickets, a few cottonwoods scattered up and down the creek, and loose shalus flowing from the hillsides down into the meadows. All the green grasses were nearly blotted from view by a solid blanket of dandelions. I couldn't help but stare at them, thinking, "Boy, I thought my yard at home was bad. Look at all the damned dandelions." A home-owner's lawn nightmare.

My adversary headed up the creek. I was tired, so I sat down against a big, old cottonwood. I knew the creek broke into rough country a short ways upstream, so had an inkling the old turkey wasn't going too far that way. He'd hold up back in that corner, probably hang around there all day, then at dusk, march back over the trail we'd just followed and go to

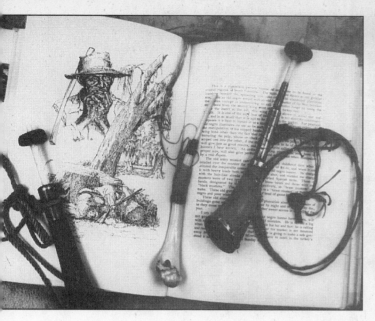

Practice, practice, practice is a must for the turkey hunter who hopes to lure wild turkeys to him, but more so with the trumpet-type call than any other.

Here's a sought-after call made and sold many, many years ago by M.L. Lynch. The Big Chief call was a peg'n'slate affair with a movable pegboard which gave the user the option of making several kinds of notes. This call, with its small pamphlet of instructions, was sold for the princely sum of $4.95.

roost back where it had all began that morning before daylight.

But, from habit, and from knowing turkeys never do what's expected of them, I fished out my old box call. Make another yelp, hear the turkey gobble, another, oh, Hell, it can go on for hours.

I called.

The bird gobbled.

I called.

He gobbled.

I called.

He gobbled.

Hell, wake up, Bland, that bird's making tracks. I slouched down hard against the rough bark.

I called.

A gobble, this time damn close. Hey, there's his red head. *BOOOMMM.*

Turkey calls are what you make 'em. You and the turkey. Why that old turkey came to me only he knows. My first thought was that there was another gobbler back in that nook, so I walked back there. There was no sign of turkeys anywhere, couldn't even find tracks for the one I'd just shot. Obviously, there was only the one bird.

Did the call suddenly sound different? I doubt it. My hen cadence never varies, so it wasn't that. I'd been tailing that gobbler for three miles, but had quit calling to him once he began moving. I'd tried to make a visual contact so maybe I could make a stalk, or bushwack him somehow. But, he'd walked too fast for that. Who knows, perhaps the old gobbler had been doing that every day for two weeks. I'd not hunted the area earlier that week.

Turkey calls work magic at times. For many years, about the only call I used was the diaphragm call, or as we referred to it then, the horseshoe call. I handmade mine from condom rubber and fishing sinkers pounded flat.

Mouth calls are truly fine, but often the darned things are just too handy. Once a person gets used to having one in his mouth, he often keeps it there for hours on end. With it in place all the time, it's very tempting to use it. The fact is, the calling sounds so damned good to the hunter he just can't help but make another call, or two. Then he makes some more. Boy, those sound good. Mouth calls are great, but just don't overdo it.

At times, wild turkeys do no end of calling, particularly during the early fall hunts. I've heard droves of birds talk up a storm for hours as they meander from feeding ground to feeding ground, with an old hen or two doing most of the talking. Or, perhaps a drove will become noisy during the afternoon, with some of the months-old gobblers trying their hand at gobbling, which will make you laugh it's so sorry. If you can sneak close enough to watch, you may see these young gobblers also trying out their strutting technique, even though spring is months away.

Turkey calls are overrated—by this I mean a great many hunters think a call guarantees them a turkey if the call is used properly. If the bird doesn't come, they presume they've used the call incorrectly. The fact is, on any given day the birds that come to your call would have responded to any hunter's call, and those that didn't probably wouldn't have. You'll talk to hunters who will tell you they've called in umpteen hundred turkeys. But one thing for sure. You'll probably never hear mentioned how many turkeys they *couldn't call up.*

In the Spring, When a Turkey's Fancy Turns to...

GOBBLING TIME is springtime. New green shoots are spearing upward across the great palmetto pastures that have been burned in Florida; Indian turnips stand like tiny sentinels at lonely guard posts in a Vermont woods; woodhens ring the piney woods with their jack-hammering in search of wood borers; and a thin blanket of an overnight snow still lies dazzling white in the Rocky Mountain sun, etched with the drag marks of an old turkey's strutting. With all this, the gobbling of a wild turkey is just more icing on the cake.

Why does a turkey gobble? Biologists tell us this is the male bird's love song, though it doesn't much seem in the same category with a mockingbird or a cardinal. But obviously it is, because the birds seldom gobble at other times of the year. All of us who have hunted fall and winter turkeys extensively have heard gobbling then, but it is sporadic.

The hunter's fondness for spring turkey hunting has resulted in slang terms for the turkey's gobbling. It is oftentimes referred to as "sounding off," "firing back" or "cutting loose." You may hear a hunter remark that he heard a bird "bellering his head off." All are terms of endearment to men who love the sport.

Folks who do not hunt may wonder why there is a spring hunt for wild turkeys. A few simple facts will help explain. Wild turkeys mate during the spring, and unlike ducks, doves, and other game birds, do not pair during the mating period. A single adult gobbler will gather from one to several hens and mate each many times over a period spanning several weeks. Turkey hunters refer to a group of hens as a gobbler's "harem."

Once that adult gobbler mates with a hen, the hen no longer needs further mating; this one time will see her through the egg laying season for one year. Once an adult gobbler has mated with the local hen populace, he can be considered "surplus," insofar as turkey numbers are considered. His demise will not have any bearing on continued turkey populations.

But, to lessen hunter disturbance of nesting hens, the season must be set so as not to interfere with hens incubating a full nest of eggs. The result is a season that opens after the birds have mated the one time necessary, but before the hens have laid the clutch of eggs and while the adult male is still gobbling. Once the hen has laid all her eggs and has begun incubating them, she no longer seeks out the male's company. Soon the gobbler's mating instincts wane, causing him to cease gobbling.

Numerous states open their spring hunts when all the hens are still with the gobbler. This causes much gnashing of teeth for the turkey hunter who hopes to lure the male with a hen call. Others end each day's hunt at noon, or thereabouts, to prevent disturbing the turkeys the remainder of the day. According to hunting pressures, there are states with long seasons, and others with seasons that last but a week or two. Obviously, the hunting of wild turkey gobblers during the springtime has little effect on future populations. A great many states have had such hunts for decades, with turkey populations today as good as the terrain will permit.

Gobbling season is by far the most popular of the two hunting seasons for wild turkeys. Why? Because the turkey gobbles. This reason alone causes people to jump out of bed at

For so many thousands of hunters, a spring gobbler is by far the finest trophy found in the country's woods. Ed Norwood (left) and Mike Monier pose with a spring kill made by Monier at Ed's camp in Mississippi.

ridiculously early hours, leave home without breakfast, file for divorce, spend outlandish sums of money—all for the privilege of lollygagging around on some wooded hill, listening for a bird to make a crazy sound. And it is this crazy sound that causes so many hunters to take to the woods in March, April and May. The hunter hears the quarry, so knows it is there to hunt. Without the gobble, the average hunter is lost insofar as knowing how to cope with the shooting of a turkey. If all the turkeys in this country would quit gobbling next spring, the country could return to some sort of normalcy. Bosses would see employees they ordinarily do not see in April, and little children just might get daddy to take them to school.

The daily habits of a gobbler with his bunch of hens are important to all turkey hunting enthusiasts. For it is around these habits that the groundwork for hunting methods are laid. An average April morning finds the old male perched high on a branch, the hens scattered among nearby trees. At the first inkling of coming daylight, he will have the urge to gobble. Though it in no way sounds like a song, it is said to be the male's song. Supposedly, his gobbling also lets the hens know where he is, and once he has flown to ground, they go to him. Sometimes he will leave the tree after only a gobble or two, while on another morning he may remain in the tree until after sun up, having gobbled maybe a hundred times.

Very often, he will fly to ground, gobble a time or two, whereon the hens will join him, and then will cease gobbling. There will then be mating activities, after which the hens begin walking toward a favored feeding area. Mating may take place other times of the day, particularly when the mating season is at its peak. If so, the adult may gobble anytime during the day, though the average male will gobble predominantly before 10:00 A.M.

A spring turkey season is feasible because a hen needs to be mated only once to proliferate the race. The hunting season is also set to open during prime gobbling season. Such gobbling indicates a lessening in male and female relations, causing the male to gobble frequently in order to lure hens to him. It is at this time that the male bird is by far the easiest to hunt. Like I've heard it said about men, "He's a sucker for a skirt."

Spring turkey time is also tick time. With all the talk today about Lyme disease, the savvy hunter will use a tick spray to ward off the beasts. Use the stuff liberally, but read the instructions before doing so. Don't spray it on bare skin.

A handful of today's turkey hunters have turned to hunting the big birds with old-time muzzleloaders. Tom Preston, hoisting this fine old gobbler, has been toting such guns for fifteen years, having bagged a great many birds with the one he's holding.

Diane Damuth holds up the head of a wild gobbler being worked on in the taxidermy shop she and her husband run, located in Brady, Texas. Diane's specialty is wild turkeys.

Ranney Moran, a hunter new to the sport, with a jake bagged on his first hunt. Hunting turkeys is the fastest growing hunting sport in the United States.

The older gobblers throughout much of the turkey range will be removed by the hunters each year, particularly where pursued by veteran hunters. Numerous areas, where my buddies and I have hunted for the past 20 years, have not produced what could be classified as an outstanding "trophy gobbler" in the past umpteen years. Bluntly, we keep them shot out. There simply are no hermit gobblers, nor birds which attain the long, lean, curved spurs of the trophy adult. There are no five- to ten-year-old gobblers in the woods I hunt each year.

Many, many hunters would quit hunting turkeys if the birds ceased all gobbling, mainly because they would no longer be able to locate them so easily. This is why spring turkey hunting far outstrips fall hunting in popularity.

How many times have we all had someone ask us, "Did you hear a bird gobble this morning?" I think I've heard that question a thousand times. It's akin to asking the man who catches great numbers of fish what he's using for bait, and where he's been catching 'em. I'd be a fool to tell some stranger where I

heard two birds gobbling this morning after he has just told me he hasn't heard a single one.

The hunter who attempts to cause a turkey to gobble is invariably attempting to "raise a gobbler." You may overhear a hunter remark, "I was owling, but couldn't raise one." What this means is that the hunter was imitating the call of an owl in hopes that a wild gobbler would sound off. Or, a hunter who does much calling may be attempting to "crank up a turkey," to cause a bird to gobble over and over. Many different sounds can stimulate a turkey into gobbling. Apparently, these are simply what could be referred to as reaction gobbles. The most common sounds which elicit gobbling are the hooting of owls and the cawing of crows.

"Owling," what we turkey hunters know as imitating an owl's hooting, has gotten completely out of hand in much of the country's turkey woods. No doubt all the hooplah surrounding "owling" at turkey calling contests is what's brought all this about. And, all things considered, why not have a contest to see who can slam a pickup door best, or caw like a

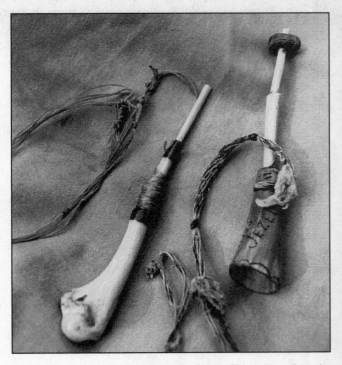

Wingbone calls are excellent for spring hunts. They will easily make the yelps and clucks of the wild turkey hen. Notes made on the wingbone call will carry a considerable distance.

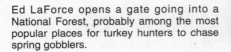

Ed LaForce opens a gate going into a National Forest, probably among the most popular places for turkey hunters to chase spring gobblers.

crow? Or bark like a coyote? Gobblers cut back at all these sounds, too. Anyhow, it's got to the point that a real live owl hasn't got a chance once turkey season opens. Can you imagine how confusing this is to the owls?

I suppose there are a great many hunters who haven't made an owl hoot in years while hunting. I haven't. I do carry a

Many, many hunters would quit hunting turkeys if the birds ceased all gobbling.

crow call, but never use it until later in the day. After I've located a gobbling bird, have moved in nearer to his location, and want to pinpoint where the gobbler is, but don't want to use a hen yelp to do so.

I've found that a good gobble is more apt to make a turkey gobble in today's woods than an owl hoot. Gobblers always

gobble at each other. However, the only problem in today's woods is that making a gobble can be risky. So if you make gobbles with your box or mouth call, do it when you are out in plain view so you won't get shot. There isn't a call made which will boom forth a gobble as well, and as loud, as a mouth call. Takes some practice. Of course, the old Lynch-style box makes good gobbles, handled properly. I've heard gobbles made on other type callers, but none were really worth a damn. Most of them were too faint for too many places. Whatever you decide to use, just be careful 'cause the woods are full of nuts who'd shoot first, then go see what they'd shot!!!

Reminds me of a slob who was popular with some folks and who had won a bunch of calling contests. He told a friend of mine to "shoot anything that moves," then look to see if it was a gobbler. This was a spring hunt. He'd invited my buddy to come down and hunt, after they had met at a calling contest over at Yellville back when I was judging.

Honking a car horn will sometimes cause a gobbler to

Here's a sight that will make any turkey hunter's blood pressure go up a bunch of points, the marks made by a strutting gobbler's wings dragging in the soil.

Ed Norwood, old-time veteran of the turkey wars, shows how to hold a box call so the notes will be heard at maximum distance. This is a must for locating spring gobblers that may be roosting on distant ridges. The box should be held at eye level, or even higher, and the box's edge stroked vigorously with the paddle. If the box is held so the open part faces toward the area the hunter thinks birds may be, the notes will be louder than if the bottom of the box is facing that way.

sound off, as will slamming a door, clapping of hands, or shooting a gun. The turkey will usually gobble only one time at these sudden sounds, and further attempts to entice more responses will be ignored. Continued gobbling is often brought about by only two sounds—the calling of hen turkeys, or the gobbling of other males.

There will be spring mornings when you will hear no gobbles even though you are certain the birds are present. Shutmouth turkeys defy all explanation. Weather, time of day, any or all conditions can be exactly the same as other days when the birds cut loose time after time. After a few days of this silence, it is common to hear hunters remark, "they ain't gobbling," or "they was gobbling two weeks ago, but they quit since then." When the birds are "shutmouthed," the hunter can either pack up and go home, or endure the long, hard days of still-hunting, ambushing, or just hope to call a bird to the gun. The hunting of "shutmouth" birds in the spring season is probably the toughest there is.

Finder's Keepers

How do we locate a turkey gobbler if he is not gobbling yet? Or make a bird sound off? Let's presume we have done our homework, and through scouting, or further endeavor, are positive that we are in known turkey country. We did not arrive before season, so we must begin hunting as soon as we can find a bird to hunt. We need to make a turkey gobble.

There are countless ranches in Texas, Oklahoma and New Mexico where hunting is a business with agriculture and cattle ranching taking a backseat to commercial hunting programs. By writing the Chamber of Commerce of countless larger towns and cities, a hunter can often learn the names and addresses of places which offer these hunts.

Pam Johnson with a spring gobbler she nailed on a ranch in western Oklahoma. She's put in many days on fall hunts, so she knows both sides of hunting the birds. The author can recall when she began hunting, and like today's ad goes, "we've come a long way, baby." She's a heckuva better hunter today.

The hunter on strange ground will do best to remain near a road until he can make contact with a gobbler. It's too easy to walk a jillion miles in unknown country. To the beginner, I suggest the best chance of finding a turkey, or getting one to gobble, is to drive country roads, woods trails, or even little-used blacktops and listen for a gobbling bird. This is best done just as daylight is washing white onto the eastern sky and can last well past sunrise. Throughout hilly or mountainous terrain, it is wise to stop the vehicle every $1/2$- to $3/4$-mile, shut off the engine, quietly get out of the vehicle, and listen. Since I personally do not like to waste time waiting for a bird to gobble, I try to get a gobbler to sound off by using my mouth call.

If the hunter is on foot, a gobble should be made every couple hundred yards. It is wise, during the few hours just past daybreak, to cover ground fast to increase your exposure to gobbling birds. Don't give up too early though; many gobbling turkeys have been heard at high noon. I can recall hearing gobbling turkeys several times when I have been at the truck eating lunch. Turkeys can and do gobble all day.

There are areas where the local turkey populations will be so good the hunter need not drive the backwoods roads, but rather can walk through the woods and listen.

If you hear a gobbler, there are times when it's best not to return the call until you know more about the circumstances. Just this past spring I heard an old bird cut loose, and not fully acquainted with the countryside, I held back until I'd eased

nearer to him. It was a good thing I didn't call since he was on the neighboring ranch where I didn't have permission to hunt, nor could the turkey get to where I was because of hog wire fencing. I did eventually kill the bird, but only after finding a place in the fence where the gobbler could crawl under, then taking up calling from there. Quite often I will hear a gobbler from a distance, then study and look over the situation before making my play. I may decide not to call, but rather to bushwack the bird.

Of course, some gobblers come unexpectedly, and close

Some gobblers come unexpectedly, and close enough to be in a person's hip pocket.

enough to be in a person's hip pocket. Pam Johnson, the editor of this book, and I were on a stand and had been for some time. We hadn't heard a thing all morning. Just like a shot, a gobble wracked our position, very obviously so near we should have had no trouble seeing the bird. Moments later we did, but we were too close for me to make a hen call, yet beyond gunshot range. The gobbler walked off. Once out of sight, I slipped out the call and made a couple hen clucks. Never saw the bird again, nor did we hear him again. A cou-

75

ple days later we tried the same stand. The gobbler suddenly gobbled again, but this time probably a hundred yards from us, and below us, from in a slight hollow. I could make a call, but like the previous day, the bird would not gobble back. Suddenly, like a black vapor, there stood a big, beautiful gobbler, inside twenty yards, almost in back of us. Thankfully, we were located in deep shade and Pam got the gun on him. Though she had to shoot through a small but clear opening, she made the kill.

Shutmouth, or loudmouth, any turkey that gobbles, and that you've called to, may or may not come to your call. Never

---

*S**uddenly, like a black vapor, there stood a big, beautiful gobbler, inside twenty yards, almost in back of us.*

---

lose sight of the fact that in turkey hunting, the exception can become quite common. Time was when I did all my listening while afoot, but after having hunted so much unfamiliar country the past couple decades, I drive back roads, pinning my hopes on hearing a bird sound off from the pickup. Areas I hunt extensively are still hunted on foot, since I know where the birds will be found, though there are some exceptions. The exceptions are the historic ranges of the Merriam and Rio Grande wild turkeys. These two subspecies can, and very often do, travel long distances migrating from their wintering

flock range to their spring residence. Though a flock winters in the same area for years on end, the birds making up this flock may not take up spring residence in the same area year after year. This is particularly true of Merriams.

Rio Grande turkeys often do not return to the flock's spring breakup-nesting area. These variances can be attributed to food supplies, the quality of nesting habitats, land use changes, water and winter flock populations. My observations indicate that small wintering flocks of Osceolas, Easterns, and some Rio Grandes will nest nearer to the wintering area. Where large wintering flocks are evident, fifty birds or more, the birds are scattered over a larger area at nesting time.

After Locating the Turkeys

Regardless of how you locate a gobbling turkey, the next thing is, "What now?" Before you do anything, make sure the sound is a gobble. But if you are positive you've heard a bird, be certain you have a fairly good bearing on the direction the gobble came from. Invariably I try to get a bird to gobble two or three times, then I decide my next moves. Very often the gobbling of one bird will cause another to gobble and this bird could be closer.

What about topography? Can you get to the gobbler's location? Can you tell how far the bird is from you? Can you tell if the gobbler is up on a tree branch, or has flown down to the ground? Did the turkey gobble without your stimulating it, or could you tell? Has it gobbled since? Are the yelps those of a hen or could it be a hunter calling? Can you hear an owl hooting? Maybe it isn't an owl.

W.C. Boyd (right) and his grandad, Oscar Boyd, admire the old bird bagged by the boy on a spring hunt, certainly a trophy any eleven-year-old, or for that matter any hunter, would be proud of.

A hunter must consider all these variables, but in less time than it takes to read this. So long as you are some distance from the bird, each second counts. You need to get within a couple hundred yards, preferably before the bird quits gobbling and while it is still in the tree. Gobblers are apt to sound off to a greater degree while on a branch. Once they go to ground, the hens (if present, and you must always assume they are, until you know otherwise) will join them. Very often after the hens have made company with the gobbler, he will then go silent. If you are in a position to observe the group at this time, the gobbler will prance about in full strut, often continuously, and tag along behind the hens as they begin walking away toward feeding areas.

Judging the distance to a gobbling bird can be extremely difficult if the hunter is on unfamiliar ground. Sounds bounce back and forth over differing types of terrain and can change based on barometric pressure and the effects of wind, rain, fog, heat and cold.

If the hunter overestimates the distance, then gets too close, there is also the chance that the bird will see him and spook. Getting a "fix" on the location of a gobbling bird becomes critical if the gobbler is located on a spur ridge, point, or any location the hunter must circle and approach from another angle to get close. Often it is necessary to lose contact with the bird for a short period of time and, then as you draw nearer, hope you are close enough to regain contact through calling or even sight.

The early morning habits of Merriams differ from many Eastern gobblers. Merriams tend to go downhill; the average

Throughout the states where all-day hunting is allowed, a hunter can get mighty thirsty when the sun breaks out full blast. Do like Bland does—get a canteen and lug it along.

Once in a great while a hunter may bag a full-size spring gobbler, but on closer examination will discover the bird doesn't have all the adornments usually found on older turkeys. Ed La Force exhibits the beard and spurs taken from a gobbler, the bird having what's termed in turkey talk as a stunted beard. In truth, the spurs are darned near as long as the beard. Now, isn't that something?

It's an old saying throughout the South that when the dogwood blooms, the wild turkey gobbles. If you want to find out for yourself, you need to head for Dixie next April or late March if there's an early spring.

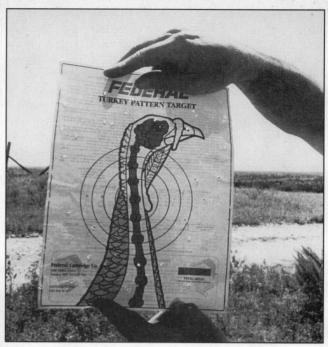

Tom Preston jolts back from the recoil as he shoots a turkey head target. He's testing to see if the load he's chosen will be a good one for spring gobblers. The average spring turkey is large, tough, and hard to bring down, so it takes a number of shots, preferrably in the head and neck area, to solidly anchor a bird. If you're like Tom, not happy with the load, it's best to try another.

Eastern gobbler remains on a ridge or some high elevation until later in the morning. If the Merriam hunter locates a gobbling bird that refuses to come down-mountain, the hunter treats the bird the same as an Eastern; he must get above or on a like level with the bird and try to call it to the gun.

Before I begin my approach, I make a quick study of the situation, and though I may be in unfamiliar country, I try to analyze the terrain. Gobblers are more easily called when the hunter is on the same ridge, within the same hunk of woods, on the same side of the creek, or along the same side of an open pasture. Throughout Old Mexico's high Sierras, a hunter is wasting his time calling a gobbler located on another mesa; the hunter must be on the same flat with the bird.

When I first hear a gobbling turkey and then hear hens clucking and yelping nearby, I quickly make a decision about what I want to do. If on unfamiliar ground, I realize that once the hens join the gobbler, the whole bunch could easily get away from me. I can run the risk of dealing with them as a group and stalk them, or charge in among them, hoping to get a good scatter, and then attempt to crank up the gobbler with hen yelps, and call him in to me. Mexican turkey country falls into this category, as does much Merriam range.

Once I decide to go toward a gobbling bird, I run if possible, wanting to get to within a hundred yards of the gobbler before he can move off. If you just lollygag along, the bird most likely will shut up before you get near, and then you won't know where the bird is. Walk fast if you aren't up to running or trotting. You may want to stop a time or two, hoping the bird will gobble, thus maintaining a good fix on its

location. I don't like to make hen yelps while approaching the bird, so I either rely on the bird to gobble again, or stimulate him with crow calls, owl hoots, or gobbling. When nothing else works, I will make a hen yelp, though I prefer to wait until I have drawn close and make the killing stand.

I seldom approach a gobbler on a straight line, particularly the last hundred yards. Utilizing screening cover, to prevent the bird from seeing me, I will take whatever route the cover provides. If I know the bird is on a ridge, I want to get on it

Before I begin my approach, I make a quick study of the situation, and though I may be in unfamiliar country, I try to analyze the terrain.

with him, and if I have an inkling that the bird's located along a flank, I want to come in on the ridge slightly above the gobbler. This could mean circling competely around a mountain, but the time will be well spent, more so if I am dealing with an Eastern gobbler. If I am hunting open prairie gobblers such as Osceolas and Rio Grandes, I want to remain in a strand of cover as long as possible and not risk crossing open pastures. Getting near a gobbler on a long slope sparsely dotted with mature timber could easily mean a mile of sneaking in order to get within a 200- or 300-yard calling range.

Once the hunter has closed the distance to less than 100 or

Mike Monier bends to gather up a fine Osceola gobbler taken at John Roger's (right) ranch in southern Florida. Notice the background foliage interspersed with pines and saw palmetto. Ideal Osceola wild turkey range.

200 yards, visual contact should be made if humanly possible. Today's endless array of small pocket-sized binoculars are excellent for searching out turkeys in thick terrain. Too many times though, the hunter will attempt to look for the birds with just the naked eye and, in moving closer to get a better look-see, is seen by the turkeys. As a result, the birds run off, spooked, leaving the hunter calling to nothing but trees, bushes, and rocks.

If visual contact is made, the hunter must then decide whether to stalk the group, attempt a scatter, call, or just maintain contact and hope a plan arises as the morning wears on. Keeping in visual contact with a group of turkeys is risky over a prolonged period of time. The birds will move a great deal, and as the hunter attempts to keep them in sight, he is often seen. Of course, if this distance is stretched out to a few hundred yards or so, he can dart among the cover to keep up. The opportunities to move may be fleeting, but the person willing to run the risk may be successful. This often calls for quick decisions, with actions to match, such as fast running, belly-crawling as fast as possible, and perhaps wading waist deep across a creek.

The hunter who has maintained eye contact with a group may see two or more gobblers. An attempt can be made to call one from the group. Only one gobbler will be the dominant bird and he will remain with the hens. The other may also be dominant, but there is always an outside chance he can be tolled away from the group. There is nothing lost in trying.

If the season is set late enough, the hens will be sneaking off from the gobbler after a few hours. In this situation, the

Mike Monier with a spring kill in a southwest New Mexico national forest. Bagged during a sudden snow shower, this fine old Merriam gobbler constitutes one of the many from the Grand Slams Mike has attained while hunting these birds all over the United States.

Pinpoint accuracy is a *must* in all turkey shooting, but it's even more important for the bowhunter. Bow shooting is much like many of the shooting sports, a hunter doesn't always get the chance to shoot from the best positions. So anyone hoping to waylay a gobbler with a bow needs to practice from different stances, like Dick Bland is doing here.

Dick put his arrows dead center of the marked area on this target. However, on this target the lethal area is much too low. Any gobbler hit through the lower chest as seen here will probably escape. The bird must be hit in the upper half of the chest area, or through the butt of the wing.

hunter can try calling the bird to the gun. All of the hens may not leave the male until near noon, but often this may be much earlier, between 8 and 10 A.M. When the hunter sees that the gobbler is alone, the time is excellent for making some hen talk.

When a hunter calls to a group of gobblers and hens, one of the hens might cluck or yelp, letting the hunter know there are hens present. Having learned this, the hunter can attempt to call the hen to him, hoping she will bring the group with her, or shut off all calling.

Who knows how many times each spring hunters sit and call for hours to a gobbler with hens, the end result being the turkeys going their way and the hunter heading back toward the pickup. I suppose it's because of the one time when the whole bunch, or a single gobbler, came to our pleading.

The hunter who cannot make visual contact will still have all these problems and decisions, and more. Hearing a bird gobble, he might, without giving it another thought, decide the gobbler is all alone. The hunter makes a hen call; the bird gobbles. This goes on for a time. After a while, the hunter makes a

call, but there is no gobble. The hunter assumes the bird has left. The truth is, the gobbler is with hens, and though he will gobble back to the hunter's calls, he is not going to leave his hens for a hen he cannot see. The hunter has made no mistakes. He just does not have all the facts laid out where he can see them.

But, suppose the hunter has heard no hens. If contact was maintained with the gobbler before and after he left the roost and, during this time no hens were heard, chances are good that no hens are present. Hens are usually noisy before leaving the trees. Exceptions are common in all turkey hunting, so the hunter can't be certain no hens exist until visual contact has verified this.

If a hunter has made contact with a gobbling turkey an hour or so past sunrise, there is no way of knowing if hens are with him. By this time of morning many hens have quit making any sounds. They are now ambling along, pecking and feeding, and may not make another note of any kind throughout the day. All turkeys are most vocal at dawn, and this is why it pays to hurry toward them then.

A gobbling turkey alone on the roost offers the best chance

A clear morning in Missouri, and a successful hunter trudges back toward camp carrying a big Eastern wild turkey gobbler.

Diane Melillo, a veteran New Jersey turkey chaser, listens for a spring gobbler to cut loose on a Pennsylvania ridge. No, Diane won't try to call the bird in without her face mask on, she's too long in the woods for that. Diane's often told me that far the worst problem she faces is in keeping her eyeglasses shaded so the reflection from them won't spook off an approaching bird.

for the hunter to bag what he came after, once the bird flies to ground. On hearing a gobbling bird and cutting the distance to less than a couple hundred yards, if it seems that he is still in a tree, I advise clucking to him. Make these sounds softly. If you get no responding gobble, make the notes slightly louder so you are assured the bird hears. If the gobbler is lusting for the company of a hen, he will gobble to your calling.

What the hunter most hopes for, and dreams of, is to have a turkey gobble back time after time to even the slightest calling.

What the hunter most hopes for, and dreams of, is to have a turkey gobble back time after time to even the slightest calling. One gobble instantly followed by another is known in turkey hunting circles as a "double gobble"; three is a "triple gobble," etc. Now and then the hunter comes across a gobbler that can be easily "cranked up," and by doing lots of calling, the hunter can stir the bird into gobbling time after time. Incessant yelp-

ing with a raspy shufflin' box is hard to beat if the hunter wants to crank up an old gobbler.

All this gobbling gives the hunter time to sneak to within a couple hundred yards while the bird is in the tree. In heavy timber, it is often very simple to walk to within 75 yards of a gobbling turkey. Just be careful not to be seen.

Having closed to within these short distances, the hunter can then attempt to call the bird into gunshot range. Few veteran hunters do much calling as long as the gobbler remains in the tree, in hopes the bird will come to the few calls already made from the calling stand. I prefer to hear lots of gobbling, so I do considerable calling from my intended shooting stand. This may delay the gobbler coming to me, either keeping him in the tree, or causing him to dawdle along the way, stopping to strut. But an added advantage to this technique is that the bird keeps me posted to his route with all his gobbling. By the time he is in near range, I have the gun well aligned. Again, let me remind the reader that I strive to call from places where the terrain prevents the bird from seeing exactly where my hen calls are coming from until he is within easy shooting range. Quite often the roll of the ground will do this, but it is

A spring turkey hunter's camp in Florida might find more than wild gobblers swinging from the trees. One hunter here shows off a small wild hog he's bagged. Ed LaForce (left), Phil Conrady (center) and Lennis Rose (far right) with game each has bagged in a morning's hunt near Fisheating Creek, near Palmdale.

otherwise accomplished with weeds, rocks, logs, brush and bushes. In many instances I will turn my head, or hide the call box, endeavoring to give the hen yelps a muffled sound, as if the hen is behind cover. Many, many times the first inkling of an approaching gobbler has been the sight of the upper tips of the bird's fanned-out tail feathers, so I watch for these in the direction of a gobbling bird. The instant I see them, I align the gun, firing when the bird's head comes into view. I have no silly qualms about shooting a turkey in full strut. A turkey's head is vulnerable whether sticking up on a long neck or pulled in on a short neck. I would shoot at a turkey's head if the old bird was standing on it. So long as the bird is in strut, I know he isn't spooky, so the mark is secure. True, a gobbler shot in full strut will have a few shot pellets in the upper body, but once I decide to shoot, I intend to end the bird's life quickly.

Anyone who has taken extensive notes on approaching gobblers, or any wild turkeys responding to a call, knows that strutting birds are far more likely to come directly to a call that is not visible and to one that does not stop. A talkative wild turkey does not suddenly quit calling unless it becomes suspicious or danger appears. Your calling has this sameness, and if a gobbler is coming to you on a course which will reveal you to the bird at forty yards, look around for a place that won't allow the bird a long-distance look. If the bird is not yet in view, hustle to it, even if it means crawling on your hands and knees. I've moved umpteen times in the last moments before a gobbler came into view, seeking a location that required the bird to walk to within easy shooting distance before it could

eyeball me. There have been times when this commotion resulted in making lots of noise in dry leaves, but since turkeys also make these sounds, I didn't fret about it.

Often the gobbler will answer a hunter's call, fly down, gobble to the call a few times, walk into shooting range, and the hunt is over. There is nothing difficult about this, except carrying the heavy body back to camp. Many, many springtime hunts did not have such happy endings, and others did, but only after an hours-long hunt, well laced with sessions of

I have no silly qualms about shooting a turkey in full strut...so long as the bird is in strut, I know he isn't spooky, so the mark is secure.

calling, sneaking from one location to another, and resorting to all the tricks in the book. Invariably, the less fortunate episodes got underway the same as the successful ones. You located a gobbling turkey and moved nearer, even got the bird to gobble back a few times, but then the whole hunt seemed to come apart. Long periods of waiting were followed by the appearance of nothing but mosquitoes and gnats. The turkey had answered, seemed interested, but the bird did not show. After a while, the gobbles ceased, and stark reality whispered in the back of your mind, "the bird is gone." What happened? The bird could have approached the hunter and caught sight of

(Above) Here's a fine kettle of turkeys, but where do you shoot? You don't. If you hunt enough springtime gobblers, you'll face this kind of a situation some day. Let 'em go if you don't get a good clean shot, one your shot pattern won't cut down a hen or two. And, if you are in one gobbler country, you don't want to put shot in that other gobbler. Save him for another day.

(Below) Perhaps even more important than camouflaging a hunter's face is keeping his hands covered. Exposed skin is liable to cause the loss of a wary old gobbler coming to the gun. Many hunters walk into the woods each spring without a pair of camo gloves. I bought three pairs at a Wal-Mart store last spring for less than two bucks—a small price to pay to bag a trophy turkey.

a tiny movement, or a shining face, or the glint of sunlight bouncing from a gun barrel. Maybe he didn't like the location from which the calls were coming, became suspicious and vamoosed. Or maybe we were dealing with a gobbler that wandered away from the call after gobbling to it earlier. What then? I would leave the area for two or three hours, then come back to it and attempt to raise the gobbler again. Stimulating the turkey into gobbling can be done by making sudden loud noises or using hen yelps. I've used both, but usually imitate the hen, often with sudden, loud yelps, noisy and fast, six to ten in number. If I decide to stay, I seldom follow the bird but make a long circling walk in hopes of intercepting him in another area. Very often I will change calls when I try to raise the bird from this new location. I usually carry a shuffling box, a wingbone, and a few mouth calls with me. I also change the rhythm of the notes—anything that will make this "hen" call sound different from my last.

There have been times when I've circled the area, hoping to get in front of a gobbler traveling with hens. I have then taken up a location where I can see and hear, waiting to see what develops. Scads of times I have been leaning against a tree when a hen would yelp nearby, or the male would gobble. After hearing the hen, I would stop calling. Hens are tough competition, and in this case I'd be better off stalking the bunch, or getting near enough to scatter them.

If I scatter them, I watch where the gobbler goes, follow him, and then my chances to call him are excellent. I don't wait long to begin calling, usually making my first calls within ten minutes after separating the birds. My first yelps will be

Dick Bland wears a short-sleeved camouflage shirt in one pattern while holding up camo coats in two other patterns. There's a pattern to fit your hunting area, from jungles to deserts, though I don't seriously think you'll find gobblers out in a desert.

83

soft, only two or three in number with just enough time lag between notes to give them a "where-are-you?" sound. If there is no answering gobble, I remain alert to the bird that comes without gobbling; birds will do this sometimes. I won't locate out on a large flat and will invariably seek out the highest ground in the area, though I won't do this if it means one of the hens could be between me and the male bird.

Should I hear the bird gobble before I begin calling, I will answer him very quickly. If he does not gobble back, I then get edgy about what the bird will do. The bird's gobble is his way of letting the hens know where he's located, and since they are in the habit of grouping at his location, the male expects them to come to his call. This is why I prefer to call soon after locating, in hopes he will come to my call before he has time to gobble.

Once the gobbler takes up a calling stand, there is always the chance he will wait for the hens to come to him, refusing to go to them. This happens umpteen thousand times each spring, particularly if the bird is four or five years of age. These older gobblers stake out a small gobbling and strutting territory, often on a narrow ridge, out in the flat of a pasture clearing, or in open woods, and go there each morning after leaving the roost tree. The birds call and strut, the hens go to them.

Long, drawn-out sessions involving a gobbling turkey and a hunter trying to coax the old bird into shooting range are often talked about or read about in hunting magazines. Turkey hunters place the ability to call a gobbler above all other endeavors in life, from making a marriage work to being top dog in the local social register. Telling long tales about one's prowess is far more important than how much money is in the bank. So long as we have turkey hunting, we will have to endure this stuff. But, these episodes probably would have never taken place if the hunter had been doing things right. If we reflect back on the tales surrounding the gobblers that took so long to call, do a little soul searching, and then be truthful with ourselves, the whole mess could have been avoided had we not made a big boo-boo.

The bulk of the time my mistake has been in locating badly. Before the birds came into range, they became wary for two reasons. One, I was making calls from open terrain where the responding gobblers realized they should be able to see the calling hen. Number two, my location found me under eye-to-eye scrutiny by the turkeys, so I couldn't continue calling. The

Well-known TV personality Butch McCain hefts a fine winter-killed gobbler for the author's camera. Butch and his brother, Ben, have long been television favorites across the Southwest, and have appeared numerous times as guests on "All My Children," and others.

All of us should take time to smell the roses, to enjoy nature to its fullest while we're hunting. What's finer than listening to a mountain brook tumbling among the rocks in Vermont's Green Mountains, or marveling at the humped loping of an otter passing through a moss hung hummock in Saint Lucie County, Florida, or, like Bland, admiring the glowing beauty of this prairie flower, called Indian Blanket, on the plains of western Oklahoma.

birds became suspicious, and though in all but a few cases I did in time kill the birds, it was only after difficult relocating and calling maneuvers. Invariably, my longest, most time-consuming kills while calling were from calling stands where there was not enough cover to screen me well. Had I selected

Turkey hunters place the ability to call a gobbler above all other endeavors in life, from making a marriage work to being top dog in the local social register.

slightly heavier cover, chances are the bird would have walked within range in short time.

There isn't much sense continuing to call a turkey that has been gobbling back for a half-hour. It's best to quit calling and move out of the area. Should the gobbler enter the area searching for the hen, there is no chance it will be spooked and then run off for good.

You will hear an endless variety of reasons why a gobbler

will answer the hunter's call, but refuse to go to him—the hunter calls too much; he does not call enough; he should have clucked instead of yelped; he made a move which the bird spied. Seldom will a person know for sure the real reason.

Whenever a bird gobbles incessantly, but does not come in, I back away, make a circle, and try to make visual contact, and, if possible, make a stalk. Having another hunter along is a tremendous asset because one hunter can keep the bird gobbling, while the other pinpoints and stalks the bird. Gobblers are far less wary when answering distant calling.

If you hear a hunter remark, "Boy, I couldn't do anything with that old bird this morning, he was traveling on me," chances are the bird was gobbling at every call the person made, but kept walking. Walking and gobbling, walking and gobbling—one of these gobblers can cover lots of distance, draw numerous hunters to an area and create no end of turkey calling efforts.

If the bird is alone, the whole thing becomes slightly maddening. I have observed this type of gobbler walking past hens without slowing down, as though they weren't even there. Though he will gobble at hen yelps, he seemingly has no urge to mate. Once in a while, he'll come to gobbles made by

The turkey hunter's vest is exceedingly popular with its numerous pockets and oversize game bag in back. The large game bag will hold a full-grown, record-size gobbler or, until you shoot him, a big lunch and enough cokes to last a week. I wouldn't be without mine. It's seen no end of use and a small army of dead turkeys.

Setting out a hen decoy isn't just sticking it in the ground anywhere, not if the hunter wants to up the odds on bringing an old bird into shooting range. Locate areas where birds have been feeding recently, places where hens have been coming each morning. After all, the hens will often have company tagging along, company with long beards.

another male, but a so-called "traveling gobbler" will seldom pay any heed to a male's gobbling either. I have had some luck when circling them, waiting in the hoped-for path. The bird's gobbling makes this hunting method easier.

Last, but not least, is the bird that remains in the general locale, gobbles now and then at the hunter's call, and though seemingly interested in the hen, refuses to come to where the hunter waits. And, there is a world's plenty of this kind of turkey gobbler. They can be encountered at any time of the day throughout any and all springtime turkey range. I have found them among all five strains of bearded and spurred turkeys, so don't think you have a corner on the market just because your woods are full of these old reprobates. A good many of these strolling gobble-machines have some hens with them, but some don't, and there is no real way of knowing unless the hunter makes visual contact. Of course, if hens are present, it is easily understood why the gobbler won't leave them to come to a call.

I can remember when I first began hunting turkeys, I would spend hours fooling with one of these turkeys. Calling, waiting, watching, calling, all the while the bird would keep up my hopes with a gobble from time to time. One bird one day would stand in place gobbling, while another the next day might walk back and forth, gobbling from one end of a ridge to the other. While still others would just start walking away

Spring not only turns on a lot of gobbling turkeys, but very often turns out all the creepy crawling and flying little beasts which can make a turkey hunter's life miserable. About the time you get an old bird to bellering back each time you call, the mosquitoes really get to chewing on your hide. There are ways to beat them at this little game. Try getting a head net or a camo jacket with a fully built-in head net. My cap is simply resting on my head over the net.

If a gobbler does not come to my calling, I go to him...many have fallen to my gun because I have been able to slip within easy killing distance.

gobbling, with me following, almost running. Some I'd see; some I wouldn't. A few I killed; a whole bunch I didn't. At least I learned how to recognize them. Today, if a gobbler does not come to my calling, or does not head my way inside of twenty to thirty minutes, I go to him. Many have fallen to my gun because I have been able to slip within easy killing distance. Aside from this, I have devised other on-the-spot tricks to bring about their demise. Anyone could do the same. It is simply a matter of studying the situation, deciding on a course of action, and then following through.

If the turkey is a traveling gobbler and on a course that the hunter feels he can intercept, this can be done. Some are fast walkers, not leaving a hunter enough time to circle around them. They are often heard gobbling as they leave the hunter's hearing range. Just let them go. They may return hours later.

I have moved away from a gobbling turkey who would not come into gunshot, only to have the bird walk to my old calling stand when I made calls from my new location. If you have a bird pull this stunt, you can do what I did one day in Arkansas. I moved to a new stand, made a call, the old turkey gobbled back, and then I ran back toward my previous calling stand and was still out of breath when I spied the gobbler coming. This trick won't work on flat terrain unless there is a lot of intervening cover. I was in the ridges and coves of a mountain-

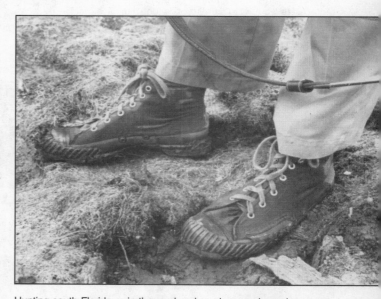

Hunting south Florida or in the mud and muck someplace else means your feet are wet all the time. Do like I do—lug along a pair of canvas wading shoes for such bogholes. Nothing beats them in wet country.

side. I have killed gobblers simply by continuing to call—loud, noisy, and plenty of it—while at the same time walking straight toward them. I've done this even when there was not a solid wall of cover, hoping that if the bird detected any movement, he might think it was the hen walking his way. My last two gobblers I tried this trick with—both were gobbling considerably, both were all alone and had been for over an hour, and neither would budge an inch in coming to my enticements. I shot each at less than 25 yards. Risky? I guess you could say that.

A spring-killed Osceola gobbler has to be one of the finest wild turkey trophies found anywhere, due to so many of the birds sporting keen, sharp spurs. Notice the lack of barring on the wings of this bird bagged by another of Bland's long-time hunting companions, Ed La Force.

There is no other hunting sport that will come close to the excitement of the approach of an old gobbler on a damp spring morning. For a spell, you can tell he's close, but you can't see him. Then, like magic, here he comes, wings dragging in the leaves, you hear that "whooommph," as he pirouettes, tail fanned out full, head tucked against his roused back feathers. Surely he can hear your heart pounding, pounding, pounding.

I've circled turkeys, and then called them to me, though this can be risky with a bird who has ignored your calls thus far. It is possible to circle the bird, station yourself in its path and make a call. However, the gobbler may veer off, going by you one hundred yards away, or he may turn back on his course. If I try to circle a bird, and think I am within gunshot of its path, I rarely call. I would prefer to take my chances without the call, simply because the bird did not come when I had called earlier. True, he may have gobbled back at me, but he was reluctant to come to the call.

All of us who hunt spring gobblers on mountainous terrain—hills, knobs, ridges, whatever you want to call them—have run across gobblers that marched back and forth along a wooded ridge or perhaps across a glade dotted with trees, the ground littered with dry leaves. The watchful hunter may discover a hole in the bird's defenses, allowing a sneak into gun range. Again, this is risky because there is always the chance the bird will detect the hunter. But this is the chance a person must take unless he wants to sit around all spring and count gobbles.

Turkey sign, like these droppings, acquaint you with the daily habits of the birds in your area. Such a great amount of dropping are found only beneath roost trees. Do not hunt here.

By the same token, I have called reluctant gobblers with what I term too much calling. The thickest beard in my collection came from a gobbler that would not come to my calls, though I could not make a note he did not gobble back to at least once. That old monarch finally began coming my way when I began calling without letup. I detected a gobble or two, but much of the time I couldn't hear the bird for my own calling. I must have called four or five hundred times while the bird made his way, inch by inch, to a point where I could shoot.

How many times have all of us heard, "I have some good news, and I have some bad news." This applies in particular to springtime gobblers. The good news is when they gobble. The bad news is when they are "shutmouth." When the birds don't

Many spring hunters search out other hunting options to go along with a spring hunt. In much of the country, the only other pursuit is fishing. But, there are places where wild hogs can be added to turkey hunting. The tusks on this hog are being admired by Dirk Ross, famed elk hunter and guide.

David Jackman has many Royal Grand Slams to his credit and is rarely caught in turkey woods without binoculars. Going turkey hunting without them is darned near as bad as leaving the gun at home. Many areas of the country are best hunted by sitting and glassing, more so after the birds have quit gobbling.

There are many ways to try to induce a gobbler to gobble, from hooting like an owl, to banging car doors or honking a horn. And, you can buy what many of us have long called a turkey's neck and shake it. These rubber tube-like calls, if shaken properly, make a turkey gobble. Hopefully, a real one will answer yours.

gobble, very few hunters will hunt them. Why? Simple. The turkey's gobble is a beacon to the average springtime turkey hunter, and when the beacon is not working, the hunter does not know where the gobbler is located. Or he thinks "the birds have moved someplace else." This undermines morale, getting progressively worse the more the hunter thinks about it.

On mornings when the gobblers are not sounding off, the next best thing is to go into areas where it is thought the birds are, or have been when the conditions were nearly identical, and listen for hens talking. Hen talk ordinarily stimulates the male to gobbling, but I have heard hens on many mornings when the gobblers did not gobble. If hens are heard, the hunter should move in as close to them as possible without being seen, and then call with the same notes and vocabulary they are using. If the hens can be called to the hunter, any gobbler with them will tag along.

Many toms gobble but a time or two while on the roost branch, and then after flying down, won't gobble as the hens collect around him. The hunter who enters an area a moment or two after fly down will not hear anything and will think the birds are shutmouth. In reality, by the time he has arrived, this is the case. Hunting shutmouths is that way, and a hunter can hunt them day after day in prime turkey country without even a glimpse of wild turkey. Turkeys that don't gobble are hard on morale.

Beginning at dawn, I move from place to place, trying to hunt places I think a particular subspecies will inhabit, taking the time of day into consideration. Hens go to feed not long after flydown, so I want to hunt much of the morning in areas where the hens will be searching for food. If I can find the hens, the gobblers will probably be with them. During the midday hours, the hens should be nesting, leaving the gobblers to while away these hours loafing, standing in the shade, preening, and dusting. Later in the afternoon the hens will again feed, and toward sundown all of them will head for roosting sites. By constantly keeping in mind what a turkey is most apt to be doing at different times of the day, I can pace myself to hunt these areas. I must never lose sight of which strain of wild turkey I am hunting, and having studied the bird before the hunt, will have an idea of the terrain the bird seeks at various times of the day.

Calling techniques can vary according to the hunter's whims. I call considerably as the day begins, but cut back later in the morning. During the afternoon hours I call very little, simply because this is a quiet period for all wild turkeys. By late afternoon I will all but cease calling, making only inquisitive clucks, these few in number and well spaced. I will also move from one calling location to another. Turkeys cover lots of ground during the late afternoon.

Shutmouth gobblers that do come to a call do so like so

When the birds don't gobble, very few hunters will hunt them...turkeys that don't gobble are hard on morale.

much black smoke. One minute they aren't there, the next minute there they stand. When I am hunting shutmouth gobblers, I choose calling locations that give a greater field of visibility than when I am calling to a gobbling bird. This is in hopes of seeing the bird a ways from me, so I can take precautions to sit unmoving and be ready with the gun. Anyone who does considerable calling, spring or fall, will have birds show up unannounced. If the hunter has been engaged in this standoff over a period of several days, remaining alert is all but impossible. A turkey, suddenly standing at close range, quickly makes up for all the silence, but far more quickly if the hunter can take advantage of the opportunity.

There have been times when hunting shutmouth gobblers

Many times each spring a hunter will suddenly come upon a large, speckled egg lying out on open ground, a wild turkey egg. Here, Frank Dunn, a boy from Crested Butte, Colorado, who likes to hunt turkeys with his dad, Larry, has found one. No one knows exactly why the birds do this, but it's not uncommon, even among domesticated fowl.

that I've not heard a gobble for days, only to suddenly have a bird gobble back and continue gobbling as it comes to the call. This cranked-up bird is what we all hope for on such days. One hot afternoon, after not hearing a gobble for two days, I walked up a pine-flanked hill and stopped to make a call. A big bunch of slash pines had been piled on top of the little knoll, and it happened that I stopped just as I walked up to them. I called, and a gobbler cut loose on the other side of the brushpile. I fell forward and stretched out belly-down, gun up on my elbows. I slid off the safe just as a red-headed turkey gobbler came

When the dogwood blooms, it's turkey gobbling time. It is the season to hunt wild gobblers.

around the stack of dead limbs. Obviously, the old bird was coming up the hill from the opposite direction, but I would never have known the bird was there if I hadn't stopped to call. If I had walked on a few steps, the gobbler would have seen me and skedaddled, me never being the wiser.

There is luck in all turkey hunting.

Too often, in this day and age, you will hear what seems to be another hunter calling to the bird you had considered *your* turkey. First, you should ask yourself if you are dead certain the calls are not those of other turkeys. I've known of veteran turkey hunters backing away from a situation when it seemed

another hunter was pulling a bird away from the gun, only to make visual contact and learn that the "other hunter" was a well-feathered wild turkey hen. A turkey call can be made to sound exactly like a wild turkey, and a wild turkey can also sound exactly like a turkey call. Time after time I have heard hens who were perfect imitators of box calls. To me, there is no call which sounds so like a wild turkey as does a shuffling box if the user is well versed in its use.

Anytime a gobbler gobbles back, there is always a chance the bird will come to where the call was made. Gobblers will and do gobble at almost any sound. I've heard them gobble at band-tailed pigeons cooing in Mexico's Sierra Madres, at sickle-billed curlews in Black Mesa country, at a wild hog's squeal in Osceola Indian country, or at somebody hammering nails; they'll cut loose at anything. Had one gobble back to me after I'd missed him, *but that old gobbler was flying*. I'd just killed his buddy, so swung on him as he ran into takeoff, shot just as he hopped into flight, and missed him. I was looking straight at him when he gobbled in the air, head stuck out as they do in flight, beard flowing back. I've always thought it was a rather derisive gobble, much like the bird was giving me the raspberry.

Jakes can gobble just as well as longbeards, and if you are hunting an area where very few old gobblers are left, but a good population of jakes remain, you will often hear excellent gobbling, and lots of it. In a short time, the dominant jake will take over an area, his gobbling becoming very good. I've had any number of clients, even old veteran turkey hunters, mis-

Throughout much range of the wild turkey are foods which the birds prefer over all others. Regardless of the subspecies, acorns and grasshoppers are two such foods. Anytime you kill a wild turkey during the fall hunt, particularly if late in the day, open the bird's craw to find what the bird's been eating.

Hitting the sounding edge of a box rather suddenly will make a sudden loud yelp. Do this several times and you've got a series of yelps. If made as loud as possible, the yelps will often fire up an otherwise silent gobbler. Try this trick after the birds have seemingly ceased gobbling for the day.

takenly kill jakes, thinking the bird was an adult from its excellent tones.

On the other hand, in areas where there are an abundance of older gobblers, you'll oftimes never hear a jake gobble. Not once. And, quite often, the jakes will simply vanish. You'd be very hard pressed to find and kill one. So, keeping this in mind, just remember, if you have scads of jakes, you may have very few old gobblers.

The Legend of the Dogwood

There is a legend that, at the time of the crucifixion, the dogwood was the size of the oak. So firm and strong was the tree that it was chosen as the timber for the cross. To be used thus for such a cruel purpose greatly distressed the tree, and Jesus, nailed to it, sensed this, and in His gentle pity for all sorrow and suffering, said to it:

Because of your regret and pity for my suffering, never again shall the dogwood tree grow large enough to be used as a cross. Henceforth it shall be slender and bent and twisted and its blossoms shall be in the form of a cross...two long and two short petals. And in the center of the outer edge of each petal there will be nail prints, brown with rust and stained with red, and in the center of the flower will be a crown of thorns and all who see it will remember....

Throughout all of wild turkey country, there's a saying that goes, "When the dogwood blooms, it's turkey gobbling time." It is the season to hunt wild gobblers.

6

Fall and Winter— When You Truly Earn Your Bird

Hunting old gobblers during the fall season is the ultimate challenge in all turkey hunting. A hunter won't find these birds running around looking for a girlfriend, so the gullible bird from April has become a wary, wild, wild turkey. Once you've made up your mind to hunt the old longbeards in the fall and winter months, you'll understand that real turkey hunting wasn't in spring after all.

WHEN PLANNING a fall or winter hunt, the first matter of concern is to take a hard look at the options—where to hunt and when. This is made easier for those hunters who belong to the National Wild Turkey Federation (NWTF). Each year the organization's magazine *Turkey Call* runs a report by Bob Gooch giving a state-by-state rundown of license costs, season dates, prospects, etc. Additionally, the report points out major state hunting regulation changes which may affect the turkey hunter.

The hunter should choose several states which sound appealing, and then write each, asking for a complete set of regulations governing fall turkey hunting. If the hunter is not a resident of the state, he should ask for regulations applying to non-residents. Upon receiving the material from the chosen states, the hunter can then narrow down the choice after studying bag limits, weapons allowed, daily hunting hours, etc. I prefer to hunt areas with multiple bag limits of two or three turkeys.

What birds are legal? Is it an "any turkey" season, or can "gobblers only" be killed? What about the weather? Are there public or private lands where I can hunt? It would be silly to travel several hundred miles without considering these queries, plus umpteen others which will surface. And yet I've known folks who have gone on a hunt without asking these questions and then could not understand the adversities which arose. Each year I have hunters call me searching for a place to hunt that is not overrun with people. My home state of Oklahoma does not have many public areas with good turkey hunting, so when the season opens, those few areas sporting fair turkey

A fall turkey camp is camping at its best. What can beat a campfire on a cool fall evening, cooking on a gasoline stove, and a warm, snug sleeping bag beckoning from a tent?

populations are crowded with hopeful gunners. Both Oklahoma and Texas have a great many wild turkeys, but the majority are on private lands. Obtaining permission to hunt on private property is difficult at best, and impossible much of the time.

Game departments often give glowing reports of game populations on department-managed areas. This may be true, only *if the hunter can be in the area at the season's opening and provided he also knows where the game is located.* By late afternoon on opening day, extremely hard morning pressure could result in a large kill, and assuredly this can mean the droves will be widely scattered, resulting in anything but a quality hunt.

One indicator oftentimes supplied through state game divisions is turkey kill statistics. Studying the breakdown of reported kills, a hunter can decide upon areas which warrant further investigation. This is when I study a map showing a state's county boundaries. I will note which counties have the largest kills, the size of these counties when compared to others, and if there are public hunt areas, national forests, or other areas open to hunters. Seldom will I plan on hunting the county with the greatest number of kills. Why won't I hunt a place which appears to be the obvious best choice? The answer is simple. Publicity. Once an area is listed as the top county in numbers of birds taken, hunters will gravitate to it like bees to a clover field.

Added pressure may even result in a larger kill the following year. True, the area may be the best insofar as turkey num-

"Black Dog" Kahlich (left) and Mike Monier coming into camp with a snow kill. Lone birds are often easy to call to a hunter during fall and winter hunts. Usually all that's needed is a few yelps. Since turkeys like company, they'll often answer immediately, then walk to the hunter.

Much of what's been written about turkey hunting has dealt only with spring hunts; very little in-depth material has been published about fall and winter hunting methods. These two seasons are as different as night and day.

Box calls, like this M.L. Lynch, will make excellent turkey yelps and clucks. This one-sided box will call in gobblers if the user slows the cadence and drags the notes.

bers are concerned, but probably fringe counties will have good turkey hunting, and far fewer hunters. I prefer turkey populations that exceed hunter numbers, so will always choose an area with far fewer birds, if the hunters are all but non-existent.

Kill reports are also subject to scrutiny. Hunters in one area may consider it such an honor to kill a wild turkey that they proudly take it to a check station. Checking the bird is proof of their hunting ability. Five hundred miles away hunters who have been exposed to turkey hunting for a longer period of time, while just as proud of birds taken, see no use in taking a bird by a check station.

I study kill reports, take into consideration the number of years turkeys have been hunted thereabouts, and ordinarily add 100 percent to the kill figures. This will give me a rough idea how many birds may have been taken in that county. I

will then study the areas open to hunting in surrounding counties, and if possible, look for areas which are two or more miles from roads. If these are numerous, I then catalog the area as a possibility. From there I go to bag limits. I seldom will travel far to hunt an area with a one turkey limit.

If the area is "one turkey," what then? Is the area open to "either sex," or "any turkey"? Or is it "gobblers only"? If the area is heavily wooded, I prefer "any turkey" bag limits. Why? Wild turkeys are difficult to identify in terms of sex, particularly young turkeys, and especially in the dim light often found in wooded forests. Combine this with the poor light found at dawn, and an early fall when the leaves are yet on the trees, and you have conditions that are extremely bad for identifying a young hen from a young gobbler. The average hunter has enough trouble telling them apart when the birds are dead, lying at his feet.

Locating larger droves of wild turkeys is often the name of the game during fall hunts. Very often every bird within miles will be in one single large flock, sometimes even the older gobblers, too. These hunters, on the Kansas plains, will watch for turkeys from afar. Once birds are located, it's a matter of waiting until they are in a position for the hunters to stalk them to within shooting range.

There are numerous hunters who are heard to say, "I don't kill any hens. I don't think anyone should kill a hen turkey." Such statements only tell me that the hunters know nothing of population turnovers due to natural mortality. Game department turkey biologists have made intense studies of turkey flocks within their jurisdiction. When these folks say it's okay to kill hens, then it is okay. The hens are apt to be a part of the year's natural loss, so the hunter should benefit. Doe seasons often arise for the same purposes. An area becomes overrun with deer. The answer is to cull out some does. Wild turkeys do not overrun an area in the same sense, but when the flocks have reached a saturation point, natural causes will skim off the surplus, be it hens or gobblers.

My home state of Oklahoma allows hunters in specified counties to shoot "any turkey." Hunters pursuing turkeys in another group of counties are limited to shooting gobblers, while another group of counties has no fall hunt, as the bird populations do not justify the potential kill.

I have always advised new turkey hunters to keep the weather in mind when choosing an away-from-home location for a fall turkey hunt. Never let the weather extremes escape your scrutiny and make equipment adjustments for these adversities. When hunting the larger mountains, such as the Rockies or the Sierra Madres, you should never leave the camp or your vehicle without a map of the nearby surroundings, a matchsafe, compass and sharp knife. White coveralls, or a snow parka, can also add to your hunting comfort should you suddenly find the landscape blanketed in snow.

Having settled on an area you intend to hunt, your hunting success often hinges on what you do once you arrive. Chances are you have decided to hunt a public hunt area, or a national forest, or its equivalent.

Hunting success often hinges on what you do once you arrive.

I don't advise anyone to just park the truck, jump out, and head into the woods. This could come later, if all else fails. But, first try some other tactics. Talking to local people is number one. Idle chatter with a gas station attendant has brought me results more than once. The same goes for folks who take your money at quick-stops. These people are in daily contact with local hunters who stop for a cup of coffee, a

W.C. Boyd, the author's eleven-year-old nephew and avid turkey hunter, demonstrates the advantages of camouflage during a hunt in Oklahoma. Few small boys (and a lot of older folks) cannot sit quietly for any period of time. So anything that will help to hide their movements is a tremendous advantage in turkey hunting. W.C. has a pair of gloves, too, but heck knows what happened to them.

doughnut, or fuel. The smaller the store, and the further its location from a large population center, the greater the chances that the proprietor will know what gives with the local hunters.

The hunter who arrives in a distant area before the season opens can often locate turkeys simply by driving forest roads, keeping watch for droppings in the trail, tracks where soil conditions permit, and the birds themselves. Eyeballing turkey sign while driving a road takes practice. The beginning hunter will have to drive at a snail's pace, but in time, he will begin to recognize areas which should be watched closely, and those which he can cover quickly. Obviously, a road covered by small pebbles and gravel will not reveal tracks, but one of sand, mud, or even better, covered with a light snow, will. Even a rocky road will not obscure a large dropping in a wheel track. Or a primary feather which has recently fallen from a bird's wing.

The smaller the store, the greater the chances that the proprietor will know what gives with the local hunters.

Making short hikes along abandoned roads can be very productive. Turkeys walk all roads within their territory, so a fast walk for a mile or so along one of these can reveal local turkey possibilities. Fall turkeys are often vocal, so there is also the added chance that the scouting hunter will hear birds. Probably the greatest factor related to walking roads is that these are built for vehicular traffic and are therefore kept on high ground. Turkeys like high ground. If there is food on it, they will use it if it is within their range. Therefore, the hunter should keep an eye open for acorns, dogwood fruits, wild grapes, grasshoppers, anything that is a preferred wild turkey food throughout the area. There are a couple of disadvantages to arriving in a strange area prior to season. Firstly, there will probably not be any locals traveling forest roads, and secondly, there will be no shots to tell the visiting hunter if others are into turkeys.

In the average turkey hunting area, once opening day arrives, there will be enough hunters traveling the roads, firing shots, and checking birds to give the visiting gunner some insight as to where birds are to be found. Throughout many areas, such as Pennsylvania, parts of Arkansas, the Virginias, western Oklahoma, and others, opening hour usually brings forth volleys of gunfire as local hunters get into droves of young birds. This is heard at some distance, and the traveling hunter can then head toward the sounds, and as he meets hunters, can locate the exact place where the birds were encountered. Hunters who are not knowledgeable of fall turkey hunting practices will ofttimes leave those areas, thinking them to be the very last place to hunt a turkey. Which, of course, at least for the first few days, is not so. Quite the contrary, the hunter should get as near as he can to the exact place

Anyone hunting fall turkeys, particularly fall droves, realizes there is no substitute for head-to-toe camouflage. The only thing that might alert a bunch of birds, if the hunter's situated so he blends in with the surroundings, could be the big, round hole at the end of the gun's barrel. Or the snoring, if he's gone to sleep.

from where the drove flushed because that is where the birds will reassemble.

I have noticed many springtime hunting addicts presume turkeys can be hunted throughout the same terrain during the fall and winter seasons. Though fall and winter birds can often be found on their spring stomping grounds, there are so many exceptions to this that we should stop here and take an in-depth look at this part of a turkey's life.

The statement can be made that all five subspecies of the bearded and spurred wild turkeys *can be found during both fall and spring seasons on some areas of their home range.*

With this statement, another can be added. Throughout the ranges of all subspecies will be areas where the birds *will be found during the spring seasons, but will never inhabit as a drove or wintering flock* during the winter season.

The magnitude of these tendencies, call them migrating habits if you wish, varies with local terrains and the subspecies of turkey being dealt with. This traveling about, migrating or just wandering, as I often refer to it, is due to several factors. Rocky Mountain wild turkeys, often known as Merriams, must travel back and forth over separate ranges because of bad weather conditions. Heavy snows and severe winters cover the food supplies and cause the birds to seek lower elevations where food can be found. This up-and-down traveling can result in birds being located here today, but forty miles distant next week.

The methods utilized in hunting autumn turkeys are so numerous they defy description. And, along with these are infinite numbers of on-the-spot tricks which a hunter can improvise to fit the situation he may suddenly be faced with. I doubt if there is a gunning sport which, by constantly changing tactics, can be so often brought to a successful culmination, time after time, than is the hunting of wild turkeys. But success will be had only by the hunter who has the ability to think, keep an open mind, and make instant decisions. The decision to act may result in instant, fast movements, or a long, slow deliberate course of delayed action. Fall turkey hunting, for any and all ages and sexes of wild turkeys, is best done by the hunter who possesses all the aforementioned capabilities. He must be able to think freely, to make lightning-like decisions, and then to act on them. Among those of us who travel incessantly in quest of wild turkeys, it must never be forgotten which bird we are hunting, thereby applying habitat adaptations to our hunting techniques.

By late fall, November and December, the hunter could bump into a drove made up of any combination of sexes, ages or numbers of turkeys in small bunches. The droves of young turkeys, hatched from the egg the previous spring and therefore six months of age, will be with the mother hen. At times,

A couple of hunters in Mexico show off some Gould's wild turkeys, these killed near a laguna (pond) where the birds came to drink and feed. Mexican hunters use whatever gun they own and shoot whatever cartridges they are able to purchase. Wild turkeys are scarce throughout much of Mexico. Fall and winter hunts are no longer allowed.

there will be added barren hens tagging along with these family broods. As the fall season progresses, such small bunches will join together, forming larger droves of fifteen, twenty, thirty, or forty turkeys. Ordinarily, the older adult males will be paling around together in groups of two to ten, perhaps even more. Or, these older gobblers will be seen wandering about as singles all by themselves. By mid-winter, these small groups will ordinarily be made up of birds of a like sex. Age can vary.

The young birds are the easiest to bag of all wild turkeys.

Assuredly, the young birds are the easiest to bag of all wild turkeys, though the droves can be extremely difficult to locate, more so for the hunter traveling into strange new country. Once a person walks into the woods on an autumn morning, he must locate the birds through any number of means, the least of which is being able to hear the birds as they call. Many turkeys call back and forth to some extent during the fall months. Sometimes it cannot be heard at any distance and the hunter will need a good deal of luck to hear the chatter.

When I am hunting strange woods, don't know where birds are located, and the morning is calm, I will walk at a brisk pace, stopping every 200 or 300 yards to call and listen a moment before continuing my journey. The mixed drove of hens and young birds are most vocal at daybreak, so my chances of walking to within hearing distance of a group is highly increased with the amount of territory I can cover. As the morning wanes, I can slow the pace, as the birds will slacken calling considerably once they arrive at feeding places.

When I am lucky enough to hear an awakening drove, I can then weigh the options. What to do? Of course, the first thing to do is to walk nearer, preferably placing myself at an elevation above them if possible.

Having drawn as near as I can without spooking them, I

While Ed Le Force looks on, Lennis Rose cups his hand behind the deformed foot of a fine old gobbler bagged in southern Florida. Osceolas are a great fall quarry for any hunter wishing to test his skill in the Sunshine State. Due to heavy cover, the birds are often noisy grouping up at the dawn flydown, so are easily located. Calling will do the trick on scattered birds, as will stalking, and if the hunter knows the habits of a local flock, he can simply set an ambush.

Turkeys often roost in flocks during the fall and winter months, as this small band of gobblers is doing. Once the trees have shed their leaves, wild turkeys are easily seen once they've flown up. Many are killed by poachers who slip into the area before daylight.

Turkey tracks in the snow—the only thing you need to know is when it snowed. Such tracks can tell you how many turkeys were in the bunch, what kind, which way they were traveling, and freshness, whether the tracks are fairly old or have just been made.

Veteran turkey hunter Gary Blakeslee, who owns a fabulous wildlife art gallery in Palm Beach, Florida, with a winter-killed bird. Hunting wild turkeys in snow can be difficult due to a lack of white camo. Gary's treebark camo outfit is in stark contrast to the snowy background. Fortunately, the author was able to place Gary in dark cover and pushed a drove past his hiding place.

then attempt to learn if the birds are yet in the tree. Birds sitting among the upmost branches can be called to in hopes one flies to the hunter. Once a few of them alight on the woods floor, chances are that all will join them there. True, some may glide to earth off to the side, but on average, the drove will assemble where the largest number has flown down.

Two hunters working together can bag birds with ease from an awakening drove at first day. It is often a case of one hunter circling them and then walking toward the birds as the other hunter also begins walking toward them. There are serious drawbacks to calling birds roosting together within a relatively small periphery. In most instances, the hunter will not be able to sneak near enough without being detected. Undisturbed turkeys, when flying down, often give just a flip of the wings and glide to earth very near the roost tree. Birds on the outer edges of the roosting flock will fly a longer glide path, but

head toward the center of the bunch. Complete flydown can take but a moment or two for a small drove. So, unless a hunter can slip close to the birds, almost in among them, his chances of calling in a bird from an unsuspecting, unmolested close-roosting drove are not good. Chances for calling kills are far greater if the hunter simply walks in among the birds, or runs, as I do, scatters them from the trees, and then after a short wait, uses the call. The birds will make all kinds of calls, and those which have not been hunted will become extremely noisy, as bird after bird joins in regrouping. Young gobbler yelps, half-gobbles, hen yelps, kees, whistles, clucks, you name it—a bunch which has been separated makes all the notes in a turkey's vocabulary when gathering.

Let's pretend you haven't heard any birds at first day, and it is now mid-morning. Still no sound of turkeys. What next? The hunter must keep in mind the routine a turkey follows on

Mark "Black Dog" Kahlich of Arizona with an old gobbler killed in a snow storm. Arizona's mountains are subject to sudden storms during both spring and fall seasons, as are the mountains of Colorado and New Mexico. Merriams go about life just the same except when the snow gets so deep they can't get around. Then they hike back down to a lower elevation. As soon as the snow melts, they head back uphill.

an ordinary fall day. The birds gather at the roost location and from there amble toward water or a feeding area. The bunch will peck at anything edible along the journey, and it should be remembered that wild turkeys, like all wildlife, spend most of their lives engaged in the pursuit of food. The drove will linger during the midday hours, preening, dusting, standing, sleeping, and in general just being lazy before again taking up the hunt for food during the mid to late afternoon hours. The fall turkey hunter must keep this routine in mind and build his game plan around it.

Thus, the mid-morning plan should involve a hunt for turkey foods, and in searching for those, the hunter should make contact with the birds. At this time of morn, I will be covering lots of country, noting what foods are abundant and if the turkeys have been feeding on these. By reading such signs, I will know where to be extra alert and where I can

probably find birds. I don't concentrate in one tiny area, but work a larger range of a few square miles and note the types of terrain that could be productive.

Chances of calling in a bird from an unsuspecting, unmolested close-roosting drove are not good.

During fall hunts to unfamiliar areas, my principal method in searching for birds is to walk fast, stop to listen from time to time, watch for signs of turkeys, keep an eye peeled for major food sources, and all the while keep alert should I bump into birds. This sounds like an unreasonable number of things to be engaged in, but with time it becomes a habit. It is no more than being extremely alert, uti-

101

lizing the senses of sight and hearing, while taking a hike through the woods. A great many hunters never truthfully see all there is around them. How many snakes have you seen while hunting? What about lizards, or snails? Deer? Hummingbirds? Mexico's mountains are laden with these. Though you may not always see the little jewels, you'll hear the buzz of their wings. Do you look up into the trees? Few hunters do. Is there a good mast crop this year, or didn't you notice? Have you noted where the bulk of the roost trees are located in your home turkey woods? In numerous areas, these will be located along a north slope. Do you know why?

You can do all of this, still remaining alert should you walk into shooting distance of unsuspecting birds. Such alertness will enhance the chances of spying a drove of turkeys. Too often a hunter ambles off into the woods, keeps his mind on what he's doing for a few hours, then becomes rather lackadaisical. From then on, he's just wandering. Won't see a turkey unless it flies into his face. Worse, he will not be able to take advantage of any nearby unexpected chances to bag a turkey.

Perhaps a major difficulty faced by inexperienced turkey hunters is in keeping up hope or maintaining a positive attitude that the hunt will be successful. With each passing hour that game is not found, morale becomes all the more difficult to keep in check. Those same gobblers that were gobbling during the spring are now silent. It is easy to give up. Thousands of fall turkey enthusiasts do give up after only one or two days of hunting. A gradual loss of hope is invariably tied to the unseen, the unknown, and the uneducated. The veteran hunter has faced these obstacles day after day and realizes that success is possible, but it is up to him to ferret it out. This is true hunting. This is hunting in its purest, rawest form.

When I am walking through the woods, popping up and down over sandhills, easing through the dark confines of an oak motte, wading a swamp, or easing through the clawing brush of a manzanita thicket on a mountain's flank, all the while searching for turkeys, I try never to lose sight of my one objective—I am hunting turkeys. Watch close, but watch at a distance, too. Listen at all times. Keep both eyes searching for recent turkey sign. Don't forget the trees, turkeys are tree-oriented birds.

Fall hunts can be miserable without the proper camping gear, tents, sleeping bags, lanterns, folding chairs. If you don't have the whole shebang, you're gonna suffer for it.

Some days a turkey may remain on a roost branch until mid-morning for seemingly no reason whatsoever. At other times the bird may be flushed into a tree by a coyote, or perhaps the hunter. I guess if you find one in a tree, your next best bet is to scare the critter out, and hope it won't alight in another one down the creek.

Perhaps a major difficulty faced by inexperienced turkey hunters is in keeping up hope or maintaining a positive attitude.

Few hunters can hunt and keep watch on the trees at the same time, it's just not human nature. I've killed a number of turkeys in trees, the great bulk of them birds that were spooked and lit on a tree. I say "on" because invariably the birds will alight smack on top regardless if it's a towering pine, spreading oak, or a spindly red cedar. The main problem with such shooting centers around identification. If you are hunting an "any turkey" area, then you haven't any worry, but if you're hunting a "gobblers only" season, telling the sex of one bird from another "way up yonder" can be difficult. Too, sometimes it's not easy to get a clear shot at a bird sitting on a tree's crown.

It is easy to discern a roosting bird from a spooked bird. The roosting birds will be down "in" the tree, usually on a larger branch. Sick birds, even badly wounded ones, particularly those near death, will sometimes remain in a tree and will allow a person to walk up to them. One afternoon Ed Norwood and I were hunting some pines in Amito county, in Mississippi. We walked right up to a hen perched on a low branch. She wasn't ten feet from dry ground. Easing gently up to the bird, we could at last see that she was blind. We were amazed. She'd only lost one eye, because when we got to a point where she saw us with her other eye, she was gone. There was no way of knowing how she had lost the eye, or how long ago. Both of us were astounded that the bird could fly so well with but one eye.

One winter day I walked up to a long-bearded gobbler sitting only fifteen feet or so from the ground. The old bird was hunkered on a big horizontal branch. I backed off, then rolled

Turkey hunts are what you make 'em. This bunch has been into the hog waylaying and turkey bushwacking business. Left to right, outfitter Jim Pepper of High Country Safaris in Arboles, Colorado; Rex Haley and Ken Tyner, guides on Dirk Ross' Rancho Rio Bonita; Dirk Ross, well-known elk guide and outfitter and maker of a very popular line of video hunting tapes; and on the far right, the author.

Many snakes are very active during the fall of the year, apparently preparing for fall hibernation. Many become extremely aggressive and are more apt to strike than at any other time of the year. This coontail western diamondback rattler is probably the most aggressive of all the many subspecies of rattlesnakes. He will give you little warning if you suddenly walk too close.

Camp Redneck near Reserve, New Mexico, where Dick Bland ponders a new snow. Snow often makes for easy hunting, as it tells the hunter where the birds are, but only after a few hours time. By evening of the first day it's just a matter of searching out tracks, deciphering what made them, then taking up the trail. Of course, if the snow quit before dawn, you may want to backtrack to learn where the birds had been roosting. The trail will take you close, but you'll have to search under the trees for fresh droppings, as most turkeys defecate just before flydown. Binoculars are a tremendous help when tracking turkeys on snow.

him from the tree. I knew the old gent had seen me so it was obvious he had bad problems. And, he did. He'd been shot earlier, so much so that both legs and the breast had turned a greenish color from severe infection. Thankfully, I'd come along; he'd suffered far too much. His beard had a maroon tint to it—I still have it.

I think some turkeys "hole up" on a tree branch when a hunter walks into view, their instincts freezing them there no differently than a gobbler making like a rock in tall grass. The birds, from poult to adulthood, are used to remaining quiet when danger presents itself, hoping the danger will pass.

When a drove of turkeys is sighted by a walking hunter, there are a number of things he should strive to learn. Of course, if the birds are within easy gunshot, the hunter should attempt to make a kill, whether the birds are running or flying. Even then, if he is with other hunters who may want to hunt the scattered turkeys, he should make an effort to ascertain where the separated birds flew, and then mark those areas in his mind's eye, so he can relay the information to his friends.

Let's assume the hunter has spied a drove of birds well beyond killing range. First, have the birds seen him? If so, he must take action instantly if he hopes to scatter them. This can sometimes be done by running toward them as fast as possible. If they do not fly, but commence running, he will need to shoot a time or two into the air. With few exceptions, this will put wild turkeys into the air. Watch where they go. Did they

all fly away in the same general direction? Did they scatter to the wind? What age were the birds? How many did you see?

Make an effort to answer all these questions while the birds fade from sight.

But let's presume you have been trodding an old logging trail, have just passed through stands of huckleberry along the road, then suddenly spot turkeys pecking beneath a few wild cherry trees scattered across a flat. They haven't seen you. They are well beyond gunshot. Freeze—but gently ease to earth, lowering your body closer to the ground. No matter what part of the country a hunter is working, turkeys at a hundred yards distance will have trouble eyeballing the hunter who has settled to a squatting position, simply due to the intervening brush, grass clumps, rocks, and the jillion other things which clutter the outdoors. Camo clothing will do the rest, helping to fade the hunter's form into the background and nearby foliage. From this lower vantage point and by moving with extreme caution when the birds are not acting wary, you can study them to determine what the best course of action should be.

If you see a bunch of birds and they have not seen you, make every attempt to drop from their view, where you can decide what to do next. An unspooked drove of turkeys is far easier to hunt than one which is hightailing it for the next county. Doubly so if the hunter is well out of range.

Turkeys that see a hunter at long distance, before or at the same time the hunter sees them, are very difficult to hunt

A good blind will shade the hunter from the eyes of any approaching turkey. The ideal blind's interior is so dark the birds can't make out any movement within, even at a distance of only a few feet.

thereafter. The birds will ordinarily head for the next county without any further notice. Super wary now that they have spotted the hunter, the drove will also not scatter. The whole bunch can stay on the alert, which means twice as many eyes to keep a vigil.

Birds the hunter sees before they have noticed him, at longer distances, are sometimes the easiest of all turkeys to hunt. This is when binoculars are extremely valuable as a visual aid. The terrain can be studied inch by inch, and seldom will there be areas where a stalk cannot be planned. Or, the birds can be kept under scrutiny with hopes that they can be hunted when moving to a different location, or travels studied in hopes of planning an intercepting route.

Two qualities a hunter needs in such situations are supreme patience and sufficient education about the everyday habits of wild turkeys to be able to decide what they will do next. Of course, of utmost importance is to cut the distance between hunter and turkeys *without them becoming suspicious*. The nearer the hunter is to the birds, the quicker he can strike should the opportunity arise. Quite often, the hunter who makes moves from time to time, in closing the distance, will suddenly realize that one more move will bring him into killing distance.

Crawling on the hands and knees, or better yet belly-crawling, is very often the only method which will bring a hunter those last few critical yards. This works well during the fall months when leaves are still clinging to bushes, and the bushes stand aloft from the summer growth of weeds. We all cuss weeds that peep up from our lawns, but if it hadn't been for weeds, a passel of wild turkeys would have escaped my gun.

I've crawled on all fours from one end of this country to the other, with part of Mexico thrown in for practice. It is the simplest method there is for stalking wild turkeys.

Invariably, the hunter who has seen turkeys at a distance can work himself to within scattering distance if not within gunshot. By making a sudden run toward them, he can create a good scatter. The birds will fan out, though all will fly off toward one general direction. That is the time to mark them down to the best measure possible and immediately go in that direction.

Why? Wild turkeys, being gregarious birds and having grown up together, are used to having each other's company. Upon being separated, even for just a few moments, they will quickly strive to find the company they have been accustomed to. So, if the birds are young, have not been hunted much, nor been separated before insofar as the hunter knows, they will begin regrouping the second they come back to earth. If the woods are open without a heavy screening canopy of leaves, and the woods floor is void of brush, the birds will probably see each other alight and get together by sight. This is also true on prairie hunts and in open meadows, or on a great many mountain hunts in the Rockies, as much of this country has a park-like topography.

When I bump into a drove of birds, I strive to learn the age and sex of the individuals. All further techniques must be built around this knowledge. Without it, the hunter has his hands tied. The hunter calling to a scattered drove of young jakes would not want to try to call one using hen yelps.

Just last fall I was guiding a couple of longtime friends, Ted Herrick and Mike Monier, both of whom have hunted with me for years. We were walking a narrow hogback ridge, well covered with oaks, when suddenly a small bunch of birds flushed from the trees just off the crest, on the ridge's flank. None of us had any inkling the birds were there so no one got in a shot. I did note that all the birds I could see appeared to be jakes, young gobblers, birds-of-the-year. Fanned out across a narrow front, the whole passel flew across a deep gulley, going to ground on a likewise steep hillside opposite us. It too was heavily treed with open spaces of heavy, short brush.

An unspooked drove of turkeys is far easier to hunt than one which is hightailing it for the next county.

Hurrying along, I took my two gunners on a longer route which got us out of the birds' view in a hurry, but which brought us back onto the ridge, just back of where I'd last seen them run after alighting. We hunkered down near the highest point on the hill, but where we could cover it with gunfire. Quietly, I fetched the slate call I was carrying, an Ashby slate, made by Ike Ashby, from Houston, Missouri. He sells a very good slate which has a sounding box far better'n most such calls. I sanded the surface and then made a few yelps, jake yelps, which are made a tad slower than hen callings. Right off I got an answer.

Two calls later, over a period of maybe five minutes, I could tell that very darned soon a turkey was going to show on top the hill, so I motioned for Mike to cover it. He did. A gobbler stuck his noggin up, and Mike give him a blast.

We ran up there and saw two young jaspers flopping around. Just one of those things which happens. We never had seen that second bird. Mike filled out both he and Ted's tags.

As the season advances, and if the birds have been hunted moderately for two to three weeks, hunting will become progressively more difficult as each day goes by. Once they've been hunted for this long by only a handful of hunters scattered throughout their territory, the birds will have attained a superior wildness, which means they will simply be tough as hell to hunt for the remainder of the season. Even if it lasts for two months. Such birds will flush at the sight of man though the range may be half a mile. They will roost with greater distances between them, and will feed less with much time devoted to standing absolutely motionless, head and eyes slowly moving to search the surroundings. They will probably be call-shy. If you think they aren't, get into a position where you can see one, then make a call. You'll know the answer if it makes for the next county like a scalded cat.

A scatter late in the afternoon could be no better than none at all, as the birds may not call so near sundown.

Late December hunts can be tough due to bad weather and a lack of foliage, to name just two adversities. When you add snow and cold, things get tough. Hunting a bunch of scattered, spooky wild turkeys makes it all but impossible. Many of the well-known "name" hunters will no longer make the scene though the birds are still in the woods. Those same good old boys who earlier had said that fall and winter hunting was easy are now hiding in the house, huddled around a fireplace, dreaming of spring. I have never bumped into one of them in turkey woods when winter's winds are howling.

Each fall when the season begins to draw near, my mind invariably drifts around to the hopes that in the weeks ahead an *old gobbler* will loom above the barrels of my side-by-side.

What are the chances that the hunter will get a shot at an old bird, perhaps at 25 yards? Such hunting can be compared to gambling, and playing cards, along with the term, "the luck of the draw." There is a little bit of luck involved, and regardless of how much work a hunter puts into an effort, if Murphy's Law is working against him, he may not be successful. The hunt for old gobblers during the fall and winter months is this way. These birds are all of the things which the word *unpredictable* is meant to be. No matter how hard the hunter hunts, he could go the entire season without firing at one of the older turkeys. Perhaps they've ranged over onto a neighboring area, and this could be miles from where the bird was during the spring months.

There are no "best" methods for hunting older gobblers from October to January. All of the techniques utilized in fall

Fall turkey hunting means hunting the droves, which boils down to facing a whole woods of turkeys on the watch for your skulking figure. Bide your time. It may be easier than you think. Patience is the key.

One hunter calls, the other shoots, probably one of the best team efforts in all of hunting. But, if you try this technique, keep in mind that the bird might come to the call. So don't call from a place the bird may approach, only to be too far away for a shot.

Knowing where to find a small gang of old gobblers during a winter hunt is the secret to bagging one. These little droves usually use the same area day after day if it has all the food and shelter they want, which includes roost trees. But, don't hunt them near where they roost or look for them thereabouts, because such turkeys never dally around the roost once they fly down. They'll be somewhere else on their range.

Steven Preston (left) and his dad, Tom, talk over a big whitetail buck Steven downed the day after the fall turkey hunt ended in Oklahoma. What a life! Turkeys one day—big bucks the next.

hunting for any turkey will work on an older male bird, be it bushwacking, stalking, calling, plain walking, or lying in ambush. The one difference is that it often requires a greater number of attempts to bring about a successful hunt. By this, I mean that whereas a hunter might walk three miles before flushing a drove of young turkeys, he could very well walk ten, or even twenty, before crossing paths with a big gobbler. There just aren't as many of these birds, so it will take more time to find and kill one.

If the hunter will take his time, but hang tough, stick with it and make up his mind that he wants to hunt until he bags an adult bird, in time this can be possible. But, this is possible only if he is a good shot, hunts with dedication to the hunt itself, can make quick decisions, and has a complete knowledge of the turkey he is pursuing. For instance, consider that numerous adult gobblers can often be found alone.

This little fact, seemingly harmless, has cost many older gobblers their lives. The bird has but two eyes, so when it is engaged in feeding, watering, or whatever, it is then susceptible to a predator. If the hunter can detect a tiny drove of these old birds from a distance, sneaking or stalking them is often possible. I've made kills from a good many droves numbering four to ten or twelve, older gobblers. Throughout the bulk of these incidents, the birds had their heads down busily feeding, which made the sneak easier. During these crawling stalks, there is no way a person can be too careful. If the woods are silent, noise is magnified, and this must be minimized to below a whisper. Of course, the main worry is being seen. This includes taking care that none of the brush suddenly moves, should the hunter bump it. He cannot move a twig. The birds will catch quick movement like it's a magnet, so a crawling hunter must pass through cover as silently and easily as a copperhead snake. Moving when the quarry is not alert, being stone-still when it is alert, and having the patience of a 'gator watching a young deer come to water, is all necessary for a successful sneak.

Calling long-bearded gobblers during the fall and winter months is truthfully a lesson in very little calling, lots of listening, and the patience to watch a leaf turn brown. There are two situations which make calling a viable hunting method—calling separated birds and calling adult gobblers that are roaming and feeding. Calling feeding adults is done only by a person very well acquainted with the patterns of resident gobblers. Even then the plans can go awry, as older gobblers are extremely unpredictable.

If the hunter can scatter a small gang of old gobblers, the chances become far greater to call one of them to the gun. Of course, the hunter must realize he is dealing with long-bearded turkeys, so identification is a must, along with knowing which way the scattered birds flew, how far it appears they have gone, and at what time of the day the scatter takes place. A scatter late in the afternoon could be no better than none at all, as the birds may not call so near sundown.

If the birds fly away on a like quadrant, the hunter should take after them on the dead run because they will regroup by

Fall hunts can and do mean mixed bags if a person takes advantage of what the area has to offer. There is nothing finer than mixing ruffed grouse or partridge with Eastern Wild Turkeys.

Now, when speaking of regrouping in relation to adult long-bearded gobblers, this can mean simply the getting together of just two birds, or perhaps more; I have never known of older birds lolling around until all the members were together before moving off. Once old gobblers are spooked, they do not hang around the neighborhood. One or two may join up, perhaps others if they are along the trail. Very often when a hunter comes up near older gobblers, and suddenly flushes them, the birds will fly away on a like quadrant, fanned out in a like direction. After the hunter has hurried to the area and worked it thoroughly, further scattering them, it is best to go beyond the area up to a quarter-mile, take a calling stand uphill from where the birds seemed to go, and do any calling from there. Sit facing back toward the scatter area.

I would not advise making the first note for at least fifteen minutes after sitting down; if the birds are in a hard-hunted area, it would be best to wait a half-hour. The calling should only be an occasional cluck with a yelp or two after the first hour. A couple of hours of calling should add up to three or four clucks, and two or three yelps. Should your clucking be answered by a cluck, or yelp, it is very advisable to instantly call back with two or three clucks. But, *do not get carried away with the calling.*

Old gobblers are shutmouth throughout all of the year, except during the spring gobbling season.

Old gobblers are shutmouth throughout all of the year, except during the spring gobbling season, so excessive calling will only arouse wariness in an answering gobbler. Once the bird has answered your calls, the gobbler knows where you are, and if he has decided to come to you, he will. If he has decided not to come to you, all of your calling, or your not calling, won't change his mind. Make yourself confortable when you begin calling because the session may last until dark, and you may never hear a cluck, or see a feather. Forget the time. Make like a stump. Keep your gun in hand.

I guarantee you this—if you have nothing but troubles in April, you just *think* you've seen "hard times" in the turkey woods. Go back out in the woods next fall, those *old* birds will still be there. No, there won't be any gobbling to tell you where. Then you'll know what it is like to hunt a wild turkey.

You've heard the phrase, "people can help their luck," or "luck is what you make it." I think these were coined about turkey hunters. Some folks have it, some don't. But, all of us can make it better. The turkey hunter can do this by being alert, always ready to take advantage of the least opportunity, practicing to improve both his hunting and shooting abilities, and by using the one sense which makes man the primary predator—the ability to think and reason.

sight quickly once they have landed. The hunter must get to where the birds appeared to be going as fast as possible, and then scour over a hundred to two hundred acres of the woods, always keeping in mind that regrouping adults seek high ground. This doesn't mean that the birds will go to the top of the nearest hill. If it appears they flew toward bottom land, the birds will regroup on lands up from the bottom unless it is a very large area.

7

Real Turkey Hunters Shoot Shotguns

Breech-loading shotguns date back into the last century and didn't have the excellent choking found on today's guns. That is evident when reading the accounts of those early hunts for wild turkeys. General William Strong and his Army cronies had all kinds of problems trying to kill birds on the roost with big 10-gauge guns.

WHEN WE OKIES were in the middle of the Dust Bowl years back in the 1930s (we called it the Dirty Thirties), there wasn't enough water in western Oklahoma to wash a big man's feet. In most places there wasn't even enough for a little guy's feet. And though all of us farm boys, by the time we were six or seven, loved to hunt, our duck shooting education had to wait until we were about ten. Then we tied into the sport with a vengeance. The "we" I speak of was me and my brother Dick. My first shotgun was a borrowed side-by-side 410 which dad got from an old boy who ran a mechanic's shop there in town. Dick wasn't much better off than me, as he got to carry a family gun, a bolt-action 410 with a three-shot magazine.

After the dust quit blowing, there was a good bit of rain, and the ducks poured into a big bunch of easily flooded flats that lay about twelve miles from the house. Since we were too young to drive, grandmother Simmons would haul us out there, dump us and our old wooden decoys, bid us goodbye (and probably good riddance), go back home, and then return at dark to retrieve us and any ducks we'd taken that day. By the end of the day we'd shot up all our shells but made up for the lightness of our load by bringing back home an equal (at least) weight of mud. For the next many years we waged our own private war on the ducks of the Drummond Flats.

If there were a legal hunting season we didn't know about it, or at least didn't care. A game warden lived in our home town, but we figured he had better things to do—like go hunting. I do recall one day, while hunting from a tiny hunk of high ground a good half-mile long, encountering a couple of hunters running past me, one of 'em telling me the game warden was coming and I'd best "git." I soon went, but by evening everybody was back to usual, blasting away. There wasn't a game man living who could outrun me or Dick, even with us loaded down by a gunny sack of decoys, shotguns and shells. Times were hard then. If you got arrested, you just had to sit it out. And jail "ain't no place for a freedom lovin' man. Ain't gonna catch me there again." Perhaps I should add, "No, I didn't go there 'cause the game warden caught me."

Anyhow, the two of us learned how to shoot a shotgun the best way I can recommend—shooting ducks. Back then a good winter flyway had all kinds of ducks—teals, widgeon, pintails, scaups, redheads, cans, ruddies, woodies, greenheads, spoonies. Once in a great spell you might even knock down a black or a bufflehead. Later on we'd see a few gold-eye, but aside from these last few, the great bulk were teals, pintails and greenies.

Hunting methods ranged from using a stool (decoys to you all), to jump-shooting pasture potholes, or shooting passing ducks beelining from one place to another. You began shooting with first light when you could see, and you quit when you couldn't, 'cause it was dark. Barrels some-

times got so hot you'd lay the gun down in the marsh to cool it off. None of us will ever forget the last shot of the day at a lone teal whizzing by at dusk and the cussing as the damned bird escaped into the night; the tongue of blue flame licking out of the gun barrel seeming only to give the bird a boost in the butt.

The tongue of blue flame licking out of the gun barrel seemed only to give the bird a boost in the butt.

Dick and I finally talked Dad into trading in our little boy shotguns for some *men's guns*. A Sears & Roebuck side-by-side 12-bore for Dick and a side-by-side Montgomery Wards 12-bore for me 'cause stores didn't ever stock but one gun at a time.

The birds at the Flats got a hard bunch of lessons after that—

W.C. Boyd checks to make sure his gun, a National Wild Turkey Federation commemorative Winchester, is on safe. The Model 1300 has a 3-inch chamber and is in 20-gauge. W.C. shoots Federal shells in it, loaded with #6 shot. It's a good looking gun and laid low a big old gobbler last spring.

Getting the gun to shoulder seems to be the most critical part of turkey shooting. A hunter can spook the bird by raising the gun with the bird running away before the shot can be made. If the hunter waits until the bird is well inside range, and then, if there isn't any cover between them, wait for the bird to look away, he can ease the gun up in a deliberate move, not slow, not fast. This invariably will freeze the bird for just a second—enough time to bring the gun to bear and make the shot.

they had no idea the toy guns were no longer around. What few survived became the smart ducks you all hunt today.

No other gunning sport offers as many different kinds of shots as does waterfowl hunting—particularly if a great many subspecies are flying and various hunting methods are used. Ducks will flare and climb over decoys, drop and bore across, or, perhaps, fly over time after time just looking 'em over like the wary pintails. Jump-shooting or pass-shooting at redheads or scaup as they highball it down the lake is unbeatable. Throw in some high prairie winds, and all the makings are there for either getting to be a purty good shot, or going home and settling for duck track soup.

But, the point is, a boy used the gun that was handed him. No arguin' back in those times. And, there wasn't a boy I knew who wasn't thrilled with what he got—those years after the Big Depression and the Dust Bowl made you realize that money truly didn't grow on trees. So, we all learned to shoot the gun we had which made it easy for us to shoot about any-

thing later in life. It's not the gun anyhow, it's the guy holding it that makes it or breaks it.

Today's Turkey Shotgun

Of course, today guns are plentiful, so a hunter can select one made especially for the task at hand. But, before any turkey hunter goes out to buy a shotgun, he should read his state hunting regulations, then buy accordingly.

Obviously, the 12-gauge is hands down the number one choice for turkey shooting in this country. A versatile 12 can handle 3$\frac{1}{2}$-inch as well as 3-inch or 2$\frac{3}{4}$-inch loads. Mossberg's new 835 Ulti-Mag is probably the most versatile 12-gauge shotgun on today's market. It comes in full camouflage RealTree finish with a short 24-inch barrel and ventilated rib, a camo'd quick detachable sling, plus a special turkey tube choked Extra Full. It can also be had in 10-gauge for the 3$\frac{1}{2}$-inch shell. There're two beads on the short barrel, which is good, because the lack of a longer sighting plane makes it

Any turkey hunter will try to shoot a walking or standing turkey in the head or neck area. All shotguns will cover part of the bird's neck with the pattern, even a Full choked gun. A large old gobbler is a pretty tough old geezer, so what's needed is a good dense pattern. By my way of thinking, a hunter who is any kind of hunter at all won't shoot a gobbler beyond thirty yards.

(Top, above and right) Chuck Hartigan and Pam Johnson use entirely different styles of guns for turkeys. Chuck's gun is a 12-gauge Model B-80 Browning with a Full choked Invector barrel with vent rib. Chuck loads Federal Premium shells, shooting two ounces of #6 shot. Pam's over-under is a rare blued-receiver Ruger Red Label, and it sports one Full choked barrel and one Modified barrel. The cartridges are standard 2³/₄-inch hulls loaded with 1¹/₄ ounces of #6 shot. Both cartridges are copper-plated buffered loads, a damned fine turkey load.

easy to be off your mark just a tad which can translate into a miss at twenty yards. The Extra Full choke tube keeps the shot pattern hemmed in at close range and with the two beads should make for a better hold and effective shot on approaching gobblers. The Ulti-Mag holds five 2³/₄-inch shells. Sho' looks like a damned fine gun. Wish I owned one. Or, better, yet, wish I had one of the Model 9200s with the Mossy Oak Camo.

The Remington people could see that turkey hunting was here to stay and so they have done it up the way only Remington would with a good selection of turkey killing firearms. Probably most hunters would choose the ever popular pump-action 12-gauge 870, but on this go-'round I'd want the new Special Purpose Deer/Turkey model with full Mossy Oak Bottomland camo finish, quick detachable sling, buttpad, sights and Super Full Turkey Rem-Choke tube. Boy, this should be a turkey killing machine. Now, unlike the Ulti-Mag, this gun chambers only the 3-inch shell. But, the barrel is even shorter, only 20 inches. The gun has rifle sights which it should have with the shorter barrel. Remington, of course, didn't quit there. They also have a 12- and 10-gauge automatic Model 11-87 and, like the Model 870, it has the full camo finish and synthetic stock, plus all the goodies the 870 has. The 10-gauge 3¹/₂-inch holds three shells. Of course, these guns sell for a little more.

If you never bumped into an old, tough gobbler, a 20 would be just fine, but who doesn't want to bump into old gobblers.

In general, gun prices have risen over the years, but there are still a few very reasonable shotguns available on the market. Maverick Arms offers a 12-gauge auto and pump, both chambered for 3-inch shells, for less than $300. Mossberg's Model 500 pump action, camo'd with 3-inch chamber goes for around $350. Magtech imports a slide-action pump, also chambered for 3-inch in 12-gauge, which brings down $250.

Winchester has yet to get its teeth in the specialized turkey market, but still offers its lightweight pump Model 1300 in 3-inch 12-gauge, with the proven Winchoke system. Ithaca makes a fine 12 pump gun, a good value for turkey hunters. Besides the 12, it has a short barrel version in 10-gauge.

You may have noticed I never mention 20-gauge shotguns. For many years I shot an over/under 20, which was and is a fine gun. With the 3-inch shell it will darned sure nail turkeys because I've used it on them. But, for the average hunter, a 20 might be just a bit too light. Turkeys can be tough, and like Robert Ruark said, "use enough gun," which couldn't be truer when hunting these birds. If you never bumped into an old, tough gobbler, a 20 would be just fine, but who doesn't want to bump into old gobblers. That's what we all bought tickets for. And, though a 20 may be okay in the hands of a hunter who's hunted lots of turkeys, I won't recommend them for general turkey use. Just like I darned sure wouldn't advise a

The small 20-gauge isn't often seen in the turkey woods. My hunts in Mexico have given me a chance to see what others might use in a country where turkey hunting is still in its infancy. I've never taken a gun as I can instantly adjust to whatever is handed me. Learning that my friend Marcelo Delgado was toting a small 20 was no surprise. His gun is a Zarrasqueta-Eibar side-by-side choked Modified and Full. The most popular cartridge in Mexico is the Mexican-made Union brand.

person to get a single shot—don't go in the woods without a backup shot.

Over/unders are excellent turkey guns as are side-by-sides if the guns have double triggers. Selective triggers are nice, but too often the hunter doesn't know which barrel he's got the selector on and so shoots with the Modified choke tube when he wanted the Full. Double triggers help ease this problem. Its easy to just move a finger from one trigger to the other. But, the catch is, few double trigger guns can be found these days. Good used guns can be found as trade-ins and in pawn shops and will be much cheaper than any over/under made today.

For many years I hunted turkeys with an old Valmet over/under, one like the Baby Bretton, imported today by Mandall Shooting Supplies. The barrels aren't, as we call it in doubles language, "married," that is, not soldered together but

Dixie Gun Works handles numerous modern breech-loading shotguns, many of them valuable side-by-side doubles, plus quality over/unders, in addition to pumps and autoloaders. Butch Winters is showing here a fine old blackpowder muzzleloader.

Knowing how to handle a shotgun is what puts meat on the table and turkeys in the oven. Nothing substitutes for experience so whether a person shoots on a Skeet or trap range or is just busting cans with friends, the simple act of shooting over and over is what makes a hunter a better shot.

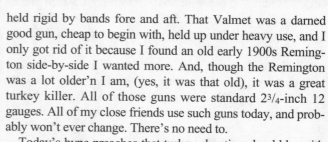

held rigid by bands fore and aft. That Valmet was a darned good gun, cheap to begin with, held up under heavy use, and I only got rid of it because I found an old early 1900s Remington side-by-side I wanted more. And, though the Remington was a lot older'n I am, (yes, it was that old), it was a great turkey killer. All of those guns were standard 2³/₄-inch 12 gauges. All of my close friends use such guns today, and probably won't ever change. There's no need to.

Today's hype preaches that turkey shooting should be with big guns, 3- or 3¹/₂-inch chambered 10 and 12 gauges. Kinda reminds me of the old market days—you weren't a man until you could handle a 6- or 8-bore. If the law would allow, I'm positive that many hunters believing the bigger is better hype, would immediately throw out the 10s and get a 6-gauge.

The truth is, the hunter should be running the show, not the other way around. Range should be the foremost consideration in all kinds of hunting. Shorter ranges result in fewer cripples, which are usually lost birds. A gobbler that has been hit hard but flies or runs from sight can almost invariably be marked as gone for good.

Few hunters take time to clean a gun, particularly shotgunners. And, this can be critical if the gun is an autoloader which is easily disabled by sand and mud. Doubles, either side-by-side or stacked, are easy to clean. If a person thinks there's dirt in the barrel, it's not a problem to open the breech, pull out the shells and look to see if the barrels have been plugged with mud or snow. If so, it can oftentimes be blown out or, at the worst, a tree branch can be cut and the object pushed out.

But, this can be reversed. If you think you got a solid hit, then you'd be wise to keep a couple things in mind. Number one, always try to get a good fix on the bird's path as it leaves the area. A flying turkey will normally hold to a fairly straight course, unless it has flown out over a valley, or from a mountain, as it will have to fly back into the mountainside in landing.

Last fall I had called up a small gang of turkeys, a mixed bunch of jakes and young hens, with maybe an old hen. My young hunter had killed a pair of birds the year previous, so he knew how to hold on the birds. When I whispered for him to shoot, he knocked over the best of the jakes only some twenty-odd yards from us, his 3-inch 12 more'n enough gun. But, the bird only flopped around three or four times, and like magic was on its feet and off to the races. I'm hollering "shoot, shoot" but my hunter's next two blasts at the running turkey had no effect, except to encourage the young gobbler that its wings would get it outta there a helluva lot faster'n its feet. I tried to keep it in sight, but it soon disappeared, flying out across the oak woods which lay all around our location.

We jumped up, heading toward where I hoped we'd find the bird. I knew the gobbler had taken a hard blow from the hunter's first shot. We searched for about fifteen minutes, then heard the calls of the scattered birds as they began to group back together. I decided to take my hunter back to the shooting location where he might have a chance to snag one of the other turkeys as they regrouped. Not much of a chance for this to happen with no one there to call. But he'd do better there than with me, and with him there I could keep searching for the turkey he'd shot but lost.

I was soon back to looking—this time trying as best I could to hold the straight line as I worked through cover away from where we'd been sitting. Back and forth I searched, but looking for a gobbler in thick oak woods, with the leaves still on the trees isn't easy. Three hundred yards from our calling setup I found our gobbler, lodged about eight feet from the ground in the limbs of a blackjack oak. Dying in full flight, the gobbler had tumbled into the tree at full force, one wing breaking upon impact. My hunter was very happy when I laid it down alongside him and amazed when I took him through the woods to show him where I'd found the bird.

Patterning and Ammo

Regardless of how much effort is put into making close shots, there'll come that day when a bird escapes, often badly crippled. Obviously, the best defense against this is to be sure of the backup shot and make it count. When I first got into muzzle-loading, I had a number of old gobblers try to leave the scene after my first shot, but I killed them all with the number two barrel. I'd not found the best load for the old guns, but after a lot of diligent work at the patterning board I came up with one that lays 'em out. Nowadays I have no birds trying to run off crippled.

My advice to anyone who has purchased a new gun or buys a box of shells they've never tried is to get out there and do some patterning. No two guns shoot alike, neither do two different lots of shotgun shells. A box of #6s manufactured by one company may pattern far better than one from another maker.

And as for the gun, you may find out it doesn't shoot the best pattern at the point of aim, may not shoot your old favorite loads well at all, or could shoot high or low. Over/unders, as well as short barreled guns, all have a tendency to shoot high. But the gun doesn't bring this about; it's due to the shooter not getting "into" the gun. Instead of the hunter looking along the barrel, he's really looking down onto it. This might not even be evident, as such a slight deviance can result in shooting off the mark.

The hunter should be running the show, not the other way around.

Patterning should also include the backup loads as their pellets are ordinarily of a slightly larger size than the initial load. I would hazard a guess the number one first load fired at turkeys today are #6s, probably followed by #5s or #4s; I certainly don't like to see a hunter using #2s for any kind of shot on turkeys. A long-range shot at a fleeing gobbler will often only add to the misery, perhaps breaking a wing on the bird. Very few turkeys that escape on foot are found, and one making tracks with a busted wing is a sickening sight.

Probably at least twenty-five years ago my buddy and I were hunting Merriams late one afternoon in a light sleet storm when we suddenly spied six or seven young gobblers

just as they ran up a draw above us. I didn't consider shooting since the birds were a good sixty yards distant. But, my buddy who was using #2s threw up his old magazine gun and blasted away at the birds just as the gang skedaddled from sight, at about eighty yards. A miracle shot hit one young gobbler which flopped around in the oaks and pines long enough for my friend to get it in hand. I've lost track of him in the years since, but the last time we hunted together he was still shooting at turkeys with #2 loads. I have no idea how many turkeys he's crippled since the hunt years ago but fifteen or so years back I ran into him just as he was coming out of the woods. He'd lost another turkey that morning. The bird had been hard hit but flew off. What was he shooting? Yep, the same old #2s.

The gun isn't any better than the person holding it.

Lady Luck took my hand and we went and found his gobbler—stretched out dead on some oak leaves, lying flat on its back. Feathers scattered about told the story. The jake had died in flight, tumbling to earth some four hundred yards from the place my buddy told me he'd fired his fatal shots—of #2. Don't even think of using such stuff for turkeys; it only encourages a hunter to make longer and longer shots.

There is plenty of darned good turkey ammunition out there but none of it works miracles. Not too long ago I was reading an article by one of this country's better known turkey experts, who made a statement that I'm sure he didn't mean, 'cause he knows better. Perhaps he was hoping by saying some nice things about a particular shotgun the manufacturer would thank him profusely and send him one of their guns. Anyhow, he said single shots were fine for turkey hunting. Then, later on, he makes the remark that turkeys are tough to nail down, so use the best shells you can get.

Every hunter leaving the house in search of a wild turkey owes it to himself, to all of mankind in general, and in particular to the turkey, to be the best shot he can be.

Now, if a gobbler is tough to keep down, then wouldn't it be logical to carry a shotgun that has more than a single load in it, *just in case of a running cripple?* Sure it would. Don't hunt turkeys with a little single shot. And, don't use these combination guns, the ones with a rifle barrel and a shotgun barrel matched together. They're just as worthless. Maybe even worse. There is still only one shot of each, and too often in the heat of getting a bird to stand still out toward the far end of the barrels, it is forgotten which barrel the selector is set to fire.

While there are a great many loads on the market for turkey, none are miracle killers. Shotgun pellets quickly lose penetrating power the farther they travel away from the barrel. And, the smaller the shot size, the faster it loses that power. It's the number of hits that kill, and at distances of even thirty yards, it's the number of hits *to the bird's head and neck* that do the killing.

Spending time on a trap range, as these men are doing, is what all turkey hunters should do. After all, don't we owe it to the game we hunt to become "the best we can be."

Though just a teenager, Zac Stover from Enid, Oklahoma, has, in just a very few years, become a crack shotgunner. Trophies he's won at state and national contests attest to just how good he is. When he raises his shotgun on a wild gobbler, that bird is indeed in trouble.

Someday perhaps all states will have laws which prohibit using any shot larger than #4s for turkey hunting—and none smaller than #6s. Nobody should go after turkeys with anything but #4s, #5s and #6s. Perhaps, then, this ridiculous long-range blasting will end. No shot size will consistently kill a bird as large and as tough as a wild turkey at forty to fifty yards.

Federal, Remington, Winchester, all of these companies make excellent loads for turkeys. The best loads I found are buffered copper-plated, extra hard shot, often in shot cups. By using the maximum load the gun will handle and keeping the range short, you'll become a good turkey hunter. Most importantly, *think for yourself.*

Having been around for so long and a hunter for over sixty years, it's been my privilege to know many of this country's best hunters. None of them use a $3^1/_2$-inch bored gun for turkey hunting and only one uses a 3-inch, it being in 12-gauge. Almost to the person, they carry a $2^3/_4$-inch 12-gauge. All of them learned years ago that a standard old 12 would kill any turkey in the woods; it was just a matter of getting the bird into range.

So, if you own one of the many fine new guns on today's market, or have an old favorite, fine. Just try to become a better hunter. Get the bird in close and you'll never have to agonize over one running off with a busted wing. Get a gun that gives you a backup shot. Someday, if you hunt long enough, regardless of how much you concentrate on making only short-range shots, there will come a time when you'll need that quick second shot. And, use the best shells you can buy.

But always keep in mind this one thing.

The gun isn't any better than the person holding it.

It can't think.

But, you can. Only you can decide whether to make the shot or wait for a better one.

So, if you bump into an old gobbler that is tough and woods smart, that won't come into where you know Ole Sue Betsy will lay him out, bide your time. Study the layout. I know you can do it. And certainly that gun you're toting will do the job. But, it's up to you to tell it when.

117

8

Hunting Turkeys the Hard Way— With a Rifle

THERE ISN'T ANY part of turkey hunting which can stir up folks more than mentioning hunting the birds with a rifle. The subject just fires up most older turkey hunters—they've never done it, don't want you to do it, and don't want anyone else to even think about doing it.

For years I never gave it a thought. Oh, I did when somebody said he thought he'd get himself a rifle because he couldn't get close enough to the birds to hit them with the old scattergun. So by gosh, he'd show those turkeys. A good scoped rifle would put an end to this business of standing out there beyond shotgun killing distance.

It's been my good fortune to have hunted turkeys many times with about anything that's legal—pump, double, automatic, over/under, single shot, some borrowed, some new, none camouflaged though. I once borrowed a sawed-off riot shotgun. I had loaned a well-known hunting magazine writer my shotgun as his got lost on the airlines, and borrowed the half pint from an Apache lawman friend of mine. Later, after the airline had located my writer friend's gun, he wrote up our hunt in an article and stated that he was awfully happy to get his own gun back in his hands since the one loaned to him wasn't much of a turkey gun. Of course, he's probably yet to kill as many turkeys with all his guns as my old gun had at that time, and that's been twenty years ago. Just proves that some folks don't know how to use a gun—nor can they adapt. This world's full of guns that will kill turkeys. It's still the shooter's task to know how, and when to use it.

I've also killed turkeys with a bow—and also with rifles, both modern cartridge shooters and muzzleloaders. I haven't used a crossbow, mainly because I don't own one, and too many places won't allow them. I have caught birds with my bare hands, but those aren't listed as being legal either, so turned them loose.

To my way of thinking, the rifle is the most difficult tool to use for slaying wild turkeys. Now, I'm talking about slaying turkeys, not just shooting them. You can shoot a turkey with many things, but some are better for *killing* the birds than others. Rifles too often aren't the best for the *killing* part.

Throughout all my years of chasing turkeys, I've come across a good many cripples in the last stages of dying, all but one was too weak to escape. Four of these were old gobblers, all spring birds, and all hit fatally by rifle fire. But, not bad enough to yield the hunter a prize turkey. The last one I ran across, over near the back fence of the Seminole Management Area in Florida, was a bird I spied hunkered down under a palmetto. I shot him to put him out of his misery. No good to eat, the bird had been badly hit, one leg nearly shot away. Undoubtedly he had flown from where he had been shot, coming to rest very near where I found him. I had no way of knowing how long he had suffered, but his emaciated condition told me the bird was very near death. I can tell you more stories, all with the same sad ending.

After several such incidents, I decided to learn more about this rifle thing. I wanted to know *why* rifles wounded more often than killed. Amazingly, you only have to hunt turkeys with a rifle once to learn the answer. It hits you square between the eyes the first time you look at a wild turkey across the sights or through the scope. The rifle is a long-range

If the hunter is a responsible person, rifle shots at wild turkeys will be at fairly short ranges—inside 100 yards, or even better, inside 60 yards. The bird's vital parts are small compared to its actual size as it walks through cover. So a thorough knowledge of the bird's anatomy, as well as careful bullet placement, are necessary for successful hunting.

Extreme rifle accuracy calls for the use of scopes. The lethal area for instant kills on wild turkeys is small, and if not hit there, the bird can easily escape. The author has killed a number of turkeys which, after examination, had obviously been hit earlier by rifle fire. Though in mortal condition, the bird had lived several days before being bagged by the author. It is very easy to cripple and lose a turkey when using a rifle.

weapon and the second you begin taking long shots at gobblers, the more quickly the problems add up.

First of all, wild turkeys do not often remain still for any length of time, and the birds have a very small vital area. Add to this weeds, brush, or trees, which easily deflect a rifle bullet and you begin to see why rifles and long shots often maim. The only time a rifleman has a good chance of killing a turkey is when the shot is made while the bird is in the open.

Of course, there are doubters among you, so do me a favor. Go into the woods with a rifle, during deer season if you must, when it's legal, and put your sights on any wild turkey you see. Take a fine bead, just like you'd do if you wanted one of them so bad you could see it browning in the oven. You'll immediately notice two things: one, the birds don't care about standing stone still; and two, the sights cover up too much turkey. Oh, you're using a scope? Scopes magnify the movements of the birds and just about the time you get settled into squeezing the trigger, the bird will walk off, turn, or peck at a busted acorn.

For a rifleman, the vital areas of wild turkeys are well known—the backbone or spinal area and the wing butts, which cover the heart-lung area. Shotgunners can take head shots but the head is too small for a rifle, except when the bird is very close, which again, isn't a rifle shot. No use toting a rifle if all the shots you make are inside easy shotgun range.

The maximum distance anyone should attempt to kill a gobbler with an ironsighted rifle would be about fifty yards. Even then, too much of the turkey is hidden behind the sights. In dense woods, this shot would be impossible. Fifty yards is the

Of course, the more a person shoots a gun, any gun, the better he'll get with it, and this becomes critical when in the woods hunting wild turkeys. When shooting a rifle, accuracy is absolutely necessary because there is no fringe of pellets to down game on the outer edge of a pattern.

Muzzleloaders are excellent for hunting wild turkeys because the gun can be easily downloaded, so the projectile hasn't got the souped-up wallop that a centerfire cartridge would have. A hit with a hot cartridge projectile can destroy far too much meat. A round ball, with its much lower velocity, will destroy very little meat. As with all rifles, pinpoint accuracy is an absolute must.

limit if the bird is in the open, unmoving and the shooter knows the gun, and knows the vital areas of a turkey. A scope cannot be relied on beyond a hundred yards and then only by an expert rifleman who has sighted in at that distance.

Turkeys are hunted with rifles in many areas. Much of the West allows rifles. My home state has a crazy rule on this. Turkeys can be hunted during the fall with rifles, but not during the spring season. Nobody has ever explained this to my satisfaction, but I certainly would not want to attempt to kill a mature gobbler in full strut with a rifle. I've seen many gobblers at long distances on the prairies with my naked eye, often in full strut. I could have taken a pop at one if I'd had a rifle. But, while a shotgun can easily kill an old bird in full blossom with a head shot, shooting at this ball of feathers with a rifle is another matter altogether.

There are areas where gobblers are easily killed with rifles from blinds. Texas is famous for this practice. Many times the rifle is a 22 rimfire. In the hands of a person who has shot such a gun many, many times, the little 22 is certainly a turkey slayer. Sally Jackman, my cousin, who lives in Kansas with her husband David, a veteran turkey hunter, is a dead shot with a 22. She practices year 'round on sunning turtles so turkeys are in deep trouble when they wander in front of Sally. The last gobbler I saw her shoot simply never knew what hit him. A fine longbeard, the bird had a neat small hole just beneath the eye, and back about an inch.

Her rifle is scoped, but all of her shots are inside easy shotgun range. Since Sally is very small, no bigger'n a bar of soap,

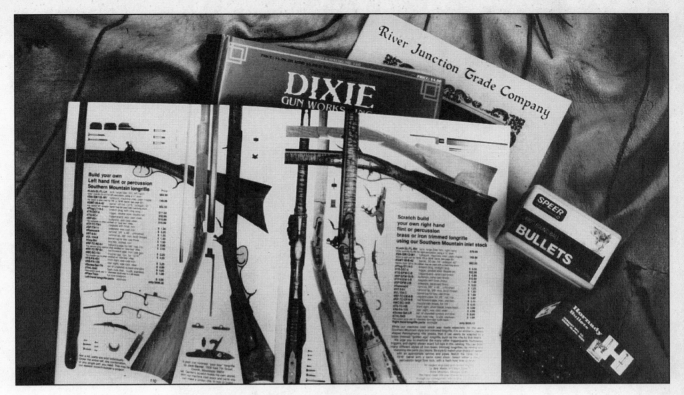

Today's blackpowder hunter can buy all the parts and plans to build his own rifle. But for a nice longrifle, the project could set back a person upwards of $400-$500.

she doesn't like the recoil of a shotgun and has gone to the little 22. Anyone who's hunted much in the Lone Star state has seen hunting blinds scattered all across the ranches in west Texas. Some are elaborate affairs, others just a framework with tarpaper stretched over it. Of course, the advantage of blinds is that body movements are hidden, and invariably, a shot can be made across a rest. No offhand stuff. Rancho Rio Bonita, near Junction, Texas, where I do some guest guiding, has many such blinds. Dirk Ross, who leases the ranch for hunting, is constantly working to make these better. I haven't been able to talk him into installing air conditioning as yet.

While a shotgun can easily kill an old bird in full blossom with a head shot, shooting at this ball of feathers with a rifle is another matter.

But, wherever you hunt, or intend to hunt, read the regulations before lugging out your rifle. Colorado has the same law as Oklahoma—no rifles during spring hunts, but fall hunts, yes. Florida allows about anything, except on management areas. That old gobbler I found near the west fence had probably been shot on private property, since the season had been open for a couple of weeks. The bird had fled onto management land where no rifles are allowed. Read the rules.

All but one of my few rifle kills have been with muzzle-loading rifles, a 45-caliber long Kentucky-style and a scoped

50-caliber. When I decided to see what turkey shooting was like with a rifle, I began with the long Kentucky rifle. The gun handles like a dream, has a long sighting plane, and the 45 round ball doesn't destroy lots of meat. To learn the best load for turkeys I began shooting the gun at turkey profile targets. Fifty-yard shots were iffy due to my eyesight not being what it was years ago and to the front blade of the sight covering up too much turkey to pinpoint the bird's small vital area.

I settled on a 50-grain load that still held on the same sight picture I'd been using for deer, but at longer distances bullet drop became more significant. Since my shooting was limited to under fifty yards that didn't matter. I was loading 45-caliber Buffalo Bullets. Recently I was reading an article by one of the country's foremost blackpowder experts. He mentioned "shooting through the breast meat." Well, he can shoot his gobblers through the breast, but I'm darned sure not going to, and I hope nobody else takes his advice. Very few turkeys will be killed if shot through the breast, unless a hunter is shooting front to back in hopes of breaking its spine. Far the best shot is side-on. You won't tear up any meat if you hit the bird properly through the wing butts or into the backbone. Two old birds I sniped with the 45 last spring were bagged with Buffalo Bullets. I lost no meat because both were side-on shots. If you're shooting side-on, shoot high when you aim at the wing butts. That way if you miss, you may shoot completely over the bird, or crease the skin on its back, a wound which will quickly heal. I missed a fine old bird two years ago due to shooting too high, but I'd much prefer to miss than to cripple it with a hit into the gut area. A gut hit

The accuracy needed for killing wild turkeys with a rifle is best done from a rest. Hunting from a blind also prevents the birds from becoming spooked by your presence.

bird may be upended, but it'll be gone before the hunter can get his hands on the bird's neck. Rifles in this sense are much like bows—it's a one-shot hunt, so it must be made *right* the first time. Trying to nail down fleeing cripples is about as hard to do with a rifle as it is with a bow.

Only shooting practice with a rifle at turkey profiles or

Trying to nail down fleeing cripples is about as hard to do with a rifle as it is with a bow

bowhunting targets will make a person realize how small the vital area really is and, as the range lengthens, how small this area becomes through the guns sights.

Many states do not allow scopes on muzzleloaders, so you best check your rules before getting into this. Scopes are allowed on all modern rifles wherever rifles are legal for turkeys and undoubtedly rifles used for turkey hunting are for the most part modern guns. Many modern rifles will fill the

bill for hunting wild turkeys. Using them the overall range can be extended to 125 yards due to their flat trajectory. But even then, 125 yards should be the maximum distance and then only by a person who has considerable experience with the gun, knows the loads, and has the confidence plus the patience to make killing shots at long range.

Years ago I hunted on several thousand acres with four hunters who toted centerfire rifles. I knew none of them personally but was always endeavoring to set them close to birds, mainly because the hot cartridges they were using could carry a long way in that flat country. All of them were extremely patient in making a shot. They just didn't blaze away. Each carried a small cushion on the shoulder strap, and when a gobbler was sighted, or a flock of turkeys, the rifleman would flop down on the belly, get into the sling, rest the gun in a prone position, then bide his time in making the shot. Rarely, very rarely, did any of these guys ever kill a bird. In fact, they very seldom made a shot. Seemed that the birds would never hold still. All these guys had beautiful rifles fitted with fine scopes. I was easily taking birds with my old muzzle-loading shotgun

The average turkey hunter has never given a thought to using a rifle, and probably for two or three reasons—the state in which he hunts doesn't allow them; he's heard rifles aren't the thing to use; and he's not a good enough shot to hit a bird with one anyhow.

while they roamed the hills, probably cursing me and my gun.

Two of these fellas were shooting 222 Remingtons; one was shooting a 22-250; and I never did learn what the other one guy was toting. All were loading their own cartridges since they believed factory loads were too hot and tore up a bird too much. A rancher friend of mine has killed a great many turkeys with a 222, and like those men I just mentioned, he also handloads. He also told me how he had upended a huge gobbler but on getting to the area he couldn't find anything but feathers. He never knew whether he'd hit the bird good (bad to me), or just made the feathers fly.

All of the riflemen I've discussed turkey hunting with have agreed that it's not easy to get a good standing shot at a turkey unless the bird is in a tree. Of course, this gets into roost shooting, and such shooting with a high-powered rifle means the projectile will land heck knows where if it misses the bird. Other problems are getting permission, as many farmers and ranchers don't want rifles used on their lands.

Many turkeys are taken each fall by deer hunters, using their old standby deer rifle. Ordinarily such cartridges will destroy a lot of meat. Although such guns and cartridges aren't ideal for turkeys, I'm sure as long as states have coinciding seasons there will be lots of turkeys shot at. I certainly don't recommend hunting turkeys from tree stands either, but a scoped rifle from a tree is vastly superior in range to a shotgun from a tree stand. If the hunter is completely camouflaged, the birds aren't so apt to eyeball him. If the hunter is wearing hunter orange, the birds will see him every time—at least in many areas where I hunt. Don't kid yourself—turkeys see as much of what's above them as they do at eye level.

It's downright funny now, but back when I first got into turkey hunting I learned that down in the Deep South some of the so-called best turkey hunters used rifles. It didn't take long for me to decipher this one. These old boys weren't the best *hunters*, they were the best rifle shots. If they'd been good *hunters*, they'd have learned that any good scattergunner will kill a whole passel of turkeys to each one laid out with a rifle. No contest.

But, to each his own. Edward McIlhenny, in his old book, *The Wild Turkey, And It's Hunting*, published and sold in 1914

Neal Wildman (left) and Dick Bland (far right) look on while Don Wildman stuffs a cartridge into the chamber of his Model 70 Winchester. The rifle, when loaded with solids, is one of two rifles he favors for hunting turkeys; the other is a Remington Model 700.

for $2.50, held the opinion that nothing surpassed the rifle for killing wild turkeys. On the other hand, Simon Everitt, also known as "The Kurnel," in his *Tales Of Wild Turkey Hunting*, published in the year 1928, remarked that he gave up using rifles "because of the many birds I lost after making a clean hit."

The old-timers mentioned the 219 Bee, the 220, the old Winchester 32-20 using a full-jacketed bullet, and the old 22 Hornet pushing a 45-grain full jacket. All of them stressed the same thing: a good rest to shoot from; a long hold; a firm crisp but moderate trigger pull; and a keen scope. Then, with patience born of expert riflemen, a choice is made. Folks who lack any of the above should not hunt turkeys with a rifle. It's a whole bunch easier with a shotgun.

Twenty-five or twenty-six years ago I happened to hunt with a fella from Alabama. I met him while searching around down there for a place to hunt. He was carrying a well-used little 22 Hornet shooter and he was also carrying a small box call on a string around his neck. I do mean small. It wasn't more'n an inch wide anywhere and maybe four inches long. He stroked it on a chalked area on the gun's stock, just on top of the wrist where the stock is narrow. Wasn't any way even a keen-hearing old gobbler could've heard that box more'n a couple hundred yards, *if that far*.

We'd part ways in the morning at the gate, him going one way, me the other. We kinda hunted that way for three days. I killed two birds but, you know, he never did show up at the gate with a turkey, nor did I ever hear his gun. He told me one

Don has killed many gobblers with his 22-250 and 222 Savage rifles—the longest range being 300 yards—and he can't recall losing a bird. There are few cattlemen who take as good care of their animals as Don Wildman, and certainly none takes better care. Nor is as good a rifle shot.

evening that he'd had a long shot at a gobbler up on a branch of a big pine but "supposed maybe I missed 'em."

Still wish I'd tried to buy that little gunstock box off that fella. Had no use for his gun.

All the turkey killing I intend on doing with a rifle (which won't be much) will probably be with my old long gun loaded with maybe a Buffalo Bullet, or perhaps a patched ball. And you can bet money, marbles, and chalk, the shot will have to be pretty close for this old coot to even try it. Turkey hunting ain't turkey hunting if the bird's a city block from the end of the barrel. That's sky-busting—laid out flat. A good turkey hunter shoots 'em close. Even with rifles.

9

Bows and Arrows for Short-Range Turkeys

STEVEN PRESTON, my grandson, and I were camped high in a mountain pasture which was surrounded by Gambel's oak thickets and a scattering of ponderosa pines which got thicker the further up a man climbed. The gulches that cut the pasture in places were dry but during the thaw these would carry off the snow melt. The area was rugged with lots of ups and downs to it and no end of rocks and timber too thick to hunt. Nevertheless, it had some mulies, which is what we were after and a pretty good crop of Merriam turkeys. Colorado's muzzleloader deer season was on, as was bow season, and also wild turkey. I'd drawn a permit for the old sootblower; Steven had bought a bow license; and both of us had turkey licenses.

I'd hunted the area for years, always for turkeys, but it was my grandson's first hunt there. So after we'd pitched our tent the afternoon we arrived, I told Steven we'd go the next morning over south of camp and look that country over. It was too early to get serious about turkeys, so I lugged my 50 carbine along, a Deerstalker made by the Lyman folks. It's a gun I can count on, easy to carry through thickets and has great knockdown power. Steven was toting his bow, a compound in the 80-pound range.

We'd no sooner left camp when we ran into the first bunch of turkeys, a hen and her brood. Obviously, the little band was heading downhill towards the cattle watering tanks as the country that year was very dry. Had been all summer I was told.

We'd heard the birds calling to each other while we were still amid the trees. I motioned Steven to hunker down near a big pine and I did the same. I then began making a series of whistles much like young turkeys make in the early fall. Through the dense forest we soon could make out birds flying down to our left front, then the old hen clucked and here they

Bowhunter's greatest hunting achievement is to bag a wild turkey gobbler. Steven Preston hefts a fine Merriam gobbler he bagged during a fall hunt while scouting for mule deer. One shot at thirty yards cut the bird's heart into two pieces.

came. All the tanks were behind us and from all the tracks in the mud it was clear the deer and turkeys and bears had put these watering holes to good use.

My whistling brought the birds close, but we weren't really interested in shooting one. They stood around perting and putting for a spell, then headed off downhill.

We crossed a big canyon, and by the time we broke out onto a long mesa, we'd seen three or four other bunches of

---

From all the tracks in the mud it was clear the deer and turkeys and bears had put these watering holes to good use.

---

turkeys. Seemed we couldn't get away from the beasts. Deer sign south of camp was nowhere as plentiful as that seen north of camp the evening before.

Glassing further along the mesa, we spotted another small gang of turkeys, but *whoa*, these babies had beards. Right about then we forgot the deer business. Old long beards were another matter—now it was about time to get *real* serious about this turkey chasing.

A stalk didn't look too difficult, and so twenty minutes later, we'd closed the range to about sixty yards. Too far for me with open iron sights, and way the hell too far for Steven's bow. But now we'd run out of cover and we weren't carrying a turkey call. But then, calling wouldn't have brought the birds to us anyhow. Too often calling to a bunch of old gobblers will have the opposite effect the caller had in mind, that is, they take off running *the other way*. If you can get the birds scattered and separated, then a turkey can be called to the hunter. But if old long-whiskered gobblers are meandering around in a bunch, forget the call. You have to stalk them, or get in a line with their direction of travel and bushwack 'em.

Steven and I weren't going to do either with this bunch as they were holed up around a small stand of huge pines, smack out on a bare knoll. No way to get nearer, and as it was now mid-morning, it appeared they may spend a few hours lollygagging where they were.

Reaching out in front of me, I grabbed an oak bush, and just simply shook the hell out of it. I figured, nothing ventured, nothing gained. Nothing was gained, so I shook it again. There wasn't a breath of wind, the sun was shining, the whole country was quiet as a cemetary. With the second shake, every one of those gobblers stood straight up. I knew one thing. That bush was getting a real looking over.

One of them stepped out into the sunshine—walking a few steps our way. I shook it again, then again, trying to shake the green leaves off the branches. I could hear a bird "putting." Pretty soon that lone gobbler began ambling toward us, stopping at last in a small clump of oaks about forty yards distant. Until that moment, I hadn't noticed a clump there. Now what? I shook the bush some more but the bird stood his ground, then turned and walked back to where his buddies were standing in the shade of the big pines. Well, so much for that.

I grabbed the little bush one more time and gave it a real

shaking; I mean *big time*. Aha-ha. I could see what appeared to be the same gobbler ambling over our way, followed by a second bird. Both were headed for the same tiny clump, walking into it and standing there in the shade watching my bush. By now, you probably have doubts about my sanity. I've done lots of these kinds of things around wild birds and animals, just to see what will happen. The results are entertaining, in fact, at times getting downright funny. Try whatever comes to mind, but just don't show your whole body or silhouette as the turkey will recognize the human shape.

I couldn't see Steven, but knew he was right behind me. I had no idea whether he was stretched out belly to the ground like me, or hunkered on his knees. The clump of trees we were in was thick, but I knew he could get clear to draw if he got the itch to try a shot. Steven had never shot a Merriam, in fact, this morning was his first dealings with them.

Dick Bland admires all the necessary equipment for nailing wild turkeys with a compound bow—arrow rest, sight, bow quiver and finely headed arrows.

A couple of shakes later the second bird ambled out from the hiding place, working across the open ground straight toward us. I could hear Steven rustling leaves but presumed he was trying to make himself less visible. At about thirty yards the gobbler stopped, standing head high, eyeballs searching out the little oak bush.

I never saw the arrow hit the bird. All I knew was that a second later the gobbler was lying on its side, kinda flopping, but not doing a very good job of that. When my brain finally told my legs that Steven had shot, I jumped up and took off like a turpentined cat. But Steven beat me to the bird.

Later, we stepped it off—exactly thirty yards. Steven said he'd sighted on the thirty-yard pin. He holed the gobbler right through the boiler works. When we cleaned the bird, its heart had been severed into two pieces. Steven's first Merriam had a seven-inch beard, gorgeous rounded tail, lots of white in the

Turkey feathers provide excellent fletching for arrow shafts. A section peeled from the feather with a flexible portion of the feather shaft intact can be easily cut to length and, with a few straight pins or a fletching jig, be glued to the arrow shaft. The author, his brother and their bowhunting friends some 55 years ago used this method; the author's brother still uses it.

The many excellent bowhunting magazines on today's stands have articles on every phase of bowhunting and offer a full array of bowhunting manufacturers advertising their equipment.

Killing a wild turkey requires pinpoint accuracy. And pinpoint accuracy can only be achieved with lots of practice. A bowhunter going afield for turkeys without studying the lethal areas on the bird will lose more than he'll bring to the table.

wing primaries and on the lower rump feathers. Though we didn't have a scale, his trophy probably weighed around fifteen or sixteen pounds. His first shot at a Merriam, and with a bow. He's killed a number of Rio Grandes, all at closer ranges. He remarked at the campfire that night that he was darned glad the bird had come to within thirty yards of us, since thirty yards was the outside distance at which he'd take a shot. Fortunately he'd been practice shooting at both twenty and thirty yards all week before we had headed west.

I'm not a bowhunter—though I have killed two turkeys with a bow. While writing the first *Turkey Hunter's Digest* I got interested in the use of bows for turkeys and decided, perhaps I should try the sport. Now, back during the '30s, a few of us farm boys got to fooling with bows and arrows, making it all on our own. We had no idea what we were doing, so we came up with some very unorthodox "equipment" if you could call it that. The arrows didn't "match" the bows, nor did they match each other. But, we killed scads of cottontails, jackrabbits, I even killed a duck once (purely an accident). We even killed a good many squirrels, but also left a majority of our good homemade broadheads stuck up in tree branches. It wasn't until somebody opened an archery shop in Oklahoma City that we found out up-to-date bowhunters used "blunts" for critters like bushytails. Even the term "bowhunter" was brand

new back in the '30s. Using bows for deer hunting was just getting a start, and all the talk was about those bowmen in Michigan, Wisconsin, and Pennsylvania, killing whitetails with longbows and its new rival, the recurve.

In our old milkbarn, using an ancient drawknife and doing the finish work with broken hunks of beer bottles, I made the best bow I knew how from an old bois d'arc fence post. If you've never driven staples into such stuff, you have no idea just how hard this wood is. Bois d'arc is the same tree many folks today know as osage orange, or hedgeapple. There's lots of it growing in the old Dust Bowl country throughout Kansas, parts of Nebraska and Colorado, and the northern and western halves of Oklahoma. This tree was planted in the "shelterbelts" which were blockades to slow the wind, and stop soil erosion. I hunted many, many days with my bois d'arc bow, and the arrows I made there in the barn.

All of us boys learned to solder, burn nocks, and make bow strings from the saddle linen we bought at the harness shop. (We also bought hunks of beeswax there as all saddlemakers used it on the linen when sewing.) And each of us had favorite patterns for making the blades of the broadheads.

I never picked up the old bow once I came home from the Big War, perhaps because it seemed kinda puny after using a pair of pounding 50-caliber machine guns. But, here I was,

Numerous types of broadheads will scrag a turkey. Shown here is a broadhead with a star added behind the main point. The star helps keep the arrow shaft in the turkey and was once a desired add-on for many bowhunters.

Mark Mueller, a Missouri bowman, skewered this fine gobbler with a Browning compound bow. Mark is the developer and manufacturer of the Invisiblind, a quickly assembled bowhunter blind.

late in life, digging out the old bow, making a few arrows and after building a dirt "butt" in the backyard, practicing. Boy, was I bad. For the first couple months I was lucky to hit the pile of dirt on which I fastened my targets. But, in time, I could hit a 3x3-inch cardboard from distances of *five to ten yards*.

Why so close? I've hunted turkeys too long to think just any kind of hit was going to bring down one of these big tough

Why so close? I've hunted turkeys too long to think just any kind of hit was going to bring down one of these big tough birds.

birds. I also knew I could wait until I got a close shot. Practicing at longer distances left me feeling that though I *might* kill a bird, I might also just cripple one, leaving it to run off and die a lingering death.

That fall I scouted out a small drove of turkeys that were watering at a windmill high in a pasture dotted with clumps of mixed oaks and dense cedars. The birds passed by one of the dense clumps of trees along the route—an excellent place for

an ambush. With a saw I cut out the heart of the clump, leaving plenty of elbow room to draw the short bow. On my first morning in the hide, about an hour past sunup, I could hear turkeys talking, which told me the bunch was soon to pass by. And, right on schedule, a bird walked past, a hen, then another and another, Range, about four to five yards. Then came a fine jake. Just as quickly, I drew and released, using the old Indian draw where the arrow is let loose just as the peak of the draw is reached. Arrows from the old bows don't have the velocity of those thrown by a compound, so arrow flight is easy to follow. The shaft went into the jake just back of the bird's wing butts and nearly to the feather fletching. The bird took the hit and ran from sight. Try as I might, I could see only the bird's general direction of flight, but did notice that all of the other turkeys in the bunch were following it. Anyone who's been raised on a farm where chickens were kept, or sometimes turkeys, has seen the birds chase each other when any blood was present. For example, if we'd just cleaned some cottontails and the birds found the entrails, there would soon be chickens running all over the backyard. Those without a hunk of gut would be chasing the ones with some. The bloodier the entrails, the harder the chase. So, I wasn't surprised when these wild turkeys chased the one with blood on it. Quite natural.

Slipping from my hiding place, I ran up to the top of the ridge and saw several birds standing near a big cedar. Yes sir, I'll bet my jake is holed up right there, I thought. Slowly I walked toward the tree, then began circling it, peering into the crannies made back under its long overhanging boughs. Very quickly I spotted the bird, hunkered down on its breast. I couldn't see its head, but I could see the arrow. Stringing another arrow, I put this one in the bird. Nothing happened. The bird was dead.

Fetching it from under the limbs, I could see the iron blade protruding from the bird's off side. I'd patterned my blades after the old vintage "trade points" used by settlers to barter with the Indians back in the 1800s. Handmade from flat iron sheeting, such as 55-gallon drum lids or wagon wheel rims, the point is hand-tied onto the shaft at a slot cut back from the front of the arrow.

The fletching is made from the primary wing feathers of a turkey. A strip of feathering can be peeled back from the outer end of the long primary and hand-tied onto the arrow shaft with sinew.

Continued practice throughout the following year made me anxious to try for a second bird the next fall. This time, I tried another type arrow. I'd arranged for a Comanche friend to make me a few arrows from the old tried-and-true dogwood switches that are found along so many prairie creeks. The switches are peeled of bark, left to dry for several months, then heated gently over a campfire and straightened. My new shafts were fletched with feathers from my first bird and then I had my Indian friend make me flint heads for the killing part of the arrows. He can make a good flint arrowhead in about fifteen minutes, sometimes less.

My second hunt lasted no longer than the first. When an old hen passed by my hide, I decided to try for her. I didn't have to chase *this* turkey. Running perhaps twenty yards, it fell dead. Like the iron point, the flint had passed through the bird's body.

I hung up the old bow. Haven't drawn it since. I figured it would only be a matter of time until I crippled and lost a bird. So today I let my grandson, his dad, my brother, and other

I hung up the old bow....I figured it would only be a matter of time until I crippled and lost a bird.

friends "do in" the turkeys with their bows, I just have a good time being around them.

Today's bow, and the arrows it shoots, are very lethal weapons. Whereas an arrow shot from my old bois d'arc seems to just kinda lope along, I often can't see the arrows fired from some of these bows today. Just a flash of color, and there it sticks, usually very near the mark and upwards of forty yards distant.

One fall afternoon, Mark Mueller, from up in Missouri, and I were hunting on my lease in western Oklahoma. Mark wanted to demonstrate his Invisiblind, so we'd set it up near a place I'd been seeing lots of birds pass. A feed strip lay on the other side of a farm road not far from there, and the birds walked the road to get there. Mark hadn't been settled in his blind more than an hour when a small drove came into view, hotfooting it down the road smack at us. I was hidden some ten yards away. Hidden in the dark area behind the netting, Mark easily made

These two bowhunters have had a successful fall morning. Andy Wiley and Steven Preston hold up their birds for the author's camera.

his draw, held, and released, without any chance of spooking the birds. I didn't see the arrow come from the blind because Mark simply shoots right through the lightweight camo netting. The jake fell over dead, right there. Didn't flop, wiggle, nothing. Range, about ten yards.

Inspecting the Invisiblind afterwards, I could see the small triangle-shaped hole in the netting where the broadhead had passed through. Both the Invisiblind and the bow worked perfectly. Mark has killed a good many whitetails and turkeys from his blinds which he markets from his place of business at Catawissa, Missouri.

Hunting from a blind undoubtedly offers a bowhunter the best shots at turkeys because the range can be short and the movement of the draw can be made without having to worry about being seen. Once turkeys detect predatory movements at distances inside ten yards you can bet they will begin taking evasive action. Of course, decoys are an excellent aid, helping to divert the bird's attention away from the hunter.

When putting together permanent blinds that allow full movement for drawing a long-bow, it's a must to have a bow present so the blind can be built around the measurements required for its use in hunting. Hunters who have hunted once from a good blind will always want to do so again. More so, if the blind is sight-proof so a hunter can move around without danger of being seen. Comfort is a must, and folding lawnchairs with armrests are far nicer than the standard hard wooden bench seat found in many old duck and goose blinds. They can be folded up when not in use and tucked away in one end of the blind. This allows for more room for bowhunting also. I've constructed one-man, two-man, three-man and four-man blinds various places, all extremely comfortable even when

Dick Bland with custom-made longbow. Custom bows are becoming increasingly popular with bowhunters across the U.S. Dick is fully camouflaged, including gloves, face mask and short-billed cap.

Troy Hardesty studies the fletching on the wood shaft arrow he's made. Like the Indians, Troy reinforced the shaft at the nock to prevent it from splitting from the recoil of a strong bow.

rain or snow sets in. I have clients who have traveled hundreds of miles to hunt. They don't book a guide to sit in camp; they want to hunt. With the blinds, they can. And kill game. However, it's imperative that blinds are built where there are turkeys. If you aren't sure where the turkeys are, don't waste time, money and materials until you do.

Portable blinds, like the Invisiblind I mentioned are becoming quite popular. They are lightweight and can be put together and taken down in a short time. Some I've looked at didn't seem to be big enough for bowhunting. If I were intending to bowhunt from a portable blind, I'd take my bow with me when I went shopping. Many kinds of extremely lightweight decoys are available too, so with a few of these tucked away, a person could make a very nice setup for decoying gobblers during spring hunts.

Free-lancing for turkeys, as Steven and I were doing in the mountains, is a much tougher way to kill turkeys. The ranges are longer and the movements made in drawing and holding to sight are not hidden completely. Full camouflage—face, hands, pants, shirt, anything which will help the hunter to blend in—is a must.

Keeping any approaching turkey in view is a tremendous help; when the bird passes behind any obstacle, the bow can be drawn. A mouth call helps the hunter keep in contact with the bird and assists in tracking the bird's movements. Decoys add to this setup.

Pinpoint accuracy is a must. Shotgunners have read many times that a gobbler in full strut should never be shot. However, this is the easiest time to kill one. I've killed a truckload of old strutters with my shotguns. A head shot is a head shot, regardless of it's stuck out on a long neck, or on a neck drawn back as when the he-turkey is in full blossom. For a bowman, the best shot would be when the bird is in full strut and facing directly away from the hunter. Shooting for dead center of the tail and lined up perfectly vertical on dead center, you will hit the backbone, even if you shoot slightly high. A dead center shot otherwise will strike the bird's heart-lung area.

On the plains, where stiff gales blow, a strutting bird will have trouble holding his tail erect. If the wind is side-on, the tail will blow over to the side. So if a bowman is drawing his bow under these conditions, he wants to take the wind into consideration. Many times I've seen old gobblers strutting in a

The only problem any of us have with hens coming to the call is getting a good clean shot at their male escort.

hard wind, so don't get the idea they won't do this. Winds bother old turkeys about as much as rain bothers a fish.

Dave Harbour, an old friend of mind who's now gone, also felt that the best time to draw was when the bird was strutting. When it wheeled, with its tail to the hunter, the bow was drawn, and with compounds, held until a good sighting was made. Whether it is a head-on or side-on wing butts shot. Dave, who was an excellent turkey hunter, tells of his bow skills in his classic book, *Hunting The American Wild Turkey*.

Many bowhunters use an arrow release on their bowstrings. Using a trigger as the release mechanism, it holds the arrow to bowstring.

Like many turkey hunters, he found full camouflage a must, from head to foot, and also utilized whatever blind material was on hand. Dave hunted a lot in Florida, and as those of us who've hunted there many times know, there isn't any finer cover for screening a hunter from a gobbler's prying eyeballs as there is in Florida's jungle-like outback.

Dave Harbour, my brother Dick, my grandson, and his dad Tom Preston, all have killed a number of wild turkeys with bows and all basically hunt in much the same manner. They locate turkeys, close the distance as much as possible, then often use a call to lure the bird into shooting range. Many wild turkeys can be easily stalked into shotgun killing range, inside thirty yards, and while this is also inside bow range, most good bowhunters have misgivings about shooting turkeys at that distance due to the vital area of the bird being so small. The

Cam Stewart, custom bowyer from Mesa, Arizona, crafts long-bows under the trade name Superstition Longbow. They are truly pieces of artwork.

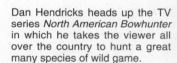

Dan Hendricks heads up the TV series *North American Bowhunter* in which he takes the viewer all over the country to hunt a great many species of wild game.

veteran turkey hunter also knows that the range can be short-ened with some patience and some work. It's best to wait and make the surer close-range shot than to risk crippling, and per-haps losing the bird at the thirty-yard mark. Ten to fifteen yards offers more dead cinch opportunities if there are such chances in turkey hunting.

My brother Dick tells me that during spring hunting he prefers to pass up calling in a gobbler when the old bird is with hens. Hens aren't much of a concern for a shotgunner. I can only recall one time, in Merriam country, when a hen came in too far ahead of the old strutter, saw me and spooked, telling the old he-bird to scat also. But, as the bow-man can't make the kills at longer ranges (or doesn't want to), a hen coming to the call well ahead of an old gobbler can truly mess things up. And, if she didn't spot the hunter

immediately, she very well will when the bow is drawn, and her putting and perting will alarm the gobbler, which may result in no shot.

Ordinarily, the only problem any of us have with hens com-ing to the call is getting a good clean shot at their male escort if there's a bunch of them. The nice thing about calling in such a group is the gobbler is so intent on hustling along with the hens he doesn't see the hunter until far too late. Many times as I've eased the gun out the hens would begin clucking and perting and raisin' general hell, but the old bird would just become more excited in his strutting, seeming never to notice the warning.

And, any hunter can raise the excitement level of a strutting bird by simply cranking him up with the call. Many expert turkey hunters feel hunters call too much. This is often true.

Veteran bowhunter Jim Pepper with the recurve bow he uses. His Indian-style, over-the-shoulder quiver holds his hunting broadhead arrows. Jim owns a hunter/outfitter service in Colorado called High Country Safaris.

However, there are also just as many times when a hunter does not call enough. Lord knows how many gobblers have wandered off because the caller quit and the bird lost interest and left.

If a turkey coming to the call is alone and called to many times, he will become so excited with mating desire that he will gobble over and over. Such a bird, once inside easy range, will pirouette, fan, display, strut, gobble, turn and wheel and become an easy mark for bow or gun. Mouths calls will crank up an old bird just as quickly as a box, or any other call. The idea is to simply keep it going. Don't stop when the bird gobbles; keep winding him up. It only adds to the hunt. Sure, it

may cause the gobbler to take a little longer getting there, but what the heck. If you got a bus to catch, you don't have any business being there in the first place. Take it easy, make him beller back time after time, then you'll begin enjoying turkey hunting instead of all that sweating and fidgeting you've been doing.

I got tickled at my brother when he first got into turkey hunting with a bow. He was always trying to hit the bird through the wing butts, which is where a bowman should kill them. This means the arrow passes through the heart-liver-lung area, very lethal. I think the first three Dick bagged with a bow, two of them he almost cut the bird's neck in two. And

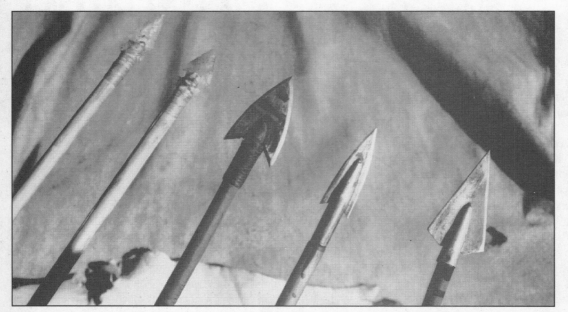

Arrow heads have been crafted from a variety of materials over the centuries. But, all have one thing in common—placed in a lethal area with a strong bow, they will all kill quickly. From far left: two flint-tipped arrows; center is a homemade trade point style blade; second from the right, a homemade broadhead from the '30s made by the author out of a field point; far right is a '30s commercial broadhead.

A growing number of bowhunters are using the old traditional longbow, both the straight-limb version and the recurve shown here in the hands of Dan Hendricks.

the third bird he hit in the head. Of course, all died there on the spot. Dick wasn't shooting at the bird's neck but he was simply shooting too high.

So, whatever you do, shoot high when you're shooting turkeys. Regardless of what you're carrying. You will cripple fewer birds.

Practice is what makes a bowhunter deadly. Practice, practice, practice. Dick, Tom, Steven, and other hunters I know all stress this one thing. Killing a big gobbler requires pinpoint accuracy as the upper chest vital area isn't any bigger than a

Lord knows how many gobblers have wandered off because the caller quit and the bird lost interest and left.

small grapefruit—the backbone only an inch wide. The smaller the turkey, the smaller these will be.

Today's bowhunter has the best of all worlds. The whole country is up to its neck in bows and arrows and many stores have such an array of equipment that I would become confused. Certainly the manufacturers have not been lax in producing bowhunting paraphernalia for the hunter.

Compound bows are still the average bowman's choice, but I see more longbows and recurves each year. And many of the handmade wood bows are a thing of beauty as well as a fine hunting weapon. Custom handcrafted bows are offered these days by such people as Bill Stewart, Bill Forman's Great Plains Co., Black Swan, Black Widow, and Martin Archery. My brother hunts with a Martin longbow. He's like many of the older compound shooters who are switching back to traditional stuff. Longbows require more strength than compounds and a longbowman must shoot them over a

longer period of time to build up the arm, shoulder, neck and back muscles to hold full draw. A hunter just getting into shooting longbows and recurves should study some of the new books on the market dealing with instinctive shooting. It's a whole new ball game for anyone who has never shot anything but a compound with its highly technical sighting system.

Of course, compounds can be purchased from the older companies. Pearson, Bear, and York, all have offered fine archery equipment for many years. Browning has its excellent line, as does Martin, Hoyt, Jennings, and High Country, but there are many others who manufacture excellent bows. Darten makes a very good bow—my brother has killed many whitetails with his Darten.

Broadheads, hunting heads, come in many weights these days, the bulk of them from 100 grains to 160. Muzzy has a new 100-grain three-blade model. Thunderhead sells 100-, 125-, 150-, and 160-grain weights. Rocky Mountain makes 100s and 125s. Bear has a full line as do the Zephyr people, and don't forget the Anderson Magnums. Easton still seems to have the finest complete line of aluminum hunting shafts, available both in light- and heavyweight arrows.

I seriously advise any hunter, old or new, and anyone wanting or thinking about getting into archery and bowhunting, to subscribe to one of the many bowhunting magazines published today. *Bowhunter* and *Bow & Arrow Hunting* are excellent reading and will keep the hunter abreast of all the new developments each issue. You'll not regret the money spent; it may be the wisest thing you've done.

Just leafing through one of these magazines makes me realize how primitive this bow of mine and these wooden arrows with their homemade points really are. *Kinda Primitive!!!!*

Hell, I ain't sure Alley Oop would've even used this stuff.

Grand Slammin' Turkeys With Muzzle-Loading Guns

LOOKING DOWN the barrel of a muzzleloader at an old longbeard, you see two hammers sticking up, kinda like looking between a mule's ears. You pull the trigger, some fire, smoke, maybe even some bits of hot metal explode next to your cheek, right alongside your face. There's a jolt along with a roaring *BOOMMM*, followed by copious white smoke. The smoke's blotted out the old gobbler you've been fiddling with so long, and in your mind you scream, "Where'n hell did the turkey go??" Long 'bout then, you can do one of four things.

1. You can jump up and run like hell through the smoke to see if you got the old turkey.
2. You can just sit on your backside, wait for the smoke to clear, then see if he's flopping around.
3. You can cuss 'cause you didn't get him.
4. Holler with joy, "You got him."

To my way of thinking, there's nothing this side of The Happy Hunting Grounds that can beat hunting turkeys with a side-by-side soot-belching muzzle-loading shotgun. I've laid out turkeys with all of 'em—cartridge busters, rifles, all kinds of shotguns, bows and arrows, but nothing gives me the thrill of easing a blackpowder burner to my shoulder, and setting on fire what's inside the barrels.

You won't understand my feelings until you follow my lead. Get rid of your fancy camouflage clothes, lay your hands on some old-timey clothing, getcha a slouchy felt hat, an old pair of brogans, a sack coat (what used to be called a law dog coat), then you'll have an inkling of what it must have been like to hunt wild turkeys back before the turn of the century.

Oh, sure, you need a turkey call. Nope, you can't use a mouth call or one of these new-fangled plastic things. You need a wingbone, or a box, maybe a peg'n'slate. The wild Indians called turkeys with their mouths; settlers first began using the ones I've mentioned. Calling a wild gobbler to the gun was soon considered the badge of excellence worn only by the most expert hunters. Very few hunters were known as excellent turkey hunters.

There are a number of modern-made muzzle-loading shotguns on today's market. Side-by-side's are offered by Dixie Gun Works, CVA, Navy Arms, Cabela's and Trail Guns Armory. Don't buy a singleshot because you won't have a backup barrel should you suddenly find yourself looking at a cripple leaving for the next county. Of course, two shots are always better than one. Most of these modern steel doubles will set you back upward of $400.

While I don't recommend using the old vintage antique guns, these are all I carry. Made back during the middle of the last century, during the 1800s, these old guns are made of what today we call inferior metals. With time and stress, original blackpowder shotguns may come unglued at any time. I've run hundreds of loads through the ones I own without any such accident, but it's my neck if one does blow up in my face. Unlike today's firearms, the old guns can be had in any gauge; it was a case of whatever came off the gunmaker's mandrel. So, when you hear me mention my old 11-gauge, the gun I call old Cough & Groan or Old C&G, don't think

The author has hunted wild turkeys for nearly twenty years with muzzle-loading rifles and shotguns, after he read of old-time hunters who had hunted the birds with these guns. Having killed a number of Grand Slams with muzzleloaders, he's learned what a hunter can expect when hunting with blackpowder in all parts of the country, from the wet swamps of Florida to the sudden snow squalls in the Rocky Mountains.

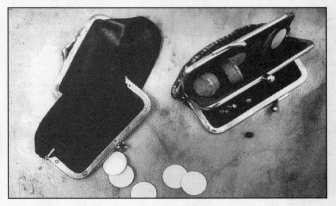

Old coin purses are excellent for toting some of the makings a blackpowder shotgunner needs for reloading a fired gun. These often have two compartments, one of which can hold a number of percussion caps, while the other can be used for wads.

the gauge has been misprinted because it really is an 11-gauge. Made back in Boston somewhere between 1840 and 1860, by a Captain Joab Hapgood, it's been my favorite turkey slayer for many years.

Loading a muzzleloader isn't a simple task of thumbing a couple of cartridges into a broken open double—far from it. This, and perhaps the cleaning, may be two of the reasons why muzzle-loading for turkeys hasn't caught on in this country. The third reason deals with a complete lack of self-confidence on the part of the shooter.

The breakdown in self-confidence invariably surfaces after the gun fails to fire or misfires. This can be the result of the percussion cap not exploding; or if the cap does explode, it fails to ignite the powder charge in the barrel; or the charge finally explodes, but during the time interval, the shooter has lost his sight picture. Of course, there is one other possibility—the cap has fallen off of the nipple.

With flintlocks, failure to fire can be caused by the powder in the pan, or the face of the frizzen, getting damp, the flint

going bad, or perhaps the touchhole being plugged. Of course, if the touchhole is "burnt out" from use, powder from the main charge could trickle out, filling the channel and hole, so it will take longer for the main charge to ignite, increasing the firing time lag further. Keep the touchhole picked clean. And, don't overfill the pan with powder; all you need to ignite the main charge is a good flame. Too much pan powder only adds to lag time plus can be very disconcerting to some shooters, especially if you're a lefty shooting a right-handed shotgun. The burning pan powder close to a person's face is damned disturbing. I've run lots of powder through pans on rifles, but finally gave it up. Figured sooner or later I'd have an eye damaged with the closeness of the pan to my face.

The primary cause of muzzleloaders failing to fire isn't in the actual loading, but rather in the use of a gun that hasn't been readied. The real culprit for the average blackpowder hunter is a shotgun that has been overcleaned, leaving moisture in the barrel in the form of gun oil. The gun must be dry to operate unfailingly. The nipples, the chamber into which the nipples are screwed, and the insides of the barrels *all must be bone dry.*

Run a few dry patches down each barrel. Do this until the patch comes out as clean as it was when first stuck in the barrel—no black, no nothing. Run a pipe cleaner into each nipple to dry it out. Then fire a couple of caps on each barrel while pointing the gun at and holding the end of the barrel close to a blade of grass, or a feather. The grass or feather will flutter, telling you the nipple and cap worked perfectly and the barrel is clear of obstructions. I invariably reverse the gun after firing caps and then blow down the barrel, watching the nipple as I do. The smoke will scoot back out of the nipple orifice, telling me the chamber is not only open and free, but that the nipple is also open. Only after all this do I load the gun.

Loading Blackpowder

Do not exceed the manufacturer's recommended maximum load. This is number one. And, if you do not have this information, I'd suggest you write for it.

I've included a chart from Dixie Gun Works' catalog which gives loading data for 10- and 12-gauge guns. I don't go along with anyone wanting to hunt gobblers with a smaller gauge gun.

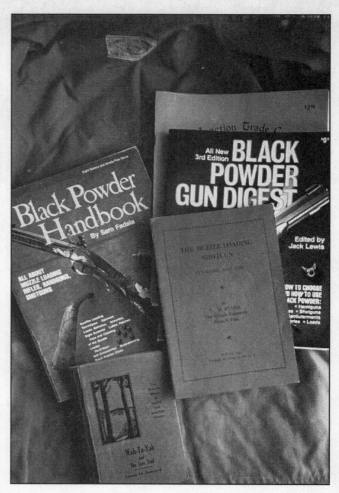

There are numerous publications available for those wanting to take up blackpowder hunting and shooting. Some of these cover every facet of the sport from advice on what to buy to how to clean the guns.

BLACKPOWDER LOADING DATA FOR MUZZLE-LOADING SHOTGUNS

Gauge	Powder Type	Powder Charge (grs.)	Shot Wgt. (oz.)	MV (fps)
10	FFg	109	1½	1033
10	FFg	102	1¼	1059
12	FFg	82	1¼	1035
12	FFg	76	1⅛	1062

There are numerous catalog houses from which all the components for loading can be ordered. Usually bags of shot and Pyrodex, or blackpowder, can be located locally. But wads and overshot cardboards aren't always found near home. Dixie handles all this stuff, but so do places like Track of the Wolf and Mountain States Muzzleloading. And, you'll need a measuring device for getting the right amount of shot or powder each time.

Finding a good load for killing wild turkeys with any muzzle-loading shotgun takes some time, a good deal of patience, and a resolve to learn the gun—what it does, where it shoots, some general "getting used to." After all, the sequence when shooting a blackpowder burner isn't as instantly quick as pulling the trigger on a cartridge-busting shotgun. This isn't too important for all standing shots, but if the bird flushes, this time lag becomes very evident.

I usually begin with a light field load, such as the 1¼-ounce load in Dixie's chart, if this is within the maker's recommendations. For turkey shooting, there are only a few sizes of shot which should be used: #4s, #5s, and #6s. I have used #5s for

many years for both season birds, though at times I have fallen back to #6 shot during the fall season hunts when I'm fairly certain the only turkeys I'll be seeing are young birds. They're not as tough to keep on the ground as older gobblers and #6s have more pellets per ounce. See the chart below and you'll see what I mean.

QUANTITIES OF BIRD SHOT TO THE OUNCE— AMERICAN STANDARD

Shot Size	Pellets Per Ounce
#4	132
#5	168
#6	218

It's easy to see that an ounce of #6s will give a far more dense pattern than will a like weight of #4s. However, shot size may be governed by what size the gun patterns best.

When I pick up a muzzle-loading shotgun I've never fired,

The selection at Dixie Gun Works offers a buyer just about any kind of old muzzleloader found on today's market. Turner Kirkland founded Dixie many, many years ago, and the business is run today by his two sons shown here.

Well-known Colorado turkey hunters Gary and Greg Miketa examine a Dixie Gun Works double-barrel side-by-side in 12-gauge. These modern-made guns have the fine steel of today's technology, making them much safer than the older guns.

I always hope the first load I stick in will pattern perfectly. But, that's never happened. Finding a good killing and hunting load invariably involves trying various wad combinations, with various sizes of shot, and varying powder loads. It's best to start with the manufacturer's recommendations, then work from that. Try varying the overpowder wads; never vary the overshot cardboard. Use what's listed by blackpowder suppliers as an overshot cardboard. It's the one thing you'll not change.

Ordinarily, I'll begin with an ⅛-inch overpowder wad, then stack a ½-inch felt wad on top of it, then pour in the shot and seat the shot cardboard. I've had good patterns with this combination. Once I've settled on the powder load, I vary the shot load to find a good pattern. I'll subtract shot in very small increments, using the exact same powder and wad combinations, and shoot a number of loads. True, this all takes time, and if you intend on doing it properly, you'll have to swab the barrels after each shot to preserve consistency shot to shot. A fouled barrel will result in a different pattern.

Knowing what you want to hunt, and what size shot you want to shoot, is what determines the powder charge. For instance, to hunt turkeys, you know you want to use a heavy

Anyone who hopes to get into blackpowder shotgunning should realize that these guns are individually loaded after each shot, so patterns vary. Therefore, a great amount of time must be spent shooting the gun to find the best combination of shot, wads and powder for the best pattern. Blackpowder shooting takes dedication if the hunter expects good results.

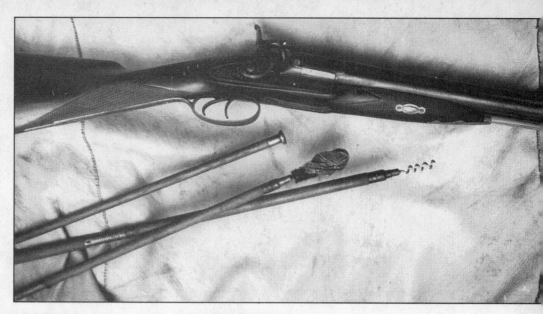

Cleaning these old guns, any muzzleloader, can be a job, a tough job, and may be why some hunters never get into the sport. Good, sturdy cleaning and wiping rods make the task much easier. The ramrods on today's newer blackpowder guns are cheap and easily broken, so it's best to replace them as soon as possible with stout ramrods offered by many supply houses.

Original accessories can enhance the use of old vintage guns. The powder flask at center made of copper, the shot pouch on the left and the old Indian knife on the far right are for folks who desire to remain completely authentic. There are also outlets that sell old-time clothing, boots, hats, gloves—everything from suspenders to sleeve garters.

load. If you were toting a Winchester pump 12, you'd want to use a cartridge loaded with at least 1³/₈ ounces of shot, probably #5s. Set your measure to hold exactly this amount of #5 lead shot. Now, use this same measure of powder. *Do not use the same weight—use the same volume.* This is an old rule-of-thumb among muzzle-loading shotgunners. Determine your shot load then use this same volume measure of powder.

You should make it a habit to "settle" both powder and shot in the barrels. Once you've poured in the powder charge, grab the ends of the barrels and tap the gunstock on the ground three or four times. Just use the gun's weight to do this; it will help the powder settle. Then you can run the overpowder cardboard and the ¹/₈-inch hard cardboard down the barrel. Push down with good pressure on the ramrod, but don't try to mash the powder. Just push it down firm, and then try to maintain this same pressure throughout all your loadings afterward.

When you pour the shot down the barrels, repeat the settling step by tapping the gunstock on the ground. Some hunters bump the gunstock a few times with the heel of their hands. Whichever you do, try to always use the same force for each

tap. This is handloading at its best. To maintain consistent patterns you need to duplicate the same load each time you load the gun.

Once the gun is loaded, the last thing you'll do is place a cap on the nipples. Make certain the cap fits snugly and that it is down on the nipple completely. If the cap isn't seated, the gun may fail to fire. The next time you try the gun it probably

To maintain consistent patterns you need to duplicate the same load each time you load the gun.

will shoot, but few old turkeys are going to hang around while you recock the gun in hopes it'll go off. Caps are dirt cheap, so learn all you can about using them when you are patterning. Some caps are "hotter" than others, though after using most all the brands, I've had no trouble or seen much difference in performance from one to the other. I do like the fluted skirt caps

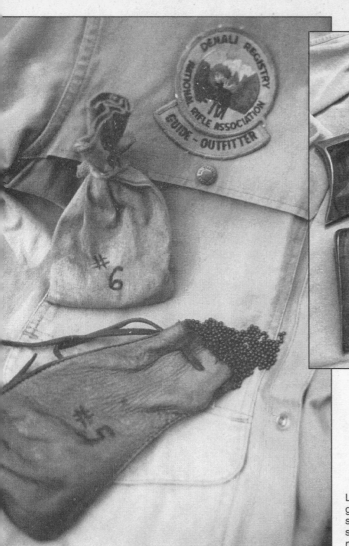

In many states a hunter can pursue wild turkeys with either rifle or shotgun, and it's up to the hunter to make his choice. Using a good side-by-side shotgun is much easier because of the pinpoint accuracy required for killing the birds with a rifle. Hunting the birds with a rifle is only for those who are dead-on shots and have the infinite patience required waiting for such a shot to present itself.

Loose shot for muzzle-loading shotguns is no different than the good grade of shot found in modern shotgun shells. Carrying the stuff afield can present problems, but the author has long carried small amounts with him in either a small canvas bag or an old bag made for carrying marbles.

because they are not easily dislodged. And, if you have to make a long sneak, bellycrawl, or make your way through thick cover, a cap can dislodge and fall off. It's safest to keep the hammers in the "safe" half-cock notches, but I often keep the hammers down on the nipples when crawling to protect against losing a cap. However, since I took to using only the fluted skirt cap, I no longer worry about one coming off. The only problem with using a tight cap is that a pair of pliers will be needed to remove one.

From the hunters I've talked to over the years about the problems they've had using a muzzleloader, far the greatest mentioned has been either the hassle of cleaning or failure to fire. The latter is invariably due to moisture or an unsettled powder charge in the powder chamber (with rifles, in the bolster area). This last problem is easily remedied by tapping the stock, but the other is just as easily solved if caps are fired to dry out the nipple area. Like I said, caps are dirt cheap. It's silly to risk ignition failure over the few pennies a cap costs.

Another practice I often hear of is firing the gun each night after the day's hunt is over. This is fine, but don't think you must completely clean the gun just because you shot it. Simply

run a few dry patches down the barrel. And why wait until the next morning to reload it—do it then. But, again, fire a couple caps before you do, watching the nipple orifices to make certain they didn't get clogged when you ran the patches down the barrels.

I never unload the gun at the end of the day; I just remove the caps. Then I let the hammers down onto the nipples to keep out any moisture from the air. I keep small leather tabs between the hammers and the nipples and let the hammers rest on these to completely seal the nipples. The next morning I'll put on two new caps, and I'm back in business. I never reuse caps I've pulled from the nipples.

You'll hear or read of old-timers who used all sorts of stuff for wadding and for shot. Swan shot, which was misshapen shot with a tail on it, made for very poor patterns. Wadding, well, they made do with what was at hand. I'd heard so much about the use of hornet's nests, I once tore up a big nest I'd lugged home from over in the Aux Arcs (Ozarks to folks today) and used it to wad both barrels of a shotgun I affectionately call Bloody Mary. The gun is a 10-bore side-by-side made by Westley Richards, the famous firm in London.

Not long afterward I bellied up onto a pair of old gobblers feeding in a dry lake bed. I snaked the old gun forward and set loose the bees in the right barrel. Killed the gobbler I'd picked out of the twosome. Bloody Mary laid the bird out dead'ern a hammer. But I never tried it again. Also tried newspaper wadding—but it's dangerous. In very dry country it could very well set some grass or leaves on fire.

For the beginning muzzleloader, the first major obstacle is killing distances. You probably won't be able to kill at those longer ranges you felt confident of when using a cartridge-shooting shotgun. In time, you may find a load which will overcome this, but usually in the beginning, the range just isn't there. Thirty yards will be about the far end of your sure killing range. But, there's a plus to this. It will make a hunter out of the shooter. Today we're inundated with new long-range guns and new loads for them. A turkey is supposedly not safe any longer at 50 yards. So, the woods are filled with what I call "shooters." These are folks who can't get a bird into short range, so fire at turkeys at long range. This is the major reason so many hunters are being shot in today's turkey woods. A great many of these so-called accidents wouldn't have taken place if the guy doing the shooting had made an effort to get close.

Though my old guns will pattern well at 40 to 50 yards, I've yet to kill a gobbler at that range. There's no need when the bird can be shot at 25 yards. You can get nearer, or wait until the birds walk in toward you if they're being called. Just have patience. Work at it. You'll be a much finer hunter for it.

Muzzleloaders don't work the same as your shell-busting shotgun. You can't throw it to shoulder, thumb off safe and shoot. You have two hammers to cock. These weren't always

Not long afterward I bellied up onto a pair of old gobblers feeding in a dry lake bed.

called hammers; they used to be known as "cocks." In time, this became offensive slang for male genitals; the cocks became hammers. Now, you'll hear that once an old wary gobbler gets within 25 yards or less, the bird may spook when you ease back a hammer. That's not true, unless you let him see you make the move. I've killed scads of old birds at distances inside 20 yards and have yet to spook a bird due to noise or movement. Of course, I usually hunt from behind

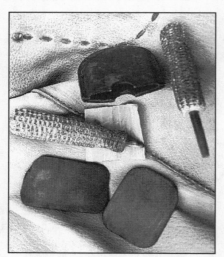

Any hunter who wants to make his own turkey call can quickly and easily make a peg'n'slate call from a small section of slate and a corncob. Slate is easily sanded to a thickness which will make the notes desired. The corncob has a short small section of cedar stick, or a like section of laurel, or maple will do, inserted into the pithy center as the peg.

The author holds up a wild gobbler killed on a fall hunt. This young Merriam was downed with a double-barreled muzzleloader at twenty yards. What greater sport can there be than camping out in Merriam country and hunting with old vintage scatterguns, particularly if you're hunting wild turkeys.

Lennis Rose, of Washburn, Missouri, in full hunting regalia, including old-time eyeglasses, slouch hat, and riverboat shirt. Lennis shoots a side-by-side 12-bore flintlock double, custom made. The gun's fiddle-back stock is a thing of beauty. Lennis has killed many turkeys with the gun he's holding, but he also has a couple vintage percussion cap double shotguns which he also uses when hunting turkeys.

some cover I've thrown together on the spot. Not wearing camouflage, I have to make use with whatever I can. When stalking, parts of the terrain will hide my approach. Once you have a bird show up at close range, simply ease back the hammer and you won't have any trouble.

Perhaps long-time experiences help in such instances, as I'll wait until the bird walks behind a tree, if that appears to be in the offing, or until the bird pecks at the forest floor, or if the bird's in full strut, wait until it turns its tail toward me. An old he-turkey that has come to a call will invariably keep looking about for the hen, so it's best that you have your hands full of gun to resist making another call. Such calling pinpoints your location for the tom, making it more difficult to get the gun on him. Let him look for the hen once he's within gunshot range, then pick your shot when he's not concentrating on the source of the call.

It is ideal if the bird is seen approaching at a longer distance and the hammer's drawn back to shooting position while the bird is still out of range. I much prefer calling a bird to a location where the bird cannot be seen until it's inside killing distance, as such birds are far less likely to hang up. When you read about "circling" turkeys, you know the birds were called into a poor calling location. Many times these are call sites in large, flat areas where the approaching bird can see no other birds, gets wary and stops, resulting in a hangup. Or, he walks around the location searching for the other turkeys he can't see.

We've all heard some hunter say, "You can't shoot a gobbler in full strut." This is about the silliest thing known in turkey shooting. Recently I read an article in which the author stated a bowhunter could shoot a gobbler in a strut, but a shotgunner could not. This guy was obviously a rank beginner, or a nut, or both. And, any hunting magazine editor worth his typewriter should know better than to print such stuff.

Let me put this question to any hunter in the country.

Do you have a preference how I shoot you? Would you prefer standing straight up, or your head pulled in on your shoul-

Lennis Rose examines a freshly fallen feather while fall hunting for Merriams in the Rockies. The serious blackpowder shooter soon realizes that the average muzzleloader does not have the range of modern shotguns, so every effort must be made to become a better hunter. The result is an expert turkey hunter, one who not only makes kills at nearer distances, but also does not have trouble locating and getting shots.

Determining Shotgun Chokes

Draw a 30-inch circle on a large piece of cardboard and place it against a shooting range backstop. Then, from 40 yards shoot for dead-center of the circle. While counting the number of holes made where pellets have hit, notice if the gun seems to be shooting to one side, away from the point of aim. Perhaps you were holding wrong, not shouldering the gun properly, nor ensuring a true sighting picture. You may need help determining if the fault is with the gun or with you. You should also note if the pattern has blanketed the circle completely, or if it has holes in it.

Count the numbers of holes in the circle, then divide by the number of shot in the load.

Full Choke = 70 percent
Modified Choke = 50 percent
Improved Cylinder = 60 percent
Cylinder = 30 percent

There are 400 pellets in one ounce of #8 shot. Let's assume you have shot one ounce of #8 shot at the target, then counted 200 holes in the target. Two hundred divided by 400 equals 50 percent. The gun has shot a Modified choke pattern. The great bulk of old muzzleloaders, and some modern ones, seldom shoot better than Improved Cylinder, many being Cylinder bore. This is why if you want to shoot game-killing loads, you must shoot at shorter ranges to ensure a dense pattern. Theoretically, to obtain the same 70 percent pattern that a Full choke gun shoots at forty yards, a Cylinder bore must be cut back to twenty-five yards. That's only five yards shy of being half the distance. So, you just need to be a better hunter if you want to kill all your turkeys with a Cylinder-bore shotgun.

Bearded hens are found throughout all the subspecies of wild turkeys, though many hunters have never seen one. This bird fell to the author's old 11-gauge, while the gun was stoked with 120 grains of FFg blackpowder, a hard cardboard wad and a 1/2-inch felt wad on the powder, followed by 1 5/8 ounces of chilled shot, then capped off with an overshot thin cardboard.

Muzzleloaders must be cleaned from time to time if the shooter expects the gun to continue shooting. This duty can be confined to camp since so few shots will be made in a day's hunt. If the gun hasn't been fired, put it away where it will remain dry for the night, but do remove the caps. Replace them the next morning, and you'll be back in business.

ders? Buddy, I don't want you to shoot at me no matter what I'm doing. If you shoot at my head, it makes not a damn bit of difference if I'm standing *on my head*.

Probably nobody in this land has killed as many gobblers in full blossom as I have. I've yet to lose one. And, there's a reason why. A gobbler in full strut is intent on finding the hen. He's not wary or spooky. True, I'll get some shot into the bird's body, but a few shot have never slowed down my eating wild turkey, or any other gamebird, so what the heck.

No bowman I know will shoot a gobbler in full strut because they want the lethal areas better defined. I'm not a bowhunter, but I would prefer shooting at a bird walking away from me, facing me head-on, or broadside, to shooting at a gobbler in full strut with a bow. With a shotgun I'm shooting at the head; with a bow I'd be shooting at wing butts or the backbone.

Some areas of the country are easier for muzzleloader hunt-

Probably nobody in this land has killed as many gobblers in full blossom as I have.

ing than others. Florida's Osceola wild turkey lives in basically wet country, where at times it's not easy to keep the gun dry. I've replaced caps as many as three times a day in such conditions. Perhaps the ones I removed would have fired, but I wasn't taking chances. Winter hunts, or spring hunts in the Rockies, can also be wet, with snow or cold rains.

Some hunting methods are easier than others. For instance, hunting from what I call commercial blinds is a cinch. Your movements are hidden and you can relax and

enjoy the scen-ery while waiting for a gobbler to amble by. You'll find commercial blinds in use all across the South; Texas must have hundreds and hundreds of them on huge hunting ranches. I guide out of Rancho Rio Bonita, down near Junction in Kimble County, Texas, and we have many blinds on the ranch. True, many serious hunters won't go in one, but such hidey holes are fine for inexperienced folks, or photographers, and disabled hunters. I've built two or three on my spread in Oklahoma just for such use. Of course, when it rains there is nothing better than to have a place to continue hunting. Clients who come to hunt haven't paid to sit in camp, and I think most of them would much prefer hanging out in a blind than following me around. 'Course, maybe I walk too much.

I'm always throwing together an impromptu hide, somewhere in the woods, where I'll sit for periods during the day when it's useless to be stillhunting. Extremely calm days are the worst for stillhunting, so if I'm tired and know of a place turkeys use a lot, I'll build a makeshift hide there and retire to it for sometimes hours. Such a blind must be sightproof to be comfortable, and large enough that you can stretch out in it and take a snooze without having to worry about whether a turkey walking past can see you.

In some places, wild turkeys can be hunted with rifles. But read the state laws wherever you plan to hunt, since these vary from state to state. I don't recommend anyone hunting wild turkeys with a rifle, simply because a shotgun is far more lethal. But, many hunters love to hunt with rifles, and if you fall in this category, fine. Muzzle-loading rifles for turkeys can be any gun you've been shooting—your deer rifle, a squirrel gun, a target rifle. Just so long as it's legal by law.

144

Nothing equals shooting a wild turkey in flight with an old soot-throwing shotgun. The author steps from a run-down shed, flushing a drove, making for a perfect angling-away shot. Easy pickin's.

Most 50-caliber deer rifles can be down-loaded for turkeys. In other words, instead of using the 85-grain load you use for whitetails, back off to maybe 40 grains or less. You'll need to get to the shooting range and learn what load will plunk them in there at whatever range you intend as your maximum. And, this is the hairy part of using rifles for wild turkeys. Most states do not allow scopes, so you will probably have to go with the open iron sights.

Killing wild turkeys with any rifle is not as simple as it seems on the surface. Too often the bird rolls over and flops around at the shot, but seconds later runs over the far hill, never to be seen again. Too many times, the knock-down power of the gun bowled the turkey over, but it wasn't hit in a lethal area. It's been my luck to kill a number of turkeys which, when I began cleaning them, had obviously been hit earlier by rifle fire. And by earlier I mean a couple of these birds had been shot at least a week previously.

Bullet placement is critical when shooting turkeys with rifles. The bullet must be placed exactly, no different than when using a bow. The bird must be hit in the wing butts,

Fall hunting for older gobblers is often a matter of building a hide where it's thought the birds may feed, then simply waiting 'em out.

Having killed wild turkeys with all sorts of things, from Indian bows with flint-tipped arrows to sawed-off barrel riot shotguns, to rifles and bare hands thrown in for good measure, Bland still considers the use of an old-time shotgun far the greatest for getting pure pleasure from the hunting of the country's grandest game bird.

Seldom will anyone run into a hunter clad in old-timey clothing in today's modern world. Lennis Rose, a long-time hunting buddy of the author, often heads into the woods decked out head to toe in such stuff, toting either a flinter or caplock.

which means a hit in the heart-lung area, or somewhere in the backbone or spinal column. Of course, a head shot will anchor any turkey, though a turkey's head is a poor target for any but the best marksman. Leave head shooting for shotgunners.

I've killed a number of birds with a rifle. One of my rifles is a Kentucky long rifle in 45-caliber; the other, a scoped CVA 50. I much prefer the scoped gun, but it's not legal in many of the states I hunt. The scope gives me that excellent sight picture which so often isn't there with iron sights. Longer shots are made easily. But since most good shots with open iron sights are only made at shorter distances, then why tote the rifle when you're now within shotgun range?

Muzzle-loading round balls are fine for turkeys, but so are Buffalo Bullets and sabots. Just remember, down load the powder charge, but don't sacrifice bullet drop over the distance you will limit your shots. And, if you hit the bird where you should, you won't ruin any meat. If you do hit the bird in the breast meat, chances are you have not only ruined a lot of meat, but probably won't get the bird anyhow. It'll escape. Let's hope a varmint gets it and it dies a quick death.

Hunting with muzzleloaders has something about it that takes you back in time, if you'll let it. And if you carry the whole thing one step further and wear old-timey looking clothes, then about the only thing left is for you to make your own turkey calls.

Peg'n'slates are the easiest. Perhaps you know where a hunk of slate is, but if not, scout around the five-and-dime

stores, or browse through the toy section of your local stores. If you keep your eyes open, you'll spot one of the small blackboards used by children. I've also found many small old-timey blackboards in antique or junk shops. After you've located a hunk of slate, cut it into small 2x3-inch or 3x4-inch sections with a fine-blade hacksaw or a handsaw. Slate is fairly soft and easy to work with. You need to sand the pieces until they are about 1/16-inch thick. This size makes excellent turkey talk. For the peg, or striker, the easiest thing to use is a plain, old corncob and a small pencil-sized hunk of maple dowel rod, cedar bough, or seasoned laurel or hard maple. Many kinds of hard woods will probably do, but these are the ones I've tried. Having whittled the wood of choice down to less than the

Hunting with muzzleloaders has something about it that takes you back in time.

diameter of a pencil, you can run it through the center of the smaller end of the corncob, as it's very soft and pithlike. If the cob has hardened a bit, this pith can be easily removed with a 1/4-inch bit used in an electric drill or a hand brace. You want to leave enough pith to hold the wooden rod securely so that scraping it back and forth across the slate will not dislodge it.

Leave an inch or so protruding and round it off with your

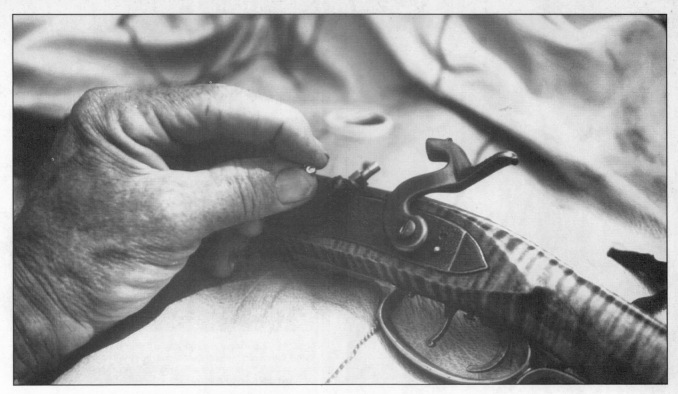

Percussion cap muzzleloaders simply won't fire unless a cap is in place on the gun's nipple, and if these don't fit snugly there is always a chance the cap will jar loose and fall off, often unnoticed. This can be remedied by grasping the cap between thumb and forefinger, and with a gentle squeeze, slightly goose-egging its shape. It'll stay in place much better.

pocketknife, then hold a lighted match to it and allow it to barely catch afire. Then blow it out. You just want to barely char the wooden "peg" as it's now called. Lightly sand off the char and now you are ready to call.

Cup the hunk of slate in one hand, and with the peg slanted at a 45-degree angle to the surface, make large "O"-like motions across the slate. You'll soon learn to make the clucks, yelps, and purrs made by wild turkeys. A series of yelps result from one group of three "Os", then two groups of five "Os", and the last clucks are made by placing the peg against the slate and quickly jerking it across, but away from the slate. All it takes is practice. Peg'n'slates are an old part of turkey hunting. Try it. You'll like it.

Wingbone calls are coming back, probably to some extent because I've been using and mentioning them for most of thirty years. Wingbones use to be very popular back in the good old days when turkeys were plentiful, the late 1800s. But, when turkeys went downhill, hunting more or less went by the wayside over much of the nation, so turkey calling of all kinds was forgotten.

Wingbone calls are available from several sources. However, most of these commercial calls are made from the wing bones of gobblers, either jakes or older birds. If you want to call jakes, fine, use jake bones. But, if you want a call for the spring turkey season, when you want to imitate a hen turkey, then you damned well don't want to use bones from a male turkey. You want to use hen bones.

The hunter may make some surprise kills while fall hunting for wild turkeys, that is, if he's prepared for such sport. This ruffed grouse fell to the author's gun while on a hunt to Vermont's Green Mountains. Woodcock, doves, quail, prairie chickens, all have been bagged while pursuing turkeys.

Vintage muzzle-loading guns are a thing of beauty, but anyone shooting these old guns should never forget that it could blow apart due to metal fatigue from excessive age. A person shooting one of these guns does so at his own risk.

Hefting a big Eastern gobbler, one you've shot with an old soot-blowing side-by-side caplock muzzleloader, is to the author the ultimate challenge in all turkey hunting. Bows never misfire, nor do modern shotguns and rifles, but sometimes when cutting a fine bead on a big, old longbeard you're not sure if it's going to go off. No matter how careful you've been, sometimes Murphy's Law takes control. If anything bad is going to happen, it'll happen.

Of course, why buy one—go out this fall and shoot a hen and make your own. You'll have a greater attachment to the call anyhow if it's from a bird you killed. Once you've bagged a hen, pick, clean, and eat the bird. Then, keep the bones from the first and second joints of the wings. You'll have one bone from the wing section next to the bird's body, and two bones from the second section. Throw these into a pan of hot water, boil them a short while and add a little dish soap if you want the bones nice and clean. Then let them cool. With a hacksaw,

Success in the woods depends not on what kind of call a hunter uses, but rather how he uses it.

cut off the knobby ends, and using a small wire and a few pipe cleaners, clean all the marrow from inside the bones.

You can then fit the ends of the smaller bones into the ends of the larger ones. You may have to cut back short sections of the bones to make them fit. Once fitted together, glue them with Elmer's Woodworking glue. Using a sucking, smacking action, you should be able to make turkey clucks. If you prefer a mouthpiece, and most hunters do, this can be made with a bottle cork, drilling a hole through it large enough to slip over the small end of the call.

Cupping the hands over the larger end of the call moderates the volume of your notes as you suck and pull air through the small end, which is held just inside the lips. The best calling is done with a kissing action, or for clucks, a sucking, jerking action. Wingbones are a dandy call; no other makes as fine a cluck, tree call, or yelp as a good wingbone. Few hunters will practice with one to the point of becoming really good. Practice, practice, practice is what it takes to be good.

Of course, box calls are not difficult to make for the hunter who has woodworking tools at his disposal. Many of my friends have boxes they've made at home. And like all calls, success in the woods depends not on what kind of call a hunter uses, but rather how he uses it. Turkeys make all sorts of crazy notes, but all are made for a reason, and often with some sort of rhythm. So make your own call, but when you use it for hunting, learn when and why turkeys "talk," and you'll be your own hunter. You called the birds to you with your own call.

Let me remind you that hunting with a muzzleloader ain't the same as carrying a cartridge-shooting firearm. Blackpowder can be dangerous stuff. Read these rules and *don't forget 'em.*

- Do not use anything in muzzleloaders but blackpowder or replica blackpowder.
- Treat every gun as a loaded gun.

What greater challenge than hunting wild turkeys as our forefathers did, utilizing learned hunting skills and shooting an old side-by-side "soot-blower." Lennis Rose pauses on a slope in Merriam turkey country.

- Be "dead sure" of your target before shooting.
- Keep the gun pointed downrange if you have a misfire or failure to fire. Wait at least a full minute before attempting to learn why; even then, do not point the muzzle at yourself or others.
- Remove the cap from an unfired barrel before reloading a fired barrel.
- Remove the caps before storing for the night, and before taking inside or placing in a vehicle.
- Never smoke while handling blackpowder.
- Never drink while hunting or shooting.
- Use some good old common sense.

When you get your frontloader, you'll begin searching out the best pattern for your gun. And this is when you shoot the gun over and over. Get acquainted with the gun. Strive to load in exactly the same manner each time so you'll build good habits. Shoot as often as possible, but particularly before the season opens.

While patterning, you may learn the gun isn't shooting the best pattern at the aiming point, or that you seem to be shooting high. As with so many muzzleloaders having the old straight English stock, there is a tendency to shoot high, so you may have to adjust for this. I still do and have been shooting the things for going-on twenty years.

When you feel you have worked up the best turkey load for

The author with his Westley Richards 10-bore side-by-side, studying a couple of freshly fallen feathers found at a small mountain pond and dropped there by some of the Eastern wild turkeys found in Missouri and Arkansas Ozarks.

Teaching young folks to hunt means that first you need to teach them to be a good, but safe, shooter. They'll get more fun from it all if you let them shoot a smoke-blowing blackpowder gun. Makes it all the more fun. And what youngster doesn't like to see where he shoots. Put your target in water, then they'll see where the shot charge strikes. And, don't forget to teach them that it is a no-no to shoot a rifle at anything on water, because the bullet just skips and keeps on going.

Nothing beats a walk in the North woods, falling leaves underfoot, a soot-belching shotgun in hand, topped off by bumping into a drove of Eastern wild turkeys.

your gun, buy some of the turkey targets on today's market. Bowhunting suppliers always stock these if you cannot find them elsewhere. Shoot a few of them at 30 yards, aiming toward the top of the bird's neck. This is the showdown. If you still put a number of pellets in the target bird's head and neck with each shot, then you can kill a real turkey.

You shouldn't have any problems hitting a bird if you always wait until the bird is inside easy gunshot range, at

You won't ever get tired of hunting turkeys with a soot-burning, bad-smelling, side-by-side muzzle-loading shotgun.

least twenty-five yards. If you don't kill the bird with the first load, you still have a good shot with the number two barrel. This is a habit any shotgunner should always remember when hunting turkeys. Don't take your first shot at the bird at long range. Your chances of crippling it are greater,

and you don't have much chance of anchoring the bird with your backup shot.

For those who give up the camouflage stuff in favor of old-style clothing, the crucial part of killing wild turkeys will be where you locate to call and make your kill. After years of hiding behind face paint and being decked out head to toe, taking it off made me feel naked as a jaybird.

Once an old bird begins stalking the call, a sudden feeling of "where in Hell am I going to hide" hits you in the face. Very often I hide behind trees which are down or take up residence near the edge of thickets, vine tangles, dense stands of low brush, behind rocks, dirt banks, creek banks, anything that completely hides me from the bird's searching eyeballs until he's in range, and then, of course, it's too late. It is said turkeys will not go into thick stuff like canebrakes, cedarbrakes and the like, but they darn sure walk the edge, and at times I've had them walk into such cover. Water, rivers, lakes, big creeks, hogwire fences—all these obstacles often mess up a hunter's plans. Locate well back from these barriers or, if it's possible to kill the bird across the obstacle, then near it. I've

Anyone who's fired a shot at a big, old gobbler with a muzzle-loading shotgun will know what I mean when I say you're always so darned glad the gun went off. That is, if it did go off. There is always the slimmest of chances something's gone haywire.

taken my clothes off more'n once to cross a river or deep stream and fetch a damn bird that I'd called but wouldn't come across to me.

Last spring I called to an old bird in some nasty live oak thickets. The gobbler had been hassled earlier that morning by another member of my party and wouldn't come to me. He'd march back and forth at about thirty-five yards, but with all the brush there just wasn't a shot. This went on for a spell and I could see that nothing was coming of it, so I quit calling. In a few minutes he walked off, beckoned by the calling of some hens, which probably weren't real hens at all.

Soon as the old rascal cut out of sight, I trotted back around the grove of trees, working my way parallel to his course for a couple hundred yards, or what I hoped was his course. I slipped in toward a stand of trees which I hoped was his destination. Switching from a wingbone to a small one-sided box call, I made a couple of clucks. And, hey, the gobbler bellered back. Right on cue, and right on course. I was standing up, kinda hunkered into the backside of a huge, green bush. Limbs

and branches were sticking and poking me from head to toe, but aside from having to stand the gun on the ground, I could make do. Calling wasn't easy because the tree was in my way. But, that gobbler marched right to me. At twenty yards the turkey walked behind a big oak. As he did, I stuck the box in a pocket, eased up the old cannon, and when he walked out from back of the trunk I caved him in. No, I wasn't camouflaged in the modern sense of the word, but I'd kept perfectly still and, with my old, dull clothing, had easily stayed hidden from the bird's sight. Of course, in that setting, the turkey was swallowed up in the smoke clouds when I fired. I always run through the stuff as fast as I can to finish the flopping bird. Such close-in shooting very, very seldom results in any cripples.

They tell us folks get tired of Coke and switch to Pepsi, or they get tired of Pepsi Cola and switch to Coca Cola. I doubt any of that bunk. And, I'll tell you something else, you won't ever get tired of hunting turkeys with a soot-burning, bad-smelling, side-by-side muzzle-loading shotgun.

11

Ambushin', Bellycrawlin' and Bushwackin'

The savvy turkey hunter will always use any and all cover to hide his form from the intense scrutiny of the wild turkey's eyesight. Very often such approaches may be painful, due to thorns, stickers or water, snow and even cow manure. A hunter bent on working into easy gunshot will not mind these little annoyances.

A hunter should try to plan a stalk so at the end he arrives at some object that allows him to bring the gun to bear and yet have a screening of cover. Stalking to a tree stump, a pile of rocks, a dense clump of weeds, even a fence post could bring this hunt to a successful end.

LET'S DEFINE STALKING. To begin with, it's invariably pronounced "stawk." To stalk means to approach using cover to hide one's movements. And that is exactly what it means when hunting wild turkeys. If the hunter doesn't use cover to mask his approach himself, he'll never get his gun to within killing range.

Throughout the varying terrains of all five subspecies of bearded and spurred wild turkeys are areas where the birds can be stalked. The easiest stalking cover is among small, rolling hills covered with trees, rocks and brush. By far the most difficult places are flat, open woods where the hunter must also concentrate on being quiet, which makes for hard times if the hunter is on dry leaves. The wind is particularly helpful when the hunter moves through the woods making noise. Besides rustling the leaves, it also stirs tree branches, brush, grass, all of which minimizes the moves being made by the hunter—movements that could be eyed by turkeys. Rain obliterates sounds as well, though rain gear made of synthetic material is noisy as brush and tree limbs brush against them. Running streams, tumbling among rocks, hide nearly all sounds.

I can't overemphasize to a new wild turkey hunter the importance of remaining behind cover if a stalk is planned. Though it is possible to stalk a buck deer from out in open terrain, easing along only when the deer is looking the other direction or feeding, this can't be done with a wild turkey. Oh, it's possible, but the conditions must be perfect, and then only by a hunter who knows wild turkeys thoroughly. For the average or beginning hunter, a stalk must be made behind cover at all times.

The worst headache for a stalker is when wild turkeys linger in one place for an hour, then begin walking, perhaps pecking at this and that, but covering a lot of ground. Except for those times when the birds move toward the hunter, which is exceedingly rare, the hunter must initiate another strategy—he must stalk to a point where *he can intercept them.*

Seldom can a complete stalk be made on foot. Those last fifty yards for a hunter trying to draw himself to within thirty yards of a turkey or turkeys should be traversed by crawling on hands and knees, or by bellycrawling. The hunter's will and desire will make or break a kill. I can't begin to recall the many physically painful stalks I've made.

Binoculars are a must for anyone who stalks wild turkeys. Slight elevations not easily discernible to the naked eye often become apparent when viewed through field glasses. They also enable the hunter to study the terrain he has planned to stalk to find the proper course for slipping to within gun range. Further study may reveal a route which, though longer, may present fewer chances of the hunter being seen or heard. There will be times when it's wisest to stay put, waiting to see where the birds go, and then hope to stalk them. This can be a gamble (nothing new to a turkey hunter), as the birds could move into a less advantageous position.

Water in one form or another has cost me shots at a number of turkeys. Invariably, this was when bellycrawling. I have

Bellycrawling is exactly what the term implies, pulling yourself along on your stomach. This is most easily done with both hands, knees, elbows and feet. Bellying allows a hunter to stalk turkeys in scant cover, but as with crawling on hands and knees, bellying can be hazardous due to all the stuff underfoot, so to speak. Rocks, mud, water, snow, thorns and manure are only a few. Bellycrawling is a very lethal method for approaching wild turkeys. It allows a close approach with a very low profile. The author has bellied into many small gangs of old gobblers which would not respond to calling.

Wherever a person hunts turkeys, there's always a chance a called bird will eyeball the hunter as it approaches. However the birds are hunted, there's no more lethal method for waylaying a wild turkey than from a prone shooting position. The author and his brother weren't surprised to find the U.S. Army teaching this technique back during the early '40s. Bland, along with many other long-time hunters, had been using this method for many years. Enemies are seldom looked for at ground level.

bellied through water several inches deep, but not so deep that I couldn't keep the gun out of water, or at least the bulk of it. Of course, not all hunters want cold water running through their shirt and pants and boots as they wallow from point to point.

Stalking turkeys in snow is as bad or worse, and is best done with white coveralls. Coveralls don't allow the white stuff to infiltrate clothing as easily. The greatest hazard is getting snow packed up in the gun barrel, though this is a problem faced by any who stalk, and must be guarded against continuously.

All of turkey hunting has endless decisions that must be made, but stalking seems overladen with them. And, once a person has sneaked into easy gunshot, deciding what to do isn't over even then. Can you slip the gun into shooting position without spooking the birds? Are you positive of range? What if you only knock a bird down with the first shot, but it regains its feet or wings and attempts to escape? Will you be in a position where you can get in a final killing shot? Is the gun barrel free of obstructions?

It is a relatively easy matter to bring a gun into shooting position on stalked turkeys. Before attempting to bring it to bear, make certain the area is free of obstacles which could be brushed in your attempt to aim, and thus spook the birds. Positive that you can ease the gun forward, keep your eyes riveted on the birds, and when you are dead sure none are looking around, slip it into the shooting position. Whatever you do, *don't make any quick, jerky moves.* Predators attack like a bolt of lightning, so all birds are sensitive and take instant action when quick moves are detected.

The average shot at stalked turkeys will be from a crouched position, or perhaps a prone position, and a hunter should familiarize himself with these positions prior to hunting. I learned long ago that only a handful of people have fired a shotgun while lying on their bellies. In this firing position the gun will not feel the same, hold the same, or aim the same as

Ed LaForce, one of the author's long-time hunting buddies, certainly isn't any stranger to setting an ambush for wild turkeys. He's got the proverbial patience of Job, and like the author, will stake out a place until he turns to rock, if that's what it takes to get a good shot at a gobbler.

when standing. To make matters worse, estimating range is a whole new ball game when the hunter's eyes are but a few inches from ground level. Flat country—open prairie, palmetto pastures which have recently been burned, large tree-lined meadows, and rolling sagebrush hills—have few reference points to give the hunter something with which to compare a turkey. A hunter who chased spring adult gobblers can be easily misled by a late-hatch young turkey in October. Chances are he will pass up a shot thinking the bird is well beyond gunshot because at 25 yards it will appear about the same size as the old gobbler did at 40 or more yards. Reverse the situation, and the fall hunter will be blasting at old birds well before they come into range.

Probably the number one quality with which a hunter must be endowed if he is to stalk turkeys is patience...a tremendous amount of time is required.

More than once I have judged distances by waiting for the turkey to look away from me, then rising up quickly onto my knees, comparing the bird to the surroundings, then ducking back behind cover before being seen. Obviously, this is best accomplished with strutting gobblers, facing away from the hunter. The upraised tails prevent them from seeing the hunter as he takes a look from a raised position to figure the range to the bird. This bobbing up and down is risky, but if the hunter keeps watch on the birds, and does it only when they are feeding or otherwise involved, he shouldn't be seen.

Probably the number one quality with which a hunter must be endowed if he is to stalk turkeys is patience. A tremendous amount of time is required in making a successful sneak. The worst thing a hunter can do is commit himself to the shot, and

once having done so, realize the bird is at the fringe of a solid killing pattern. Or even beyond it. This is less apt to happen to the hunter who only hunts spring gobblers of the same subspecies throughout the same type of terrain. Hunters who travel both spring and fall and hunt all ages and sizes of wild turkeys are the ones who must guard against making bad range judgments. Estimating distance is easy in open hardwoods, more so if there is a slight roll to the topography. Tree trunks can be used as range guides when a bird comes into view. A hunter often does this without realizing it.

Shooting from a prone position automatically eliminates the bulk of out-of-range shots. The average terrain permits a turkey, including the biggest, long-legged gobbler, to come in rather close to the hunter if there is a reasonable amount of cover. In addition, a hunter can very easily rise up and down by bending his elbows. This gives him the added advantage of keeping a bird in view as it draws closer, and it can be done so slowly from an extremely low vantage point that it's rare for a turkey to notice the hunter until the bird is well within killing distance.

Stalking takes time. Your heart will pound as you draw nearer. But, what makes it so exciting is that all the while you are easing closer, you don't know what the birds may be doing. You could end the stalk looking at bare woods. So, it's wise to maintain contact with them as you make your sneak. In doing so, you will always run the risk of being seen. This can, however, be minimized, and a good percentage of the time, virtually eliminated. Choose the shadows when you want to elevate yourself to study the birds, but keep within a part of the terrain above ground features. Crawl right into clumps of grass, weeds, bushes, tiny saplings, vines, until you are so close to the cover that the stuff brushes your face. You must become a part of it. Don't raise up over a bare log, or peak over a rock; locate a bush, dead limbs, a tiny clump of grass, and take a look through these.

155

Once I realize a bird has zeroed in on where I am hiding, I make like a rock, and remain that way even after the bird has gone back to its activities. Invariably, a wary bird will look toward any suspicious area again, perhaps several times, its head held high. Camouflage is a tremendous asset to a turkey hunter, especially when stalking and still-hunting. Facial camo is especially important. The face is the body part most likely to be seen, with its bright and shiny appearance.

When you are this close to the turkeys, the last bit of raising your head up to see the birds is the delicate part. Do this *slowly*. Once you can see them, *freeze*. If the birds seem content, you can study them and plan for your next move. If *they are heads up, one eye toward you, don't move until they relax.* You may need to stay in this position for quite a while, and you may even develop all sorts of cramps and aches. But the slightest stir could end the hunt with the birds spooking for the next county.

Stalking wild turkeys is a heart-pounding experience, not easily accomplished by all, certainly not successfully. For the hunter who has never attempted it, I can only say that until you stalk, you have never really hunted wild turkeys. Nothing teaches woodsmanship in larger doses. The hunter who studies turkey country and tries to work himself into gunshot range will begin to understand the what, why, and wherefore of these birds. The person who has never stalked them will never truly appreciate the turkey's fantastic eyesight, nor will he realize how well these birds hear, and interpret what they hear.

To me, a long stalk has more heart-pounding excitement than calling in the bird. I've also made stalks that were nothing more than a walk. One spring morning I eyed a passel of hens, escorted by two fine, old longbeards. Since the season allowed three gobblers, all of which could be taken on a single day, I wanted to bag both birds. There wasn't truly any stalk; the birds were near an old, abandoned house. I eased around until the house was between me and the turkeys, then walked very fast until alongside it, finally sneaking over to a corner and very gingerly peeking around. In full strut, both birds were inside twenty yards. Luckily, the hens were pecking at the ground. Not a bird

Planning a successful ambush requires knowing where turkeys are during the course of the drove's daily wandering. Still-hunting and stalking also are much more successful if you have a good idea where local birds are feeding, watering and nooning, which is a loafing period usually during the middle of the day. Slipping into easy gunshot is then accomplished by periods of watching the birds, then making your move when things are to your advantage.

saw me. I eased back, checked the nipples on the old smokemaker, then stepped out, gun up. One old bird went down at the first blast; the second was no trouble to nail on the flush, making sure I wouldn't also kill any hens. The worst part of the whole thing was lugging both back to the truck. I like those kinds of "worst parts."

S talking wild turkeys is a heart-pounding experience, not easily accomplished by all...until you stalk, you have never really hunted wild turkeys.

Few stalks are so easy. I have put in hours on a sneak in open woods, only to not get a shot. One morning in the Deep South my stalk lasted three hours as I bade my time, moving only when I knew it was safe, holding steady as a rock when the birds were head up. No, I didn't shoot one. The season didn't open until the next morning. And no, I didn't find them opening day. In fact, never saw those birds again.

Florida is excellent stalking country. I've killed a number of gobblers by stalking oak hummocks, cypress strands, and creek swamps. One morning, I spotted three gobblers out on a palmetto burn. From the creek swamp I was hunting, the terrain didn't look to be stalkable. But I eased nearer, then decided if I didn't mind getting black from the burnt vegetation, maybe, just *maybe*, I could get close. So I began bellying.

Those birds were feeding so intently on tiny seeds that I gradually made my way out toward them. I was black when I slid the gun out front, scragging the best of the threesome, but I doubt if I ever enjoyed a bellycrawl so much as that one on wide-open prairie.

You don't need full camouflage to pull off such stalks. Few hunters realize how much cover there is down near ground level, or how much roll and undulation there is on average terrain. I learned this as a farm boy in Oklahoma, flat-country duck hunting and sneaking up on a flock of geese. Stalking has become a lost art, but full camouflage is bringing it back. Few of these camoued hunters could make a successful stalk without the stuff.

This hunter posed for the camera purposely in a bad location. What's wrong? Well, the hunter's large outline will be instantly detected by any approaching turkey, even though he is in full camouflage. Anyone hunting areas of small pole-thin trees will do well to pile up brush to help screen the hunter's form, build a complete blind or, as the author has often done, dig a small, shallow, narrow coffin blind from which to lay in hiding.

Very little wild game has all the well-developed senses of a wild turkey. A whole bunch of them, a drove, makes things all the worse for a hunter new to turkey chasing. Few beginners truly have any idea just how well a wild turkey can see and hear.

The only thing a wary, old turkey will see of this hunter is the end of his gun barrel, if the bird lives that long.

Ambushing

Have you ever ambushed a turkey? By this I mean, have you ever hidden someplace *hoping* a turkey would come by, and then waited there for the bird? An ambush can be the result of a failed stalk, the hunter realizing he can't get within killing distance, so waits in ambush for the bird come to him. But the average ambush is a result of a hunter's scheming. This is particularly true if the hunter notices a lot of turkey sign at a location, causing him to think turkeys come there on a daily basis. This is when it pays to know the habits of wild turkeys, as ambushes are best located where the birds travel, feed and drink. I don't go along with ambushes laid at favored roosting places.

An ambush can be planned for whenever and wherever a hunter wishes, spring or fall. The person who desires to wait in ambush should study wild turkeys intensely—study turkey terrain, read all available game department reports, particularly those reporting what wild turkeys are feeding upon in the area being hunted. But there is no finer method than to spend days in turkey country prior to opening day, especially if it can be done shortly before the season opens. Notice where the birds have been leaving tracks. Can you locate feeding areas? How many foods can you locate? What age of birds made the tracks? Could you be standing in the roost area?

Laying a proper ambush is not for the average turkey hunting buff. Why? To begin with, today's lifestyle has led mankind into living a fast life! We aren't geared to spending several hours idly sitting in the woods, waiting and watching for turkeys we know are there. We'll have the fidgets in an hour. Two hours are an eternity.

The hunter who thoroughly studies the birds, reads all he can about them from egg to adulthood, and spends what time

Sitting an ambush along an old forest trail is often productive, particularly in fall and winter hunts. The droves are more likely to walk the roads than in springtime. Much food is found along woods roads by droves of fall birds, berries fall into the road, as do acorns and other mast. In many areas, a forest road will have grass growing along its borders, where the birds find insects and grass seeds. Still-hunting is an excellent method for hunting old roads and trails. Take your time as you stroll along. You'll have an easier hunt, and in time you'll probably walk smack into a bunch.

There are hunting methods which simply aren't made for nailing turkeys. Hunting from a treestand is one of them. True, you may have a drove pass under the tree you're in, but just as often you'll be seen from a distance, and the birds will skedaddle. Full camouflage is a must if you want to hunt a treestand, and you'd best be very still. Keep that gun down; don't wave it like a flag.

he can with them in the woods, can set up a successful ambush. A hunter doing this won't come out of the woods so frazzled.

An ambush ordinarily has the hunter sitting, but like a bowhunter in a treestand, the hunter may be standing. Today's ambush can be made in the open, without any blind or vision screening aids; full camouflage makes this all possible. However, a blind makes the waiting game much more comfortable. And, since wild turkeys are very tree oriented, the last place I'd recommend for an ambush would be from a treestand. I've had the birds walk right under me while in a tree, but I've also had them eyeball me and then light out as though their tails were afire.

Locating an ambush can be exceedingly easy if you are good at finding sign and are adept at interpreting the sign. You're wasting time locating where the birds pass perhaps but once a month—unless you have a month to sit, and God knows, the stamina to carry that through. Just last spring I sat a bushwack for two full days, over a hog wallow, hoping to kill

an old, black boar in that area. Two days is an eternity if nothing's moving. All of the local pig population had gone on the graveyard shift. I never fired a shot. Only two weeks earlier I had made several turkey ambushes, seeing hogs every day. Killed a fine porker, too. Killed gobblers, too. But, what I'm getting at is that waiting in ambush takes a very, very, *very great amount of patience*. If you get the fidgets, then ambushing's not your baby.

Ambushes are best located where the birds travel, feed and drink.

Far the best place for an ambush is where turkeys are feeding. ***Do not ambush turkeys at, or near, a roost. And, if water is very scarce, don't ambush where the birds are watering***. I've killed birds near water, but in each case I knew there were other local watering places. Shooting birds near roosts or water can and does drive them from an area, sometimes for

Camouflage is a must for the average turkey hunter. These two would fade into the shadows if they had their face masks in place. Camos are a must for still-hunting, stalking, ambushing and calling from a stand.

Stalking, still-hunting and ambushing—and a turkey call? You bet. Many times the author was located a drove of birds, or just one or two, with a call. However, they wouldn't come near. So, the only thing left was to go to them. Locating a drove is often the difficult part—stalking is sometimes the easy end of the hunt.

good. Only recently, on a ranch adjoining my Rio Grande lease in west Oklahoma, hunters waited, then blasted birds coming to a place where the birds had been roosting forever. *No longer are the birds there*. Now I have to stand guard that these idiots don't sneak onto my place. Shooting turkeys at a roost or over the only water available is simply cutting off your own turkey hunting.

Paths going to and from feeding areas are good, too. I prefer this over ambushing a favorite feeding location. Shooting birds at a feeding area can drive them over onto another range, perhaps beyond hunting limits. Spring gobblers are often alone, so hunting them where the hens are feeding isn't as critical as when shooting a fall drove. Kill the one bird, and you'll probably move elsewhere anyhow. Last spring in an area where the birds had completely ceased gobbling, I set an ambush at dawn, waiting along a path which appeared to connect the roosting area with a favored meadow. I was very surprised when not one but three old gobblers came along—not so surprised it kept me from culling out the best one. A year earlier in that same area the birds were using a path probably two hundred yards further south, one on which I'd killed a gobbler.

Once you've found an area where you think the chances are good for birds to eventually walk past, you have to decide where to locate. You'll need to consider several things; the various angles the birds may come from; the subspecies you're dealing with; how long you can sit there; what time of day, or how much of the day, you can take the stand; and the sun, since you want to be in the shadows as much as possible. Unless they have been hunted hard, young fall turkeys will walk into a feeding area, or on a path to one, with much less wariness than will an old gobbler, or a gang of old gobblers. Whoever thought up the term "spooky" must've been hunting old gobblers when he thought it up. I prefer building some kind of blind, or "hide." Invariably, I'll build it with old birds in mind, knowing full well that if an older turkey, hen or gob-

bler will not notice it, then any younger birds will definitely pay such a blind no mind whatsoever.

Last spring hunting an area where several hunters had been hunting, I found a couple blinds. In talking to the hunter overseeing the place I learned that no turkeys had been killed in those areas. *No wonder*. Not only were the blinds placed incorrectly on turkey routes, but obviously those hunters were sitting in sunlight much of the time. A wild turkey's terrific eyesight will detect any slight movement in open sunlight, a movement the same bird might never see if made in deep shade. I'll work three times as hard to have a blind in full shade as opposed to one in sunlight.

How long a hunter remains in an ambush is definitely tied to how comfortable he is. Anyone who's sat on the ground for hours has an inkling of just how quick that same ground begins to feel *awful*. Roots, sticks, rocks, all sorts of things soon get to poking you in the butt. With no arm rests, your arms begin to feel like a couple of somethings you haven't any place for. You itch; your back hurts.

There's only one answer; build a good blind, even if it takes a bit longer. Then you can move more with less chance of being seen. I carry a couple of things in my hunting vest if I'm in an area where I think I may want to build a hide, these being a folding saw and a good pair of shrub clippers, you know, the kind you prune bushes with at home in the garden. I wouldn't be without these, and, if these won't do, I also keep a small

Oscar Boyd with a bird killed through a knothole. Only three of us belong to the Knothole Gang. Initiation involves shooting turkeys through a small knothole in a shed located where a rancher was feeding cattle. One spring, all the birds in that area hung out around that shed. Though the birds weren't visible in front of it, they certainly were through that single knothole. A bushwack deluxe.

bow saw in the pickup. Many days I've spent a couple hours building an excellent blind, one that fades so well into the surroundings even the wariest of old hard-hunted gobblers have walked right up to it without hesitation. Several times I tried to fool an old hermit gobbler on some of those up-and-down hills you find in Mississippi, and that old bird would undoubtedly still be gobbling if I hadn't built a leaf pile blind where he hung out. Calling only kept him away. The old dickens never had an inkling I was holed up in that pile of pine needles and dead oak leaves. At twenty yards, he went out like a light.

Still-Hunting

What is still-hunting? It is simply what the word says: hunting quietly throughout terrain where the game being sought is known to live. Still-hunting is a hunting method applied to virtually all wild game. A grouse hunter in New York State walks silently toward an abandoned apple orchard, among the hemlocks, and as easily as possible among the thornapples, hoping to jump the feathered rockets at close range. This increases his chances of getting an open shot before the bird can put cover between it and the hunter. Deer, elk, prairie chickens, even cottontail rabbits—all are far easier to approach by the silent hunter than by one making noise.

Thus, a still-hunting turkey hunter is one who quietly hunts through cover known to be good habitat, trying to place himself in shotgun range through the use of his eyes, his ears, his

Shooting from a blind has many advantages. First, the hunter can be comfortable, if the blind is weatherproof and sight proof. By this, I mean the turkey cannot see into the blind, therefore the hunter can move about, drink a Coke, read a book, whatever. The disadvantage comes when turkeys get close to a blind and the hunter can't get a shot. If the blind's built well, there will be one solid side so the hunter's silhouette won't be visible.

knowledge of the bird's habits, and his ability to read the woods. To be successful at least some of the time, the hunter must be able to interpret what he sees and hears, and then make a decision on what actions are to be taken. Very often this decision must be made in a split second. Truly, the finest still-hunters are those who adore the great outdoors. People who like "being out," who like listening to a tiny spring brook as it trickles from rock to rock, or gazing at the black leaves lying dead in a stagnant pool. The hunter who trods along, not finding anything to give him pause as he passes through the woods, will not make a good still-hunter.

A wild turkey's terrific eyesight will detect any slight movement in open sunlight.

Together with this, the still-hunter/stalker will need physical stamina. Walking, leaning against trees, sitting, bending will take its toll on the still-hunter who is not physically tough. Much still-hunting requires little but walking. If the hunter has studied local turkey flocks, he will be able to place himself where these birds are known to spend the bulk of their time, increasing his chances of making contact quickly. But, still-hunting a strange area requires covering a lot of ground by foot, seeking out sign of turkey habitations, and locating the birds themselves. I've eyeballed turkeys from behind soap yuccas, dense strands of bluestem grasses, sawgrass, palmetto fronds, blackberry bushes, and a jillion other natural features found throughout this country's turkey habitat.

There is no substitute for a "game eye." A game eye can only be achieved through countless sightings of the intended quarry, at varying distances, in good light and bad, and throughout the physical makeup of the terrain. Wild turkeys will not let the hunter walk to within several yards before hightailing it, so the turkey hunter should sometimes look for the whole bird at longer distances. At other times, he may hope to glimpse a slight movement. All such sightings depend greatly on a simple little thing like whether the turkey is facing the hunter, or facing the opposite direction. A bird facing the hunter will appear black at a distance, regardless of sex, and will therefore be readily discernible. But, with the bird facing the hunter, the chances the hunter will be seen increases.

Hunkered-down birds have a built-in defense which goes into action. This is eye contact with the predator. Numerous times I have spotted wild turkeys "frozen" on the ground, squatted flat on their bellies, heads usually drawn in on their shoulders at the wing butts, feet tucked underneath so they can catapult skyward. In every instance, the split-second our eyes meet, the bird flushes. No waiting, no twisting about to get a good jump, just immediate booming from cover. I've killed a number of turkeys flushed in this manner.

A turkey's eye seems to detect movement at greater distances than does man's. The bird has a wide field of vision and understands what it sees faster than do humans. When alert to a danger, it will turn its head so that only one eye is focused upon the subject, at which time it will take a real hard look.

Understanding the turkey's eyesight is a part of still-hunting, as only then can the hunter realize how best to hunt. I've made it a habit to continually scan the woods as far as I can see, intent on dark objects at ground level, along with movement. Cloudy days are preferable over bright, sunshiny days where there is a vivid contrast between open areas and deep shade. Turkeys have an inclination to remain in the shade, making them less discernible. When walking over hilltops, or from behind any topographical structure, be it rock piles, bulldozed mounds of earth, or solid brush-screening thickets, I do so slowly, letting my eyes work back and forth as the terrain before and around me flows into view.

Turkeys have excellent hearing, plus an ability to pinpoint a sound to within feet of its origin.

A turkey facing away from the hunter presents its "camouflaged" side, making it difficult to see. All of a wild turkey's back, lower rump, and tail feathering is patterned in nature's colors, so that when the bird is hunkered belly-to-the-ground, it becomes all but invisible. The camouflage coloring is present at a very early age in the bird's life, enabling it to hunker frozen, and hopefully escape the keen eyes of predators. Man will walk within feet, and not see the bird.

The still-hunter should make the terrain work for him, which means wisely utilizing terrain cover and features. It's far better when working your way along a ridge to keep slightly beneath the highest elevation since you will be easily seen on the summit. In easing up for a looksee into the next cove, slip up behind a bush, using its screening branches to hide your face. Camouflage is a must for the still-hunting turkey addict, but even then he will need the added cover of trees,

bushes, rocks or any other ground cover found within turkey country.

Long ago I made it a habit to use shadows to my advantage. When I ease over a knoll, drop from the side of a ridge across to the other, or stroll along an abandoned trail, I stick to any available shadows to mask my movements. Additionally, a hunter's camouflage fades into the darkness of shadows.

Many hunters will have an urge to eyeball terrain that is well out of gunshot range, overlooking the terrain that is within shotgun range. Make a concentrated effort to only hunt terrain that is within easy killing distance, but at the same time scan the woods further out as it comes in sight. Once a hunter has done this, he will be aware of areas that can be approached in this manner. This is stunningly evident when hunting old logging roads. These will be grown up along the edges with tall weeds, small seedling pines, and myriad quick growth plants. This waist-high cover screens a hunter approaching bends in the trail, enabling him to walk around short curves which could place him within gun range of a turkey walking the road. This tactic can be further enhanced by always walking on the inside of these bends, moving to the opposite side of the trail if the bend goes toward that side. Ordinarily, walking on such

Small boys are all alike; all of 'em get the fidgets. W.C. Boyd, the author's nephew, nailed this old gobbler from a blind.

trails will be very quiet. On this type of still-hunt it pays to walk fast, particularly at the moment when the trail ahead is flowing into view and it is within gunshot. If the hunt is during the early fall season, when ground and woods cover is still leafy, chances can be quite good for a hunter to walk into killing distance of a drove, whether it is on the trail or off of it in nearby woods. There are hundreds and thousands of acres in Eastern wild turkey range made to order for this technique. I've killed a great many Eastern gobblers while still-hunting in this manner, both on fall and spring hunts. After heavy rains, throughout light rains, during periods of fog, at any and all hours of the day, turkeys walk trails and old, abandoned roads.

Turkeys have excellent hearing, plus an ability to pinpoint a sound to within feet of its origin. The hunter still-hunting among open forest will be heard well before he walks into sight of the great bulk of turkeys. Wild turkeys have favored routes throughout their range and a good percentage of these will be among leaf bearing trees. Invariably, the ground beneath these trees will be solidly carpeted with leaves, most often dry and brittle. It's a waste of time and energy to even attempt to still-hunt such terrain. The hunter crossing such areas will cause less suspicion among any listening wild creatures if he walks slowly, stops often, and tries to act like

another ambling turkey or a deer. A wild turkey hearing the slow, steady creeping step made by a sneaking hunter will immediately think the sounds are made by a predator. When I must cross dead leaves, I amble along a ways, perhaps pick up a length of dead limb, and scratch the leaves with it as I move through the woods. I make every effort to work my way to less noisy ground when at all possible. But, as long as I'm on the leaves, I try to sound like a gobbler feeding. Hunters who have heard solitary gobblers feeding and scratching will agree that these old birds sound identical to a lone human's movements.

I walk the edges of cultivated fields that border uncultivated areas. Such edges will have weedy cover which, in addition to offering weed seeds as food, will attract insects and bugs. Recently cultivated soils are sometimes used by turkeys in their daily dusting ritual, presumably as a deterrent against mites. The birds will wallow out dish-shaped depressions, and lying in these on their sides, will pull the powdery soil up into the feathers with their wings. A still-hunter working edges will soon know if turkeys have been there as he will find feathers, droppings, and perhaps an abundance of tracks. Young turkeys will lose scads of small feathers throughout the fall, which can indicate an area being used by a drove almost daily. Many times I have located in an area where I found large quantities

Greg Miketa, a veteran turkey shooter hailing from Pueblo, Colorado, long ago learned the value of a good pair of binoculars. Greg and his brother Gary guide for bighorns, too. Surely there aren't any two species of wild game with better vision that a wild gobbler and bighorn ram. So if the hunter wants to be successful on these, he's got to take a cue from the Miketas. Get a good pair of glasses and use them.

Plains country turkey hunting takes a little getting used to. Many hunters are intimidated by the openness, thinking it all but impossible to move about without being seen. To some extent, this can be true. But, like the mountains, like the creek swamp, like hunting in cabbage palmetto, each requires a different hunting approach.

of newly dropped feathers and have invariably bagged turkeys. Such ambushes can take a few hours, or days.

The still-hunter must be quiet for another reason though, and this is so he can hear any sounds nearby turkeys may be making. This could be far off yelping and keeing made by early morning droves when leaving the roost trees and assembling; or later in the day, he may hear the calling of lost birds and/or birds that are answering them. It is possible for a springtime still-hunter to hear a gobbler cut loose any time of the day.

There will be times that the hunter will hear the clear, unmistakable "putt" or "pertt" of spooked turkeys, birds which have seen the hunter and are alarmed. Young, unhunted turkeys may not instantly take flight, though they will walk away at a fast pace. Others will invariably run or fly. The hunter should make an effort to identify the birds by sex and age, as these facts could be valuable to him as he continues the hunt, probably by calling.

During fall and winter hunts, I make a run toward spooked birds, going all out in getting them separated from each other. In doing so, it's often possible to learn if the birds are a small drove of old gobblers, or if the drove is a hen or two with their young. Too, I'll know how they scattered; all these facts will help determine what calling methods should be settled on, and where to call from.

During the spring season when I hear a deep "putt" while still-hunting, I'll usually be able to identify it as a gobbler. If he is alone and has an inclination to run off through the woods, I'll let him go. Chances are I might be able to cut a half-mile circle around him and call him to me. But, if he has hens and I can hear them sounding the alarm, I'll make a run into the birds, spooking them badly. This results in a wild flush and hopefully in the hens being separated from the gobbler.

Chances are that if I can get between him and any hens I will hear calling over the next hour, I will be able to call him to me instead. So, the still-hunter should train himself to gain all the knowledge he can at every turn, which will allow him to use all the wrinkles in the book, so to speak.

Of course, the hunter hopes to spot the birds before they spot him, and when this happens, there are a number of alternatives. Number one is to ease to the ground, as this is where a person will be most comfortable and far less apt to be seen when the turkeys raise their heads. When I see turkeys that appear undisturbed and apparently have not detected my presence, I drop to the ground quickly, but do not take my eyes

Dick Bland, the author's brother, sits on a calling stand, the chill breeze blowing across patches of old snow, hoping a bunch of turkeys will amble into sight. Most bushwackers use a call from time to time, hoping birds will talk back.

Logan Clarke, a seafood exporter from Maine, with a grand, old gobbler bagged on his first turkey hunt. Logan has the one must ingredient for becoming good at hunting turkeys—lots of patience. My advice to those with little patience is for them to take up race car driving or ice hockey. Turkey hunting's not for folks who can't sit still.

from them in doing this. Thus, as they leave my view, I know whether they were pecking at the ground, strutting, or whatever. Or, perhaps one of them spies me just as I sink from sight, and all heads jerk erect. It makes a considerable amount of difference what is done next if the birds are alerted.

If, as I fall to earth, the birds have not seen me, I can ease behind cover, raise myself behind screening foliage, and study them to decide what action to take. In flat country, a hunter lying on open ground will learn that few turkeys will see him beyond fifty yards.

If the birds are not wary, a hunter can take his time in choosing what to do. Can they be stalked through bellycrawling? Are they coming toward the hunter? Will the turkeys walk behind a solid screen which would allow the hunter to ease within shooting distance? Would it be advisable to call to them? These are but a few of the questions which can and do arise in such circumstances.

Let's presume the birds had spotted me, but only enough to realize there was a movement they didn't have time to understand. Once I had fallen to cover, I would then want to be extremely cautious in taking a looksee to study the situation. I can't stress how important it is at this time to use terrain to your best advantage while looking over these wary birds. Of course, full camouflage will be of tremendous benefit, but even then the hunter should try to come up behind a screen of brush, grass, a low, leafy bush, anything which will break his outline and prevent the birds from noticing his moves. Such moves must be made very, very slowly. Once you can see the birds, stay put. Don't move, because after they decide that there is no apparent danger, they'll go back to whatever they had been doing. Then the hunter can analyze the situation, make a decision on how or what is to be done, and attempt to carry it through.

The still-hunter must be quiet for another reason though, and this is so he can hear any sounds nearby turkeys may be making.

There are times when slightly spooked turkeys will linger a short time, remain alert and wary, and then decide to leave. They will simply begin walking away, usually at a brisk walk, strung out in a unit. Such birds won't stop just over the next rise. The hunter must make up his mind as to the next course of action, and quickly, or he can let them walk away. If the birds are within a hundred yards or so and the terrain is fairly level, it's best to run toward them, making a scatter. If the birds are in an area which will cause them to pass from view quickly, there are times when the hunter should wait until they are out of sight, and then run to where he hopes to either intercept them, or bring himself within gunshot.

There is another factor which comes into play. All human hunters are ground oriented. We seldom look up. If you don't believe me, ask yourself how many times a bowhunter has called out, but you couldn't locate him—*until you looked up*.

Here's a clue to make any turkey hunter's heart beat just a bit faster if he hasn't seen or heard any birds. Often soil conditions will not allow for much ground sign. Many times I've been out for a period of a couple days, not once finding droppings, or tracks, then eyeballed a fresh feather caught in a weed or lying on a bed of oak leaves.

And, those were the ones who called out. How many others remained silent, while you walked on by?

In never looking up, we're never prepared for the wild turkey which flushes from overhead. Many springtime gobblers roost above old tote roads, logging roads, even little-traveled blacktops. Also, spooked gobblers often flop into trees above such trails, standing on a branch until they're satisfied danger no longer exists. The point is, a still-hunting turkey hunter is very apt to walk smack under one of these birds, which will invariably catch him completely unprepared at its thundering flush. It pays to look up into the trees while still-hunting, more so if it is during the early morning hours, or if it is raining, or if the hunter suspects that other hunters have scattered a drove in the past hour. Stray dogs barking can be an indication of turkeys having been spooked into the trees.

If the hunter has reason to believe the area contains wild turkeys, he will need physical proof. Walking will answer the question one way or another. Interpreting sign, then, is the key, and this can open up a whole new can of worms. Finding a lot of droppings, feathers, and tracks ordinarily indicates a good population of turkeys, but this also can be misleading. The most important factor in utilizing sign to determine local drove size is to always keep in mind the subspecies of bird being dealt with, plus local feeding conditions, and how much acreage may be found in uninterrupted tracts.

A hunter from West Virginia, spring hunting the Merriam wild turkey for the first time in Arizona, would think he had found a bonanza should he stumble onto a tiny mountain brook where a drove had spent the winter months. Snow on surrounding mountains had perhaps driven them to this area, where the winter afternoon sun melted the snow along the mountain stream, revealing green meadow grasses, and innu-

Regardless of what a person hunts with, if he can't hit anything with it he'd better stay home. I have known men who spent days endeavoring to get a shot at a wild turkey, and when the chance came, they weren't ready. A good friend once lay in ambush from first daylight until smack at sundown when along came a small gang of old longbeards. Nope, neither barrel on his muzzleloader would shoot!

merable spring seeps. Nearby, Gambel's oak thickets provided scratching for acorns, and a towering ponderosa gave the birds a safe roost branch for the night. But, the snows had ceased and gave way before the spring sun's intense rays, and the dry air had preserved the droppings. The birds had drifted to other haunts at higher elevations. Yet a person walking along that trickling water would say to himself, "Hey, man, look at all the sign. Those droppings look like they were made yesterday." Add this to the tracks he had spied in the dust on the logging road, and together it spelled turkeys all around. Of course, as it hadn't rained since the last snow, he couldn't know those tracks were three weeks old. A lack of wind and very little traffic can cause few changes. But, the knowing still-hunter, the person who has studied the Merriam before traveling 1,000 miles to hunt it, is aware that these birds migrate up to forty miles due to weather and feeding conditions. Living in country of varying elevations such as New Mexico, Arizona, and Colorado, where weather varies with altitude, Merriams must travel up and down with the snow line during the winter, as deep snows will prevent them from feeding.

Farther south, the Gould's wild turkey found back in Mexico's Sierra Madre Range doesn't need to migrate so widely, though it, too, is a high mountain bird. Why? Mainly due to a lack of snow. An abundance of water is the only limiting factor in Gould's range, and this is brought about by lack of rainfall. Nor do Rio Grandes, Osceolas, and the bulk of Eastern wild turkeys wander great distances, in comparison to the Merriam.

A Colorado hunter journeying to West Virginia in November would be hard pressed to find any sign at all. The Eastern wild turkey wanders daily across a large portion of its range, and seemingly leaves little to note its passing. Leaf fall continues to cover droppings as winter progresses. The terrain, with scant patches of bare ground, doesn't make for sighting of tracks. Add to this a greater abundance of annual rainfall, along with tremendous increased hunting pressures, and the Coloradan will come from the woods with the idea that there weren't many turkeys there.

Let's go to Florida, a large cattle ranch in Saint Lucie county, not far northeast of Lake Okeechobee. Or to a spread in west Texas where the ranch buckaroos drive the whitefaces to gathering pens and chase Rio Grande gobblers from the hurricane deck of the same pony. Turkeys in both locals are apt to be hanging together in large droves, perhaps thirty to one hundred to a bunch. The country thereabouts will be solid with tracks, feathers, droppings, and be little different from what one would expect to find at a turkey farm. In fact, the signs can oftimes be so thick that it becomes confusing, lulling the hunter into thinking he can kill a turkey with his eyes shut. But, fire a shot or two and it's a whole new ball game. Turkeys can see a hunter a mile distant and he'll have to still-hunt with greater respect.

Local turkey hunters are wont to steer strangers to any place but where the birds can be found. I know, I've done it.

In addition to using sign to determine turkey populations, the hunter can rely on local hunter numbers. The fewer hunters, the fewer birds. Now, I am speaking here of *average* turkey country with its numerous backwoods roads, not of many areas in Rocky Mountain Merriam turkey range, as the human population there is considerably smaller than the great bulk of ranges for the other subspecies of wild birds. Like the turkeys themselves, hunter populations can be related to the number of birds found locally. Merriams are apt to be scattered across mountain ranges, whereas a mile square area in Virginia may have several native droves.

Throughout average Eastern wild turkey range, if I notice very few local hunters and realize I am not within what is considered the best place to hunt, round-about conversation can bring out much information from the locals. This alone should be given careful consideration, as turkey hunters are wont to steer strangers to any place but where the birds can be found. I know, I've done it.

The author's brother Dick stakes out a ragweed patch where birds have been coming each morning to feed. Plains country hunting offers unexcelled long-range observation of approaching droves. The hunter has to keep in mind that the turkeys can eye him from afar. Sitting still, and seated where the hunter blends into the surroundings, will solve that problem.

The author, looking across a valley in Sonora, Mexico. This picture will give the reader some idea of the immenseness of that country's mountain range, the Sierra Madres. The name means Mother of Mountains, and to those of us who hunt these hills from time to time, the name certainly fits. As far as the eye can see in all directions, nothing but mountains. And, there's not many Gould's turkeys in this range, certainly not a fraction of what the terrain once supported, back during a time when Juh, Victorio, Geronimo and Cochise called the place home.

Game rangers will pass out the whereabouts of droves, particularly in areas where poachers are operating. The last thing a poacher wants is company, especially if it is a stranger. And, while it seems best to hunt in the areas with the greatest number of birds, it should also be remembered that fringe areas, with fewer birds, can produce a better quality hunt. As long as I'm in country with even a fair population of turkeys, I will hunt it rather than go to one with more birds and an army of hunters.

Large, uninterrupted tracts of land, like that found within our national forests, often have small turkey populations, particularly when compared to the number of acres. What causes this has been the subject of much speculation among wild turkey biologists. Among the reasons are lack of law enforce-ment, local attitudes toward poaching, baiting and roost shooting, lack of water the year round, scarcity of preferred foods, and wild turkey lifestyles. I have hunted a region that has huge tracts of national forest, which seem to be ideal habitat. Throughout the spring hunt, there will be gobblers scattered from end to end, over hundreds of square miles of mixed pine and hardwood terrain. During the fall it is all but impossible to locate a drove in these same woods. Where have all the turkeys gone?

Throughout this area the summers are often hot and dry, causing the bulk of the small streams to dry up. The birds then move to the larger river bottoms. In these areas, many small farms with cow pastures, cultivated fields, and many woods-lined edges are found. The birds find this to their liking and

Steven Preston and Brian Gildehaus (the author's son-in-law), with a winter kill made by Brian at inside twenty yards. A snow two or three days old will tell the hunter where the birds are feeding each day and the trails they are using to those favored areas. It's then only a matter of taking up a wait along the trail. Don't forget to locate back in the dark, under a big tree where there's no snow, or against something that allows the dark camos to blend. Of course, if the hunter has snow camos, or white coveralls, this makes locating much easier.

A favorite "hide" of the author is this old cotton house. Turkeys dust in this clearing regularly each day. The author keeps the dust holes maintained by taking a stout stick and stirring up the dirt in the holes, loosening it so it'll stay dry. When he arrives, if the dust holes are filled with mast or hard clods, he'll scoop them out, make three or four more nearby, and pound the soil until it's got the consistency of dust. Hens love such stuff, and with hens come gobblers. Of course, he sits inside the house on a folding chair, where he can eat, drink and read with the door slightly propped open to shoot out of when the time comes.

can be seen daily by the locals. Local attitudes are "shoot today because you may not see one tomorrow." Baiting is common around the farms bordering the national forests. A game ranger thereabouts is simply butting his head against a stone wall in trying to enforce game laws. Only time, plus the education of young hunters, will overcome this. Meanwhile, the area is supporting only a portion of the number of turkeys that should be found there.

When the still-hunter is searching for sign, he must keep all these facts in mind. It will help if the fall and winter hunter has been to the area during the spring. If birds were gobbling there in springtime, it's a good bet they will be nearby during other seasons, except in certain Merriam and Rio Grande areas. But, the hunter must also keep in mind that when finding little sign, this doesn't necessarily mean there are no turkeys; nor does a great amount of sign mean wall-to-wall birds. The hunter should study the birds before beginning the hunt, read all he can about their habits, study game department literature about that area, and then give it his best in the woods.

Mental toughness? What about it? As with all phases of turkey hunting, still-hunting and stalking calls for a hunter to "hang tough" until it runs out of his ears. You will sometimes be told to "hang in there," or "stick with it." These all mean the same thing—to make up your mind to stick to it and accomplish the task at hand, with little regard for the obstacles. Mental toughness comes with being educated, insofar as turkey hunting is concerned, for the person who doesn't thoroughly study the wild turkey's habits and habitats will soon be demoralized once he goes into turkey country to hunt. The farther from identifiable habitat that a hunt is conducted, the tougher will be the mental strain. This is best pointed out by recalling all those days in April when the hunter never heard a bird gobble.

For me, there have been lots of such hunts. Throughout much of my early turkey hunting travels years ago, there was no one to tell me where the best areas were, so I had to ferret them out on my own. I would hunt an area and hear no gobbles, yet I would find sign indicating that there were birds in the area. Were the birds still there, or had they migrated to another segment of their range? Should I move my hunting location, or hang tough? No gobbles, no turkeys? Or were the birds just being silent? If so, why?

Any time I mention at near or close range, it should be understood that I'm discussing the shooting of a shotgun, which to me is within thirty yards. I'm known as a hardhead on close-range shooting, but it is wise to look at it in the following manner. If the hunter shoots at a wild turkey beyond thirty yards and only cripples the bird, his follow-up shot will be in the neighborhood of forty yards—too far to prevent the bird's escape. Many, many turkeys are fired on by today's hunters at distances up to, and beyond, fifty yards. Sadly, gun and shell manufacturers are responsible for much of this, as they continually besiege the hunter with ads making all sorts of claims about long-range killing guns and loads. I have come upon a number of crippled birds which I've finished off, saving a bird that another hunter crippled. And, I have found dead birds, recently crippled, which escaped the hunter, but then died. Don't cripple. Become a dyed-in-the-wool true turkey hunter, shoot them inside of thirty yards. Twenty-five yards is best.

Down through the years I've run, walked, crawled, bellied, elbowed, hunkered and all but dog-paddled my way to where it was a near-range shot at all six of the world's bearded and spurred wild turkeys. There've been times when I couldn't pull off a stalk or a sneak, whichever you want to call it. But, there have been lots of days when I could burn powder. And the turkeys felt what was in front of it.

12

If There's a Turkey, There's a Way

Ed Norwood surveys the terrain surrounding an old abandoned house deep in the Mississippi woods. Wild turkeys haunt such areas, in this case, roosting just a short distance away. You reckon perhaps a man just might take it easy on the front porch and maybe a big gobbler just might come strolling past!

I COULD SAY HERE that whenever so-and-so happens, you should do such-and-such. This all sounds good when read, but as we both know, each hunt is just as much an individual event as are all human beings different from other. Year after year, a hunter might kill an adult gobbler while sitting against the same tree, but you can bet the hunter would tell you none of those kills were even close to being identical. Planning stratagems to bring about a turkey's demise invariably begins after a turkey is either heard or seen. There could be a number of birds involved, too, and two or more hunters.

Wild turkeys have a habit of seeking high ground once they have been spooked. Fall or springtime, a single bird or a drove—turkeys simply hike for "high ground" when danger is near. The elevation could be nothing more than a long low hill in prairie country, a short spur ridge in Ozark mountains, a towering rock strewn crest in Mexico, or a long rolling summit in Pennsylvania. In low, flat, river-bottom areas, the birds often alight in trees. Knowing all these things, and keeping them in mind, will put birds in the oven.

Years ago, I made it a habit to ease over hills in turkey country like the moon coming up, very slowly. I always utilize cover, using trees, bushes, rocks, weed clumps, cactus, anything to break up my outline. When possible, I always use the shadows. I keep my gun barrels down; no use sticking them up like a periscope for a bird to see. As I gain height on the hill's crest, I scan the opposite hillside as it flows into view, taking great care to study shadowy areas beneath trees for birds feeding on acorns, other mast, berries, and the bugs and insects drawn to these foods.

As I rise behind the screening brush, I not only scan the opposite slopes, but also the other side of the one I am on. Turkeys could just as easily be below, perhaps within gun-

This passel of birds sneaked in behind the author on this stand. A turkey hunter needs a neck like an owl, to allow him to see in all directions.

shot. Remember, try to remain in any shadows, make no sudden moves, and make all movements as slow as ice melting. Certainly, this takes time, but if you can't get into easy killing distance, all the turkeys in the county won't do you any good. I've seen scads of spooked turkeys remain motionless for long periods of time, heads scarcely turning, as they eyeballed the landscape. Such birds are looking for the slightest movement, which is all they'll need to tell them to "git." Spooked wild turkeys are not easy to stalk, so it is best to surprise them and do it fast. Catch them in a fast rush, so to speak.

I've come to the conclusion from years of observation that the birds which gather on a high slope are waiting for those on watch on the hill's summit. The birds who tarry cause the birds in front to do likewise, and in the end, the drove comes together where the main group has assembled. Invariably, this will be just below a hill's topmost elevation. If the day is cold, the birds will most often gang up on the sunny side. Ordinarily, droves of recently spooked turkeys will hole up there for upwards of a half-hour, then they'll go back to wandering and feeding. The hunter who has the will and the stamina to charge over a hill, knowing birds just walked across it, will very often be rewarded.

I don't recommend this tactic unless you're hunting in an "any turkey" area. Fall turkeys, particularly during an early fall season, are not easily told apart, more so when flying full tilt in the opposite direction. Young gobblers and hens look the same under such conditions. Nor do I recommend wingshooting for the hunter who is not a good wingshot. Flushing turkeys are extremely fast, though to a veteran hunter who has lived a lifetime of shooting flying targets they are much akin to shooting at a flying barn.

A hunter should be a good wingshot. If he's not, then he owes it to himself to go to the trap and Skeet range, burn a small mountain of shotshells and get good at flying targets. True, Skeet and trap are not exactly what the hunter will be up against in the woods, but these sports teach the fundamentals of wingshooting—tracking targets, shouldering the gun, shooting from all sorts of angles and follow-through.

The strategy I have just described—observing turkeys, walking over a hill, and then rushing them—is like all turkey hunting strategies; it doesn't always work. If you have no gambling spirit, you probably won't try hill-busting turkeys. It's risky. But then all of turkey hunting has a tad of luck, risk or the spirit of gambling to it. Some folks just have a knack for culling out which.

Next to finding the real thing, there's nothing better'n picking up a fresh feather. Telling the age of a feather is easy. Just look at the quill, or the base, and the tiny hairs where the main feathering begins. If these show no sign of dirt or particles of clinging dust, threads of leaves, grass or weeds, and the fine hairs are separate, then you can bet the feather hasn't been long from the turkey's body.

Killing a big gobbler with a bow is a great accomplishment. Doing it freelance is more so, as the great bulk of bow kills are from a pre-built blind or stand, using decoys. Taking quick advantage of having located a gobbler, then knowing the right moves to make, brought this old bird into killing range.

Charging after turkeys can also work on a single bird or can be used in the spring on a group of hens with an adult gobbler. Adult gobblers among a group of hens are easily identifiable, even on the flush. Also, bunches of feeding hens with a strutting gobbler move rather slowly, so once they fade from sight, a fast trotting hunter should find them very near where he last saw them. The old bird usually brings up the rear, being behind the hens aways. I've popped over hills many times when all the hens would be feeding, the gobbler in full strut, and none of them would even be aware I was on the premises.

The hunter who walks, trots or runs over a hill in hopes of getting into gunshot of turkeys should make a habit of understanding the path a turkey will most likely follow. For instance, turkeys crossing from one ridge to another, given the choice of dropping down into a deep cut with its rocks, brush, etc., or walking around a long slope connecting the two hills, will always make the walk on the adjoining slope. Pressed hard, they would probably fly across the cut.

When you break over a ridge, hot on the trail of a drove of birds you assume are not within range, let your eyes dart back and forth as the landscape flows into view. You will have to pick your path and watch for the birds at the same time. If they

are beyond range, 30 to 35 yards, you will either have to put it in high gear, or shoot into the air, make a scatter, then call one back to you. You may want to do this anyhow if you want to kill only a gobbler.

You should be aware that given the proper circumstances, the presence of ample brush, grass and other low ground cover, the birds might not flush, but instead could run from you. And let me tell you, birds on the wing are far

> **L**et me tell you, birds on the wing are far easier to hit than birds dodging and ducking around in a bunch of brush.

easier to hit than birds dodging and ducking around in a bunch of brush. Many times, when young birds-of-the-year are flushed, they alight on a nearby tree, oftentimes on the topmost part or crown. The bird will then sit there, watching and waiting. Once satisfied all danger is gone, they will fly back to ground. A rule of thumb is that the older the bird, the longer it will stay there on its high perch. Adult

Crossing the trail of a bunch of turkeys after an overnight snow may seem like good fortune. Such luck, however, will need to be watered down with a great amount of patience, as the hunter must locate the birds before any hunting strategies can be made. And the hunter must avoid being seen while making these observations, as spooked turkeys on snow can be darned cagey when it comes time to get a shot at one.

This hunter chanced on a fine gobbler as it fed where a rancher had been feeding cattle. Turkeys just naturally gravitate to such areas toward mid-morning and again late in the afternoon, whether in the fall or the spring.

Many hunters think that a light snow is a great advantage to any kind of hunting. But too often the white stuff simply makes it easier for the turkey to see the approaching hunter. This is the time to back off, move slowly, use binoculars, and spot the turkey first. Then the hunter is holding the trump card.

Two fall hunters admire old birds bagged after a sighting proved the birds would move into a situation where the hunters could make a stalk. Splitting up, they came at the birds from different directions. Yes, one did make a kill at the end of the stalk—and drove the other bird into the path of the second hunter.

bang, down tumbles the turkey. Easy as shooting fish in a barrel, except you don't get water in your eyes.

When the leaves are still on the trees, the shot will invariably be when the bird flushes, and this high-tree crossing shot is perhaps the hardest to make in all turkey hunting. The bird can present any angle to the hunter as it leaves the tree—going away, to either side, or coming directly across the hunter. A big gobbler can flush fast, gain momentum even faster and, as he booms from a high pine, is a veritable hurricane on wings as he heads for the next county.

Turkeys alighting in trees located on steep hillsides, or inclined mountain slopes, can be hunted by the stealthy stalking hunter, so long as he keeps in mind that such birds, when flushed, will fly either along the side of the mountain or downhill. The exception is the bird that has settled in a tree on the terrain's crest; this bird might choose to fly over the hilltop.

A rule of thumb is that the older the bird, the longer it will stay there on its high perch.

Mountain gobbler hunters know this and, when a bird refuses to respond to calling, can hope for a shot if they approach the bird's tree from directly downhill. I would not advise shooting at such birds unless the hunter has made positive identification in terms of sex. Hens are oftentimes perched very near the gobbler, so the hunter must take extreme care in making correct identification. During fall hunts, in "any turkey" legal areas, this would not matter, except to those hunters who prefer not to shoot a hen.

Pushing or Driving Turkeys

There are a number of strategies two hunters can apply to both fall and spring turkeys. Probably the one most used is in pushing, or driving, a bird or birds past another hunter. This tactic works well with all subspecies, at any time of the year. As with all hunting methods employing two or more shooters, teamwork, plus unselfishness, is what hangs birds in camp. The game hog who wants to get in his shot first has no place in team killing of wild turkeys. His impatience will mess up the plan for everyone.

The old-fashioned Southern turkey drive is nothing but a group of beaters herding a bunch of birds toward a line of shooters. Very often the birds will be running and flying. This hunting method should only be utilized in an any turkey area because identification will be impossible when the shooting begins. The size of the drive depends on the turkey population and the number of shooters.

The average drive is conducted by two buddies who hunt together a lot. It will be an impromptu affair, brought about by the conditions at hand. It seems I've been involved in many of them from New England to Mexico, with any number of friends. All have been the result of seeing a group of turkeys in a position that one hunter could circle behind and push the birds into gunshot range of the other hunter. It must be

turkeys will stay there until they turn to stone. Leastways, you'll think so. If you like a little spice in your turkeyin', then the next time you flush a drove, keep your eyes peeled for a bird landing atop a tree crown.

Your next move, plus the speed of its execution, will determine whether you carry that bird back to camp. You'll need to be a good fast shot, willing to gamble on a daring chance, reasonably fast afoot and, regardless of how the episode ends, satisfied to go back to camp with a grin on your face, fully aware that you win some, lose some.

Before that bird gets itself settled on that branch, head for it on a run, marking your course so that when you get inside easy gunshot you will be just off to the side of the tree, where you can angle a shot into its uppermost part. If the leaves are off the tree, you should be able to keep the bird in view until you stop to make the shot. If the leaves are on, the risk is greater that you will lose sight of the bird and may not get off a shot when it flushes. The hunter's running toward the tree seems to freeze the bird; it possibly hopes that by remaining motionless it will not be seen. Also, the bird has probably not seen a man running before, and this action is new to his escape senses.

Most of my shots have been at the bird as it still sat quietly atop the tree. I simply run up into easy range, slam to a jolting halt, heave the gun to face lightning fast, get a quick bead, and

A single turkey feather, in this case a primary wing feather from a young Osceola gobbler, tells the author that a drove of these birds are in the area. It's only a matter of locating them. This may seem like an impossible task, but what better definition of the word hunting than to be searching for a small drove of wild birds in a Florida creek swamp?

Merriam country is big, often open, with scattered patches of trees and brush, usually excellent places where a turkey can see a hunter a mile off. Many times the hunter will never know a turkey has been in view. The best answer to this stuff is to carry, and use, a good set of binoculars. Once a bunch is located, the hunter can make a decision on how best to hunt them.

planned so there is no chance of either hunter being shot, which is unlikely if all parties follow the plan and identify the mark before shooting.

I've made so many one-man drives I've lost all count—some to just a single waiting hunter, others to three or four people and even upward of fifteen to twenty on a more or less firing line. Placed properly, a bunch of good shots can play havoc with a large drove of turkeys. Numerous times my party has killed from ten to twenty birds at one stand.

Driving wild turkeys to a stand of hunters can be hilarious, though, if they aren't used to seeing a big flight of oncoming birds. Some pretty fair shots can suddenly become lousy shooters. Not long ago I located a drove of birds in an old feed patch, this the morning after a winter storm. Ice and snow covered everything which made the birds easy to locate, smack out in the field far from cover. It was colder'n an outhouse in the Klondike, but the five of us laughed at all the slipping and sliding involved in getting ourselves into position near the field. I was guiding a group of four men, all usually darned good shots. Having stationed them at thirty-yard intervals to fit my plan, I then backed off, making a huge circle in some canyons so's I could push the birds over them.

Good cover, on an incline, had made it easy to get my party exactly where I wanted them. When I left them, I'd given them instructions to keep a sharp watch toward the direction of the drove, but for gosh sakes, not to let the birds know they were there or I'd never get the turkeys to fly in that direction. The snow had stopped, but a little breeze felt like it was right off the polar ice cap. Easing into position at an angle that seemed correct, I then began bellycrawling out toward the birds. The nearer I could get, the better the flush. Too often if you can't get near enough, they'll run.

Placed properly, a bunch of good shots can play havoc with a large drove of turkeys.

Everything went hunky dory. I bellied almost into gunshot, though I had no gun. When I jumped to my feet, those turkeys left there like rats leaving a sinking ship. Fanned out across a hundred-yard front, the whole passel lit out straight for the picket line I'd set. I stood there in the ice and the cold, a ringside seat to the very soon-to-be broad-

We old boys who guide sometimes have our work cut out for us—like taking, of all people, the president and vice-president of DBI Books, Inc., Chuck Hartigan and Pam Johnson, into the wooley wilds after gobblers. Anyhow, who has more fun? Chuck's mad 'cause Pam's gobbler weighs more than his bearded hen. Pam's upset 'cause the beard on Chuck's hen is longer'n the beard on the gobbler she's holding. I'm mad 'cause nobody let me shoot. Oh well, there's always next year!

side which I knew was coming. My hunters had a total of seventeen shells in the four guns. All were 12-gauges, most of them 3-inch jobs.

The cannonade began and was over almost as quick. I needn't have had any concerns about the bag limit, which was one turkey, either sex. Seventeen cartridges later, *one lone unfortunate* turkey, a smallish hen, cartwheeled into a canyon behind the blasting. I couldn't help but laugh crossing the snow-covered feed patch. And when I got to them, I never heard a single excuse. Of course, there weren't any. Just damned poor shooting. But, perhaps they had too much time to see the birds coming. After all, a big bunch of oncoming turkeys will get your heart to stirring.

Another method that works extremely well in hill country, or with mountain turkeys, requires two hunters. The next time you and a buddy encounter a springtime gobbler that keeps gobbling to the call, and yet won't come to it, try this on him. Once you have made voice contact and the bird is answering your calls regularly, you can assume one of two things quickly: Either the bird has hens with him or he simply wants the hen (you) to come to him. Now, one of you must stay put and call while the other must circle the gobbler, coming in toward him from behind, preferably from higher ground. This can be

nothing more than a foot or two in elevation. If the bird is on a hill, make an effort to work yourself into position, at or above his elevation. Sneak in as close as possible. Bellycrawl, get down on your hands and knees, whatever it takes to bring yourself to within sixty yards. Do not call until you are as near him as possible.

Certain that you are close, you can now make a few hen yelps. This trick has worked each time I've used it, often after one short series of calls. I've called in strutting single gobblers and gobblers accompanied by hens. Invariably, the birds will come to me a minute or two after the call is made. The ideal situation is when you have cranked up a gobbling turkey located above you on a hillside, or along a slope or crest of a mountain. Many of these birds, though located originally on the hill's crest, will work their way slightly off the summit when you call, but will refuse to come any lower.

There will be times when the circling hunter can sneak into easy killing distance of the bird, too. A lone hunter can try to work the same trick, but the drawback is nobody is left to call from the original point of contact and the bird will often cease gobbling, perhaps ambling off. A lone circling hunter will often spook the turkey or lose track of its exact location. When team hunting, we can assume that once the bird was raised, or

Two happy hunters, Dr. Gary Miller (left) and Dr. Dennis McIntyre, with a pair of winter-killed young gobblers. These birds were first seen at long range with field glasses, then after discerning where the birds were headed, a plan was made to get in their path. After a long dogged hike up a snow-filled canyon, a scramble up a steep bank, and a quick peek, there they were inside twenty yards. Dennis bagged his bird on the ground; Gary nailed his on the flush with his old Manton side-by-side, a vintage 1800s muzzleloader.

Hunters listening to a gobbler cutting loose on a ridge above them. What to do? First, they'd best back off and ascertain if there's a route they can take which will put them on the ridge with the bird, slightly above him. And without being seen or heard. Or they could call from where they are, and if the bird won't come to them but gobbles at each call, one of them can remain to keep the bird gobbling, while the other circles the turkey, hoping to either bushwack it or take up calling once in position. All such plans should be discussed before separating. Teamwork very often will bag a gobbler where a single hunter wouldn't have a prayer of a chance. But to succeed requires unselfish friendship.

heard to gobble, both hunters closed the distance to within a couple hundred yards. The hunter who remains behind to keep the bird gobbling is in an advantageous position to shoot at the bird should the circling hunter spook it. At best, he can watch to see where it goes. Remember, mountain turkeys flush downhill.

Many times I have been with another hunter or two when we saw a drove of wintering birds or perhaps an old gobbler or two with a passel of hens. Even though at first there appeared to be nothing we could do about them after watching a spell, a plan would slowly evolve. Invariably, this was little more than moving around them and placing ourselves in locations we hoped would be in their path. By separating, the chances became much greater that one of us would get in a killing shot. There was also the chance that, if spooked, the fleeing birds would pass the other hunters, or that a bird might fly up into a tree and one of us could make a run for it. At the very least, the birds would probably pass within easy spooking range of someone, and once scattered, the chances for a kill increased. Of course, this applies to spring gobblers, too. As long as the old birds are consorting with hens, the hunter is left out. The bulk of all turkey hunters feel they must hunt alone, but their chances for success would increase tremendously if they would hunt with a buddy. Having guided for so many years, I have hunted with groups of two to ten or twenty men, all expecting to get a turkey, and all of them fairly new at turkey hunting. By working together, I've been witness to an awful lot of turkeys killed by such groups. And, I have never noted even a near-miss in terms of a shooting accident while engaged in multiple-hunter outings.

A tremendous number of hunters would make proper strategy decisions, if they would just relax, and allow their minds to think.

However, the average turkey hunt is a single hunter in the spring of the year. He hopes for success by using a call to lure the bird to him. The strategy is simple. A gobbler cuts loose from its roost branch, the hunter sneaks to within a couple hundred yards of it, finds a comfortable place to lean back against a tree trunk, makes a few calls, then kills the bird when it walks into gunshot. Nothing to it.

We wouldn't have any turkeys left if this technique worked even half the time. The birds would all be shot out. There are ways to combat the various things that go wrong. Let's say the bird cuts loose like the Bells of St. Mary's just at first day. We get set up a hundred yards from him, and he is still in the tree. We haven't called to him. Oh-Oh! A hen sounds off. Her pips and clucks tell us she is in a tree near the old bird. Now we have a problem. What to do? The average hunter will call at this time. The gobbler will gobble back. The hen will continue to cluck and chirp. This goes on and on, the birds fly down, get together, and march off. The hunter gets zip. He would have at least had a fighting chance if he had easily walked in among the roost trees and scattered the birds. It's a dead cinch he wasn't going to bag the gobbler if the bunch waltzed off together, so if by flushing them, if nothing comes of it later, it's all the same.

When turkeys are flushed from the roost area without a shot being fired, chances are good the old bird will soon get over the fright and commence gobbling again. Separated from the hens, a gobbler very often is a pushover for a caller. On terrain that lends itself to stalking and sneaking, the hunter could wait for the birds to group on the ground, then attempt to waylay the old adult in this manner.

The one ingredient the average hunter lacks in pulling off such a stalk is patience. The hunter must hold back, study the group and wait until they are in a situation advantageous to the hunter. Oftentimes, he will not have visual contact, but must keep track of the birds through their gobbling, the sound of the strut itself, and the talking of the hens. Once the hens begin moving toward their feeding grounds, the group will move along at a good pace, the old gobbler bringing up the end of the procession.

While the hens are traveling to wherever it is they have in mind, they will usually be head down, pecking at the ground all along the way. The group is extremely vulnerable now. It is often best to try to waylay the old gobbler who is tagging along behind a passel of hens by coming up on him from the rear. The hens are looking ahead, and the old bird, usually in strut, can't see behind him because of his fanned tail. The hunter who has patience and waits until the group has just passed over a knoll, dropped into a cover, or faded from view behind a rock outcropping can then quickly slip forward, check the birds out, move, and check again, until the opportunity to kill the gobbler presents itself. Often I have had to whistle to make the old bird stick his head up so I could cut a fine bead on him.

There is absolutely no end of tricks a hunter can try with turkeys. Some are just foolish gambles, coupled with the crazy idea they might work. A tremendous number of hunters would make proper strategy decisions if they would just relax and allow their minds to think. A bird gobbling, or a bunch having flushed then flying to all quadrants, mesmerizes many hunters, causing their thought processes to go blank. From there on, they do the first thing that comes to mind, not turning over all the alternatives prior to acting.

Undoubtedly, if the hunter doesn't take a chance, certainly

An old woods road in Dixie. How many days have some of us trod these paths? Hopefully, many more to come. Hunting such a trail, while walking, is the ultimate lesson in still-hunting if you're after wild turkeys. The number one secret is always be ready, and by this I mean coiled like a copperhead ready to strike. A drove of birds, or a single, can blast upwards at every turn in the trail. The hunter who is always gun ready and is a good shot can make a kill. I've done it many times all across this country, so can you. But you must walk quietly.

he is not going to be successful. How many times have you read about a hunter who sat still and called a bird into gunshot only to have the bird approach from behind? He could hear the turkey gobbling and walking, but couldn't see it, nor did he attempt to turn toward the turkey. At last, the story ended with the bird walking away, making some deep clucks as he made tracks. Immediately, we can draw some conclusions. First, why did the hunter sit there and let the bird walk in on his blind side? Was he so comfortable he just hated to move? Surely not. Could he observe the bird the last hundred yards as it approached? Probably not. Therefore, he could have moved, keeping his gun aimed in the general direction of the turkey. But, if there was no explanation, why not make a play for the bird once it came into easy range? After all, once the bird walked up close and spied the waiting gunner, he was spooked, and the chances are heavily against the hunter calling it back into gunshot that day. The fact is, the hunter's chances were no worse than if he made an effort to bring the gun to bear on the turkey before it was within shooting distance.

The what-to-dos when a turkey is answering a hunter's calls are probably the trickiest part in all turkey hunting. Fall or spring, it doesn't matter. There have been so many conflicting how-tos on what a hunter should do that all this has just confused a lot of folks. My advice is to read what you can, try to keep it in mind the next time you hear a bird answer your call, but think. Don't try so-and-so just because you read it. Study the situation. Look over the terrain where you are calling from. Does it resemble a place you have known turkeys to use? Are you sitting out in a park-like opening against a lone tree with brush scattered

The what-to-dos when a turkey is answering a hunter's calls are probably the trickiest part in all turkey hunting. Fall or spring, it doesn't matter.

about? Could this be a situation where you will be seen first by the turkey? Have you got visibility which would allow you to move if the bird is within what you would estimate as fifty yards? Dense brush does not make a screen for any of the above. You can't see through it, but a turkey can. You can't shoot through it with any degree of confidence. You would not be able to move, as you are not certain the bird wouldn't see you. In such a location, chances are you

Florida's turkey woods offer great possibilities for scragging birds. Calling is often used due to low visibility. Stalking is excellent due to thick screening cover, most often in the form of saw palmetto, tall grasses and undergrowth. Florida is made for the turkey hunter.

would never get a shot, as the gobbler would eyeball you before you'd get a shot.

I just mention this in hopes that hunters will loosen up, study the facts at hand and then think. All of us, given enough time in the woods, will soon weave enough rope to hang ourselves.

Late one afternoon when hunting near Junction, Texas, a spring hunt, I was walking a fence line separating the ranch I was on from the YO Ranch, a well-known spread for the well-heeled. I was searching for holes in the fence, holes big enough for a turkey gobbler to sneak through. A couple days earlier, I'd heard the over-and-over gobbling of an old bird across on the YO. Knowing he wasn't about to fly over the eight feet of stacked hog wire, mixed with barbed wire, I'd not taken the trouble to call to the gobbler, thinking I'd deal with him later. Now, the time had come. The way he'd belted out those gobbles, I had every hunch he'd gobble late in the afternoon as well unless, that is, somebody had done him in the meanwhile.

There weren't any holes where I'd like them located, but there was one which would have to do. Tracks in the dust under the fence told me it was being used by wild hogs which made it plenty big enough for a gobbler. It wasn't exactly

where I wanted, but some hundred yards from it was a hill covered with brush. I could take up a calling stand there.

Getting settled back under a big live oak, I felt pretty good about the affair. Brush, junipers, oak scrub—one thing about it, I needn't stew about anything coming in from behind. Maybe an hour later after I'd called a number of times, guess what. A damned gobbler went to clucking, right behind me. *Behind me!* In the damned brush. Easing around, I just caught a glimpse of a big red, white and blue head sneaking back through the stuff. I could hear the darned fool clucking until it went out of earshot. I turned the air blue all over south Texas. What darned crazy turkey would come through that stuff when there was wide open ground twenty yards out, parallel to where the bird must've walked? One thing was clear. I was just as crazy to stay under that tree. Had to move.

No, I didn't think the bird was the one from across on the YO. Oh, don't get me wrong, I'd have stacked him up in the oak leaves given a chance, but, no, I was sure the bird was one that just happened to hear me and came looking. Of course, not knowing my plans, the danged gobbler came in *wrong*.

Well, I studied the situation again—I certainly didn't like the location, but it seemed my next choice would be a nearby

If there's a will, there's a way. All told, there's five Merriams hanging on this big Gambel's oak, killed with calls, stalking, and one bird driven by one of these guys to the other. Mark Kahlich (left) and Mike Monier on a spring hunt into the Gila country in New Mexico.

Excellent Eastern wild turkey country in the Northeast with lots of ridges, areas of open pasture and many, many small cultivated fields. This is tough hunting in late fall. Too often the hunter will be seen from a distance, so the birds skedaddle. Use binoculars, listen for other hunters shooting, but mainly do a lot of sitting and watching. Use a call, but do it sparingly, and after the first week of the season, you may want to leave it in your pocket. Search out the places where turkeys have been feeding recently, and if nobody's got these staked out, keep watch over them. Listen for a single yelp; calling hunters rarely quit with one or two notes.

All turkeys want water, some seemingly more than others. Tracks just below the gun butt tell us that the birds are using this watering trough. A wait here just might be the ticket to success. But if water is scarce, and no other water is available, do not hunt there. That's taking undue advantage of the thirsty birds. Back off and hunt them on paths leading toward water a couple hundred yards from the source.

open stand of oaks. The hole in the fence was out of sight, but with my back to another portion of fence, at least I felt *satisfied that no other gobbler would sneak in from behind.*

When I began calling this next time, the bird over on the YO got into the act. In jig time, he was wound up like a clock. Then he quit. Didn't seem like he'd come much closer either. An hour and a few calls later, he still didn't gobble. Probably he'd been joined by a hen, *or hens.* The sun was sliding pretty far down when I eased around, so's I could see over toward the hole. *Great daddy longlegs,* here comes a big, black-as-tar *turkey gobbler.* Just hustling along like they do when the old birds have *sex* in mind. The YO lost a gobbler just a tad later, as I slew the bird with the Hapgood 11-bore. But, when I walked back toward the truck, carrying that old turkey, I still thought the first place would've been a better place to shoot a turkey from. Maybe if I'm ever back down in that area, I'll try it again. This time I'll face sideways—then I can watch out front *and* behind for that sneaky gobbler that's still snickering in those parts.

I hadn't hunted turkeys for many years before I knew that the sport would lose its flavor for me, providing I just kept drifting along, killing turkeys in the same area year after year. I'd already taken to making birds flush, shooting them on the fly. I'd been raised as a wingshot. Ground sluicing any game bird was strictly for slobs. Wingshooting helped, but I felt the urge to find the real challenge in turkeyin.' I found it when I began hunting turkeys in "new" country—places I'd never been.

Back in my early days when traveling to Dixie, I was hunting in a piney woods one morning in Mississippi. The morning began at first day on a high ridge, but as I heard a gobbler sounding off to the west, I worked my way down into a creek bottom and eased up onto the gentle slope of the ridge with him. Like so many places, I'd never set foot thereabouts before, but had an idea what the terrain was like. A person can do this by "reading" the countryside while traveling in a car or on foot. It's simply studying the terrain as it comes into view. Notice how the land lies. Is it gentle or is it rough and hilly with lots of water-cut gullies and erosion? Has there been much timbering done recently? What about underbrush? Is there water in all the creeks? What about open fields with those clean grassy edges that strutting gobblers like? Is there any cultivation?

I worked my way to the top of the rise, well studded with mature pines. Obviously, the bird had been roosting somewhere thereabouts when I first heard him at daybreak. I called from time to time, and he was still answering me off to my southwest, at maybe two hundred yards. His muffled gobbles told me he was either behind a knoll or in a draw. Could be either, as the country had lots of small hills and gullies. Simple. He'd flown down, the hens had come to him, and the whole passel had wandered to where they were now. My first contacts had been from so far distant that until now I hadn't been able to tell what the situation was. Calling again, I got another quick answer. Getting a good fix on his position, I sneaked ahead, easing off to the left as I didn't want to risk going straight toward him.

Just in case the bird suddenly decided to come to me, I didn't want to bump into him coming through the woods and spook him off, so I drifted off to one side, more or less a circling move. Turkeys are always doing it to other folks, so I do it to them. If I get to where the bird has been, and he has gone to my calling place, I'll soon know it and can make amends for "standing him up."

There was my gobbler—my wild gobbler—in a chicken wire pen.

Drawing near, I called again. His muffled gobble was inside a hundred yards. I'd have to be very sneaky from here on in. Didn't want to blow it now. Slipping ahead, a step at a time, I suddenly caught sight of a farm building ahead. That would explain the muffled gobbles. The bird was behind the old barn. A few more steps—what's that? Looks like a car. It hit me in the face like a sack full of mush. I eased forward, taking a look from where the brush ended. Of all the damned fools! There was my gobbler—my wild gobbler—in a chicken wire pen. No wonder his gobbles weren't loud and clear. Domestic turkeys have a gobble that doesn't carry like a wild bird's ren-

Being at the right place at the right time can be luck or, as in this case, planned well ahead. The truth is, I'd noticed so much sign passing this old tree that I presumed it was only a matter of how long a hunter had to wait there before a drove of birds walked past. Lady Luck was with me; it wasn't but a few hours.

Many times a hunter won't hear any turkeys gobbling on spring mornings, so it's either head for the house, hunt them shutmouth or try to get one to gobble any way you can. Crows often hassle turkey gobblers, particularly if the old bird is in strut. Or they may surround a bird on the roost and get him to gobbling time after time. Last season, the author heard a gang of crows hassle a number of gobblers for well over an hour, and when it seemed the turkeys were about to quit, the crows' continual cawing would get them going again. Earl Woodbury's an old Oklahoma turkey hunter, so he's aware that toting a crow call makes sense when hunting gobblers.

spurs have formed from the main ridge. Are there small coves tucked into mountainsides? Do the main ridges all tend to run in like directions? What about the underbrush—is it open or is it in new leaf? Are there lots of dead leaves on the slopes? I lost an easy chance at an old Merriam one morning in the Rockies simply because the sky was clouded over. I'd been fooling with the bird for a half hour or so, and it finally became obvious I would have to get above him. I hadn't done so earlier, hoping he'd come down to me. Climbing can be hard work at an elevation of 8,000 feet, but he wouldn't budge, so-oo-oo...

Studying the face of the mountain, I could see that it wouldn't be difficult to back away from where I was calling, make a circle up a dry arroyo to the summit, walk along the backside of the main ridge until I was even with the bird's gobblings, make a call, and shoot him as he came up to me. Any hunter who has done this a great many times is aware that it is easily done. I made it to the arroyo, climbed it until I broke out on the summit ridge, dropped over the backside, and walked the flank around toward where the gobbler had been. He'd stopped gobbling, but with a call I was certain he'd get fired up again. I eased out near where the mountain broke downward and called. No answer. I slipped along fifty yards or so and made another series of calls. I was mystified as to why he wouldn't answer. He had been so cranked up, gobbling time after time, it was unbelievable he had quit. Perhaps the old boy had hotfooted it down to where I'd been earlier. No. If he had, I could easily hear him from where I was. I couldn't understand how, but apparently I'd spooked him. I headed off the mountain.

Pulling the compass, I took a reading. I was going the wrong direction. Turning around, I climbed back to the summit. Taking a reading there, I then had the uneasy feeling that somewhere along the way I had taken a wrong turn. Retracing my path, I soon found out what had happened. Not knowing the mountain, I had walked along its backside and had simply walked onto the flank of an adjoining ridge jutting from the mountain's backside. I'd been calling into a canyon that was one ridge removed from the one where the old bird was gobbling. With the course straightened out, I made my way back toward where the bird had been. Never heard him after that. He'd probably gotten disgusted with the hen's "fiddling around" and stalked off looking for another lady friend. Had the sun been shining, I'd have been aware of the change in direction there on the mountain's flank. And had I been there before, I'd have not made such a goof.

ditions. He was penned alongside a falling down shed which deadened the sound. I was mad 'cause I'd spent the morning fooling with a tame turkey, but I couldn't help laughing either. I'd been had!

To this day I'm leery of gobblers that won't come to me in areas I've never hunted. I'm always watching for houses and fences if I have to move toward them—and creeks, rivers, streams and beaver ponds, too. It helps to know where water is located because many turkeys will hang up on reaching water. The larger the body of water, the greater the chance they won't try to cross it. Birds will also react the same to ravines, gullies, draws, cuts and arroyos. Many times I've had turkeys come to me across these obstacles, but it's best to presume the bird won't if you know the area and make provisions beforehand. Too often the gypsy turkey hunter finds out such things after the bird has refused to come to him. I called to two gobblers one morning and upon easing toward them came to where I could see a large stream. In short time, I could see the two birds pacing the opposite bank, gobbling back at each of my calls. Luckily, they flew across to me after I began a session of non-stop calling. Yet, on a similar occasion, a bird called to an intervening creek wouldn't budge. He could have hopped over if he'd had any gumption.

The number one rule in hunting Eastern mountain turkeys is to call to them from the ridge they are on and, if humanly possible, from slightly above them or at least the same level. Of course, if you haven't seen the ridge until you hear a bird whooping and a hollering from there, the odds are stacked against you. This is why it's so important to study an area even as you drive through it. Notice how many little side

How many times have you heard about a turkey that seemed to be coming to the hunter, but the bird was across a river, or a swamp pond, and is still alive because it would not come over to the hunter? Once in a while, one will fly across, but the best thing for anyone to do is back off, once you think you've made contact across such a barrier, then work to where it'll be possible for the bird to come to your call, if you don't want to do some of the walking yourself.

Successfully hunting wild turkeys is akin to putting a puzzle together. Grasshoppers are a favored food of wild turkeys, so if you bag a bird that has been eating hoppers, catalog it in your memory and hunt where there are grasshoppers, too.

The traveling turkey hunter can do two things that will far exceed all others in preparing to hunt on unfamiliar terrain. Using a map, he can study the region beforehand and then read books on the turkey subspecies that lives there. Both can be done off-season, at home, or riding the commuter train to work. Once a site has been chosen, which needs to be little less than a general area—a national forest, a county or simply one corner of a state—the hunter can then ask for information from that state's game department

Studying and observing will help immensely in hunting and killing wild turkeys on strange terrain.

concerning turkey studies that have been made, along with annual kill dates, etc. Subscribe to the department's wildlife magazine, many of which are published monthly. Reading these will bring an education in game laws, what to expect in terms of wild animals, trees, flowers and geography, and they'll also give you a general feeling of having been there once you arrive. If a national forest is chosen, order maps of it. Once the area has been selected, topographical maps can be ordered. These indicate the contours of the area, wooded sections, streams, plus an endless variety of landmarks valuable to an outsider. Many of us want to learn all we can about the flora and fauna thereabouts, so we buy books identifying trees, flowers, grasses and birds. A few years of traveling and hunting for wild turkeys will make a person realize that the real America is found along the lit-

tle-known roads and backtrails, and in small towns and people's homes.

The five subspecies of bearded and spurred wild turkeys are classified in regions of varying amounts of annual precipitation. Anyone who has studied the birds knows this, which is why anyone who wants to gypsy around over the country hunting these birds should study them intensely. Learn what each one eats at different times of the year. Do they flock together in large droves and, if so, why?

Consider gobbling. There is a marked difference among turkeys along this vein, too. Throughout much of the Old South—Mississippi, Alabama, Louisiana, Georgia and Florida—the birds don't gobble as frequently in the late afternoon as the birds in Arkansas and Missouri. However, both are Eastern wild turkeys. Perhaps other hunters have found otherwise, but this has been true in my observations. Nor does the average Merriam gobbler sound off to such a degree during the afternoon and evening hours.

"Roosting a gobbler" is practiced in many parts of the country, but sitting quietly in hopes of hearing a bird fly up and gobble would be a waste of time in many areas. Day after day I've hunted Rio Grandes, seldom hearing one gobble at dusk. (They can be located after dark by yodeling like a coyote from time to time. They gobble at coyotes.) Studying and observing will help immensely in hunting and killing wild turkeys on strange terrain. A flat-land turkey's gobble will not carry the long distances that the gobble of a bird in the mountains will. Very often, the flat-land gobble will not be heard at 500 yards, less if the bird is behind a slight rise or if a breeze is blowing away from the hunter. An Osceola gobbler, far out among pal-

Turkey hunting can get awful tiring, more so if you haven't heard a gobbler all morning. But if there's a turkey, there's more'n one way to skin him, and that's to wait him out. Now this waiting can also get awful tiring, 'cause sitting on sticks and stones while leaning against a tree soon takes all the fun out of the hunt. My advice—build some permanent blinds.

mettoes, could go easily unheard by a hunter several hundred yards distant. Yet, an Eastern bird on a ridge in Georgia could be heard at four times the distance. Knowing this, a hunter can brace himself to not overrun a gobbler, spooking it before he can make an attempt to call. In addition, a gobbler can gobble at varying degrees of intensity, making the sounds carry far or not at all.

My experiences lead me to concur that a wild turkey gobbler gobbles as loud as he thinks he needs to. While on the roost branch during the spring of the year, he gobbles loud in hopes of attracting hens to him. Later in the morning, on hearing a hen nearby, he gobbles only loud enough for her to hear him. Once she has left his presence, he again might gobble loudly, wanting all hens in his area to know his location. Many times I have been slowly walking through heavy woods, calling now and then, hoping to raise a bird, and have had answering gobbles from very close, yet the gobble seemed "small," not very loud. I can recall other hunts when the gobble would cause me to misjudge the distance, and I would overrun the bird's position, spooking him. Loud, distinct, clear gobbling makes the bird far easier to hunt.

My experiences lead me to concur that a wild turkey gobbler gobbles as loud as he thinks he needs to.

There is a hunt in strange and new country which should be given special consideration, one that I've long referred to as the "one-day stand." When planned for a bird so wild and wary as a wild turkey, this hunt stands apart when measured alongside its chances of success. This "there is no tomorrow" turkey hunt isn't for those with no faith in their hunting abilities. Most one-day stands require hard hunting, luck and a knack for always being at the right place at the right time.

If I'm on a one-day stand and hear a gobbling turkey at dawn, I hunt him much like I would any strange country hunt. But, I never forget that I won't be back tomorrow. I must plan my hand for each card it holds. Several states don't allow all-day hunting for springtime gobblers, which cuts hunting time to half, or even less. For the one-day hunt, this means any turkey heard gobbling may be the only one you have a chance at. This separates the turkey hunters from the gobble listeners. One-day hunts are only for the aggressive.

The average hunter may not care for this type of pressure-cooker hunt. I have been invited to areas from Arizona to New York, some of them with veteran hunters, some with local hunters. But my reputation as a turkey hunter usually has preceded me, and when I go into the woods, I'm expected to come out with a bird.

The bulk of the hunts begin with a drive into the area before daylight, a crude map sketched in the dirt with a stick, and with a few "you can hunt heres" and "don't hunt theres."

To me, one-day hunts test my abilities to the maximum as I don't know the terrain, won't have time to scout it out nor will I be able to study the habits of the birds and use that information against them. The hunt is done, more or less, on the birds' terms.

One-day stands during the fall and winter hunts are another story, for a number of reasons. Number one, there isn't any gobbling to tell a hunter, "Here I am, come and get me." Number two, all the birds have bunched in small droves and, later on in the winter, in larger gangs, which makes them harder to find than single birds scattered over the same range. Number three, in many areas the birds will have migrated from their spring range to another. Number four, such droves seldom make any calls after the early morning get-together. Therefore, the hunter is looking for a bunch of birds with umpteen ears to hear him and as many eyes to see him.

Reading about the various subspecies, particularly indepth studies such as The Wildlife Society's *The Wild Turkey and Its Management*, are of extreme importance to the traveling

Blinds are best constructed of worn and weathered old lumber, but build them where you've seen lots of turkey sign over the years. Leave a shooting slot across the front and the sides, too, if you like, then put in a couple lawn chairs with armrests and you can sit here for hours on end, comfortable, out of the weather. You don't have to make like a rock, unmoving for hours. If you took care in placing the blind where turkeys travel a lot, you'll very likely bag that old bird. Stick your call out the shooting slot from time to time. Many times a nearby gobbler has hollered right back to me.

turkey hunter. There is no one book from which to learn all there is to know about any one of the subspecies, much less all five. Read all you can, then add to this your own observations while hunting. For example, though I've never read this in any book, it is a fact that springtime Merriam gobblers are often found scattered far and wide with a mile, or several miles, between gobbling birds. Why?

It's not because the intervening areas wouldn't support additional turkeys, but there is so much terrain for widespread scattering during the spring breakup. Anyone who's hunted on and below the Mogollon rim country, down into the Tonto Basin, knows those birds can and do travel long distances when heavy snows force the birds into low country, but the following thaw allows them to travel back on top. It's not uncommon to locate a gobbler or two, but then not find another for miles in such country.

Two years ago in early May, I was hunting Merriams in Colorado. Hearing a gobbler cut loose, I hightailed it toward him. Turned out he was really out for a walk, not paying any mind to my message to meet me in the pines and perhaps we could get to know each other better. Hiking south, the gobbler soon was out of hearing. Luckily, I tagged along, as there was so much brush the bird simply stayed on an old road. Those parts had been dry, so the roadbed was just like powder. Trailing the turkey was like reading a map. This went on for what later proved to be nearly three miles. At that juncture, the trail ended in a small valley with one of those picture-perfect mountain brooks coursing its way across an emerald green meadow. Bright green cottonwood leaves framed a clear blue sky. What a beautiful place to shoot a gobbler.

Moments later, I did. Not getting an answer at the first place I tried, the old Merriam blasted back with one of those "Hello World" gobbles when I hit the box a couple hundred yards farther up the creek. A fifteen-yard shot ended a three-mile hike. Merriams are like that.

If you have started a bird toward you, "raised a bird" so to speak, but on looking around don't like anything about your

Taking aim with his handgun, Neal Wildman shoots a 25-yard turkey target with a 223 Thompson Contender scoped with a 2-6x Weaver. There are a few hunters around the country bagging turkeys with handguns, but this calls for accuracy like that needed in rifle shooting. It is best done from a rest.

location, get moving. Find a spot you can live with. If the bird is a good distance from you, move toward him if you see a place where you think you can make the kill. I've moved umpteen times in dealing with gobblers. Turkeys move, so it is natural for someone using a turkey call to do likewise. During the spring, hens wander considerably. Calling from one location time after time could make a gobbler suspicious.

Making the actual decision to move is the hardest part of a hunt for many a hunter. Possibly, the fear that the bird will see or hear him prevents the hunter from moving. And while these are distinct possibilities, I learned long ago not to be concerned with them. Few gobblers will see a hunter changing positions at a hundred yards, or even at much over fifty yards, due to slight rolls in terrain, brush, trees and what-have-you. This is evident each time a hunter sits down to call. When he leans

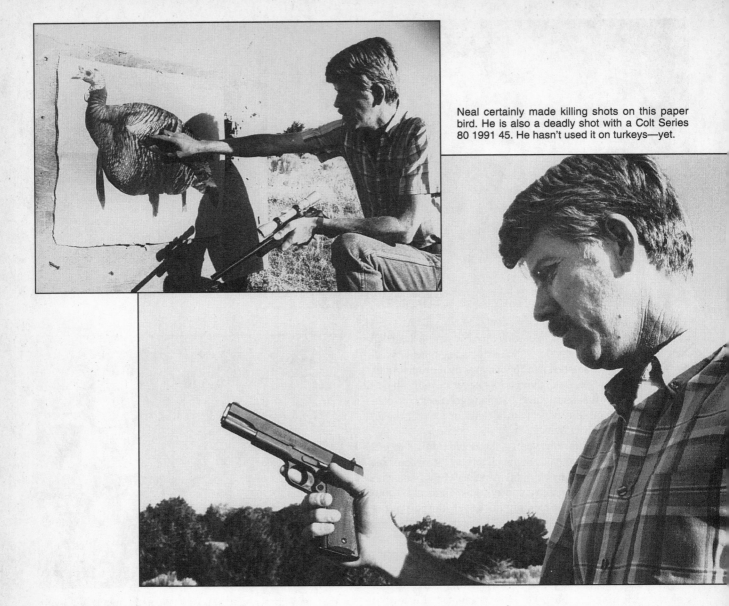

Neal certainly made killing shots on this paper bird. He is also a deadly shot with a Colt Series 80 1991 45. He hasn't used it on turkeys—yet.

back and fetches out "Old Faithful," before he even makes a note, he realizes he can't see anywhere. Of course, folks who hunt nothing but flat prairie pastures and bald mountain meadows will have excellent visibility, and moving while a gobbler is coming becomes very risky.

The hunter hopes to make a few calls, have the bird respond, come to the gun, and the hunt is over. No strategy is required. But when the bird answers time after time, yet fails to come to the hunter, then it's time to think of what can be done. Chances are fair that the bird is with hens. There is no way of knowing unless they have been heard or can be seen. I've often noticed that gobblers with hens will be moving, but at a very slow pace. So, if the bird gives you the notion that he is on the move, and doesn't seem to be in a hurry, you should then make an effort to make visual contact. Invariably, a gobbler with hens will not answer your calls but a few times, then he is apt to quit. This can mislead the hunter into thinking the bird is coming to him, when it is simply following hens, so it no longer gobbles to the hunter's yelps.

The gobbler that answers time after time is often alone. If the bird is moving about considerably, hotfooting from one knob to another, walking back and forth the length of a ridge, it's almost a certainty he is alone. The bulk of these turkeys are first-year adults, have a beard about six to eight inches in length, with spurs one-half inch long. These gobblers lack but a month or so of being two years of age. Who knows why one will act so silly, gobbling at every call, but not coming to the hunter. Many times I have seen these birds walk past hens as if they were invisible. But, the hunter's main clue that he is dealing with such a turkey is that it walks a lot. As mentioned earlier, these birds are more easily dealt with by two hunters working together, one remaining behind to keep the bird gobbling, the second attempting to waylay it where it stands. Some of these gobblers can be had by intercepting their paths, particularly those that stroll back and forth on a ridge.

Sometimes these birds come to where I had been calling from, but only after I had left that place and was calling at a new location. In my early turkey hunting years, I presumed I

There's been so much said about the actual shooting of a wild turkey from a sitting position that many hunters think that's the only way it's done. A shotgun shoots most accurately from a standing position, and many of us have killed lots of turkeys while standing. For a truly wary gobbler, one hard-hunted, there's no position better than lying on one's belly.

was leaving a calling stand too soon, or perhaps I should shut off all calling, the thought being that the hen had fallen silent and wandered off. So, I tried these tactics on the walking gobblers. But while I might kill one occasionally, very often it's the same old tune, gobble, gobble, gobble, but no turkey comes to the call. Walk and gobble.

Sometimes these birds come to where I had been calling from, but only after I had left that place and was calling at a new location.

I have killed them by moving to a new location, calling from there several times, making the bird gobble, then running back to my last stand. I never sit down at the exact place where I had made the calls earlier, but take a location within twenty-five yards, and bring the gun to bear on my calling stand. Of course, I can't make a call, as I want the gobbler to

think I am still at the place he last heard me. I must point out that the birds I've killed in this manner were standing within feet of my old location when I pulled the trigger. It's uncanny how a bird can pinpoint sound locations.

I've bushwacked a number of these strolling gobbling turkeys. This required patience above all in waiting until the bird has located on terrain favorable for closing the distance to him. Jakes, those young bucks with beards an inch, perhaps two or three, in length, will also wander about gobbling during the spring hunt. Of course, scads of them are killed by hunters making hen yelps. But while one may come to a call, the next will seem stone deaf. Springtime jakes are often easily bushwacked because their gobbling attracts hunters, and sooner or later the bird will find itself in a place where a hunter can sneak into killing distance. They run in bunches, too, so when one answers a call, or comes to it, he could bring lots of company. Only last spring I had a group of six jakes walk up to me. That was followed two weeks later by a bunch of four some 700 miles from there. All subspecies of jake turkeys will come to hen calls.

What I've hoped to get across in this chapter is to get the hunter to think, to rationalize, to study what he is planning on doing *before* he does it. There are times when it's wise not to let the turkey hear your call. There are times when it is better to scratch in the leaves with a stick, imitating a feeding hen than to make a hen call. Particularly, if the bird you're after has been hunted hard with calls, and you now think he is close on the mountain with you.

But the hunter will also have to keep in mind that some opportunities must be taken advantage of with lightning-like quickness, or the chance will be gone. Perhaps it's little else than "skootching" around to bring the gun to bear on another tangent or to make a run for another tree thirty yards distant. True, with these no-time-to-speculate decisions there is a great amount of risk—the hunter might be seen and the gobbler may vamoose—but it's far better to try and fail, than not try at all.

Long, long ago, I learned that the myths about waiting in a place for hours in hopes a turkey answers our calls, or not to bat an eyelash though the gobbler is not in sight (but could be), is a whole bunch of hogwash. The great percentage of this malarky is put out by folks who have killed a couple or three dozen birds and set themselves up on a pedestal as turkey hunters.

A perfectly thought out, perfectly executed plan to bring a wild turkey into easy gunshot is not too often accomplished. Why? Because it is not possible for the hunter to draw up the perfect strategy prior to the hunt. Only when he is in the field with the birds at hand can he put together a hunting strategy. Even then, the plan depends on the time of year, the number of birds available, and the number of hunters executing the plan. Other factors affecting a hunting strategy are time of day and the extent to which the birds have been hunted. Young unhunted turkeys, for example, can be a pushover compared to a small gang of old gobblers.

Adult gobblers, whether a single bird or one in a drove, seem to hone their spooky nature to a razor's edge once the mating season wanes, which together with summer molting, makes backwoods recluses of them by September. Seldom will a person see adult gobblers throughout the summer months—they just disappear. So, when fall rolls around, and the hunting season is on, we have a bird absolutely unmatched for wariness.

Turkey hunting is a sport of exceptions. Nothing is iron-clad, except the coming day, last light, and taxes.

These birds can be killed by all of the methods we are discussing, but conditions must be perfect. A bunch of old gobblers that are "nooning" (a turkey hunter term for loafing) may appear to be relaxed, pecking at the mast, or hunkered up asleep, but don't let this fool you. Old gobblers never for a second let down their guard. I swear they sleep with just one eye closed at a time. They do.

When I sneak into easy gunshot of a small gang of long-whiskered gobblers, I never raise myself for a looksee from behind cover, I raise up *in cover*. And just as slow as the sun coming up. You can never be any such thing as too careful when stalking these birds. The hunter who is bellycrawling a bunch of them can't get too near the ground. Nor can he be too quiet. Seldom will an entire drove have their heads down, feeding at the same time. And if one of them gets an inkling a stranger is nearby, you can kiss them all goodbye. Once spooked, you will need all the luck in the stars to get within killing range the next time.

One problem facing a hunter who has sneaked to within shooting range of a drove of adult gobblers is in shooting the best of the bunch. Locating the number one bird is best done at very close range, where beards can be studied and, if possible, the spurs seen. Quite often, the bird with the longest beard will not have the longest, sharpest spurs. Binoculars will be an asset. But the hunter must do this studying while looking through cover, be it weeds, grass, bushes, leafy tree branches or whatever screening cover is available. All movements must be made when the gobblers are looking in other directions or, better yet, when their heads down, feeding or pecking at the ground.

By far the best method that any of us can develop for hunting wild turkeys is to get out there in the woods with them and hunt. Turkey hunting is a sport of exceptions. Nothing is iron-clad, except the coming day, last light, and taxes. Read what you want, but when you get in the woods with a turkey, it all gets back to the old axiom, "Do as I do, not as I say." And I never know what I'll do, until I do it.

Do whatever it takes to put yourself on the same side of water with the turkey. Wet feet can be dried out. So what if you do catch cold, you might've been catching it anyhow. No, there's no iron-clad guarantee you'll get the bird either, but you damned sure won't if you don't try.

13

The Gould's Turkey Survived, the Apache Went Under

GENERAL GEORGE CROOK (with both the blessings of this country, and Mexico) was given the onerous task of teaching a bunch of Apaches a few things along the lines of being nice, which they weren't, nor did they intend to be. Geronimo, Cochise, along with other old warriors like Juh, simply had no use for being cooped up on some windy, dirty reservation. They took to the hills in Mexico when Crook made it too hot for them in the states. Gen. Crook and his troops lit out after them in 1883. By 1886 they had begun to get the message, but by then there were only a handful of the once infamous Chiricahua Apache warriors left.

The Apache forever abandoned the rock ledges back in the Sierra Madre Mountains and were hauled off to jail in Florida where most died of white man's diseases. Geronimo, in time, was sent back to old Fort Sill, in Oklahoma, staying there until he cashed his chips.

Those big, old mountains down in Mexico, which make up the country's backbone, would "no more forever" feel the light footstep of this fabulous fighting band of Indians. But, a witness to the past would hang on, a tough old wild turkey, a bird whose ancestors had heard the hideous Apache yell—the Gould's.

We who've hunted this turkey never think of anything but Mexico when it's mentioned. And Mexico makes me look toward the back of my old rolltop desk. There's a bottle of tequila sitting there, a part of a glass set marketed as the Cuervo 1800 Tequila set. It's good stuff. You give a jackrabbit a slug of 1800 tequila and he'll spit in a coyote's eye.

No, I won't drink it. Gary Blakeslee gave me that bottle. It'd spoil the back of the desk if I'd empty that container. So long as it's back there, each time I sit at the desk my mind wanders to Mexico and Apache country, and Gary.

Mexico's High Sierras, the Sierra Madre mountain range, is a tough land. You may be hotter'n the Devil in longhandles in the afternoon, but by sundown those longjohns got goosebumps on 'em. And it's dry. A lack of water is the main factor limiting so much excellent turkey terrain. It's possible to travel for miles without locating water. I've walked stream beds for miles finding one small pool, then nothing. Where water is found in any abundance, turkeys may be nearby.

Probably the major limiting factor throughout all Gould's range is that the locals shoot the birds for food whenever they can get them into range, and this has nothing to do with a hunting season. It's very difficult to criticize a person for wanting food, so although I hope in time these mountain people will have a more plentiful supply, it's obvious that for the present they'll still live on a main meal of beans and tortillas. Sadly, the recent assassination of President-elect Colosio was a tragedy. He was so much loved by the common people in all Mexico. They had elected him to office hoping he could head the country toward much better times—a better economy and better living conditions for all. So, I can't find fault with the mountain folks killing wild turkeys for food. It's been going on forever; I doubt if this will change for many years.

However changes are taking place. Years ago, a fall hunt was traditional, but today it no longer exists. Only spring hunts are legal. Time was when the spring season was not set

A hunter traveling to Mexico for the Gould's gobblers would be wise to obtain a passport in advance of going there and should see a doctor about any shots for eating and drinking in a country where sanitary conditions aren't at their highest. Write for a rule book on Mexico's hunting season and study it.

according to the gobbling season, but David Jackman and I convinced the authorities to set hunting dates that coincide with gobbling. Back in those days, a hunting license was "negotiable"; by this, I mean that with enough money applied to the right hands, a person could get a license with the dates written in. Of course, game wardens and game laws are for the "outside" when hunting with natives back in the mountains. Ducks, quail, deer, all wildlife comes under the gun at all times—the small whitetails *(cola blanco)* and mulies *(bura venado)* are virtually non-existent throughout many areas of ideal habitat. I've trod for miles across excellent deer lands, acorns aplenty, grass, browse, but in visiting one of the tiny mountain towns or a family home back at the end of the trail, observe dried skulls and racks, all that remained of the local deer herds. And on asking, I'm told that "yes, they were killed here, but they are very few." Certainly no surprise.

Nowhere have I found an abundance of wild turkeys in Chihuahua, Sonora, and Durango. I have skirmished large flocks on winter hunts, but these are rare, ordinarily bunched due to a local feeding condition such as a tiny mountain cornfield. The following year the land may be planted to marijuana, so the turkeys are gone, and once I get this information, so am I. You never hear about "marrywanna" today while hunting the back-

The pure strain Gould wild turkey is found only back in the high mountains, so don't settle for any lowland hunt.

country in old Mexico, so hopefully that era has passed.

Locating a place to hunt is the hard part in hunting Goulds. I don't know any of the so-called guides there, though I understand one of them tells his prospective clients I have hunted with him. This is simply a lie as I wouldn't know the guy if he walked up on my front porch. He has called me, asking me

The immense sprawl of Mexico's Sierra Madre mountain range can very well intimidate hunters who are accustomed to roads and trails and the presense of water.

All of the best hunting in Mexico is found on private property. This sign says no hunting is allowed. You don't want to get caught trespassing in Mexico.

down, but he uses bait to bag turkeys. This man promises game, which tells me he uses corn. I also question his location, because unless a hunter is back in the mountains above 6,500 feet among the small clump oaks, the Chihuahua and Mexico pine, where the scrub is thick with manzanita and madrone, he may be hunting Rio Grandes instead or local feral birds. The pure strain Gould wild turkey is found only back in the high mountains, so don't settle for any lowland hunt.

Lands in Mexico are either what I term communal or private. The former is pastured and used by everyone, the latter fenced off, usually posted and is where the game is found.

On a hunt far southwest of Durango, in the state of Durango, a bunch of us camped and hunted some forty miles back from the road on private land. Only after I'd made some kills did I learn we didn't have permission on the exact ground we were hunting so we'd best leave. My companions had meanwhile tied into some greenwing teal and gadwall, along with getting in a lick at the local Mon-

tezuma quail. The only reason no deer were laid out was none were seen. We left.

Taking your own gun back into Mexico is risky. Borrow one from your guide or the local native you're with. It's so much easier. Of course, there's no end to what you'll be offered, from tired old Remingtons and Winchesters to some old beat up cannon made in Brazil that handles about like a tire-iron. If you're a real hunter, you can easily switch. I've killed gobblers with everything but a tire-iron, and if I live long enough but get caught someday without a gun, I may have to try that, too. I have caught the birds by hand. Met an old boy down in Mexico who had killed a "havaleanee" (javalina) with a rock. He found himself surrounded by a bunch of the critters, excited and milling in the thick brush, so he chunked a large rock at one, nailing that wild pig in the side of the head.

Anyhow, I wouldn't take a favorite gun back into Mexico. Ain't worth the hassle. Should you fall in with a big

You may want to do some sightseeing while hunting in Mexico.
These ruins are found in Mexico's Valley of The Caves.

bunch of hunters, you will see a variety of guns from well-worn old 30-30s, to single shot 22s. Shotguns run the gamut, magazine guns, single barrels, bolt actions, doubles, anything that will shoot. Shells are no different. The hunt I mentioned where the turkey hunters lit into the quail and ducks, they were using #2 shot. That was all they had which is why they didn't do too well on either game. One of them

And if you're one of these "Norteamericanos" who's always in a hurry, then stay home. Things go slow and easy down there.

was toting a little 22 bolt action, but he ended up empty handed as can be imagined.

You'll be smart to obtain a passport well beforehand as this makes entering and leaving the country easier. And, you must realize that health conditions are not up to what us gringos are used to here in the States, so you may want to get shots for malaria, etc. I'd also suggest immunization for the old "yellow jack," yellow fever, and, of course, consult your doctor before you go because so many folks get deathly ill when eating food in Mexico and Central America. Your doctor can give you pills to combat this. I'm one of those lucky few who has never

had "Montezuma's revenge" or as it's also known, the "Mexican quickstep." Boil your water if it's taken from a mountain stream or fill a few collapsible plastic five-gallon containers to take with you across the border. In many small mountain towns the only utility is a tiny creek running through the village. It's used by the kids as a playground and by burros, horses, chickens and cattle for a watering hole. Most towns have a small cantina or store where a few supplies can be bought, but very few.

And if you're one of these "Norteamericanos" who's always in a hurry, then stay home. Things go slow and easy down there. You may not get to hunt today. Maybe tomorrow. Truly a land of *poco tiempo*.

Turkey hunting has been many things to me, but the people I've met, and the places they've taken me, have been as much a part of the hunting as pulling a trigger. And if you want to truly love hunting, you should learn the lands where you want to set your boots. Far the warmest people I've met have been from Mexico and Central America. It's sad how the people of the United States treat other races, including the Native American Indian, all Mexicans, along with all the dark-skinned races below the border and above. For decades in this country we've believed that the good old U.S. was top dog in the world, and where each of us traveled we were King. That's no longer true. And, while all of these folks have for so long

Rock fences are seen throughout Mexico's mountainous areas—this one surrounding a ranch in the state of Durango. These keep cattle or other livestock from drifting into other pastures.

admired "Americans," we didn't even share our title with them. After all, a person from Mexico is just as much from the Americas as you or I. But, no, today he is still "Mexican." These people are wonderful.

And once you get to Mexico, in your chase for the Gould's, see the country. I've asked a jillion questions and while I can't speak the language, I have gotten by. Many natives speak English, and together with my sign language we communicate.

I love Mexican music. Today's chart favorite is a very popular group known as Bronco, a solid hit with both young and old. A lover of guitar music, I have tapes by guitarist Antonio Bribiesca, a national favorite. Bull rings, cock fights, it's all there. They'd never heard the small VW's referred to as "bugs," and asked me what I was talking about when one day I said, "Gosh, look at all the bugs."

Travel on the few toll roads in that country is very expensive so be prepared for that expense. Of course, few people can afford them so you'll have the toll roads almost for your private use.

Hunting and fishing are both popular. Fishing Lake Guerra still tops the list, but excellent saltwater fishing for bill fish is excellent off the Pacific coast, from further south down into Nicaragua where I've hunted along the coastal mountains on the Pacific side.

Sign language is often the only way for many "gringos" to get across whatever it is they'd like to say. It's easier than you might think to work things out in this manner.

Hunting for large cats, jaguars (big tigre) and ocelots (little tigre) is popular, but mostly done at night with dogs. Sadly, much night hunting is done throughout the Central American countries and Mexico, and the new lighted reticle scopes have made the sport more enjoyable for all those folks who happen to own one. Such scopes are "the only thing" for places like Nicaragua where the bulk of whitetail hunting is done after dark with a powerful spotlight. Jaguar and ocelot are killed in the same manner.

Duck hunting is extremely popular in the lowland countries where "lagunas" are found, with all species, mainly puddle ducks like pintails, teal, widgeon, spoonies and often many pink-billed tree ducks. Quail hunting can be found across much of Mexico—the bulk of it in the lower brush country, the birds being the scaled variety. Mexico has a number of subspecies of these birds, from the beautiful Mearns to the just as pretty Montezumas.

Turkey hunting back in Mexico's mountains is a rugged sport. Huge canyons, rocky hillsides, cliffs, pinnacles, cold mountain air, terribly hot afternoons, and all at high elevations making for hard hunting. Hazards are spraining ankles, falling, shortness of breath, snake and insect bites not to mention other things like bad water and food. Durango is noted for the black scorpions that like to climb into a hunter's sleeping bag. I use a heavy canvas ground cloth around my bag to prevent entry. Nor does a person want to cross the local Federales or he may end up in jail. Looking at them on the outside, Hell's Home Guard would look like a bunch of Sunday school kids alongside the occupants of a Mexican jail.

Bag limit there is one gobbler, and in this macho land it's spelled as such in the rules book—"macho adult," male adult. Seasons are all set for late March and part of April, but the dates do vary from state to state as is the case here in this country.

Turkeys go by so many names a hunter must keep alert if he

The Gould's range can be overpowering, but if you are a hunter who'll tighten up your belt and wade into things, you won't have any problems.

hopes to catch mention of the birds. Names like guajolote, (pronounced "wah-ha-loh-tii"), cocono, gallapavo, silvestris, pavo (popular in some places), toto, pipilo, and further south into Central America another raft of names surfaces. Some birds are called turkeys though these aren't wild turkeys at all. Feral birds (tame gone wild), and birds of the old strain of gallopavo. Gallopavo are evidently scattered in places also. You'll hear many stories about where the birds can be found, and while you may have your doubts, very often I've found birds at these locations.

Hunting the Gould is akin to hunting any mountain gobbler, particularly Merriams in New Mexico, Arizona, and Colorado where rough, tough country may be encountered. The vastness of Gould's range can be overpowering to a less aggressive person, but if you are a hunter who'll tighten up your belt and

Sylvia Zavala (smiling, second from the left) and friends enjoy a burrito at a sidewalk vendor near the football stadium in Durango. No, it's not American football, it's a soccer field. The friendliness of the Mexican people is all but unbelieveable, particularly to any U.S. citizen who has just left the stuck-up air found in places like the air terminal at San Antonio or Austin.

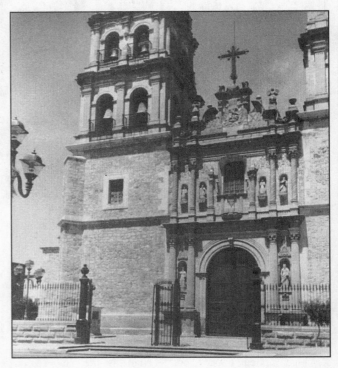

A gorgeous old cathedral in the downtown Durango public square or plaza. These plazas are very popular meeting places on Sunday afternoon.

wade into things, you won't have any problems. So very many of today's hunters are afraid of getting lost, or afraid of snakes, or the dark, or all such junk, that it seriously limits where they can and will hunt. Standing near the peak of a tall mountain, gazing at mountains for as far as the eye will see, not a town in sight, not a sound of a plane, nor a gunshot, that's a turkey hunter's world in Mexico. That's a domain for me. I hope for an old Gould's gobbler, too.

Gould's gobblers are big birds, maybe not as heavy as some of this stuff being claimed as world records, but big-boned, large in measurement. Going through my notes, I measured a bird years ago up near the Sonora-Chihuahua line 54 inches in

(Left) Sidewalk vendors are just as popular in the big cities of Mexico as downtown Manhattan. The man with apron, with the help of one of my companions, holds aloft a giant tortilla he whipped up, apparently just for the heck of it. Marceloa Delgado, wearing cap, looks on as I take the gentleman's photo.

(Below) Farming methods are still primitive back in Mexico's mountain ranges. Tractors are seldom seen due to a lack of fuel and cost of repairs. Horses can get along on grass and grain and don't have a carburetor that might go on the blink.

(Below) A wild cow trap is truly a work of art. They are built completely by hand without any power tools by cowhands who learned the trade from their ancestors. A pair of posthole diggers, a good pair of fence pliers, some baling wire and a couple of very sharp axes are all that's needed plus a lot of hard work.

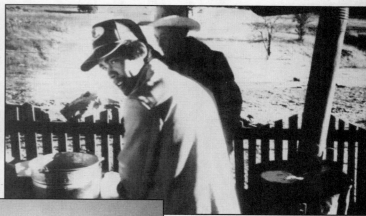

(Right) The very mention of deer, *venado*, around a mountain village, will bring forth all the trophies hanging on porches locally. The whitetail head displayed here by the old gent in the baseball cap is a very nice rack for back in Mexico's mountain country. Few heads obtain this size. The average buck is like the ones nailed to the board held by the boy.

(Above) All meals back in mountain camps are very primitive as are the cooking conditions. Tortillas (on top the stove) are definitely the mainstay and if you don't care for tortillas and beans then I'd say you'd best stay at home. Mexico's mountains ain't for you. But don't pass up the *tesvino* if it's offered you. It is green corn beer, has a muddy water look, and isn't what the average American would drink back home.

An adult Gould's gobbler can be a very large bird, with a huge wingspan and great length. Beard development is not too good, and spur growth is slow. The author has killed adult gobblers with no spurs on either leg, while other birds will have spurs not unlike the gobblers from other subspecies.

length with a 73-inch wing span. Beard length is comparable to the Merriam as is spur growth, though I have killed several gobblers with no spurs whatsoever. While brooming of the wing primaries was much like others I have killed, Gould gobblers with the middle tail feathers badly broomed were birds I'd taken in areas that had many steep inclines. Apparently the feathers were worn from dragging the rocky soil. I can recall an old bird coming to my call one day that made such a racket crossing loose shalus it was very easy to mark his progress toward me. That incline was probably at least a 70 percent grade.

The hen problem is no different than anywhere else. So if

Allen Hawkins, of Colonia Juarez, with a large Gould's gobbler. The birds are found throughout the backbone of the Sierra Madres range, from Sonora and Chihuahua in the north on south down into Durango. Acorns seem to be the main food source, though the birds are very fond of madrano and manzanita berries. Grasses are also eaten as are insects of various kinds.

Jose Llama spreads the tail on a Gould's showing the brilliant white tipped tail and lower rump feathers. Jose has bagged several kinds of big game both in Mexico and in the U.S. His home sports a number of beautiful game mounts.

Marcelo Delgado, in the camo cap, can serve a delicious meal from no more than a small grill and a couple of pans placed on a bed of embers far back in Mexico's Sierra Madres. Tortillas, refried beans, tamales, avocado, tomatoes, some diced pork, and last but certainly not least, some green chilies, are the making of a meal a hungry hunter will never forget. Just makes my mouth water thinking about it. I'm looking forward to the next one, Marcelo.

hens mess up your morning, don't think you're alone. By noon they are ordinarily away from the gobbler.

Calling is very effective for Gould's. Few have ever been near a hen yelp except those made by hens, so the birds haven't been overcalled. Back when I first hunted Mexico, a turkey call was unheard of; those I took were probably the first. Today turkey calls can be purchased in all the large cities. I've seen Lynch, Haydel, Quaker Boy, Penn's Woods, and surely there are others. The most experienced hunter I've met in Mexico, Angel Diaz Cebbalos, uses a Lynch box. He showed me pictures of several fine old gobblers he'd called, all of which he claimed were in the twenty to twenty-four pound range. Like so many Mexican nationals, Angel (pronounced Ann-jell) totes a Remington 1100, stoking it's 2³/₄-inch chamber with Mexican-manufactured Union brand cartridges.

Lying in ambush, dry-gulch, bushwack, any of these will work should you locate an area turkeys are using each day. Jose Llama, Marcelo Delgado, and I located such a place one afternoon down in Durango. I staked it out until dark that day, and with Marcelo near me staked it out the following morning. Marcelo had never hunted turkeys before. I built a tiny blind, told him to follow my lead when any birds approached, and not to shoot me as I was directly in front of him. His first turkey ever hit the dusty gray meadow not twenty yards from me. I was too busy to take notice since I had my hands full laying out a jake that had walked past my hide so close I could have grabbed it by the neck. What's more, at my shot a gob-

bler cut loose back of me, so I whirled around, missed it with the first shot, pumped the old Winchester and nailed him with the second load of #2.

Still-hunting on Mexican terrain is not the best method for killing turkeys down that way. There's either not enough cover or there's too much, particularly if you are in much manzanita and madrone. This latter grows into small tree size, sometimes called a "strawberry tree" because of its beautiful red bark. Manzanita has a darker red bark also. Both are very interesting and have berries the turkeys eat. Acorns are plentiful and the birds live where these various oaks thrive.

The maguey, also found in many areas, is a large dagger-leafed plant much like the yucca; the larger Century plant is

Calling is very effective for Goulds. Few have ever been near a hen yelp except for those made by hens.

also seen on the lower slopes. The spines of the maguey are extremely sharp, so beware of falling into any of these, or any of the many cacti found in Mexico.

Throughout the areas I have hunted this turkey, the terrain is volcanic with some steep faulting on north, northeast and northwest slopes due to uplift when the earth was cooling. South slopes are gradual, with mesas predominating at the peak, gradually giving way to southern quadrants at a lesser

Many of our hunting methods are unknown in Mexico. Marcelo Delgado had never before hunted from a makeshift blind. He adapted to it instantly, sitting very quietly as turkeys walked so near he could all but reach out and grab them by the neck.

(Right) Marcelo Delgado with a young Gould's jake gobbler. Such birds are highly prized for food by all the mountain folks back in the High Sierras. After many years of hunting the birds there, it is a fact that game laws are completely unheeded and game is hunted the year 'round, largely due to the lack of game enforcement officers.

Though there is not as much activity today as there was many years ago, the locals still dig for ancient pottery, resulting in the upheaval of old Indian graves.

A beautiful Montezuma quail bagged by one of my companions on a hunt back into the High Sierras. The gorgeous black and white dotted and striped plumage makes the birds fairly easy to see while driving ranch trails. These birds are invariably found in areas of dense manzanita thickets, and also where the handsome Madroneo tree is found.

I handed a peg'n'slate call to a man who said he knew where there were some wild turkeys. After he watched me a few times, he was making very nice yelps. Since he admired the call, I left it with him though the only gun he seemed to own was a very well-worn 22 rifle. Obviously it had seen a jillion rounds through its barrel.

degree of grade. Invariably these northern slopes contain predominant roost sites, of chihuahua pines and, if left undisturbed, will be used year after year by the birds. Too often, local hunters roostshoot the birds, causing them to move.

This roost-site information seems to be passed down from one generation of hunters to another, and if it weren't for a lack of guns and shells, there wouldn't be any turkeys. From my contacts with Tarahumara Indians in Mexico, they obviously never forget where the birds roost and can go there on the darkest of nights without artificial light to show the way. Once there, they have no qualms about building a fire to keep themselves warm while awaiting better light to shoot. Roost trees are invariably just below the summit and are not as large a tree as many we would find in areas in the United States. Like all of the civilized world, Mexico's virgin forests were timbered off way back when, and due to scant precipitation, large trees are few and far between.

North slopes are often extremely rugged in character with rock outcroppings and rock walls heavily cloaked in underbrush. Slopes are covered with loose shale rock which makes walking difficult. During the spring hunt, gobblers will often be heard sounding off along these high rims. It's hoped by the hunter that the bird will come down once he has called together his entourage of hens, saving the hunter the horrendous climb. What usually happens is that the birds are heard assembling, then march off out of hearing range, traveling out on the gradual inclines to the south of the roost areas. If the hunter decides to fool 'em and makes the climb in the dark before sunrise, the birds gather below the roost sites, on the steep brush-cloaked slopes just below the summits, and drop to the valley floor for an early morning drink.

The gradual slopes of the southern quadrants have reddish to brown soils, strewn with rock which appears volcanic. These mesas are dotted with various junipers, scrub oaks much like the shinnery oaks found in the ranges of the Rio Grande turkey, or Gambel's oak which grows in Merriam habitat.

The alligator juniper is far the most productive, having a large brown fruit with the consistency of a nut when ripe. These brown fruits will often carpet the ground beneath a mature tree. The alligator gets its name from the bark configuration which looks like the armor plating on an alligator. It is found in much of New Mexico's and Arizona's Merriam turkey range, but less abundant.

On ridges where there is excellent grass growth, chances are much greater that you will find turkeys. Invariably, the choice pastures are those in private ownership. It's not unusual to drive through a gate back in the mountains and find one side of the fence bare of grasses, while on the other side grass clumps protrude everywhere from among the volcanic rock. The predominant grasses are of bunch-grass formation, what I would classify as muhly grass. Another is what could be termed a short white grass, much like our buffalo grass here in western Oklahoma, and still another is similar to our tickle grasses.

Gould's turkeys are no different from other turkeys. They seek out cultivated foods, particularly corn.

I've found large balls of these grasses in the crops of Gould's turkeys, so obviously the bird finds them to its liking.

Gould's turkeys are no different from other turkeys. They seek out cultivated foods, particularly corn and maize. Up among the rugged mountain chains, very few cultivated fields are found, and when they are, they are often small. Ground cover is lacking in vines, creepers and grass carpet. I've seen Apache Rose on rocky slopes along with a small thorny bush known as Johnny-Jump-Up, derived from the way its thorns grab at you when you brush against it. Much of Mexico is deemed open range, though the meaning of the term is not the same in Mexico. "Open range" in America means it isn't cross-fenced, therefore a traveler touring by vehicle should be

Very seldom are gates encountered throughout much of Mexico's high country which tells us that the pastures are very large. Pine trees are never seen in abundance at least not big ones. Big trees are cut as quickly as the tree grows to marketable size.

(Below) There's so much cactus in Mexico that it's easy to understand why it is on the country's flag, along with the eagle and the rattlesnake.

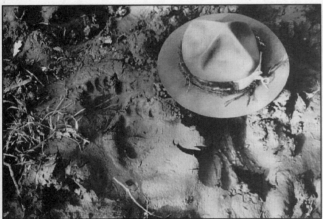

(Above) Bear sign, as well as lion tracks and droppings, are not uncommon back in the high mountains. Both are hunted with dogs if predation becomes a problem. Range cattle, small game and plentiful supplies of berries and acorns probably sustain the animals much of the time.

Much of the mature timber has been cut in Mexico leaving few decent roost trees in many areas. This lone Chihuahua pine stands all alone atop a ridge far back in the mountains near the Sonora border.

alert to cattle on the road. "Open range" in Mexico allows local inhabitants to pasture cattle on such lands.

Gould's wild turkeys will travel long distances each day to seek a cultivated field and will make excursions to that field long after the harvest. The Gould's habitat encompasses areas within the Upper Sonoran zone with elevations from 4,500 to 7,500 feet and extends into the lower reaches of the Transition zone, closely resembling the habitat of the Merriam subspecie.

Among the oaks found within the Gould's range are the Mexican blue oak, Arizona white oak, gray oak, silverleaf oak, and the Fremont oak, which has bark much like the alligator juniper. The Sonoran fantailed deer utilizes these acorns, as do the many squirrels found in the Sierra Madres.

The Gould's wild turkey lives in extremely rough, rugged mountain country. Elevations vary but can reach 9,000 feet. You must remember this if you have any type of heart trouble. Breathing can be difficult on a long, hard climb before daybreak, when the cold early morning air burns holes in your lungs as you gasp for breath.

A hunter intent on pursuing a Gould's turkey should give his health a good second look. Far back in the high Sierras is not the place to decide it's time to go to the hospital, as there aren't any. First aid is just as far unless you or someone in your party is equipped with a first aid kit. When you pack it, remember it could be subject to scrutiny at the border when you enter Mexico, and unmarked drugs could mean a delay. If you wear eyeglasses, carry an extra pair in your coat pocket. The same goes for hearing aids.

Folks with back or leg trouble would be wise to stay out of the high Sierras. These old mountain gobblers have a liking for hiking up and down the steep slopes, and though I've never understood how they've come by steel legs, I keep looking at the dead ones to see if that is what they have. The chill air encourages leg cramps, which are also brought about by sitting too long before continuing the climb. Take it easy when you first begin your hunt, and after a few days time you'll get both your legs and your lungs accustomed to the thinner mountain air. This is even more important if you are wearing a backpack or fanny pack.

I never leave camp without a belt knife, a small belt bag which contains a compass, and a small match safe. I never leave camp without a sling on whatever gun I'm toting. I've

***G**ould's wild turkeys will travel long distances each day to seek a cultivated field and will make excursions to that field long after the harvest.*

taken simple leather strips with me, and on more than one occasion, custom tied a sling then and there. This leaves both hands free, particularly for the predawn climb, when one hand will be needed to aim the flashlight, and the other for fighting brush or grasping limbs to haul yourself up-mountain. Should you decide to make any hunts from horseback, the sling comes in very handy. Too, if hunting from a horse, you could make an overnight hunt in some remote region, requiring a sleeping bag. Small, extremely compact bags are best, along with an outside tarp to be used as both a ground cloth and in case of rain provide some protection. Rain isn't a great concern in the arid mountains of Mexico though.

Additional items to pack are extra boots, long-handled underwear, gloves, soap and towel. A hunter is wise to carry along his own mess kit, including a spoon, knife and fork set. You'll appreciate having your own drinking cup. Don't forget your camera and extra film. Special foods, paper plates, throw-a-way cups, these items are all up to the individual. Some folks carry water purification tablets.

Much of the terrain in the back country of the huge Sierra Madre range is very rough, hard on both hunter and whatever he's using as a means of travel. Often the road or a trail will be down a dry creekbed. Don't head for the mountains with nothing but the best of tires.

The towns found back in Mexico's mountains are very primitive with no utilities except perhaps the creek which runs through all the little settlements. Life is very simple here. Perhaps a way of life many of us *Norte Americano's* would find much easier than the stressful ones we live.

If you are in strange country you haven't hunted, you have your work cut out for you. It becomes a matter of finding sign—tracks, droppings, feathers and what-have-you—and following these to where they become thick. Then, you'll know you are in the area of the roost site. You will be on a mesa, and somewhere along its northern face where the mountain drops off steeply, you'll find scattered pines, perhaps both Apache and Chihuahua. If the stand of pines is small, dotted here and there over several acres, and you feel up to clambering around over the steep mountainside where these trees are located, you can drop off the rim and search beneath them for droppings. If you locate several trees with droppings near the base, your chances are improving.

Once you've hunted an area for several days, you will have located several of these roost rims, with adjoining mesas, and you can rotate among them until you make contact. If you want to keep busy during the midday hours when the birds are not near the roost areas, you can look for dust sites along old cultivated fields, or along dry washes. Once you've located a dust area, you can check it from time to time for birds. Again, concentrate on areas where you find the greatest amount of fresh sign. Mountain air will dry the droppings very quickly, so don't be deceived. Tracks remain for long periods too, as there is little wind to disturb them.

Tracks two to three weeks old can appear to be made yesterday, or a couple days ago. Once you've found lots of sign, search around among it and look for other indications of age. Have any leaves fallen on the tracks where they pass under overhanging bushes? A tiny grass blade is growing from the bottom of a track. Look, and closer examination reveals that the soil at its base is undisturbed. It's popped up since the track was made. That dropping, it looks very fresh. If you don't want to pinch it with your fingers, as us old turkey hunters are prone to do, then use a stick. It's soft. That bird has been by here today.

Whenever you think you're up to it, and you've got a hankering to hunt the King of the Mountain, hike yourself off to the lands south of the border, to Mexico. Go west to the mountains that straddle the states of Sonora, Chihuahua and Durango. Hunt with somebody who knows the country.

They say there's gold in the Sierra Madres. The only gold I want to see back in those hills is the yellow glint of sunlight bouncing off the feathers of a big old Mexico gobbler.

Oh, beat the drums slowly,
and play the fife lowly,
Oh, what a long and lonely go,
As we rode the trail to Mexico.

14

You Can't Hunt Turkeys In a Rose Garden

SURELY THERE'S no profession where you are as apt to meet so many truly fine people as being a hunting guide. Oh, it's true that some of your clients can't hit the side of a barn; perhaps have never fired a gun; never killed a turkey or even seen a wild turkey; can't sit still; can't walk; the list goes on.

But these things don't keep you from liking them—many become good friends for life. You look forward from one season to the next to having them back.

But there's probably no profession with as much inherent danger as being a hunting guide. It seems gun safety takes a backseat when a hunter is following his guide. The only person who looks down the bad end of a gun barrel more than a hunting guide is a gunsmith. And, the ones he works on are unloaded.

The average traveling hunter won't remember to load his gun until I tell him to. In fact, there have been times when, in the heat of the hunt, the hunter has just plain forgot to stick in some shells.

Of course, as the guide you ask the hunter not to point the gun in your direction, but after so much of this most guides give up and hope the odds continue in their favor. The worst part about any of it is that should the client's gun discharge, it would be at very close range. Rifles are bad at close range; a load of turkey shot is devastating. Some day when you are near an old junk pile, fire a load into the side of a junked automobile or an abandoned refrigerator. You'll then realize what a terrific force is at hand.

Not only are guns a hazard to the guide but to other hunters. Recent publicity concerning hunting accidents has made

turkey hunting far the most dangerous of the hunting sports. And, as the number of hunters in the woods increases each year, the accident rate climbs. What's even more disturbing about this is that nearly every one of these accidents began as a purposeful act; the act of one hunter shooting straight toward another. No, I'm not talking about two hunters being on opposite sides of a turkey, with one shooting at the turkey and striking the other on the far side of the bird. The distances involved in this type of incident result in little more than being sprinkled with shot. These things happen. I remember late one afternoon after bellycrawling into gunshot of a bird, I made my shot. The bird went to flopping. I ran to it, grabbed the bird by the neck, gave it a quick flip, then watched as it kept flopping. I'd not noticed, but suddenly I became aware of a man walking up to me, already no more than ten yards away. I turned and spoke, noticed his gun, and only then realized that perhaps the two of us were hunting the same turkey, I made mention of this, and he pointed to where he'd been hiding. Though he was slightly out of my line of fire, he might as well have been straight down my barrel. I had no idea he was there, so would have made my shot. The only reason he hadn't fired was that he had come to the end of cover and was out of range. Otherwise, he might have shot in my direction.

At such distances #4, #5 or #6 shot probably isn't going to harm a person, but one pellet could destroy an eye. And, who knows, maybe the man had #2 shot, or even BBs in his gun. Just because BBs are illegal in that state doesn't mean hunters aren't using them.

The hunting accidents that present a clearer danger are those

involving a hunter purposely shooting toward another hunter, with intent to kill.

This is the leading cause of turkey hunting accidents. A hunter *thinks* a turkey is in view, because he sees a slight movement and hears what he assumes is a turkey calling. He shoots into the area where that movement and that sound came from. Though he never actually sees a wild turkey, his imagination, his desire, his wanting to see a turkey, takes over, and he shoots. This simply boils down to the bald truth: The mark being shot at has never really been identified.

Before any of us remark "I'll never do that," let me remind you that our worst fault as human beings is being human beings. I'm no different. Any and each of us can make mistakes—we all have, none of us are perfect. Sure, I tell myself that never will I ever shoot someone because I mistook a tiny hint of black moving near a big oak, a yelp, a hint of blue from a shirt not covered by camouflage, for a turkey and fire. No, I'll never do that. I hope I don't. I pray I won't.

A hunter can do a few things to prevent such a scenario. Wearing solid-colored clothing is one—even though the hues may be dark browns, grays or greens, these colors do not meld into the landscape like camouflage. And, all these folks getting shot are togged out in camos. The person shooting cannot see a human being due to the camos so assumes it is a turkey.

(Left) Shooting a crossbow in turkey hunting calls for close-in shooting. It is best done when a steady aim can be maintained and demands the same fine pinpoint accuracy as bowhunting.

(Below) Like many of today's modern weapons, the modern crossbow in no way resembles those carried into battle centuries ago. A scoped sighting arrangement, with crosshairs, allows Ed La Force to make various range adjustments.

You may want to wear a fluorescent orange jacket or nail a hunk of orange cloth to the tree next to you. *Don't use red.* A gobbler wears red on his head so anyone wearing red may be inviting trouble. The same goes for blue and white.

Hunting with a partner with the two of you facing in opposite directions helps to cover all points, not allowing anyone to approach unseen. Sitting with your back to a large tree, or against a rock protects your back but not your sides. There is no way to fully protect yourself.

Shotguns were a short-range weapon and hunters didn't

W*e have become a nation of shooters. Too often a shot is fired at a gobbler fifty, sixty, seventy, maybe even eighty yards distant.*

have to worry about getting shot with them at distances of seventy or eighty yards. But those days are over. With today's highly touted long-range shells stuffed into guns which can throw lethal patterns at sixty yards, the chances of being hit by shotgun pellets in today's woods has increased considerably. And, taken much of the hunting out of hunting.

We've become a nation of shooters. Too often a shot is fired at a gobbler fifty, sixty, seventy, maybe even eighty yards distant. This isn't turkey hunting; instead, this is irresponsible blasting. This is the big woods answer to "sky busting."

If today's turkey hunters would stop long-range shooting, accident rates would plummet. It is obvious the shotgun and ammunition manufacturers aren't going to accept the responsibility and produce only short-range guns and shells. So we, as hunters, must practice responsible shooting.

Health Safety

The major task faced by most guides, big game guides in particular, is placing a client to within fair shooting distance of the quarry. However, that job is hindered by hunters who arrive in very poor physical condition.

Turkey hunting can be a very strenuous sport—lots of walking, much of it on mountainous terrain, some at high elevations in thin air, through thick swamps, all the while decked out in heavy boots and carrying a gun, shells, plus pockets filled with all sorts of stuff. Usually all this "fun" begins well before daylight and doesn't end until well past dark.

It's been my pleasure to guide and hunt out of camps across all kinds of turkey country, from "sea to shining sea." And before the hunt begins darned near all of us have one habit which is really detrimental to the men and women leaving

Too many of today's turkey hunters are being shot—not by anti-hunters but by another turkey hunter. There are a few things a hunter can do to stem the tide like keeping a very large tree at one's back or, better yet, a rock pile. But probably one of the best tactics is to hunt in pairs. It won't do any good if you both face the same direction like these hunters are doing. Another turkey or hunter can easily sneak in on these boys.

camp each morning, headed for the woods—too much breakfast. Yes, far too much.

Back when the Indians were boss, warriors would get all riled up, decide that the tribe over yonder had given them trouble once too often, round up a war party, and go take a few scalps. These sorties would last for days, weeks, or months. Very often just before the party left camp, they'd feast until their bellies stuck out. After all, that might be the last plentiful meal they'd have for a while.

Today's hunter doesn't need to eat like that since few stay out all day. In fact, I seldom find one who'll stay out all morning. Most want to go back to camp for a late breakfast, or, if a shot is heard, to see if old so-and-so got a turkey. Today's hunter is a patsy; soft, no legs, no wind, no guts. And sorrowfully, so are our children. More and more we see young boys and girls who are flabby, overweight and obviously couch potatoes. It's a national disgrace.

I do have clients who are in good physical condition, men who hike, swim, exercise, and therefore are trim, can stick to my heels, and when I am ready to hunt, are there. But good physical condition goes further than just making a hard hunt an enjoyable one. A body that is agile yet muscular will be able to take the falls and bruises without injury. A bunch of us were on a hunt in the rain forest of Central America. After a very rugged three-mile hike back into the jungle, one man sprained an ankle. Of course, he was in great pain, crying out, and had fallen behind the rest of us a hundred yards or so. He gave me some concern as I trudged back to see what had happened. I was truly grateful he wasn't badly hurt. I borrowed our native boy's machete and made him a pair of make-do crutches. I ended up toting out his gun and the native boy carried his hunting jacket. Luckily, we bumped into another native lad on a small horse a ways down the mountain. He very generously climbed off his horse and with the help of a nearby boulder, we got my buddy on the beast.

Only the day before another of the hunters had to have all of his things toted back to camp as he just couldn't make it any further. This young man is an expert at karate and other martial sports, but unfortunately is also a top candidate for a heart attack or stroke. He smokes cigars, drinks too much, and excites very easily.

Another hunter in our party didn't make it four hundred yards into the rain forest before he backed out. He's a businessman who gets no exercise, and was smart to realize his limitations. His intent to get into shape will require an iron will

M*any good turkey hunts become just the opposite because a hunter can't make the grade.*

to get it done. My personal hunch is that he'll probably be in worse shape the next time our paths cross.

This all adds up to the fact that many good turkey hunts become just the opposite because a hunter can't make the grade. If a person would only walk a few blocks each evening after work, instead of slouching in front of the TV, and build

This is truly a Devil's Club, which is the proper name for this little hunk of meanness. It's best to always keep your eyes open to such hazards and be careful what you grab a hold of.

on this until it's easy to do twenty or thirty city blocks, then a walk in the woods will come much easier.

And, don't think walking in a comfortable pair of Nike's will prepare your feet for covering ground in hunting boots. If you're going to hunt in boots, wear them on your hikes or walks. If you intend to hunt in jogging or walking shoes, fine, but too often folks condition their legs in walking shoes, then wear heavy boots into the field and their feet suffer.

If you hope to hunt Merriams, Goulds, or mountain country Easterns, you need to also increase your lung capacity so that breathing will not be difficult at higher elevations. This isn't critical in Eastern turkey range but can cripple a hunt for Merriams and Goulds from the beginning. The best method to aid in increasing lung capacity is wind sprints. If you aren't in shape for that, then I'd suggest running up and down stairs. Fast rowing on a rowing machine will also help and conditions the body at the same time. Swimming is unbeatable, but too many of us have no access to a pool.

There are things a hunter can do once he's at the hunt which

Few hunters would admit it's hazardous to your health, but scragging a big gobbler back in rough mountain country could trigger a heart attack or stroke. If you have heart problems or high blood pressure, you'd be wise to keep your turkey shooting on level ground.

Hunters aren't the only ones who have troubles. This turkey was killed because it ran across the path of a steel trap which was probably set for predators.

Flat tires are rarely a hazard, but why is it that these things never happen except in bad places or when it's just rained.

Bad roads—pictures won't do justice to such a mess. This is a slick yellow clay gumbo with a little red clay mixed in just for fun. You'll need a four-wheel drive to get through this mess, if you get through.

will make things easier—quit smoking; quit drinking coffee and tea; and quit eating so much. Drink more juices, eat more fruit.

And get plenty of rest. Rest and mental conditioning go together—a hunter who is worn out and bone-tired, has half lost the game. He's on the downhill side. He won't be ready for any unexpected chances; his mind doesn't weigh all the options when he gets a good opportunity; and if the terrain suddenly presents obstacles, he's too tired to overcome them. An old gobbler will find this guy a pushover.

You don't have to go to bed with the chickens each night to keep your energy level high, though it will go against you each day after you've been up half the night shooting the bull, drinking, or whatever. Nobody knows better'n I do. Those late night bull sessions are what life's made of, but if you still hope to get in your licks, you'd be smarter to hit the sack at a reasonable hour.

People who've hunted with me know that I do a lot of resting in the woods. Not when folks are paying me to guide, but when I'm hunting for me. Many days I've had as many as three naps, all for only a few minutes each. But when I've been up late with those campfire talkathons, and am hunting the next day, I'll watch for a good calling stand, sit down, brush all the leaves and sticks back so I can lay back comfortably, and then I'll hunt a while. I'll make a few calls, wait until the woods settle down, lay my gun alongside my left leg so

Rest and mental conditioning go together—a hunter who is worn out has half lost the game.

my southpaw can hold onto the pistol grip, and just before I lay down I'll make another call, or series of calls. Then I'll lay back, tip my hat across my eyes, stretch out my legs, and "fall apart." It's a pity that so few hunters have learned to relax. There's an art to real relaxing. The best method for most folks is to begin with the fingers, tightening them up into a fist, clinching hard, then simply letting them go limp. Work through the whole body like this, and once you've mastered the technique, you'll be "dead to the world" in a jiffy.

These short cat naps, unlike deep sleep, allows me to awake two to three moments later, feeling wild-eyed and bushy-tailed and completely refreshed.

Once a person has done this for a spell, he will also learn to wake up, without a move. When you first awaken you might have to get reoriented, thinking to yourself, "Where'n the hell am I?" But, in a heartbeat you'll remember you're in Kansas, or Mexico, or heck knows where and that you are hunting turkeys. And, you'll feel your hand tighten around the small of the shotgun's stock. Then it dawns on you that, yes, indeed, you are hunting.

Unless the birds or bird that came to your calls have awakened you, you won't know any are nearby until you raise back to a sitting position. Whether you've been awakened, or simply woke up, and then sat up, not knowing if a bird is close, this is strictly fast draw time. You stir, the nearby turkeys are going to sell out for faroff places.

I've killed a good many turkeys just after a snooze—all very near when I woke up. Three or four woke me with clucking; the others I had no idea were near. An old Eastern Ozarks gobbler brought me to my senses one day just after lunch, when he got too near me (probably couldn't figure out what all of my snoring was all about) so he began this deep clucking. I nailed him inside twenty-five yards with Old C&G. I'd eaten my lunch from the pack, and like a lazy old hog, got sleepy and was soon cutting the woodpile.

Yet another day after killing one fine old he-bird, I'd laid him back of me in the shade, made a call or two to his buddies which had run off on the scatter, then laid back to nap since I presumed they wouldn't show for at least an hour or two. Ironically, one of the old birds came in, spotted the dead bird, and like any turkey began making a fuss over it; the noise woke me up.

Woven wire fences aren't ordinarily a hazard, but can be a real headache if you're trying to call a turkey through one. A wild gobbler will run alongside all day and, unless he finds a hole, will very rarely fly over. Locate a hole and call from within gunshot of it, then you can zero in on the bird when he crosses to your side.

So, you never know when you lie down in turkey country what situation you'll face on stirring from your nap. Most times it'll be interesting. You present no profile, so turkeys or cattle, deer, squirrels, snakes, or any other critter that lives in the woods you're inhabiting approach with their guard down. I've yet to have another hunter rouse me from my sleep, and I'll never know if one has passed my way. Probably any who have passed by have thought it best to let me sleep—after all, a guy who's stretched out sawing logs doesn't appear to be much of a threat to the local turkey population.

Using Decoys Safely

I would like to mention here a word about using decoys. Place the decoy far enough away from your position so that should another hunter see it from a distance and then intend to sneak toward it, hoping to get a shot at the supposed turkey, he can't approach into gun range of you. If you keep thick cover on all but one side of you and the decoy, anyone who might shoot at the decoy must, more or less, shoot across the front of you and you won't get hit. I don't use decoys, have never killed a bird over one, but I have had clients who brought them along. I can't imagine anyone shooting at such a thing as I've yet to see a decoy which truly resembled a real bird. From what I'm told, decoys are very effective, but using them could be hazardous, so be on guard.

Many hunters use decoys, which is fine if you like to live dangerously. If you are using decoys, be careful some hunter doesn't mistake them for the real thing with you in the line of fire.

All hunters would be wise to have a well-supplied first aid chest handy, either in camp or in the car or truck. Mine has about everything I can think of which might help should any kind of minor mishap cause pain or discomfort. There's everything from scissors to a pair of tweezers, and a hundred small items in between.

Clothing

Being comfortable while hunting not only helps your physical well-being but also gives the hunter a mental advantage—if you feel good, you hunt good. Try to learn what weight clothing will be best if you're traveling to new hunting grounds. Too many times I've seen a hunter freezing his butt off, or sweat pouring down his face because he is over-clothed. One of the great advantages of the camouflaged hunting vest is that clothing can be taken off and stowed in the large cargo pocket on the back side of the vest. Rain gear can be carried along, plus water and a snack.

People who travel far from home should definitely carry plenty of prescription medicines, a well-stocked first aid kit, perhaps an extra set of eye glasses, and, I always have a small book of first aid techniques in the truck. Burn salve is a must, as is tick spray, bug repellant, (sunscreen for those who burn easily), and plenty of band-aids, etc.

Accidents are something we all try to avoid—cuts, bruises, snakebite, bad falls—but we are human, so we'll have accidents. We can guard against some hazards, though, so if you hunt a lot, keep up on your tetanus booster shots. If you go into areas where bad food and water are a problem, go to your health clinic and get malaria, yellow fever (Yellow Jack) and hepatitis shots. You'll have to spend a few bucks for all this stuff, but what's money compared to good health. Or, having a trip of a lifetime end in a belly ache and total misery.

Bad water is a problem in places like Gould's country in old Mexico. Many tourists get deathly ill traveling throughout Mexico each year, simply due to bad water, and in some cases, bad food. Any doctor will write a prescription for pills which will cure the Mexican quickstep, but probably taking your own supply of water with you is the best preventative. I always pack a collapsible five-gallon container of water for

Accidents are something we all try to avoid, but we are human, so we'll have accidents.

each hunter. While baths and all that stuff are out of the question, we can at least brush teeth and drink. When you're back in the high Sierras hunting Gould's wild turkeys, you aren't going to be on a Sunday school picnic, so you won't smell any worse than the next guy. Some of us are lucky. We can get by with things others can't, probably because we were from a tougher age. So we can eat what we want, where we want, then stick our faces into the nearest creek when we're thirsty. But, unless you know you're such an individual my advice is to leave such things alone. Sometime back while

If it weren't for all the little things, hunting would be a fairly safe sport. That is, if some other hunter doesn't shoot you by mistake. Thorns are just a nuisance, but if a person fell into one of these trees it could result in serious injury.

Turkey hunting's greatest threat today isn't hunters, it's loss of habitat. Shopping malls, housing developments, highways and clean farming all take hundreds of thousands of wildlife acres out of the picture each year. And don't forget the energy industry, which not only ruins land each year, but also pollutes the water and air.

Time was when all of the older hunters like the author drank from streams all across America, but today it's a definite no-no. If you want a drink in the woods, take your water with you.

Prickly pear cactus, like all cacti, must be given due respect. This plant will certainly cause serious injury if you fall on a clump. Rex Haley, a guide on the Ranch Rio Bonita in Texas, holds aloft a hunk of it on his hunting knife.

hunting turkeys on a volcano island in central America, I came onto a trickling mountain brook. There in the rain forest it was my good fortune to drink the same thing all the other locals were drinking. After all, if it was good enough for the monkeys, the parrots, the iguanas, the boas, and heck knows what else, then it ought to be okay for a country boy from Oklahoma. And, I suppose, the local so-called turkeys drank there, too.

Game Laws and Game Wardens

While we are talking about hazards involving mankind, we may as well mention another one, which you're going to have trouble with if you don't keep your act together. The game warden.

Now, it's the hunter's choice whether he invites or avoids problems with game wardens. I've yet to meet a warden who wasn't a pretty nice guy. All of 'em love to hunt (which is why they ended up being a game man) and they love the outdoors. If you'll give them half a chance, they'll see that hunters like you and me will have something to hunt in the years ahead. All of us live in states in which poaching is a problem. I can think of a couple such areas here in Oklahoma, where the locals think it's "smart" to shoot anything and everything on

> **H**illbilly mentality poachers are taking away from every hunter each time one kills another animal out of season and by illegal means.

sight. Of course the result is that there aren't any turkeys or deer. If this wasn't so stupid, it would be funny. The sad part is one of these regions is made up of huge tracts of National Forest lands. These hillbilly mentality poachers are taking away from every hunter in the state each time one of them kills another bird or animal out of season and by illegal means.

But, it's not up to the game warden to tell you what's right and wrong. Study the rules thoroughly before you hunt a state you've not hunted previously. If you don't understand a rule, write or call and find out the answer; it may save you a fine later on. Of course, as our country's population increases, hunting rules will become increasingly complex. Many states now have rule books which require the help of a Philadelphia lawyer to understand.

Regardless of your opinion of our game laws here, you'll find them a cakewalk compared to those across the border toward the hunting grounds of the Gould's, ocellated, and gallopavo in Mexico and Central America. Those folks get real edgy about some gringo toting a gun around in their country. And, if traveling south across the border, allow enough time to get the permits you'll need. This usually takes a couple days at the border crossing, *if you're lucky.*

Rule books for some laws in South and Central America do exist though these are hard to come by and may be out of date. There are Central American countries which truthfully have no game laws. This can be interpreted two ways; either you aren't to shoot any game, or you can shoot it all. You may go on a hunt with a party of locals none of whom have licenses or permits of any kind. They will tell you there is no season, you can shoot year-'round, *day or night.* And, as such you may see damned little game.

Weather

Weather has to be the number one problem for the average hunter. There's just no answer to old Mother Nature's wrath if she decides to mess up a hunter's plans with a snowstorm, cold, blowing rain, blistering heat, whatever. And, there's nothing you can do to stop it.

My answer to bad weather is to plan for it. Allow yourself enough hunting days so that should lousy weather set in, you still can salvage the hunt. I refuse to book out-of-state hunters for less than three days. Ordinarily one of these three days will be fair enough to hunt.

Perhaps you would like to get in a day's fishing while

Nothing hurts worse'n a rattlesnake bite. Take my word for it. Few hunters are bitten each year, as most snakes are apt to go their own way if the hunter will do the same. This big Western diamondback is considered the most aggressive of all the rattlers, but he'd prefer to just sneak off if he's given the chance.

you're hunting turkeys. Fine, I love to fish, too. But, keep your priorities in mind. If the weather's good and your top hope is to bag a wild turkey, get after the bird. Don't risk using that nice day to fish and tomorrow to hunt turkeys; tomorrow could turn into one of those days when the wind blows so bad it stacks the barbs on the fence up agin the posts. Nope, get in your turkey hunting licks when you can—tomorrow's another day.

Folks who plan to hunt Merriams should pack snow and rain gear along with warm clothing. You'll get excited the first

Hornets' nests are a thing of beauty, but best left alone. Ed Norwood admires one found near his camp in Mississippi. This one is deserted, so it's harmless and will make a nice trophy to hang in someone's den.

Probably all turkey chasers have favorite terrain they prefer over all others. If I do, I'd be hard pressed to name it. One of my favorites is south Florida, where there's scads of palmetto, oak hummocks, cypress trees and cabbage palms. Throw in some creek swamp, lots of water, a few gators and cottonmouth snakes, and if there's any finer place to do in an old gobbler, well, there you are. Where to next?

time you hunt these great birds during a spring snow storm, but if you hunt them a bunch, you'll come to find such stuff simply goes with the territory. The fact is, I'm kinda surprised if there isn't any of the white stuff when I hunt these high regions. Just learn to roll with the punches when the weather gets bad. The turkeys? Well, they can't eat the stuff so they probably could care less.

First time hunters to Osceola country are smart to tote along some lightweight clothing and canvas wading shoes. Much hunting in south Florida will be around or in water. Therefore any clothing which dries easily will be a benefit. You'll be wading water so buy shoes which have eyeholes that allow the water to drain out.

Hunters in Rio Grande country need to lug along both lightweight and heavier clothes as this country has unpredictable weather. One day you may be wearing the least you can get by with and be decent; the next you're freezing in the blast of a Blue Norther.

Insects and Snakes

Insects are a nuisance anywhere you hunt, but the worst seem to be mosquitoes and ticks. With the onset of the dreaded Lyme disease, caused by the bite of certain ticks, hunters today are more concerned with ticks than the other outdoor pests. Purchase on of the new products which repel ticks, then follow the instructions in applying.

Hunters biggest complaints are about snakes. It seems that nearly all hunters dread snakes. Snakes are something most people know little about, but all they've heard was bad. No, Irene, snakes are just another little critter which, unfortunately, can't walk, so has to wiggle its way through life. None of them

will bite if left alone. Almost all will flee just as fast as some wiggling will carry them.

But, there are a few snakes in turkey country which a hunter should guard against. Though will seldom a bite from one of these be fatal, it could end an otherwise good time. Coral snakes are small and very reclusive. You'll probably never see one. The only one I've seen was back in Mexico,

If the weather's good and your top hope is to bag a wild turkey, get after the bird. Get in your turkey hunting licks when you can.

but it fled into the rocks before I could catch it. Copperheads are plentiful in Eastern turkey range, but are rather retiring snakes, so unless bothered really present no danger. Cottonmouths are slow lethargic reptiles, usually seen near water, in swamps, along brush-laden creeks, and have to be almost badgered into striking. Like many snakes, it is attracted to light so a headlight worn while night fishing is an open invitation. Cottonmouths have a legacy far beyond their bite. Rattlesnakes are the most common of the poisonous snakes and are found far and wide among all the subspecies of wild turkeys. One day you might sidestep a lazy old canebrake rattler in Alabama, and a couple days later in south Texas it could be a sidewinder dancing across the sands, going kinda sideways like the little critter had something wrong with his steering mechanism. The rattler with the worst temperament is the big western diamondback, what most of us call the

coontail rattler with the end of its tail banded muchlike a raccoon's. Give any snake a few feet, and they'll not be a hazard.

Other Hazards

Turkey country is filled with other hazards—spiders, chiggers (just a bad itch), abandoned wells, range fires, rabid animals, cattle, to name a few. I've walked past old pits, wells, steep banks, cliffs, any of which could be bad; some could easily cause death. What's worse is that many turkey hunters are out among this stuff in the dark. So, for gosh sakes, carry a flashlight, and if you're in country new to you, *do not leave camp without one.* One afternoon Ed Norwood and I happened past a newly opened hole in Rio Grande country. Looking down into it, we couldn't see the bottom. I happened to have a flashlight in my pack so I shone it down the hole. Ed and I were dumbfounded; there at the bottom of the twenty foot cavern stood a small calf. Locating the rancher, we carted an extension ladder to the area, and three of us brought the little hereford back to higher ground. His momma had shown up by then, so she laid claim to our find. Such holes are rare any place but this points out what can happen.

We always hear about getting lost. Surely nobody gets lost. They might become lost but I don't think a hunter I know gets himself lost. It just happens.

A hunter going into strange country should certainly try to

(Above) Hunters should always be cautious about grabbing a thrashing gobbler as the spurs can inflict serious damage. The author always trots up to a thrashing bird, quickly grabs it by the neck and, before it can flop, gives the bird a quick flip, completely rotating the bird's body in mid-air and breaking its neck. It will quickly die, and there's no worry that it might regain its senses and flee the area. Whatever you do, watch the spurs.

Certainly it's not a hazard, but there's always the possibility that a downed turkey will get back on its feet and scat. Savvy hunters get to a downed bird as quickly as possible, many running to where the bird lies. Keep your gun trained toward the bird, and if it should regain its feet, take good aim at the bird's head and neck and shoot again.

locate a map of the region before arriving. If he knows where he will actually be hunting, he should buy a topographical map of that region. These, together with a compass, will keep him from having to worry about getting lost.

I don't hunt easy when I have to stew over where I might be going, and probably all hunters are much the same. Oh, I know, you're one of those old boys who never gets turned

I do carry a compass, a match safe filled with wooden matches, and a knife at all times.

around out in the woods. Fine, we won't have to look for you. But throw in some fog, a heavy snow shower, then add to this a neck of woods the likes of which you've never gazed on before, and probably you'll be just like us other such folks. You may not be lost, but you will certainly be confused for a day or two.

Lost is lost. I don't guess I can truthfully say I've been lost. I've always managed to find my way back to the truck or camp. But, I'll tell you this, I have been confused many times. The only ones who knew it were my compass and me. By taking note of the country, what I knew about the various trees and what sides of the ridges these are found on, little things

like that, I have unraveled my predicament, and made my way back. But, this is lost hunting time.

I do carry a compass, a match safe filled with wooden matches, and a knife at all times. I can make it out in the woods for a night with these three things and my gun. I may not spend the night such as you would in the Waldorf-Astoria in downtown Manhattan, but then those folks can't hunt turkeys, either.

Hazards!!! We present the biggest hazards to ourselves. If you do manage to get yourself lost, and you very well may if you hunt hard often in crazy places you never dreamed of being, the feeling that you don't know North from South will be a very strange and eerie one.

I've read what the experts say about what a hunter should do when lost, but all of the advice seems to have been written by those who had never truly been in such a fix.

Your first desire is to find your way out. You are certain that with each step you'll recognize a landmark, and you'll quickly be back where you belong. But, an hour later you seem to be getting nowhere—nothing is recognizable. It's then that your mind begins to churn and you realize you simply don't know "come here" from "sic 'em." This is when so many folks get into real trouble. They panic. There are two things none of these people probably have with them—a compass and a map of the area. I can't stress enough that if you are

When hunting big country several miles from camp or vehicle, it's good thinking to pack along a few things which take up very little space, weigh almost nothing, but are worth their weight in gold should a hunter become lost. A good knife, compass, small match safe to keep matches bone dry and map of the area being hunted should help him find his way back to civilization or spend the night in the woods.

Many hunters would truly like to hunt the back country, but fear getting lost. Obtaining a map of the area, studying it and carrying a compass will put most hunters' minds at ease.

Some hazards are worse than other, but a damned mad landowner can be pretty nasty. If you get permission to hunt, then you'll never have to face this trouble. If you can't find the owner, stay the hell out.

afraid of becoming lost, you only need to stick these two items in your pockets and not only will you probably never get lost, you'll also hunt much easier. If you have to worry about where you are going when chasing a gobbling bird, the chase won't be any fun at all.

With a compass, and a small section of map you can strike a straight line for a road, a river, anything which will take you back to mankind. Don't fret over whether you'll come out at camp, or the truck; you can always work your way to that point once you're safely out of the woods.

Sometimes you'll end up in a strange place without a map because you didn't know where your host was going to dump you. But, if you have a compass, then you can take a fix on directions before you leave the road and you'll know the basic direction you took when beginning your hunt. The reverse should take you back in the general direction of your starting point.

The hardest part is trusting your compass. Your mind will already be set on which direction is North, South, or whatever. A person hopelessly lost will have to fight with himself to believe his compass is right and his instinct is wrong. But, you must do this.

If you don't have a compass. and few of you will, then you'll have to take a bearing on trees from one point to another, or a high point. If you can maintain a true course, you can work your way to civilization in that manner. Flat country is worse for getting lost than in mountainous terrain because it's easier to keep your bearings on high points, peaks, ridges, a tall pine, perhaps a saddle between hills.

Just remember, unless you are in truly "big" country, it's darned near impossible to get away from other turkey hunters.

A person hopelessly lost will have to fight with himself to believe his compass is right and his instinct is wrong. But, you must do this.

So, just about the time you think you're so far back that the "cricks" ain't got names, and you hear an old turkey cut loose, hurry up and get headed in that direction. 'Cause if you don't get to him, somebody else'll probably shoot the turkey and then you can tag along with that old boy on his way back to our Great Society.

Boy, fewer of my days have been spent worrying about getting lost than just wishing I could lose some of the other folks.

There's one other hazard I'd like to mention—*imagination*. It's been my luck to hunt from one end of this country to the other, at least what I consider all the truly good turkey places. And, at each and every one I'm always being warned not to go across the fence and get on old so-and-so's land because he "shoots to kill" the folks who trespass on his place. Let's face it, the law isn't going to turn its back on such glaring acts as killing a person for simply getting on the wrong side of the fence. True, the man can have you arrested. But, kill you? No. And, I might add, if there are such crazy folks out there, then I would like to say: Be very careful that you kill me with your first shot. You will never shoot another man.

From one end of this country to the other I hear stories about mountain lions—seems this old U.S.A. is run over with the beasts. Such and Such saw one carrying a calf out of the pasture the other night; the guy down the way saw two run across the road yesterday. Where does all this stuff come from? You could hunt the Rockies from now 'til doomsday, and unless you are a lion man, you'll never see one of these fine big cats. You may see his tracks, or where he drug down a muley or a hereford. But, see Old Whiskers? Man, you gotta be lucky. Don't let your imagination mess up your hunt. And when you and a buddy are easing down through the creek-swamp before first day come this next April, kinda whisper to him that you think you are being followed by *something*.

Hear it?

Who knows, he may get so interested in what's back of him that you can go on and scrag that old turkey all by yourself.

Earl Woodbury, veteran turkey hunter and longtime hunting buddy, nailed this old bobcat one fall day while hunting turkeys. These critters are a sure enough hazard to any and all turkeys, whether on the ground or in a tree.

15

You Just Shot a Turkey, Now What?

SHOOTING A BIG turkey gobbler has one huge advantage over downing a fine whitetail buck, to my way of thinking. I don't have to stew about getting the truck near enough so I won't have to drag it a mile or so, nor will there be three days of packing it out back to camp, in pieces.

'Course, I'd be happy to do so if I could find such a dinosaur-sized turkey. Something like those folks were bumping into in *Jurassic Park*. I've nailed old birds back five hollows from the road which, by the time I'd lugged them four hollows, seemed all of a hundred pounds. Regardless, at least you can pick up a turkey and carry it out.

Downing a fine old bird has all the excitement associated with bagging any big game animal. But once it's down, there are other things which must be given some immediate consideration. You've probably left the camera back at the truck, but you want to take photos! Oh, I know, you want to show it off back home. Is the bird of trophy status? Will you want to have it mounted? If you have any inkling you wish to have the bird mounted then there are several things you need to do now.

Many taxidermists would just as soon a hunter bring the bird to them "as is"—whole, untouched, completely frozen. Perhaps you've checked with one back home and have been given instructions on how to bring in turkeys for mounting. If the weather is hot or even fairly warm, then you need to get the bird to refrigeration. Smooth down the plumage, comb the feathers out with the grain, using a knife blade to put them in place, or a stiff small wire, or even a long narrow comb or fingernail file. Try to preen them much as the bird did. Any blood stains should be removed with cloth wrung out in *warm* water. Blood stains present the greatest problem for taxidermists so getting them out will only help to guarantee a beautiful trophy. Wrap the bird in wax paper if you have some handy, then place it carefully in a plastic bag, and stick it in the freezer. Then you can get it to the taxidermist when he wants it.

A word to hunters who travel far from home. I've been lugging gobblers, hens too, across these United States and Mexico for going on thirty years. When I bag a bird and don't have good cleaning facilities at hand, I locate a freezer (all hotels and restaurants have them), stick my birds in it, and freeze them, feathers and all, if I intend to have the bird mounted. I always tote along an old sleeping bag and a barracks bag (army surplus) which I wrap and stuff such birds in, and then check these with my other luggage, if flying. Birds I don't intend to have mounted I simply field-dress and then freeze. I'll stow them in the freezer at home, and when we're ready to eat one, I'll simply hang the bird in the garage to thaw. Since the feathers are still on the bird, it will take longer to thaw. But they also provide the best insulation for the trip home. Once thawed, I complete the cleaning process and stick the bird in the oven.

Getting the bird home in full plumage has numerous advantages. You may want to take additional pictures; you may want to dry portions of the tail and wings as trophies; or you may simply want to keep a few of the feathers. There've been times when I did not want to burden my host with all the mess of fully cleaning birds, nor did I want to use up precious time far from home stripping a bird when I'd have plenty of it once I got back home. You will always

Before a hunter does anything after he's downed a bird, he'll want to know the bird's actual weight. This should be done before any field-cleaning is done. Here Cork Kelly and Dick Bland (right) take a look at the scale on which hangs a fall-killed gobbler taken by Cork.

Here Cork Kelly hefts a spring-killed jake gobbler which he has field-dressed before coming into camp. In this case, the entrails have been removed, and the bird's body picked, leaving the wings and tail feathers intact. The legs and beard have been left on the bird should a game warden happen along asking to see proof of sex. All hunters who travel to other states to hunt should read up on what is required to remain legal when field-dressing or cleaning wild turkeys.

want to carry along a few large plastic bags in your gear bag.

Ordinarily when a bird is downed, the hunter will want to field-dress it, tote it back to the truck, take a few pics, maybe show it off to a few envious buddies, and then dress it out completely. Of course, this will be several hours later, so the entrails should be taken out in the field to cool the bird down, even on fall and winter hunts.

Lay the bird on its back, and then pull out all the feathers for an inch or two around the anal vent. Using a thick-bladed sharp knife, cut completely around the vent an inch or so from it, deep enough that you can see into the body cavity. Be careful and take your time. Try not to cut through the large intestine at the vent. Once you've completely encircled it, the vent and large intestine can be drawn out. Now carefully enlarge the opening, which will allow you to run your hand up into the body cavity. Pull the intestines, stomach and gizzard from the bird, and then carefully run your knife blade forward of the stomach and cut off the esophagus above the stomach.

Now it is easy to feel the heart, lungs and other viscera you need to remove with your fingers. After their removal, take a dry cloth and wipe out the inside of the bird. When I don't have rags handy, I use pine needles, oak leaves, but not anything which will leave too much debris in the bird.

Field-dressing a turkey is more easily done if you have a buddy who can hold the legs apart or hold the tail out of the way so it won't get stained if you want to keep it or take photos of it.

Many hunters don't keep the giblets, which are excellent for

The hunting guide should always keep the clients wishes in mind before any kind of cleaning is begun on a turkey the client has killed. Many hunters, particularly those who've just bagged their first wild turkey, may want feathers from various parts of the bird's anatomy, and certainly these shouldn't be soiled with blood beforehand.

Wild turkeys can be hung for a time just as any game bird or animal without worry of spoilage. Fall and winter kills can often be hung for several days in areas where the nighttime temperature drops into the 30s or 40s. In warmer regions, and also during many areas of spring hunting, the birds should be field-cleaned within a couple of hours and completely cleaned within hours if daytime temperatures are above 60 degrees.

use in gravy and turkey dressing. But if the hunter does want them, they must be taken care of when, and if, the bird is field-dressed or when the entrails are removed. The giblets are made up of the heart and gizzard, finely chopped after cooking to add to dressing or gravy. Some folks also add the liver.

When field-dressing, remove the heart, cut free any veins or arteries, and place it in a small plastic bag. Ziploc bags are best. Then take the liver and carefully cut the greenish colored gall sac from the side of the liver. Do not cut through it as the bile will give a bitter taste to any meat it touches.

The large lemon-sized gizzard, which is attached to and works more or less like a second stomach, can be cut free (it's easy to see, a large hard object). Placing it on the edge, cut it open lengthways. You'll see the tiny gravel, large grains of sand and tiny rocks which help the muscles of the gizzard grind up any hard foods the bird may have ingested. All fowl-type birds have gizzards to reduce the seeds, nuts, berries and other foods into a form the bird's body can metabolize.

After splitting open the gizzard, separate with your fingernails or knife the whitish skin lining from the gizzard and peel it away. All the sand and gravel will come with it. Stick the gizzard in the bag with the heart and liver, and you have the makings for some darned good eating.

Some hunters split open the craw, or crop, when field-dressing and remove it from the bird. This is fine if later photogra-

Many times I open a craw simply to learn what the bird was feeding on, then apply this knowledge later.

phy isn't imminent. I've never done this with the hundreds of birds I've cleaned and have never had a bird spoil.

Many times I open a craw simply to learn what the bird was feeding on, then apply this knowledge to hunts later in the day. Of course, if the turkey was killed at the end of the day and has several foods in the craw, applying this information is

It's best to take any and all photography before field-cleaning begins, as too often blood stains will mar a beautiful color photo. This black and white exhibits fine clean lines and will always be a true remembrance of a hunt the shooter will cherish.

The author picks clean a young gobbler taken in south Florida during a fall hunt. Notice that all signs of the bird's identification are remaining. Though Florida allows taking birds of either sex, this is a habit with the author, as there are places which allow only male birds to be taken. And many owners of private property do not want hens killed.

more difficult than if the bird was shot at noon and feeding that morning on a single item. One fall morning while hunting some rough country in Arkansas, I scragged a fine old gobbler, surprising him as he came up from the creek where he had been drinking. The old bird's craw had only a few broken hunks of acorn, a couple walking-sticks, and several stink-beetles. The next afternoon I nailed another old-man-of-the-mountains while still-hunting an old abandoned logging road, but this old gobbler's craw was packed. I could feel it like a sack of Grape Nuts bulging on the bird's chest. I knew what it contained before I cut it open—grasshoppers. Seemed like a jillion of 'em.

Telling my two buddies of my find, they took off the next day in a truck and both of them killed turkeys feeding in the grasses along the country roads. You won't find grasshoppers back in the deep woods. You only find grasshoppers where you find grass. Simple.

If you carry your turkey back to camp slung over your shoulder, holding onto the feet with the bird's plumage not mashed down and the wings flopping free, you'll have a much prettier bird for your photos. It's certainly easier to carry it by the neck, but too often I've seen a big gobbler's neck area ruined for picture taking simply because of the way it was carried. And once the feathers set, the bird won't have the nice fluffy appearance so desirable for photos.

Back at camp, hang the field-dressed bird in a shady place and stuff the body cavity with cheesecloth if blowflies are a problem. If a large refrigerator is handy, simply lay the bird on a shelf; just don't put it in the freezer until you are certain about the bird's final destination—taxidermy or table. *Do not remove visible signs of the bird's sex* until it's reached it's final destination or until you have complied with the game laws of the state in which you are hunting. Some states supply tags and require these attached at the time and place of the kill. Ignorance of the law is no excuse. If you're reading this to someone who can't read, then you should tell him that he darned sure better learn. Who knows, you may run onto a place posted with signs saying, "Turkey Hunters Welcome."

16

Now the Good Part— Eatin'

FAR BE IT FROM ME to tell folks what's good eating and what isn't. Growing up on an old sandhill sandburr patch farm in Oklahoma's Dust Bowl and always dressed up in wornout overalls, usually barefooted, but unfailingly hungry as a hog night and day, my brother and I weren't choosey about what hit the table. We weren't any different than turkeys—we ate anything that didn't eat us first.

So, what I call *larrupin'* good may not suit some folks' taste, but let me tell you, anyone who doesn't like roast turkey has to have something bad wrong with their taster.

Years ago, I found it wasn't much of a chore to get a gobbler ready for the oven, and since Stella, my wife, was working, I could take the task off her hands. Anyhow, I'd had all the fun in bagging the bird, some of the fun of getting it ready for the table could also be mine. So, I roast all the turkeys I shoot.

When the bird's cooked, I set it out to cool, and then while it's still warm, I completely debone the carcass, putting the meat into Ziploc freezer bags and throwing the carcass out.

It's while I'm deboning the bird that I first give the meat a try—me and the dog. I'll throw him a tidbit once in a while, but mostly I get in licks for me. *Whooo-eee*, that is some kind of eating. Old Justin Wilson, who does the cajun cooking show on TV, would just go wild. I never season the birds; straight from the roaster it's like we used to say, "eatin' high off the hog." Only it's better, it's wild turkey.

But, first things first. The bird has to be prepared for cooking, which means picking, or plucking if you want to use fancy terms, and removing the entrails if that wasn't done in the field.

There's three ways to clean a turkey, well, four to some people, but the fourth is, to me, downright wasteful. It's known as breasting out the bird, cutting the breast meat away from the body and throwing away the remainder.

I have a good friend, an old boy who's always preaching and practicing conservation, but who always breasts out turkeys and waterfowl. I've never understood his reasoning, but it relates to him having grown up in a well-off home, where you never got hungry or never lacked for anything. Reminds me of a buddy who grew up in a family of ten and said he didn't know a chicken had parts but necks until he was sixteen when some of his sisters got married and left home. Then he found out there were breasts, thighs and even wings.

Don't tell me you breast out turkeys. I don't want to hear about such waste.

A turkey is best plucked when it's just been killed since the feathers haven't yet set. The longer a bird lies in the field, the more difficult it will be to dry-pick the bird. Some birds are more easily dry-picked than others, too. Young turkeys in particular pick easier than old gobblers, but also may have more tiny pin feathers.

A turkey is best picked in the woods, where the feathers will biodegrade in time. Wing tips, entrails and all of such stuff will be quickly cleaned up by local varmints.

Dry-picking a turkey is far easiest done by hanging the bird by one foot from a tree branch. Pick against the grain of the feathering. In other words, pull down if the bird is hanging by its feet. If the bird is an old gobbler, with a beard you want to keep, grasp the beard right next to the bird's body, and simply pull it free. Beards thus removed will pull free as a unit. Don't grasp the beard out toward its end or by a few hairs. Make sure you get ahold of the whole thing and right next to the body.

After all the feathers have been removed, it's easy to remove the entrails and the head and craw. Invariably I cut off the wing tips before beginning since the last two joints of a turkey's wing have virtually no meat and are the most difficult part of any fowl to defeather. The tail can also be cut off before picking.

If the feathers are difficult to remove, or the skin tears, you may want to either scald the bird or skin it. I like the skin on a turkey, although I truly can't say that this enhances the cooking or the eating qualities. Probably just a hangup from the old days on the farm as we always scalded any kind of fowl we killed for eating.

Scalding does make for a beautifully dressed bird. It comes out completely void of even the tiniest of feathers, and with a little washing, the turkey is ready to cook. Scalding is done by immersing the bird completely in a large container of water heated to between 155 and 160 degrees. You'll need a candy or cooking thermometer to get this exact temperature. If the water's too hot, the skin will tear easily, and if not hot enough, the feathers won't pull free easily. I use an old copper boiler to slosh the birds in. Slosh them around until the large wing pinions begin pulling free, hang the bird and pick quickly. Few hunters scald turkeys these days.

The last method is to skin the turkey, which is again best done by hanging the bird in a tree. With a sharp knife, cut the skin at the thighs and work it free, pulling the front parts downward and removing the skin from the rump and legs by pulling upwards toward the tail section. Again, cut off the tail and the outer two sections of the wings before beginning.

Removing the entrails from either scalded or skinned birds can be done afterwards if the bird wasn't field-dressed earlier. Regardless of the method I use to clean a turkey, I always cut off the feet last. Completely cleaning a turkey for the oven is really very simple—just hang it up and get with it. Make the feathers fly.

Among my book collection are several dealing with various ways to cut up and cook wild game. Some of these folks are like people I've heard mentioned by my longtime hunting buddy Ed Norwood, from down in Mississippi. They can take a simple little task and make a real job of it. Like he says, "they can tear up an anvil with a snowball." If it took me as long to prepare a gobbler as some of these culinary experts must take, I'd have damned little time left to hunt.

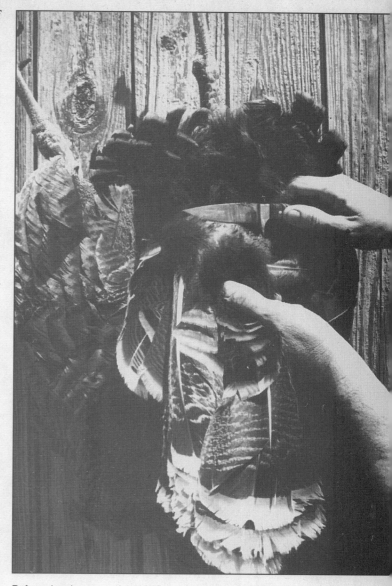

Before cleaning, many hunters first remove the tail. This can be done easily by cutting it completely free just beyond the anus opening.

If the hunter desires, the tail can then be spread, or fanned, tacked down with nails to a board, and left to dry. Powder the meaty area with Borax several times over a six-month period, and once dried,

that area can be covered with leather. The hunter can write whatever facts he deems pertinent to the kill—date, place, his name, weight, etc. This results in a nice trophy.

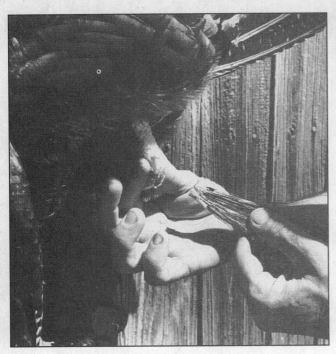

Before going any further, the beard should be removed. This is easily done by simply grasping the beard firmly in one hand, then while pushing back on the brest area, a quick pull will separate it in a sin-

gle unit. It can then be glued in a 12-gauge shell casing, or if that's too large, use a smaller 20- or 28-gauge. All but a few beards will fit into the 28-gauge.

Back during the good old days, whether the late part of the 1800s or the early decades of the 1900s, all wild game was aged before cooking. Most often fowl was hung in the shade for a few days. There were two schools of thought. One said it was best to hang the birds by the feet; the other said by the neck. Many old hunters felt it best to let game birds hang by the neck until the body fell free. I've hung gobblers for up to five days during winter, or even spring months, when the night temperatures fell into the forties and had no ill effects or ptomaine poisoning from eating such meats. Of course, I'd always removed the entrails. Some old-timers left these in the hung birds, feeling that they added to the flavor of the meat when cooked. Of course, they took them out before cooking.

There's no end to the ways a turkey can end up on a plate. Turkey breast meat can be cut into narrow strips and

There's no end to the ways a turkey can end up on a plate.

fried or cut into chunks and deep fat fried—along with hundreds of other methods you've heard about. I'd advise anyone who does cut away the breast meat to save the legs, thighs, and neck, and cook these in the roaster the next time a whole turkey is cooked. Perhaps I should tell how I roast a big gobbler. You'll probably turn around and use another method since I tend to do some things differently than most folks.

Using a large roasting pan, I'll line it completely with heavy-duty aluminum foil. Then I pour in two cups of cold water. I lay the gobbler in the roaster either breast side down

or, if the lid won't close with the bird in this position, I lay it on its side. I have previously cut off the drumsticks and lay them down alongside the bird in the water. If I'm saving the giblets for making gravy or dressing, I'll put them in the bird's body cavity, wrapped in cheesecloth. Then wrap and seal the foil with another layer over the top of the bird. Now I stick it in the oven with the setting of 275 degrees, if I intend on being away from the house a while, or at 350 degrees if I'm going to be around.

About four hours later I'll begin checking the bird, peeling back the foil just enough to see if the meat is falling away from the bones. When it is, take it out, peel the foil back off the bird, and let it cool. I never let the meat get cold because I like to remove all the meat while the bird is warm—and I can also nibble while doing this.

Now, I've heard a lot of hunters remark the legs on a turkey are worthless due to the great number of bone splints and that the meat can't be properly separated from them. Yes, and nobody wants to swallow one of these long sharp bone splints. But there's no need to. I remove the drumsticks from the bottom of the roaster, let them drain while I'm deboning the remainder of the bird, and then I debone them. The meat simply falls off, and the long narrow splints can be easily removed. As we all know, if there is a tastier meat for making casseroles than dark meat from a wild turkey, then Stella and I have never found it.

Though I do the roasting, that's as far as my cooking abilities go. Stella takes it from there. With all the deboned meat in the freezer, it's no problem to thaw a package or two, so we enjoy wild turkey all year long. Overall, poor years and good ones, I'll kill from fifteen to twenty a year—big ones, small

Next the wings should be removed at the first joint from the body. This is quickly done with a sharp knife.

(Above) The skin can now be worked forward from the bird's body, leaving skin on the legs. Once the forward part of the bird is skinned, the legskin can be split out toward the feet and pulled out and off. The wings are done in the same manner, leaving a nicely skinned bird.

(Left) If the hunter is curious about what the bird has been eating, then the craw, or crop, can be opened and the contents examined. This can also be done at the time the bird is killed if the hunter is going to continue hunting in an area where multiple kills are allowed. Knowing what foods the birds are eating will be a clue where best to hunt. Often, the older adult gobbler does little eating during the spring season so the bird's craw may be empty. Fall-hunted turkeys often have a craw completely packed by late afternoon.

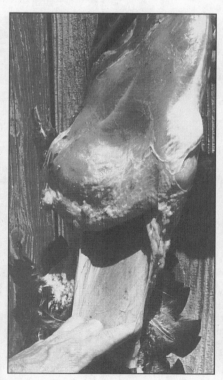

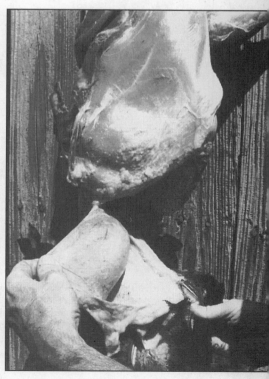

Now the craw can be pulled free by grasping it with the fingers and separating it from the bird's breast. After it is cut off, the windpipe should be removed from inside the neck area.

Popular Recipes For Wild Turkey

Many of the ways my wife prepares turkey dishes is to simply substitute cooked and deboned turkey in recipes calling for chicken. Chicken tetrazzini is turkey tetrazzini in our house. Chicken salad sandwiches are something we haven't had in heck knows when, but I eat turkey salad sandwiches very often. Chances are nine in ten that if you have a sandwich with me during turkey season—spring, fall or winter—it will be either roast sliced turkey or turkey salad. Nearby are a few recipes that are favorites of ours.

There are times when we will "rob" the breast meat from a big gobbler, but we save the rest of the meat for other recipes. Stella will take the remaining parts of the bird (wings, thighs, legs, etc.) and cook them in the pressure cooker. Stella makes absolutely delicious homemade noodles, and the boned meat from these parts often is cooked with the noodles. What do we do with the meat we've robbed from the turkey's breast? Fry it up or use it for sandwiches.

Roasted wild turkey can be eaten as a main dish or used in casseroles, salads and pot pies. It is always delicious when served as lunch meat for cold sandwiches.

WILD TURKEY AND WILD RICE

3 cups cooked turkey, boned and diced
1 cup Uncle Ben's Mixed Long Grain and Wild Rice
1 lb. fresh mushrooms, sliced
1 onion, chopped
2 Tbsp. butter
2 tsp. salt
$1/4$ tsp. pepper
3 cups turkey broth
$1/2$ cup blanched almonds, sliced
$1^{1}/2$ cups heavy cream

Preheat oven to 350°. Wash rice thoroughly. Pour into saucepan, cover with boiling water and let stand 1 hour. Drain well. Sauté mushrooms and chopped onion in skillet with butter for 10 minutes. Combine rice, onions, mushrooms, salt, pepper, turkey and almonds in greased casserole dish. Add broth and cream. Cover and bake $1^{1}/2$ hours.

TURKEY BUFFET CASSEROLE

3 cups cooked turkey, boned and diced
1 cup American cheese, cubed
1 cup celery, chopped
$1/2$ cup onion, chopped
1 can cream of mushroom soup
2 eggs, beaten
$1/4$ tsp. salt
$1/2$ tsp. pepper
1 tsp. sage
4 cups turkey or chicken broth or bouillon
4 cups round butter cracker crumbs

Preheat oven to 350°. Combine turkey, cheese, celery, onion, mushroom soup, eggs, salt, pepper and sage in large bowl. Stir in bouillon (mixture will be very thin). Place 2 cups cracker crumbs in 3 qt. casserole dish. Add turkey mixture and top with remaining crumbs. Bake 1 hour.

WILD TURKEY WITH BROCCOLI AND RICE

1/2 cup rice
Chicken broth
2 10-oz. pkgs. frozen broccoli
1/2 cup onion, chopped
1/2 cup celery, chopped
2 Tbsp. cooking oil
3 cups cooked turkey, boned and chopped
1/4 tsp. pepper
1 lb. American cheese, cubed
1 10-oz. can cream of mushroom soup
1/2 cup fine dry bread crumbs

Preheat oven to 325°. Cook rice according to package directions, using chicken broth in place of water. (Broth from a roasted turkey is preferable, but if frozen turkey meat is used, this may not be available.) Cook broccoli according to package directions and drain. Sauté onions and celery in skillet with oil. Mix cooked rice and broccoli with turkey and pepper in large bowl. Pour into greased 4-qt. casserole dish. Combine cheese and soup in small saucepan and heat over low flame until cheese melts. Pour over turkey mixture. Top with bread crumbs. Bake uncovered for about 50 minutes. Serves 6-8.

OLD-FASHIONED TURKEY PIE

3 cups cooked turkey, cut into chunks
1/4 cup flour
1/4 tsp. paprika
1/4 cup water
2 cups turkey stock
1/4 cup light cream
Salt, sprinkle
Pepper, sprinkle
Baking powder biscuit dough

Preheat oven to 450°. Blend flour, paprika and water in saucepan. Gradually add stock and cook, stirring, until thickened. Stir in cream. Season to taste with salt and pepper. Arrange turkey chunks in 1 1/2-qt. casserole dish. Pour hot sauce over turkey. Prepare baking powder biscuit dough, using enough milk or light cream to make it easy to handle. Roll or pat out dough to 1/8-inch thickness to fit top of casserole dish. Place over mixture, sealing edges. Cut slits in top. Bake 15-20 minutes, or until done.

For variation, 1/4 cup chopped onions can be added to the top biscuit dough. Also, scratch biscuits can be laid on top of the turkey mixture, in place of the dough topping.

WILD TURKEY CASSEROLE

4 cups cooked turkey, boned and chopped
1 can cream of mushroom soup
2 cups egg noodles, boiled and drained
1 can English peas or corn
1 can cream of chicken soup
Cheddar cheese, grated
Salt and pepper, sprinkle

Preheat oven to 350°. Place a layer of turkey in a large casserole dish. Add cream of mushroom soup, precooked egg noodles and peas or corn. Top with another layer of turkey and cream of chicken soup. Sprinkle with grated cheddar cheese and add salt and pepper to taste. Bake for 35 to 45 minutes. Serves 8 to 10.

TURKEY SALAD FOR SANDWICHES

2 cups cooked turkey, boned and chopped
2 hard-boiled eggs, chopped
Sweet pickles, chopped
1 small onion, chopped
Kraft Miracle Whip

Mix all ingredients with Kraft Miracle Whip in large bowl. Add Miracle Whip until mixture is easily spreadable.

FRIED TURKEY BREASTS

2 lbs. turkey breast, sliced to 1/2- to 3/4-inch thickness
1 cup flour
2 eggs, beaten
2 cups cornflakes, crushed
1 Tbsp. olive oil.

Dredge turkey breast slices in flour and dip in beaten eggs. Roll in crushed cornflakes and fry in skillet with hot oil. Let cook over low flame until turkey is tender and brown on both sides.

Last, the feet are cut off at the knee joint. If the entrails have not been removed in the field, these can now be removed. Wash the bird thoroughly in cold water and it's ready to cook.

ones, turkeys of all kinds, from many states. For over twenty years running, I've hunted at least three subspecies a year, sometimes four and five. I say this to give the reader an idea of how many turkeys I've cleaned just for my own consumption. Heck knows how many others I've field-dressed and dressed completely for other hunters. Hundreds. We still love wild turkey meat, both dark and white—the dressing, the casseroles and, in the end, the leftovers. Like me, Stella grew up on a wornout Okie farm. You'd have darned poor pickings around our house; we don't throw away food.

Wild turkeys can be smoked or cooked in a pit. Back in the mountains in Old Mexico, the natives use cooking pits quite often since they don't have an oven for such stuff. It's remarkably simple. Dig a pit about three feet deep, some eighteen inches across, then build a big fire from oak, accumulating a large bed of hot coals. Heat some fist-sized stones in the fire as you go if there are any around. When the hole is about a foot deep with live coals and rocks, layer with oak chips that have been soaked overnight in cold water. Lay the bird on the bed of coals and chips with feathers on, or plucked and wrapped completely in aluminum foil. Since there is no aluminum foil in the mountains, we coat the turkey with a thick layer of mud.

Cover the hole tightly with a hunk of tin, or brush, rocks and dirt and go off hunting if you want. In several hours, the turkey can be unwrapped or the mud busted off, and after peeling off the skin and feathers, eaten like a home-cooked bird. The mud will bake to the hardness of stone so you can crack it away with a hammer or a rock.

You may think all this a little squeamish, but after living back in the Sierra Madres range for a week or two, a few slices of this along with some *real* refried beans, a couple made-in-camp tortillas heated on the lid of an oil-drum stove, and a slice of fried *venada* alongside the tortillas will taste pretty darned good. Maybe you don't know; venada is venison—whitetail, mulie or Coues.

17

Let the Good Times Roll

ALL OF US get caught up in letting the good times roll—having so much fun today we forget about tomorrow, and yesterday, too. But, if you want to truly enjoy your cake, and eat it too, then you must preserve some of today so you can enjoy it years from now.

Luckily, years ago I began trying to learn something about this writing game. I'd been an avid reader all my life. My brother and I for years did chores, hunted for the market, trapped to sell furs, shocked wheat and oats—anything to make a little money. All went for one of several things, hunting or fishing stuff, the pool hall, eating ice cream on Saturday night when my family made the weekly trip to town, or purchasing hunting magazines. Just couldn't get enough of *Outdoor Life, Hunter-Trader-Trapper, Field & Stream, Sports Afield, Fur-Fish-Game,* these being our favorites. One time a man asked me if I'd unload a railroad car of coal, which I did. Took three days, from daylight to dark, using a sledge hammer and a scoop shovel, as the stuff was in huge hunks and had to be busted up into small enough pieces it could be shoveled out. Made $30 for that job.

Anyhow, this lifetime passion for reading gave me the idea that I could put down stuff on paper as good as the guys whose stories I'd been reading for years. So, I tied into writing and have been at it ever since. Never have learned how to write, but hell, I've had a heckuva lot of fun trying. And took no end of pictures.

That was the bonus—I didn't leave the camera back in camp, or at the truck, but lugged it with me, and today I have hundreds of 35mm slides which I can stick in the viewer and relive hunts that took place years and years ago. Many of the old boys I once laughed and kidded with are gone, but those slides bring them back in my mind. I loved all of 'em, and though you wish they were still hanging around the campfire,

you know they're lost and gone forever, just like Clementine. That's life and death. A hunter understands it better'n most folks.

What I'm getting at is hunting, turkey hunting in particular, is an important part of your life, and you'll darn well love it even more if years from now you can look back on all those chases in the woods by admiring trophies in your den, fingering the beard from the old gobbler that gave you a hard time down on Penitentary Mountain, or leafing through old photos.

With today's cameras, a person doesn't need to take a course in photography to take good pictures, though I would advise a course in photography composition if such an opportunity arises. By far the worst fault of the average Joe is that he gets so far back from his subject—the guy holding the turkey—that the yard, the house, the family car, dog, kids, etc., all end up in the picture. Which, truly, isn't worth a hang 'cause the turkey becomes just a bird the hunter is holding up like a sack of potatoes.

Move up close, forget the guy's feet, and focus on him and the bird he's so proud of. You may not even want all of the bird in the picture. If it's a fine old gobbler with a nice thick beard, have your buddy hold it up high, so the beard is profiled against the sky at eye level, and then catch just the upper parts of your friend and his turkey.

The worst photo a turkey hunter can possibly take is one showing two or three hunters, always kneeling, birds spread before them with tails fanned out. This is like taking a picture of the ass-end of a buck deer. Big turkeys have gorgeous tails, and even more so when fanned. But such photos are much prettier if the bird is hung feet first, with the hunter's face positioned close to the fanned-out tail. Have your friend look at the tail when you snap the photo and you'll both be happier with the results.

Diane and Gary Damuth, who own a taxidermy shop in Brady, Texas, are among the few I've seen who can do justice to an old gobbler only second to Mother Nature. Diane's love is bringing a wild turkey back to as near life as taxidermy skills will allow.

Good times are made of this. Dr. Dennis McIntyre (left) and Dr. Gary Miller with a couple fall gobblers, bagged on a long stalking bushwack with Bland. Dennis was toting a modern cartridge buster, but Gary is shooting a vintage Manton muzzleloader.

A person can choose from an endless variety of photo equipment today, camcorders to Polaroids, with an endless array in between. Some are too bulky to lug along on hunts, but are excellent for use around camp, the parking area, and at home. If you intend on carrying the camera into the woods, then there are many compact cameras which fit into fanny-packs or even a shirt pocket. Loading film is often as simple as inserting a roll and shutting the cover. Automatic advance, automatic focus, plus a jillion other features make today's picture taking very easy.

Wild turkeys are far from easy subjects to photograph, the birds must be standing still and in sufficient light.

Film? There's also an endless array of these, from black and white to fine-grained color prints or slides. My choice has always been slides since I can view these with a projector, have regular size or enlargements made from them, and view them by hand with a magnifying lens.

If a person wants to become a good turkey hunter, but does not want to take all the years required to do this legally, while hunting, then they should take up doing photography of these birds.

Wild turkeys are far from easy subjects to photograph, particularly close-range shots. If using a camera equipped with an average lens, then the pictures must be taken at very close distances, usually inside twenty yards or closer. For that picture

to be truly outstanding, the birds must be standing still and in sufficient light. Far, far too often turkeys are found in the dark woods, and the resulting photo shows the birds as a bunch of dark shadows or silhouettes.

For many years, I've endeavored to take pictures of the turkey and the hunter in the same frame. These are by far the finest but most difficult photos to take. Too often, simple wildlife photography is done with long-range telephoto lenses, zoom lenses, and from completely enclosed blinds. Most is also done over baited feed areas. This is how so many photographers capture large antlered whitetails and huge strutting gobblers on film.

Showing both hunter and game in the same frames can be done using a 35mm camera mounted on a clampod and using a long electronic release cable which the hunter controls. Many problems are associated with using this setup, and if you don't have lots of time to devote to each picture, forget it. All lenses have a field-of-view, the wide-angle lens having far the largest. However, using wide-angle lenses for hunter/live game photos requires the game to be very close to the hunter. If not, the game will appear to be at a good distance.

The camera must be pre-focused on the spot the hunter hopes the turkey will appear. It won't do any good to put the setup together if the bird or birds don't come to that spot once you are ready. And heck knows how often this can happen. With the camera pre-focused and the hunter positioning himself usually to one side of the planned frame, the birds must walk into that pre-planned area in order to create the illusion of a hunter just seconds away from shooting a bird. The gun must be visible and in the hunter's hands, and the hunter must be

Ed Norwood relaxes on the front porch of his hunting camp in Mississippi. Boy, how many memories I have from that bunch of hills and hollows. That's my chair next to Ed. Don't let anyone have it, Ed; I'll be back. Soon.

clearly seen. Your pictures will show the hunter more emphatically if he is not completely camouflaged. I wear old clothes which more or less blend into the surroundings.

Another problem is having enough light to show both the birds and the hunter clearly in the finished photo. Pictures made in shade are bad, and if taken in bright sunlight, will be even worse. So when choosing a location, find a place where

there's no screen of brush between the camera and the subjects; where there's plenty of light; and where turkeys will come marching to in *the middle daylight hours*. This is why you must have lots of time on your hands.

You will need a call, and you'll have to study the local birds. Choose a location where birds will either come to your call or pass through the area on their daily wanderings. Invari-

Now, I've guided for what seems like my whole life, but surprises never end. Ranney Moran (left) and Gary Blakeslee lounge next to a limo Ranney hired to bring him to western Oklahoma after he missed his regular ride. Hey, Ranney, you made our day when you pulled off this one.

You find hunters clowning around wherever you go—even far down in Mexico. Jose Llama couldn't resist when I hauled out the camera. Looks like you need a shave, boy; your whiskers are worse'n any whitetails.

How many times have you seen a hunting video or watched such stuff on TV. Well, those things have to be filmed someplace. Here Dirk Ross (in hat) is being interviewed by Daniel Hendricks, whose outdoor TV show "North American Bowhunter" is popular across the northeastern part of the U.S.

Troy Hardesty, who manages the hunting end of Ranch Rio Bonita, near Junction, Texas, is all smiles. Randi's unhappy cause I insisted she should be in this book. She just doesn't like cameras. But thanks, Randi; I'd never have felt this thing was complete without you.

ably, I try to find favored feeding areas, since many turkeys do not arrive until there is good light. Photos taken in color and without a filter too late in the day, or too early, turn out either too dark or overexposed. Photos taken midday are best.

The age of the turkeys also has a great bearing on all this. Old gobblers are very spooky, except when with hens and strutting. Young fall turkeys are by far the easiest to photograph, and fall foliage can provide a beautiful backdrop. Spring foliage can be pretty, but too often photos taken in early spring are drab and dreary as the bushes and trees haven't greened up.

I never wear camos when doing this type of photography and always try to hide from any approaching turkeys by taking pictures from a blind. This way I can, if the blind is sightproof, move around some, so as not to have to sit there like a stone. Blinds take a little work, but they're worth it when waiting hours for a turkey to come into camera range. And you don't have to worry about whether you'll be seen. I've had birds come inside easy gunshot range when on location, but before getting to within the fifteen-yard range for my pre-set field of view, they'd see me and hightail it—leaving me awfully damned mad. The whole wait was wasted.

Looking through a pile of old photos brings a smile to anyone's kisser. Every time I look at a picture of a certain cowtank near camp in western Oklahoma I have to laugh. Makes me think of the hot October afternoon I'd been guiding a

What good times wouldn't be better with a pig roast. A wild hog's over the coals at the author's Rio Grande turkey location in western Oklahoma as buddies hang around waiting for him to yell, "Grub's on." Chuck Hartigan gets a close-up of the author turning the vittles, and though I don't remember, he probably made one of his characteristic smart aleck comments about either the food or the cook or both.

bowhunter. Directly after he nailed a bird, he left for town. Now I'd worked up a sweat and felt just like the devil wearing longhandles. Right near camp is a cowtank the rancher keeps full of water for cattle in that pasture. Boy, I'd just go take me a dip in it. I got me a towel, headed down that way, stripped off naked as a jaybird, and climbed in. This tank's like many in the West; it's poured on the spot with concrete mixed right there by a bunch of cowhands. Such tanks aren't deep. In fact, sitting on your butt the water'll usually only come up to your chin. The water won't be cold if the weather's been hot, and after a hard day's hunt, it's like bathing in the Waldorf Astoria. Maybe better, since it's in a cow pasture out where there ain't any looking back at ya.

Leaning back, I was musing on what a lucky critter I was for having such an easy way of life when I hear a car coming down my little country road. Before the days of the Oil Patch, hardly a car (everything was pickups) a day went down that road. But now there was a whole lot of traffic—some days six or eight came. But I wasn't concerned with this one and watched as it passed on by.

Now, just west of the cowtank, one of these oil outfits had cut a new dirt road over a hill and drilled an oil well down in the pasture. They'd just completed the road, and the rancher and I had heard they had a pretty fair well. The road ran about a hundred yards west of the tank, angled past it, then faded from view as it went over a hill which was and still is heavily dotted with big cedar trees. Countless times, I've seen turkeys wandering across the hill, but ever since the Oil Patch put in the road I don't see 'em anymore.

Well, this big white Cadillac goes tooling past, and just when I think it's going on toward town, danged if it didn't turn in the oil field road and stop at the gate. Meanwhile, I'm

Old gobblers are very spooky, except when with hens and strutting.

"making like a alligator," all you can see of me is my nose, eyes, and the top of my wet head. Studying the big good-looking car, I thought, "What the hell are they doing?" I could see several people in the car, and I knew they had no choice but to back up and leave, since the oilies were keeping the gate locked. The rancher wanted it that way, so they were obliging.

One old boy gets out of the car and takes a look at the gate and the lock. He walks back to the car, and they all palaver for a spell. I'm thinking, "Why in hell don't they get out of here?" Hell, about that time they all get out of the car—and two *ladies*. I'm as far in the tank as I can get.

By far the easiest way to preserve memories is to take photos. The author zeroes in on longtime hunting buddy Tom Preston, who is hefting a fine old spring-killed gobbler.

Dirk Ross (right) hollers "be careful" to one of the guys who is picking cactus spines from his backside. Yep, that's what clowning around can get you into at times. Texas is not only the wild turkey capital of the U.S., but is number one in the whole world when it comes to cactus. Right, Dirk?

Turkeys are where you find them. This mural is on a building wall across the street catterwampus from the Brady, Texas, county courthouse. It's just those folks' way of saying, "Hey, pardner, you ain't seen turkeys 'til ya hunted turkeys in the Lone Star State."

Memories are made of stuff like this. Chuck Hartigan and Pam Johnson with a bearded hen skilleted by Chuck. Nobody has more fun than us turkey nuts.

A sidewalk cafe in Terreon, Mexico, with two hunting buddies smiling at the camera. The young lady? Well, when she saw me haul out the camera, she asked if she could be in the photo. The eats were delicious. The people, wonderful.

The whole bunch of 'em crawls through the gate and comes strolling down the road.

Now I'm making like a crawdad, muttering all sorts of things, all bad, not knowing where they intend on going, as I'd never seen such a thing in all my days knocking around the West. Ladies in pretty dresses and gents in nice town clothes simply don't wander around in cow pastures—*or hadn't, up to now.*

I was nothing but two eyeballs sitting on the rim of an old cowtank, watching with extreme interest in where these folks were going.

Boy, did I breathe easier when they stuck to the road and walked on past, at last fading from view behind the hill and the cedars. Man, I grabbed my towel and flat lit a shuck for camp.

Talking to Don the next day (he's the rancher), I learned those folks had some money invested in that well and had dri-

> **I** *was nothing but two eyeballs sitting on the rim of an old cowtank, watching with extreme interest in where these folks were going.*

ven clean down here from some place up in Kansas, just to see if their money had come to good use.

Don't tell me, I know, I'm a slow learner. I still crawl in that tank. And when I do I can't help but keep an eye peeled for big fancy cars—mainly white Cadillacs.

Getting back to cameras. If you have one, or get one, carry it with you. Of all the jillion folks who've hunted with me, there hasn't been but six or seven who have had a camera along when they wanted it. Fanny packs will hold one, as will all vests. Stick in the book of instructions, too, plus a roll or two of extra film and a cleaning cloth. Make it a part of your hunting gear. Lug it along just like you do your calls.

There are few mementoes as enjoyable as looking at photos,

both old and new. I laugh each time I look at one in which Dirk Ross is grabbing his backside. We'd been doing some photography on his grand Rancho Rio Bonita northwest of Kerrville, Texas, and Dirk backed into a huge cactus. I had my camera in hand, so just took a shot or two of one of the boys pulling out stickers. Dirk's well-known for his exceedingly fine hunting videos and the hunts he offers on the Rancho Rio Bonita. It's a 15,000-acre spread loaded with game—turkeys, deer, exotics, wild hogs, fishing, the works.

There's another picture which makes me think of hot afternoons—the one of me and Ken Warner on top a bare hill. Again, the scenario involves an old concrete cowtank, but this one was bone dry. We were slouched against it in the sparse shade, waiting for late afternoon and the appearance of the big old gobbler I'd been seeing there every afternoon, strutting back and forth. Hens would see the old turkey out on that bare hill, and they'd wander up that way, too. There wasn't any way a hunter's approach could go unnoticed, so the only thing to do was to arrive at midday and hold out until near dusk when the turkeys come out to feed.

The wind blew so hard out of the west that afternoon I swear the sun was two hours late going down. We waited for what seemed like an eternity. You all know Ken as the editor of *Gun Digest*, a big thick book for serious gun nuts. Ken even carried along some books to read while we hunkered there in the heat. Yep, he killed the old bird, the biggest Rio Grande I've ever had the pleasure of hanging on a scale.

You should keep a diary, too, or at least notes about each hunt. This advice comes from someone who wishes to this day that he'd done so. We all think we have good memories, but a week from now you won't be able to tell anyone what you did today except that it was a work day and you knew you were at work—or supposed to be anyhow. People soon forget the little things, and those are the things you wish you remembered.

I do keep notes, and though they are not much, I can go back through them and learn a lot about what happened. For example, I have a bunch of stuff written down about the fall of

Turkey hunting wouldn't be turkey hunting if it weren't for hunting with old friends. Lennis Rose and I have waged war on many turkeys together, though there've been times when it was questionable about who was winning the battle—us or the birds. We're still in the fight, though, ain't we, old buddy?

'89. I guided in Colorado and Oklahoma that fall. My hunters bagged twenty-four birds—nine hens and fifteen gobblers. Of the gobblers, eleven were jakes and four toms. The hens were six jennies and one bearded lady.

Here are a few other facts from that fall:

- Turkeys shot strutting or running—3
- Shot standing—14
- Shot flying, either driven, or from stalking and still-hunting, then flushed—7
- Coming to call—7
- Killed through driving technique—3
- Killed through stalking technique—5
- Walk-up flush—1
- Ambush stake-out with call—8

(The last entry means a call was being used but the primary hunting method used was waiting in ambush over a period of time, usually in well-known turkey haunts.)

Other interesting notes:

- I loaned out two pairs of camo gloves and headnets, none of which were given back.
- There were seven clean misses, and one known cripple lost.
- Four hunters had never before killed a turkey or shot at one.
- Several opportunities were lost because the hunter reacted too slowly to my commands.
- I made one small drive which resulted in two hens and one old gobbler being bagged.
- I whistled up a jake which was missed. Remaining there and calming the hunter down, I called it back a second time, also whistling, wherein the hunter made the kill. Both shots at inside twenty-five yards. This was a good-sized jake, but still a young fall turkey, not yet wise to the dangers in the woods. The bird obviously never saw us at the time of the first shot,

nor related the sound of the shot to danger. It was also separated from the drove.

- One hunter killed a young jake gobbler sitting on the top-most limbs of a huge creekbottom cottonwood, a bird I had flushed there. Heavy undergrowth allowed us to stalk the tree, where upon he fetched it groundward with a blast from his 12-gauge.

Notes from October 30, 1990, remind me that David Jackman nailed an old gobbler in full strut along the south fence on my western Oklahoma lease. Seldom will you see an old bird in full strut during fall hunts, but all the subspecies can, and do, from time to time. Invariably it's soon after flydown, though I have seen an old bird strutting at all hours of the day. Sometimes they strut when a bunch of hens and young are nearby or when a small group of gob-

You'll never regret keeping notes about your hunts—the more complete, the greater joy.

blers have gathered. I've also seen them strutting just after they've been scattered and were calling to group back together. *Kee* runs of young turkeys will sometimes trigger gobbling instincts in turkeys.

You'll never regret keeping notes about your hunts—the more complete, the greater joy these will be in future years. Writing down all the exacting details will also help you make decisions for future hunts as to what days are best, what areas, what time of day, what methods, what the birds feed on, etc.

My wife says I'm bad about carrying home just plain junk, most of which ends up in the den, where the walls are covered with such stuff—old signs, traps, decoys, Indian stuff (beaded bags, etc.), a jillion turkey calls, powder horns, pottery, guns, hunting books, not to mention a whole batch of turkey beards stuck in various display cases.

Under the meat block (no, we use it for a coffee table) is a

Shades of the Old West. Oklahoma wasn't like this back in the good old days or any other time. Ted Herrick (left) and Mike Monier, two longtime hunting buddies of the Turkey Wars, getting prepared to lay into some steamer clams and live lobsters at the author's hunting lease, Camp Redneck, in western Oklahoma. Could be that these were the first lobsters in Major County, Oklahoma. They were courtesy of Logan Clarke of Lobster Trap Co., Inc., located in Maine. Logan hunts with us guys, too.

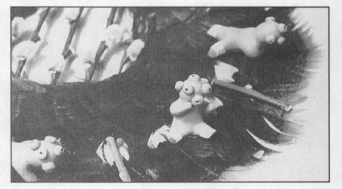

One of the author's modern mementoes from the hunt is this wall-hanging made for him by a wonderful lady in New Mexico, Loretta Valdez, of Velarde. Loretta has won many, many awards for her artistry in arranging dried flowers, nuts, feathers and other gifts of nature. The one she made for me is from the feathers of an Eastern gobbler, a few pussywillow branches and several clay mudheads, a mythological figure in the Navajo religion. It's a thing of beauty which must be seen to be appreciated. Thanks, Loretta.

As much as I mention it, you'd think I like to eat. You're right. And where better than over an iron grate back in Mexico's Sierra Madres. Tamales, tortillas, beans, meat, guacamole, home-grown tomatoes and green chiles. Boy, we turkey hunters have it tough!

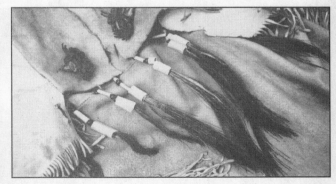

Hunters may want to use turkey beards for decoration as I've done over the years. These turkey beards were inserted and glued into small sections of the bird's larger wingbone. The beard is then tied with sinew which is pulled into the bone after being coated with glue. The sinew becomes the main tie cord, passing through other short sections of bone used for decoration along with old vintage trade beads. Spurs are also encased and sewn onto the buckskin.

You never know what'll happen next, though you are supposed to be hunting turkeys. Ed Norwood and the author skin a wild hog waylaid by a member of our party while on a hunt in Florida. Yes, there's no finer eating than such a critter roasted over a bed of live oak coals.

bunch of old cast-iron skillets. Found them under an old abandoned rundown house back in a Mississippi crick bottom. (Cricks are little bitty what's-usually-called-a-creek and sometimes dry.) Alongside them sits a small iron kettle containing a bunch of old pottery chards I picked up somewhere back in Mexico's Sierra Madres mountains. A couple of those chards have the Southwestern New Mexico look to them, stuff you'd pick up along the Mimbres River, which starts from nothing and goes nowhere. Black and white pottery chards always make me think of the people who lived along the Mimbres and the long-lost tribe some folks know as "the ancient ones," the Anasazi.

Of course, there aren't any finer trophies from a hunt than a big, nicely mounted, wild turkey gobbler. The grand and gorgeous Osceola roosting above my desk in the den carries me back to a sprawling ranch in far south Florida. Big thickets of cabbage palm, live oak hummocks, alligators, leeches (the damned blood suckers), I can still see them all and that old bird heading my way when I made a few calls lying belly down in a stand of sawgrass. I had sneaked across a little canal to get on the gobbler's side of it, then crawled over near the edge of the tall grass, knowing darn well that old gobbler was not going to come out into that stuff. The kill was all downhill, and getting to where he lay was the hard part. He's a beaut. Hope no turkey ever rakes me with hooks like he's got.

Stella can't keep all this memorabilia confined to the den, either. The fine piece of art I'm about to mention is as far from junk as you can get. It's a wall hanging that overlooks our breakfast table. Now, you're no doubt wondering how a wall hanging can relate to turkey hunting. Let me explain.

South of Taos, New Mexico, some twenty miles or so down the Rio Grande canyon and on the west side is a roadside fruit stand—a big fruit stand owned by a wonderful lady, Loretta Valdez, and her husband.

Oh, yes, I do like to eat. Just getting me to pose for this shot made me sore 'cause it took time away from that tortilla I'm munching on.

Darned few folks think of good times when they think about game wardens, but then they haven't met Dick Belding who, with his wife Marcia, lives just outside Waynesburg, Pennsylvania. If you're hunting on the wrong side of the law, you probably aren't going to get along too good with a guy like Belding. Dick and Marcia are the stuff this country should be made of. There's none better.

Well, years ago Stella and I stopped there, as we had many times before on the trip between Taos and Santa Fe. During our conversation with Mrs. Valdez, I learned she needed bird feathers for her artwork. Since then, she's become an extremely well-known Western artist. From state fair exhibits each year at Albuquerque, she's walked away with so many top honors that she's been the subject of many articles concerning native Indian art. So, over the years I've saved feathers from any number of different game birds, which I give to her when I'm out that way. In gratitude, Loretta sent me a

Of course, there aren't any finer trophies from a hunt than a big, nicely mounted, wild turkey gobbler.

number of beautiful wall-hangings. The one hanging above the table is made of a few short sections of pussywillow, feathers from an old gobbler I nailed one fall over in Arkansas, and a number of small mudhead clay figures which are a part of the Navajo mythology. It's a fascinating piece, and a reminder of the good times my sweetheart and I have had on the road to Santa Fe.

The number one trophies for any turkey hunter are the bird's beard and spurs. The beard does require care, because a tiny weevil can ruin them if they're left lying around. Years ago I was hunting in Louisiana, and one of the locals asked me to come to his house and see his trophy of beards. He fished out a cigar box from a closet, opened it up, and there was what was left of his pride and joy—just a tangle of hair that obviously had once been turkey beards. He was just sick. I would've been, too. The beards I've saved from all my turkey hunts I keep enclosed in a display case with moth crystals.

Beards are easily displayed if you'll obtain some shotshell

Anyone who's traveled the highways in southern Florida has eye-balled the signs put up by Tom Gaskins, who sells turkey calls from his home just north of the small community of Palmdale. Probably there's no one in the country who has been making and selling turkey calls longer, personally, than Tom Gaskins.

casings, 28-gauge hulls being best for most beards though 12-bore hulls may be needed for the truly large-based beard. Simply take a punch and knock out the spent percussion cap in the brass base of the shell casing. Glue a cup hook in the hole and then glue the beard in the open end, inserting it in about $1/4$-inch. Now you can hang them up, and again I use cup hooks for this. Jake beards, and hen beards, too, fit best in old 38 or 45 pistol and revolver brass.

Many turkey hunters spend midday hours at other pursuits such as fishing like these two guys. They'd hauled out several pretty nice channel cats when I took this pic.

Troy Hardesty, manager of the Rio Bonito hunting ranch, pauses beside one of the hunting vehicles commonly used throughout Texas on the many commercial hunting locations found there.

Good times include camp life, cooking over an open fire and rehashing old hunts. Keep a camera handy. You'll enjoy the memories for the rest of your life if you've taken lots of photos.

What do turkey hunters do on those long cold turkeyless nights in winter? The smart ones read *Turkey & Turkey Hunting*, edited by Gerry Blair and Jim Casada, and published by Debbie Knauer. With sales of over 105,000, it's obvious a whole army of hunters are gearing up for the spring hunts. Here's Gerry with a fine old gobbler that must'a been blind to allow somebody with that much white on his kisser to get into shotgun shooting distance.

Enid, Oklahoma, Police Chief George Stover and his son, Zac, have shared many a good time on the shooting range while Zac grew of age to become a competition shooter. Of course, being hunting friends of the author, they've also shared some time shooting wild turkeys with the author. Let the good times roll.

Spurs are another matter. Some hunters dry the feet as they come from the downed bird. But if you want the toes spread out, the dried foot resembling a walking bird, drive a sixteen-penny nail into a board, press down on the foot to spread the toes, and take a hunk of wire or stout cord and tie the leg to the nail. The foot will dry in this position. Spurs do make fine decoration for necklaces, or if you're into buckskinning, sewn on buckskin coats, hats, or whatever. Spurs are easily handled if left attached to a section of the leg bone, which is easily cut with a hacksaw just above, and below, the spur. With a sharp pocketknife, the dried skin can be cut away, and once the bone is cleaned with soap and water, you can run a leather thong through the center for hanging. Twenty years ago, I got the idea of encasing the bone in leather. That hides the raw bone, and the whole thing will be much less offensive. I've had countless strangers examine my necklaces, fingering the spurs, enthralled with them. Not one in ten thousand will know that they are actually turkey spurs, and they just stare at you when you tell them. The ideal necklace has the Royal Grand Slam of wild turkey spurs on it.

Turkey hunting is what we make it—Grand Slams, beards, spurs, stuffed birds, whatever. Probably there are hunters who keep none of that stuff, who don't have a thing to show for the birds they've bagged except the memories. Some folks can't sit still for thinking about the one bird they lack for a Royal Grand Slam, while the guy down the street just wants to go hunting. They're both right. Also reminds me of an old man who ran a tiny bait house where I'd bought my minnows. He'd called 'em "minners," not minnows. Back nearer home was another bait shop, run by an old lady. She'd been in the bait business for years and years. She called minnows "minnies."

Minnows, minners, minnies—we were all right, I suppose.

That's the way turkey hunting should be—think it out for yourself and do it your way, just stay legal. Not a soul influenced any of my early turkey hunting years 'cause there wasn't anyone who knew anything about the sport. I learned the hard way. Some things worked out OK; some I'd not try again.

But I had fun. And if you aren't laughing at your own bobbles, then you need to lean back, take a deep breath, and think about just having a good time. If you don't like getting up early, you need to eat breakfast the night before and don't get up. Those turkeys will still be in the woods when you get there.

I've probably shot as many turkeys after noon as I have before.

By far the greatest pleasure I've received from turkey hunting is all the friends I've made. It's crazy how some of us met. A few are guys I met back when I judged at the old National

> **B**y far the greatest pleasure I've received from turkey hunting is all the friends I've made. Now, I want to say thanks, for all the good times.

Turkey Calling Championships held at Yellville, Arkansas.

Many turkey hunters I've met because they called me. I've oftimes wondered how some of them found out where I lived. Heck knows how many photos I've gotten in the mail of a hunter holding up a gobbler he's shot. Keep sending 'em. There's nothing I like better than such stuff, whether it's talking turkey hunting or reading somebody's letter about how he scragged an old boss turkey one April morning.

Now, I want to say thanks, you all, for the good times.

All I ask is, if this spring you're out in the big woods, easing along, and you run into an old boy stretched out on the dead leaves and pine straw, snoring like crazy, I'd appreciate it if you'd let me get out my nap. Nothing makes a person feel better'n a little snooze in the turkey woods.

And if the past is any indication, maybe when my eyes open, and my not-so-good hearing gets tuned up, I'll realize an old gobbler is close, close enough that my left hand will tighten on the gunstock. Then *watch out* cause I'm coming up shooting.

The *good ole days!* Old buddy, we're in 'em.

Chasin' a Rainbow

"PA-VOON, PA-VOON!" My eyes shot treeward, toward the tops of a couple of towering matapalo giants. I saw the bird spring from one branch to another, a dark form. And suddenly I was face to face with the ghost we'd been seeking, the supposed jungle turkey. *Pa-voon* was what the local folks call the bird.

My old, battered Winchester whipped to my cheek. Helluva long shot went through my mind, and I squeezed.

My quest for wild turkeys has been much like chasin' a rainbow, the pot of gold replaced by the glint of gold on burnished feathers. The final quest seemingly within reach, I learn that just out of reach is another quest, another search for the Lord of the Forest. Like Coronado, it seems as though my Cibola, the Seven Cities of Gold, for which Coronado and countless conquistadores conquered Indian nations, lay at my feet in forests past. But each time, like the Phoenix, a new forest would rise up, beckoning me to search for yet another wild turkey. Perhaps in Central America, in the land of volcanoes and rain forests, my longing would end.

Nicaragua lies between the Honduras, on its northern border, and Costa Rica, to the south. The Pacific batters Nicaragua's western shores, whereas all of its eastern side makes up a part of the old Spanish Main.

Columbus had scanned those Caribbean seas in 1502, his tiny ship watched from the jungles by the Miskito tribe, along what today is known as the Mosquito Coast. My journey to this Central American country was the culmination of plans made by my old friend, Gary Blakeslee, who owns a wildlife art gallery in Palm Beach, Florida. Gary has many friends in Nicaragua. When one of them mentioned wild turkeys on his visit to the Sunshine State, Gary let it be known that he had friends too—turkey hunting friends. And, here we were, Gary, me, Mike Monier from New Jersey, and Ted Herrick from New York. But we had obtained special permission. Hunting is still an iffy proposition in Nicaragua.

Hunters who intend to hunt any country south of the Mexican border would be wise to make plans well ahead.

Immunization shots are a must—malaria, cholera, yellow fever, and hepatitis are all musts. A tetanus booster is a must also if ten years have passed since the last one. And, if you have a stomach that doesn't tolerate foreign foods, you'd be smart to get a prescription from your doctor for pills to cure Montezuma's Revenge, a.k.a. the Mexican Quickstep.

You must have gun permits if you take a gun into any of these countries. This can get messy, so if you have a resident friend, I suggest you use his.

We were guests of the Healy family and we hadn't been there but a few hours when I realized hospitality is truly something we don't have in the U.S., that is compared to that extended us in Nicaragua. Here in the states, anyone who wants real friendship needs to go south, far south. I learned this many years ago on my treks back into the Sierra Madres range while hunting Gould's turkeys in Mexico. Nowhere have I found people so warm, so down to earth, so real. No one has his nose out of joint. None of this unfriendly I'm-better-than-you-are bit that stares everyone in the face in this country. You walk in an airport terminal in Atlanta, or Miami, and it's akin to stepping into Hades—darned near everyone seems mad at the world.

The trouble with places like Mexico, and Central America, is too many folks want to please. If you're seeking wild turkeys, *great*, we'll go find some. But, which ones.

Our first hunt was into rugged hill country near the Pacific coast, down toward Costa Rica. Passing several armed checkpoints, we all stared at the passing parade of flowering foliage, trees festooned in pink blossoms, vines laden with blue, white, orange, and over all this was cast a blanketing crown of yellow-topped laurel trees. Flat-crowned roble trees stood like sentinels overlooking the small valleys, a blanket of pink flowers marking each outpost.

Mike Healy drove the four-wheeler to the end of the road—the ocean and beautiful white sands. For miles along this virgin beach not a soul could be seen, and looking out across the waters not a ship or dot of land was visible. Heck

The Healy family of Rivas, Nicaragua, son, mother and daughter, undoubtedly among the country's most gracious hosts, opened their home to four gringos from the States. Wined and dined for several days, I can't recall a time when I so hated to leave, nor could my companions.

People who have never been to Central or South American countries will see many things new to them, such as these young girls selling (and eating) fruit toted in baskets on top of their heads. Like all young people they found it amusing to see a stranger taking their picture.

knows how far to the west the first islands in the Pacific were. We backtracked, pulling off the trail, a mile or so inland. Henry Torres met us there, along with some of his hunting buddies. But they weren't interested in turkeys; they hunted deer—whitetails. Yes, our beloved whitetail hangs out in Central America. Henry pulled up moments later with five of his cronies, plus a pack of hounds. With him he'd brought a local Indian boy, Santos, who was our turkey hunting guide. Here I am, too near seventy to back out now, had never had a guide in my entire life, and this wisp of a boy was to be my man Friday.

Made me think of me when I was a barefoot (and I don't think they ever were clean) boy in Oklahoma. If anybody wanted to know where anything was on or within miles of our farm, my brother Dick and I could lead them there. Right off I knew one thing for dead sure. If this boy knew where old "cham-pee-tay" was hanging his spurs, then I'd stick to him like skin on a snake.

You'll hear turkeys called many things while hunting south of the border, any border. In northern Mexico, turkeys are very often referred to as "guajolote," properly pronounced as "wah-ya-loh-ti." Or, you may hear simply the first part of the word, "guaya," or "pavo." Further south in Mexico a turkey may be "totoe" or "pipilo." Much of the time back in the high Sierras, the locals all know turkeys by the name "cocono," the hen being a "cocona," the young birds "coconitos." So, I wasn't surprised when I was told the wild turkey's name in this land far south was "champipe." This is pronounced "cham-pee-tay." One hunter I talked with called them "pavo silvestre." Nor was I taken back on learning that in a day or two we would journey to the land of still another turkey, the "pa-voon."

We headed into the brush. Toting a borrowed, old, tired Winchester pump somebody had handed me, I glanced back as we hiked off into the now dry forest. Nicaragua has two seasons, a dry one and, when the rains come, a wet one. We'd arrived toward the last of the dry one. So with the leaves down, the low canopy had opened up. Visibility was

Gary Blakeslee, who owns the beautiful Blakeslee Wildlife Art Gallery in Palm Beach, Florida, studies a sign denoting a wildlife refuge deep in Nicaragua.

good. Easing through a non-ending thicket of vines and umbrellaed brush, our pace was slow as we ducked under looping vines or jutting branches. We passed by some papaya trees in a bottom and I noticed the long, ripe fruit dangling from the upper part of the tree. Nicaragua is a fruit eater's paradise with bananas, plantains, tangerines, dangling from trees about anyplace you go. Mangoes have to be the best of the bunch. If you keep your eyes open you'll see coffee trees, really bushes, tobacco, and, of course, the number one crop, sugar cane. Our guide, Santos, was toting a machete in a leather belt scabbard, as do so many men in this great country. When it's not hacking down the long sugar stalks, it's a must for forest travel.

Santos seemed intent on where we were headed, which after a mile of beating through the dense jungle, was obviously far back from the little-used trail we'd driven in on. Something caught my attention in a brush pile off the path a few feet—a blotchy skinned, gray and brown iguana. Though Santos would no doubt have liked for me to scrag the little beast, I didn't catch his arm and point it out to him. We weren't hunting two-foot-long lizards.

All of a sudden, a turkey gobbled—far off, to the south, toward a ridge. My three buddies behind me wore looks not only of surprise but excitement as their eyes twinkled in anticipation. It wasn't difficult to tell that we four gringos had come to hunt. Run out the turkeys, and cover your ears.

Signing to Santos to go ahead, I motioned a course which should have taken us just a bit to one side of where I thought a bird might be. Easing forward, we hadn't covered another fifty yards when the gobbler cut loose again. Santos looked back, but I motioned for him to go forward. Undoubtedly, he was also pondering why I was sticking with him like the skin on his back.

We had covered several hundred yards, slipping through the brush as silently as five hunters could, when suddenly the bird again belted out a gobble—this time inside a hundred yards. I'd noticed how different this bird's gobbles seemed compared to state-side turkeys. The notes were

Ivette, whose husband Andy Seeger runs a fishing boat out of San Juan del Sur, can and will serve your catch to you while fishing in the beautiful blue Pacific aboard their small charter boat. A charming hostess, Ivette's one of those people I'll always be glad I met.

I remarked to my companions that this turkey species must have been a descendant of today's domestic turkey.

shorter and kind of boxey sounding. Nonetheless, it was definitely a turkey gobble.

I fingered the safety. I'm an old double-barrel man, so I could only hope I'd be fast in handling the pump gun when, and if, the time came. I was given short-base light loads, 1-ounce of #6s to use. Not my choice for shooting wild turkeys, but in a country where political turmoil is still a fresh and real part of life, a gringo from the states had best leave his guns at home. I'd shoot what was given me.

Santos crept forward, just right of where we thought the last gobble had erupted. I'd signed to him that I was ready, but to take it slow. Brush was excellent for a close encounter—the slight up-and-down roll to the ground made for a dry-gulch bushwack.

Santos' head turned quickly to the left. My eyes followed and fell on a red head. The pump gun thundered in the thicket, and then like a cat, I unleashed a second charge. I could see that the bird was settling to the ground, head sluiced with #6s. I scrambled through the brush to retrieve my prize. Just as I got to the turkey, I fell into a waist-deep hole, which I learned later was created by locals digging for pre-Columbian Indian pottery and artifacts.

In that instant when a hunter pulls the trigger, he has a perception of the target in his mind. My mind's eye had told me this South American gobbler was short and my mind's eye was correct. He had very short legs, white spurs and a nice 6-inch pencil-thin beard. But, what he didn't have was barring on the wings. They were a dark tobacco brown color with extremely well-broomed tips.

Turning the gobbler over, I remarked to my companions that this turkey species must have been a descendant of today's domestic turkey.

While in pursuit of this bird, we'd heard another gobbler to the east of us. So then, with me bringing up the rear, toting my gobbler, we moved a sashay in the direction of this second

Our hunting party takes a break in rough country during our quest for the wild turkey found in those parts of Nicaragua. The terrain was rough up-and-down hill country, festooned with vines, huge trees and a seemingly endless array of flowering bushes, trees, vines and plants.

A vicious thorn tree exists in abundance throughout all the mountainous terrain of the country along Nicaragua's Pacific coast. Anyone falling into this tree would suffer serious injury due to the size, toughness and number of these protruding from each tree.

Mike Monier, veteran New Jersey turkey hunter, studies the large pods on a nameless tree among the rugged terrain where we hunted in Nicaragua.

247

Hunting in the dry off-season in Nicaragua's rain-forests results in extreme heat, which brings on exhaustion. Water should be carried by anyone planning a very long outing, and lightweight clothing should be worn. A hunter can expect to sight iguana, boa constrictors, countless birds and perhaps some of the small whitetails. Ocelot and jaguar are present, but are very seldom seen during daytime hunts.

turkey. Leaving a papaya-studded bottom, we trudged up a steep hill, stopping for a breather alongside a huge, old mata-palo tree. Mike and I popped horseshoe calls into our mouths and made a few yelps from time to time. This didn't seem to fire him up, but I figured calling could only help our cause.

Gary eased out on a point on the hill. Fetching my camera, I was taking pictures when Gary's gun suddenly exploded. Then again, and a third time. We all scrambled toward Gary's position like hound dogs on a gravy bowl.

When we neared, we could see turkeys flopping.

Gary had kept watch and nailed a pair of jakes that had come in to him shutmouth—silent. Both were young turkeys and close to the same size as the adult I'd bagged. They were

Some genetic oddity probably accounts for the lack of barring in the primaries.

short of stature with short legs and very short beards. One was intensely black with very little white except on the lower rump feathers. As with the older gobbler, the blue on the head was a gorgeous fluorescent mixed with red and touches of white. Again, no barring on the wings. Obviously, all of these turkeys were of the old race from which all the domestic turkeys were derived. Some genetic oddity in the area probably accounts for the lack of barring in the primaries.

Two days later we journeyed into rough mountainous country—a land of monkeys, both Congo and white face, umpteen kinds of parrots, along with countless crested jays and myriad other birds and animals. Several times I spotted trogons flying acros the jungle roof; twice I thought I spotted the beautiful ruby breasted trogon, the famed Quetzal.

We scouted for a guide and found a young lad who the local folks used because he seemed to know the area so well. He, like Santos, wore a machete in a scabbard at his side. However, after we left his village, that machete was never stuck back in the scabbard. Too much stuff to cut through, even though we followed a stream bed.

Nicaragua is a land of volcanoes—156 of them. Mount Concepcion and Mount Maderas lie in Lake Nicaragua, and it was the latter volcano that we found ourselves clambering up in hopes of finding the elusive "pa-voon."

Lake Nicaragua holds the distinction of being the only freshwater lake in the world with a resident population of freshwater sharks. Tarpon fishing is excellent, as is fishing for *guapota*, pronounced gwah-coat-ta. The guapota resembles a peacock bass, with a pronounced hump on top of its head, and is a delicious eating fish. It can be taken on Big-O-type lures and fights like a large-mouth. Our party caught several along the edge of the lake. The faces of these dandies are much like a piranha's, teeth and all. Needless to say, these babies would be pretty hard on wooden plugs.

Trudging up the narrow stream bed, a torture chamber of rocks, low overhanging branches and fallen trees, I tried again to stick to our guide. We'd picked up a stray dog somewhere in the jungle and I soon learned how handy the critter could be in flushing any pa-voons along the route. Jaime Delgado, a friend of our host Mike Healy, was with us and kept me posted on what our young guide had to say. That is, when he talked, which was damned seldom. But, I had endless questions, so I kept Jaime busy translating my inquiries and the boy's answers. I did learn that our quarry would probably be seen flying or sitting far up in the huge trees. From time to time, I studied the height and wondered if my gun and load could reach a bird up that high. Several tree trunks were easily fif-

The author's wild gobbler taken in the mountains not far from the Costa Rican border and a mile from the Pacific shoreline. The small, but fully grown, adult gobbler had the characteristic vivid white tips on the lower rump and tail feathers of the *Gallopavo* strain of turkey.

teen feet at the base, with canopies I'd safely judge to be one hundred and fifty feet across.

We were running short of water. The native boy had brought a small jug along, but two of our party had already consumed it. At my pestering, Jaime finally got it from the guide that we would find water far up the mountain, so we looked forward to getting tanked up there.

I was still thinking water when my boy Friday suddenly whispered "Pa-voon." Up went the old gun—BANG—the bird hopped to another branch. Though I could tell it was hit, I pumped in another load, and *bang*. As if in slow motion, the bird let go all holds and plummeted into the thick foliage below. I thought we'd seen the last of it, but the boy crawled into the brush and soon handed me my pa-voon.

Left to right, Mike Healy, Henry Torres, Sr., Mike Monier and Henry Torres, Jr., chomping down on the gobbler bagged earlier by the author. Mike Healy and his family own a plantation in Nicaragua and the Torres family are large ranchers along the coast of Lake Nicaragua.

Royal coconut palms wave in the breezes above the beach on Mt. Maderas Island far out in Lake Nicaragua. Hunting up on the sides of this volcano, our party observed countless birds, black-and-white-faced monkeys and a large variety of parrots, both large and small. Hunting in this rainforest is extremely rugged, very hot and requires very tough footwear. The bird we found there was not any subspecies of wild turkey, but a Crested Guan, a jungle fowl.

One look convinced me I had shot a fine-looking bird, but it was no turkey. It was instead some sort of jungle fowl. A long-tailed bird, about the size of a hen pheasant, once it was dressed for eating. The bird was an overall dark brown with a very long tail and a crest on its head. Bright, dark red feet were well clawed for perching, and under the bird's chin was a red sac, probably inflated during breeding and mating seasons. So much for jungle turkeys.

Our hunt ended at the water hole, a tiny series of pools high on Mt. Maderas. We lay there in the heat resting for a while, then began the long three-mile hike back down the mountain. Mike sprained an ankle, which made the return trip miserable for him. Ted bagged a white-face monkey for some locals who had instructed us to bring one in if we got a chance. The animals are good eating.

Again, I'm back on my old Hallelujah Trail—chasing the rainbows and looking for wild turkeys wherever they may be.

Like Coronado's search for the Seven Cities of Gold, another gobbler seems to swirl like a mirage above distant lands.

I hope those rainbows never end.

Beyond the Chagres River
  Are the paths that lead to death;
To fever's deadly breezes-
  To Malaria's poisonous breath!
Beyond the tropic foliage
  Where the alligator waits
Is the palace of the devil-
  His original estates.

Beyond the Chagres River
  'Tis said, the story's old-
Are paths that lead to mountains
  of purest virgin gold;
But 'tis my firm conviction
  Whatever tales they tell,
That beyond the Chagres River
  All paths lead straight to Hell!
      "Lands of The Caribbean" Carpentor, 1926

Cock fighting is an every Saturday night affair in many towns in Nicaragua, which isn't for the faint-hearted. And, like all Central and South American countries, plus Mexico, this is a macho sport; women are not allowed. Who'd I meet at the local rooster killing but a darned nice young man named John Barber, from Omaha, serving with the Peace Corps.

Wild Turkey Seasons and State Game Commissions

The following states offer hunting for wild turkeys during the spring season, and some offer fall and winter seasons, as well. License fees are not listed due to constantly changing prices. A hunter should send for the state rules and regulations governing that season, and study them carefully. Maps can be purchased from state game departments.

Wild Turkey Seasons

State	Seasons	Subspecies
Alabama	Spring/Fall	Eastern
Arizona	Spring/Fall	Merriam
Arkansas	Spring/Fall	Eastern
California	Spring/Fall	Rio Grande, Merriam
Colorado	Spring/Fall	Merriam
Connecticut	Spring/Fall	Eastern
Florida	Spring/Fall	Osceola, Eastern
Georgia	Spring	Eastern
Hawaii	Spring/Fall	Rio Grande
Idaho	Spring	Merriam
Illinois	Spring/Fall	Eastern
Indiana	Spring	Eastern
Iowa	Spring/Fall	Eastern
Kansas	Spring/Fall	Rio Grande, Eastern
Kentucky	Spring/Fall	Eastern
Louisiana	Spring	Eastern
Maine	Spring	Eastern
Maryland	Spring/Fall	Eastern
Massachusetts	Spring/Fall	Eastern
Michigan	Spring	Eastern
Minnesota	Spring/Fall	Eastern
Mississippi	Spring/Fall	Eastern
Missouri	Spring/Fall	Eastern
Montana	Spring/Fall	Merriam
Nebraska	Spring/Fall	Rio Grande, Merriam
New Hampshire	Spring/Fall	Eastern
New Jersey	Spring	Eastern
New Mexico	Spring/Fall	Merriam
New York	Spring/Fall	Eastern
North Carolina	Spring	Eastern
North Dakota	Spring/Fall	Merriam
Ohio	Spring	Eastern
Oklahoma	Spring/Fall	Merriam, Rio Grande, Eastern
Oregon	Spring/Fall	Rio Grande, Merriam
Pennsylvania	Spring/Fall	Eastern
Rhode Island	Spring	Eastern
South Carolina	Spring	Eastern
South Dakota	Spring/Fall	Merriam
Tennessee	Spring/Fall	Eastern
Texas	Spring/Fall	Eastern, Rio Grande
Utah	Spring	Merriam
Vermont	Spring/Fall	Eastern
Virginia	Spring/Fall	Eastern
Washington	Spring/Fall	Merriam
West Virginia	Spring/Fall	Eastern
Wisconsin	Spring/Fall	Eastern
Wyoming	Spring/Fall	Merriam

State Game Commissions

Alabama Department of Conservation and Natural Resources, 64 Union St., Mongomery, AL 36130/205-242-3486

Arizona Game and Fish Department, 2221 West Greenway Rd., Phoenix, AZ 85023/602-942-3000

Arkansas Game and Fish Comm., 2 Natural Resources Dr., Little Rock, AR 72205/501-223-6300

California Department of Fish and Game, 3211 S. Street, Sacramento, CA 95816/916-227-2244

Colorado Division of Wildlife, 6060 Broadway, Denver, CO 80216/303-297-1192

Connecticut Department of Environmental Protection, 79 Elm St., Hartford, CT 06106/203-424-3105

Florida Game and Fresh Water Fish Commission, 620 South Meridian St., Tallahassee, FL 32399-1660/904-488-4676

Georgia Game and Fish Comm., 270 Washington St., S.W., Atlanta, GA 30334

Hawaii Game and Fish Division, 1151 Punchbowl St., Honolulu, HI 96813/808-587-0077

Idaho Dept. of Fish and Game, Box 25, Boise, ID 83707

Illinois Dept. of Conservation, P.O. Box 19446, Springfield, IL 62794-9446/217-782-7305

Indiana Div. of Fish and Wildlife, 615 State Office Building, Indianapolis, IN 46204

Iowa Conservation Comm., Wallace State Office Building, Des Moines, IA 50319

Kansas Dept. Wildlife & Parks, 512 S.E. 25th, Pratt, KS 67124/316-672-5911

Kentucky Department of Fish and Wildlife Resources, #1 Game Farm Rd., Frankfort, KY 40601/502-564-3400

Louisiana Department of Wildlife and Fisheries, Wildlife and Fisheries Building, New Orleans, LA 70130

Maine Inland Fisheries and Wildlife Licensing, 284 State St., State House Station 41, Augusta, ME 04333

Maryland Dept. Natural Resources, Tawes State Office Building, Annapolis, MD 21401/301-974-3195

Massachusetts Division of Fisheries and Wildlife, 100 Cambridge St., Boston, MA 02202/617-727-3151

Michigan Wildlife Div., Dept. of Natural Resources, Box 30028, Lansing, MI 48909

Minnesota Dept. of Natural Resources, 500 Lafayette Rd., St. Paul, MN 55155-4040/612-296-6157

Mississippi Game and Fish Comm., P.O. Box 451, Jackson, MS 39205/601-362-9212

Missouri Dept. of Conservation, P.O. Box 180, Jefferson City, MO 65102-0180/314-751-4115

Montana Dept. of Fish Wildlife & Parks, 1420 East 6th St., Helena, MT 59620/406-444-2535

Nebraska Game and Parks Commission, P.O. Box 30370, Lincoln, NE 68503-0370/402-471-0641

New Hampshire Fish & Game Department, 2 Hazen Dr., Concord, NH 03301/603-271-3421

New Jersey Division of Fish, Game, and Wildlife, CN-400, Trenton, NJ 08625

New Mexico Dept. Game and Fish, Villagra Building, Santa Fe, NM 87503/505-827-7885

New York Fish and Wildlife Div., 50 Wolf Rd., Albany, NY 12233-4790/518-457-3521

North Carolina Wildlife Resources Comm., 325 North Salisbury St., Raleigh, NC 27611

North Dakota Game and Fish Dept., 2121 Lovett Ave., Bismarck, ND 58505

Ohio Division of Wildlife, Fountain Square, Columbus, OH 43224

Oklahoma Dept. of Wildlife Con., 1801 N. Lincoln, Oklahoma City, OK 73105/405-521-3855

Oregon Dept. of Fish & Wildlife, P.O. Box 59, Portland, OR 97207/503-229-5400

Pennsylvania Game Commission, 2001 Elmerton Ave., Harrisburg, PA 17110-9797/717-787-4250

Rhode Island Division of Fish and Wildlife, Group Center, Wakefield, RI 02879

South Carolina Wildlife Resources Dept., P.O. Box 167, Columbia, SC 29202

South Dakota Dept. of Game, Fish and Parks, Anderson Building, Pierre, SD 57501

Tennessee Valley Authority, 100 Van Morgan Dr., Golden Pond, TN 42211/502-924-5602

Texas Parks and Wildlife Dept., 4200 Smith School Rd., Austin, TX 78744/512-389-4800

Utah Div. of Wildlife Resources, 1596 West Temple, Salt Lake City, UT 84116

Vermont Fish and Wildlife Dept., 103 S. Main, Waterburg, VT 05676/802-244-7331

Virginia Comm. of Game, Box 11104, Richmond, VA 23230-1104/804-367-1000

Washington Department of Wildlife, 600 Capitol Way N., Olympia, WA 98501-1091/206-753-5700

West Virginia Department of Natural Resources, 1900 Kanawah Blvd. East, Charleston, WV 25305/304-558-2758

Wisconsin Dept. of Natural Resources, P.O. Box 7921, Madison, WI 53707/608-226-1877

Wyoming Game and Fish Dept., 5400 Bishop Blvd., Cheyenne, WY 82202/307-777-4601

Topographical Map Directory

Topography map index, and maps, may be ordered from:
For map areas east of the Mississippi River:
U.S. Geological Survey
Map Distribution Section
Washington, DC 20242

For map areas west of the Mississippi River:
U.S. Geological Survey
Map Distribution Section
Federal Center
Denver, CO 80225

United States Forest Service Maps can be ordered from:
United States Forest Service
Washington, DC 20250

And/or from Field Offices of The Forest Service:
Eastern Region, National Forest Service
633 West Wisconsin Ave.
Milwaukee, WI 53203
(National forest in Illinois, Indiana, Ohio, Michigan, Minnesota, Missouri, New Hampshire, Maine, Pennsylvania, Vermont, West Virginia, Wisconsin.)

Southern Region, National Forest Service
1720 Peachtree Rd., N.W.
Atlanta, GA 30309

(National forests in Alabama, Arkansas, Florida, Georgia, Kentucky, Louisiana, Mississippi, North Carolina, South Carolina, Tennessee, Texas, Virginia.)

North Region, National Forest Service
Federal Building
Missoula, MT 59807
(National forests in Idaho, Montana.)

Rocky Mountain Region, National Forest Service
11177 West 8th Ave.
Box 25127
Lakewood, CO 80225
(National forest in Colorado, Nebraska, South Dakota, Wyoming.)

California Region, National Forest Service
630 Sansome St.
San Francisco, CA 94111
(National forests in California.)

Pacific Northwest Region, National Forest Service
319 S.W. Pine St.
P.O. Box 3623
Portland, OR 97208
(National forests in Oregon, Washington.)

Books About Turkeys and Turkey Hunting

Some of these books I have read, some I haven't. When I first began hunting wild turkeys, there was not a single book on the market which had been done in recent times. The first book I found was in a store which sold old books, and I paid $6 for a copy of McIlhenny's *The Wild Turkey and Its Hunting*. Not long afterward I found a copy of Davis' book for a ridiculously low price. Today, both are high dollar collector's items. *Dwain Bland*

Advanced Wild Turkey Hunting and World Records, by Dave Harbour, Winchester Press, Piscataway, NJ.

The American Wild Turkey, by Henry E. Davis, available from Old Masters Publishers, Route 2, Box 217, Medon, TN 38356.

Bearded Bird, by Larry Hudson, available from L.F. Hudson, 2013 Lansdowne Way, Silver Springs, MD 20910.

The Book of the Wild Turkey, by Lovett Williams, Winchester Press, Piscataway, NJ.

Bowhunting For Turkeys, by Jack Brobst, available from Jack Brobst, R.D. 2, Box 2172, Bangor, PA 18013.

The Complete Book of the Wild Turkey, by Roger Latham, Stackpole Books, Harrisburg, PA.

The Complete Turkey Hunt, by William Daskal, El-Bar Enterprises Publishers, New York, NY.

The Complete Turkey Hunter, by W.N. Bledsoe, available from The Long Hunters, 11334 Crest Brook, Dallas, TX 75230.

Dealer's Choice, by Tom Kelly, available from Wingfeather Press, P.O. Box 50, Spanish Fort, AL 36527.

The Education of a Turkey Hunter, by Frank Hanenkrat, Winchester Press, Piscataway, NJ.

50 Years, Hunting Wild Turkeys, by Wayne Bailey, available from Wing Supply, P.O. Box 367, Greenville, KY 42345, or Penn's Woods Products, 19 W. Pittsburg St., Delmont, PA 15626.

The Grand Spring Hunt For America's Wild Turkey Gobbler, by Bart Jacob and Ben Conger, Winchester Press, Piscataway, NJ.

Happy Times Hunting in the Beautiful Woods of Alabama, by Gesna Griffith, available from Gesna Griffith, Route 1, Box 229, Camden, AL 36726.

High Ridge Gobbler, by David Stemple, William Collins Publishers, New York, NY, and Cleveland, OH.

Hunting the Wild Turkey, by Tom Turpin, available from Penn's Woods Products, 19 W. Pittsburg St., Delmont, PA 15626.

Hunting Wild Turkeys in the Everglades, by Frank Harben, Harben Publishing Co., Safety Harbor, FL.

In Search of the Wild Turkey, by Bob Gooch, Great Lakes Living Press, Waukegan, IL.

Long Beards, Long Spurs, and Fanned Tails, by Bob Clark, Northwoods Publications Inc., Boiling Springs, PA.

Modern Turkey Hunting, by James F. Brady, Crown Publishing Co., New York, NY.

On Target for Successful Turkey Hunting, by Wayne Fears, Target Communications, Mequon, WI.

Some Turkey Scratchings, by Dwain Bland, available from Wing Supply, P.O. Box 367, Greenville, KY 42345, or Penn's Woods Products, 19 W. Pittsburg St., Delmont, PA 15626.

Spring Gobblers, by John Lowther, McClain Printing Co., Parsons, WV.

Tales of Wild Turkey Hunting, by Simon Everitt, available from Old Masters Publishers, Route 2, Box 217, Medon, TN 38356.

Talking Tomfoolery, by Earl Groves, available from The National Wild Turkey Federation, P.O. Box 530, Edgefield, SC 29824.

Tall Timber Gabriels, by Charles S. Whittington, Spur Enterprises, Monroe, LA.

Tenth Legion, by Tom Kelly, Spur Enterprises, Monroe, LA.

This Love of Hunting, by Frank A. Jeffett, Tejas Press, Dallas, TX. Some chapters on turkey hunting, good reading.

Tom Tells Tall Turkey Tales, by Tom Gaskins, available from Tom Gaskins, Box 7, Palmdale, FL 33944.

The Turkey Hunter's Book, by John M. McDaniel, available from The National Wild Turkey Federation, P.O. Box 530, Edgefield, SC 29824.

Turkey Hunter's Digest, by Dwain Bland, DBI Books, Inc., Northbrook, IL.

Turkey Hunter's Guide, by Byron Dalrymple, The National Rifle Association, Washington D.C.

Turkey Hunting, Spring and Fall, by Doug Camp, Outdoor Skills Bookshelf, Nashville, TN.

Turkey Hunting with Charlie Elliott, by Charlie Elliott, David McKay Co., New York, NY.

The Voice and Vocabulary of The Wild Turkey, by Lovett E. Williams, 2201 S.E. 41st Ave., Gainesville, FL 32601.

We Talk Turkey, by Tom Gaskins, available from Tom Gaskins, Box 7, Palmdale, FL 33944.

The Wild Turkey and Its Hunting, by Edward A. McIlhenny, available from Old Masters Publishers, Route 2, Box 217, Medon, TN 38356.

The Wild Turkey Book, by Wayne Fears, Amwell Press, Clinton, NJ.

The Wild Turkey, Its History and Domestication, Publishing Division, University of Oklahoma, Norman, OK.

The World of the Wild Turkey, by James C. Lewis, J.B. Lippincott Co., Philadelphia and New York City.

Hunting Equipment Directory

AMMUNITION, COMMERCIAL

ACTIV Industries, Inc., 1000 Zigor Rd., P.O. Box 339, Kearneysville, WV 25430/304-725-0451; FAX: 304-725-2080

Ballistic Products, Inc., 20015 75th Ave. North, Corcoran, MN 55340-9456/612-494-9237; FAX: 612-494-9236

Brenneke KG, Wilhelm, Ilmenauweg 2, D-30551 Langenhagen, GERMANY/0511/97262-0; FAX: 0511/9726262

Dynamit Nobel-RWS, Inc., 81 Ruckman Rd., Closter, NJ 07624/77-93-54-69; FAX: 77-93-57-98

Estate Cartridge, Inc., 2778 FM 830, Willis, TX 77378/409-856-7277; FAX: 409-856-5486

Federal Cartridge Co., 900 Ehlen Dr., Anoka, MN 55303/612-323-2300

Fiocchi of America, Inc., 5030 Fremont Rd., Ozark, MO 65721/417-725-4118; FAX: 417-725-1039

Gamo (See U.S. importer—Dynamit Nobel-RWS, Inc.)

GDL Enterprises, 409 Le Gardeur, Slidell, LA 70460/504-649-0693

Hirtenberger Aktiengesellschaft, Leobersdorferstrasse 31, A-2552 Hirtenberg, AUSTRIA/43(0)2256 81184; FAX: 43(0)2256 81807

Hornady Mfg. Co., P.O. Box 1848, Grand Island, NE 68801/800-338-3220, 308-382-1390

Omark Industries, Div. of Blount, Inc., 2299 Snake River Ave., P.O. Box 856, Lewiston, ID 83501/800-627-3640, 208-746-2351

Polywad, Inc., P.O. Box 7916, Macon, GA 31209/912-477-0669

Remington Arms Co., Inc., 1007 Market St., Wilmington, DE 19898/302-773-5291

RWS (See U.S. importer—Dynamit Nobel-RWS, Inc.)

Star Reloading Co., Inc., 5520 Rock Hampton Ct., Indianapolis, IN 46268/317-872-5840

Victory USA, P.O. Box 1021, Pine Bush, NY 12566/914-744-2060; FAX: 914-744-5181

Winchester Div., Olin Corp., 427 N. Shamrock, E. Alton, IL 62024/618-258-3566; FAX: 618-258-3599

AMMUNITION, CUSTOM

Ballistic Products, Inc., 20015 75th Ave. North, Corcoran, MN 55340-9456/612-494-9237; FAX: 612-494-9236

Cubic Shot Shell Co., Inc., 98 Fatima Dr., Campbell, OH 44405/216-755-0349; FAX: 216-755-0349

Estate Cartridge, Inc., 2778 FM 830, Willis, TX 77378/409-856-7277; FAX: 409-856-5486

Hirtenberger Aktiengesellschaft, Leobersdorferstrasse 31, A-2552 Hirtenberg, AUSTRIA/43(0)2256 81184; FAX: 43(0)2256 81807

Hornady Mfg. Co., P.O. Box 1848, Grand Island, NE 68801/800-338-3220, 308-382-1390

M&D Munitions Ltd., 127 Verdi St., Farmingdale, NY 11735/516-752-1038; FAX: 516-752-1905

AMMUNITION, FOREIGN

Ballistic Products, Inc., 20015 75th Ave. North, Corcoran, MN 55340-9456/612-494-9237; FAX: 612-494-9236

Cubic Shot Shell Co., Inc., 98 Fatima Dr., Campbell, OH 44405/216-755-0349; FAX: 216-755-0349

Dynamit Nobel-RWS, Inc., 81 Ruckman Rd., Closter, NJ 07624/77-93-54-69; FAX: 77-93-57-98

Estate Cartridge, Inc., 2778 FM 830, Willis, TX 77378/409-856-7277; FAX: 409-856-5486

Fiocchi of America, Inc., 5030 Fremont Rd., Ozark, MO 65721/417-725-4118; FAX: 417-725-1039

RWS (See U.S. importer—Dynamit Nobel-RWS, Inc.)

AMMUNITION COMPONENTS— BULLETS, POWDER, PRIMERS, CASES

Accurate Arms Co., Inc., Rt. 1, Box 167, McEwen, TN 37101/615-729-4207; FAX 615-729-4217

ACTIV Industries, Inc., 1000 Zigor Rd., P.O. Box 339, Kearneysville, WV 25430/304-725-0451; FAX: 304-725-2080

Ballistic Products, Inc., 20015 75th Ave. North, Corcoran, MN 55340-9456/612-494-9237; FAX: 612-494-9236

Bell Reloading, Inc., 1725 Harlin Lane Rd., Villa Rica, GA 30180

Brenneke KG, Wilhelm, Ilmenauweg 2, D-30551 Langenhagen, GERMANY/0511/97262-0; FAX: 0511/9726262

Brownells, Inc., 200 S. Front St., Montezuma, IA 50171/515-623-5401; FAX: 515-623-3896

CCI, Div. of Blount, Inc., 2299 Snake River Ave., P.O. Box 856, Lewiston, ID 83501/800-627-3640, 208-746-2351

DuPont (See IMR Powder Co.)

Federal Cartridge Co., 900 Ehlen Dr., Anoka, MN 55303/612-323-2300

Fiocchi of America, Inc., 5030 Fremont Rd., Ozark, MO 65721/417-725-4118; FAX: 417-725-1039

Hercules, Inc., Hercules Plaza, 1313 N Market St., Wilmington, DE 19894/800-276-9337

Hirtenberger Aktiengesellschaft, Leobersdorferstrasse 31, A-2552 Hirtenberg, AUSTRIA/43(0)2256 81184; FAX: 43(0)2256 81807

Hodgdon Powder Co., Inc., P.O. Box 2932, Shawnee Mission, KS 66201/913-362-9455; FAX: 913-362-1307

Hornady Mfg. Co., P.O. Box 1848, Grand Island, NE 68801/800-338-3220, 308-382-1390

IMR Powder Co., 1080 Military Turnpike, Suite 2, Plattsburgh, NY 12901

Lage Uniwad, Inc., P.O. Box 446, Victor, IA 52327/319-647-3232

Pattern Control, 114 N. Third St., Garland, TX 75040/214-494-3551

Polywad, Inc., P.O. Box 7916, Macon, GA 31209/912-477-0669

Precision Ballistics Co., P.O. Box 4374, Hamden, CT 06514/203-373-2293

Precision Components, 3177 Sunrise Lake, Milford, PA 18337/717-686-4414

Rainier Ballistics Corp., 4500 15th St. East, Tacoma, WA 98424/800-638-8722, 206-922-7589; FAX: 206-922-7854

Reloading Specialties, Inc., Box 1130, Pine Island, MN 55963/507-356-8500; FAX: 507-356-8800

Remington Arms Co., Inc., 1007 Market St., Wilmington, DE 19898/302-773-5291

Scot Powder Co. of Ohio, Inc., Box HD94, Only, TN 37140/615-729-4207; FAX: 615-729-4217

Shotgun Bullets Mfg., Rt. 3, Box 41, Robinson, IL 62454/618-546-5043

Taracorp Industries, Inc., 16th & Cleveland Blvd., Granite City, IL 62040/618-451-4400

Trico Plastics, 590 S. Vincent Ave., Azusa, CA 91702

Vihtavuori Oy, FIN-41330 Vihtavuori, FINLAND/358-41-3779211; FAX: 358-41-3771643

Vihtavuori Oy/Kaltron-Pettibone, 1241 Ellis St., Bensenville, IL 60106/708-350-1116; FAX: 708-350-1606

Winchester Div., Olin Corp., 427 N. Shamrock, E. Alton, IL 62024/618-258-3566; FAX: 618-258-3599

Windjammer Tournament Wads, Inc., 750 W. Hampden Ave. Suite 170, Englewood, CO 80110/303-781-6329

BOWHUNTING EQUIPMENT

American Archery, P.O. Box 200, Florence, WI 54121

Barnett International, Inc., P.O. Box 934, Odessa, FL 33556 (also crossbows)

Bear Archery, RR 4, 4600 S.W. 41st Blvd., Gainesville, FL 32601

Black Widow Bow Co., Box 357-1, Highlandville, MO 65669

Browning, Rt. 1, Morgan, UT 84050

Cabela's, 812 13th Ave., Sidney, NE 69160 (also crossbows)

Cobra Mfg. Co., P.O. Box 667, Bixby, OK 74008

Easton, 7800 Haskell Ave., Van Nuys, CA 91406

Gander Mountain, P.O. Box 248, Wilmot, WI 53192 (also crossbows)

Golden Eagle Archery, 104 Mill St., Creswell, OR 97426

Hendricks, Dan, North American Bowhunter, 20 9th Ave., North, Glenwood MN 56334

Saunders Archery Co., Box 476, Columbus, NE 68601

Stewart, Cam, Super Station Longbows, 816 East Globe Ave., Mesa, AZ 85204

Tru-Fire Corp., 732 State St., N. Fond Du Lac, WI 54935

Wasp Archery Products, 9 W. Main St., Plymouth, CT 49651

York Archery, P.O. Box 110, Independence, MO 64051

Zwickey Archery, Inc., 2571 E. 12th Ave., N. St. Paul, MN 55109 (Zwickey Scorpio Turkey Grappler)

CLOTHING AND ACCOUTREMENTS (Old Timey)

Buffalo Hoof Trading Co., Box 103, Gowrie, IA 52302

The Buffalo Bull, P.O. Box 8, Marion, IA 52302

Mountain Man, 1001 Manitou Ave., Manitou Springs, CO 80829

Mountain Man's Trading Post, 3713 Waterway Dr., Hudson, FL 33568

River Junction Trade Co., 312 Main St., McGregor, IA 52157

Salish House, P.O. Box 27, Rollins, MT 59931

Tecumseh's Frontier Trading Post, Box 369, Shartlesville, PA 19554

Track of the Wolf, P.O. Box 6, Osseo, MN 55369

GUNS, FOREIGN—IMPORTERS (Manufacturers)

Alessandri and Son, Lou, 24 French St., Rehoboth, MA 02769/508-252-3436, 800-248-5652; FAX: 508-252-3436 (Rizzini, Battista)

American Arms, Inc., 715 E. Armour Rd., N. Kansas City, MO 64116/816-474-3161; FAX: 816-474-1225 (Stefano Fausti & Figlie s.n.c.; Luigi Franchi S.p.A.; Grulla Armes; INDESAL; Avnda Otaloa Norica; Aldo Uberti; Zabala Hermanos S.A.; blackpowder arms)

Armas Kemen S.A., Box 228, Alpha Terrace, Glendale, CA 91208-2137/310-809-1999, 818-956-0722; FAX: 818-956-5512

Armes de Chasse, P.O. Box 827, Chadds Ford, PA 19317/215-388-1146; FAX: 215-388-1147 (AYA; Auguste Francotte & Cie S.A.)

Beretta U.S.A. Corp., 17601 Beretta Drive, Accokeek, MD 20607/301-283-2191 (Pietro Beretta Firearms)

British Sporting Arms, RR1, Box 130, Millbrook, NY 12545/914-677-8303 (B.C. Miroku/Charles Daley)

Browning Arms Co. (Parts & Service), 3005 Arnold Tenbrook Rd., Arnold, MO 63010-9406/314-287-6800; FAX: 314-287-9751

Cape Outfitters, Rt. 2, Box 437C, Cape Girardeau, MO 63701/314-335-4103; FAX: 314-335-1555 (San Marco; Societa Armi Bresciane Srl.; Westley Richards & Co.; blackpowder arms)

County, 11020 Whitman Ln., Tamarac, FL 33321/305-720-2066; FAX: 305-722-6353

Dynamit Nobel-RWS, Inc., 81 Ruckman Rd., Closter, NJ 07624/201-767-1995; FAX: 201-767-1589 (Wilhelm Brenneke KG; Diana; Gamo; RWS)

Galaxy Imports Ltd., Inc., P.O. Box 3361, Victoria, TX 77903/512-573-4867; FAX: 512-576-9622 (Laurona Armas S.A.)

Giacomo Sporting, Inc., Delta Plaza, Rt. 26N, Rome, NY 13440 (Renato Gamba S.p.A.)

GSI, Inc., 108 Morrow Ave., P.O. Box 129, Trussville, AL 35173/205-655-8299; FAX: 205-655-7078 (Merkel Freres; Steyr-Daimler-Puch; Steyr-Manlicher AG.)

G.U., Inc., 4325 S. 120th St., Omaha, NE 68137/402-330-4492 (SKB Arms Co.)

Heckler & Koch, Inc., 21480 Pacific Blvd., Sterling, VA 20166/703-450-1900; FAX: 703-450-8160 (Benelli Armi S.p.A.; Heckler & Koch GmbH)

Hi-Grade Imports, 8655 Monterey Rd., Gilroy, CA 95021/408-842-9301; FAX: 408-842-2374 (Arrieta, S.L.)

Ithaca Acquisition Corp., Ithaca Gun Co., 891 Route 34B, King Ferry, NY 13081/315-364-7171; FAX: 315-364-5134 (Fabarm S.p.A.)

Jansma, Jack J., 4320 Kalamazoo Ave., Grand Rapids, MI 49508/616-455-7810; FAX: 616-455-5212 (Arrieta, S.L.)

K.B.I., Inc., P.O. Box 5440, Harrisburg, PA 17110-0440/717-540-8518; FAX: 717-540-8567 (Baikal; FEG; Kassnar; K.B.I., Inc.)

Krieghoff International, Inc., 7528 Easton Rd., Ottsville, PA 18942/215-847-5173; FAX: 215-847-8691 (H. Krieghoff Gun Co.)

London Guns Ltd., Box 3750, Santa Barbara, CA 93130/805-683-4141; FAX: 805-683-1712

Mandall Shooting Supplies, Inc., 3616 N. Scottsdale Rd., Scottsdale, AZ 85252/602-945-2553; FAX: 602-949-0734 (Arizaga; Bretton; Cabanas; Hermanos Crucelegoi; Erma Werke GmbH; Firearms Co. Ltd./Alpine; Gaucher Armes S.A.; Hammerli Ltd.; Korth; A. Krico/Kriegeskorte GmbH; Morini; SIG; Tanner; Techni-Mec; Ignacio Ugartechea S.A.; Pietro Zanoletti; blackpowder arms)

MEC-Gar U.S.A., Inc., Box 112, 500B Monroe Turnpike, Monroe, CT 06468/203-635-8662; FAX: 203-635-8662 (MEC-Gar S.R.L.)

Moore & Co., Wm. Larkin, 31360 Via Colinas, Suite 109, Westlake Village, CA 91361/818-889-4160 (Bertuzzi; FERLIB; Armas Urki Garbi; Piotti; Rizzini)

New England Arms Co., Box 278, Lawrence Lane, Kittery Point, ME 03905/207-439-0593; FAX: 207-439-6726 (Arrieta, S.L.; Bertuzzi; Cosmi Americo & Figlio s.n.c.; FERLIB; Renato Gamba S.p.A.; Lebeau-Courally; Rizzini)

Orvis Co., The, Rt. 7, Manchester, VT 05254/802-362-3622 ext. 283; FAX: 802-362-3525 (Arrieta, S.L.)

Pachmayr Ltd., 1875 S. Mountain Ave., Monrovia, CA 91016/818-357-7771, 800-423-9704; FAX: 818-358-7251 (FERLIB)

Perazzi USA, Inc., 1207 S. Shamrock Ave., Monrovia, CA 91016/818-303-0068 (Perazzi m.a.p. S.P.A.)

Precision Sales International, Inc., P.O. Box 1776, Westfield, MA 01086/413-562-5055; FAX: 413-562-5056 (Anschutz GmbH; Erma Werke GmbH; Marocchi F.lli S.p.A.)

Quality Arms, Inc., Box 19477, Dept. GD, Houston, TX 77224/713-870-8377; FAX: 713-870-8524 (Arrieta, S.L.; FERLIB)

Sile Distributors, Inc., 7 Centre Market Pl., New York, NY 10013/212-925-4389; FAX: 212-925-3149 (Benelli Armi S.p.A.; Marocchi F.lli S.p.A.; Solothurn)

Stoeger Industries, 55 Ruta Ct., S. Hackensack, NJ 07606/201-440-2700, 800-631-0722; FAX: 201-440-2707 (IGA; Sako Ltd.; Tikka)

Turkish Firearms Corp., 8487 Euclid Ave., Suite 1, Manassas Park, VA 22111/703-369-6848; FAX: 703-257-7709

Weatherby, Inc., 3100 El Camino Real, Atascadero, CA 93422/805-466-1767; FAX: 805-466-2527 (Weatherby, Inc.)

GUNS, FOREIGN—MANUFACTURERS (Importers)

Arizaga (Mandall Shooting Supplies, Inc.)

Arrieta, S.L., Morkaiko, 5, Elgoibar, E-20870, SPAIN/(43) 74 31 50; FAX: (43) 74 31 54 (U.S. importers—Hi-Grade Imports; Jack J. Jansma; New England Arms Co.; The Orvis Co., Inc.; Quality Arms, Inc.)

AYA (Armes de Chasse)

Baikal (K.B.I., Inc.)

Benelli Armi, S.p.A., Via della Stazione, 61029 Urbino, ITALY/39-722-328633; FAX: 39-722-327427 (E.A.A. Corp.; Heckler & Koch, Inc.; Sile Distributors)

Beretta Firearms, Pietro, 25063 Gardone V.T., ITALY (Beretta U.S.A. Corp.)

Brenneke KG, Wilhelm, Ilmenauweg 2, D-30551 Langenhagen, GERMANY/0511/97262-0; FAX: 0511/9726262 (Dynamit Nobel-RWS, Inc.)

Bretton, 19, rue Victor Grignard, F-42026 St.-Etienne (Cedex 1) FRANCE/77-93-54-69; FAX: 77-93-57-98 (Mandall Shooting Supplies, Inc.)

Browning Arms Co. (Parts & Service), 3005 Arnold Tenbrook Rd., Arnold, MO 63010-9406/314-287-6800; FAX: 314-287-9751

CBC, Avenida Humberto de Campos, 3220, 09400-000 Ribeirao Pires-SP-BRAZIL/55-11-742-7500; FAX: 55-11-459-7385 (MAGTECH Recreational Products, Inc.)

Churchill (Ellett Bros.)

Cosmi Americo & Figlio s.n.c., Via Flaminia 307, Ancona, ITALY I-60020/071-888208; FAX: 071-887008 (New England Arms Inc.)

Crucelegui Hermanos (Mandall Shooting Supplies, Inc.)

FERLIB, Via Costa 46, 25063 Gardone V.T. (Brescia) ITALY/30 89 12 586; FAX: 30 89 12 586 (Wm. Larkin Moore & Co.; New England Arms Co.; Pachmayr Co.; Quality Arms, Inc.)

Franchi S.p.A., Luigi, Via del Serpente, 12, 25020 Fornaci, ITALY (American Arms, Inc.)

Francotte & Cie S.A., Auguste, rue du Trois Juin 109, 4400 Herstal-Liege, BELGIUM/41-48.13.18; FAX: 41-48.11.79 (Armes de Chasse)

Gamba S.p.A., Renato, Via Artigiani, 93, 25063 Gardone V.T. (Brescia), ITALY (Giacomo Sporting, Inc.; New England Arms Co.)

Garbi, Armas Urki, #12-14, 20.600 Eibar (Guipuzcoa) SPAIN/43-11 38 73 (Moore & Co. Wm. Larkin)

Glock GmbH, P.O. Box 50, A-2232 Deutsch Wagram, AUSTRIA (Glock, Inc.)

Grulla Armes, Apartado 453, Avda Otaloa, 12, Eiber, SPAIN (U.S. importer—American Arms, Inc.

Heym GmbH & Co. KG, Friedrich Wilh, Coburger Str.8, D-97702 Muennerstadt, GERMANY (J.,gerSport, Ltd.; Swarovski Optik North America Ltd.)

IGA (Stoeger Industries)

Krieghoff Gun Co., H., Bosch Str. 22, 7900 Ulm, GERMANY (Krieghoff International, Inc.)

Lanber Armes S.A., Calle Zubiaurre 5, Zaldibar, SPAIN/34-4-6827702; FAX: 34-4-6827999

Laurona Armas S.A., P.O. Box 260, 20600 Eibar, SPAIN/34-43-700600; FAX: 34-43-700616 (Galaxy Imports Ltd., Inc.)

Marocchi F.lli S.p.A., Via Galileo Galilei, I-25068 Zanano di Sarezzo, ITALY (PSI, Inc.; Sile Distributors)

MEC-Gar S.R.L., Via Madonnina 64, Gardone V.T. (BS), ITALY 25063/39-30-8911719; FAX: 39-30-8910065 (MEC-Gar U.S.A., Inc.)

Merkel Freres, Strasse 7 October, 10, Suhl, GERMANY (GSI, Inc.)

Miroku, B.C./Daly, Charles (Bell's Legendary Country Wear; British Sporting Arms)

Perazzi m.a.p. S.P.A., Via Fontanelle 1/3, 1-25080 Botticino Mattina, ITALY (Perazzi USA, Inc.)

Perugini Visini & Co. s.r.l., Via Camprelle, 126, 25080 Nuvolera (Bs.), ITALY

Piotti (Moore & Co., Wm. Larkin)

Powell & Son (Gunmakers) Ltd., William, 35-37 Carrs Lane, Birmingham B4 7SX ENGLAND/21-643-0689; FAX: 21-631-3504 (Bell's Legendary Country Wear)

Rigby & Co., John, 66 Great Suffolk St., London SE1 0BU, ENGLAND (Griffin & Howe, Inc.)

Rizzini Battista, Via 2 Giugno, 7/7Bis-25060 Marcheno (Brescia), ITALY (Alessandri & Son, Lou)

Rizzini, F.LLI (Moore & Co. Wm. Larkin; New England Arms Co.)

San Marco (Cape Outfitters; EMF Co., Inc.)

SKB Arms Co., C.P.O. Box 1401, Tokyo, JAPAN (G.U., Inc.)

Societa Armi Bresciane Srl., Via Artigiani 93, Gardone Val Trompia, ITALY 25063/30-8911640, 30-8911648 (Cape Outfitters)

Techni-Mec, Via Gitti s.n., 25060 Marcheno, ITALY (Mandall Shooting Supplies, Inc.)

Tikka (Stoeger Industries)

Ugartechea S.A., Ignacio, Chonta 26, Eibar, SPAIN 20600/43-121257; FAX: 43-121669 (Mandall Shooting Supplies, Inc.)

Weatherby, Inc., 3100 El Camino Real, Atascadero, CA 93422/805-466-1767; FAX: 805-466-2527 (Weatherby, Inc.)

Westley Richards & Co., 40 Grange Rd., Birmingham, ENGLAND B29 6AR/010-214722953 (Cape Outfitters)

Zabala Hermanos S.A., P.O. Box 97, Eibar, SPAIN 20600/43-768085, 43-768076; FAX: 43-768201 (American Arms, Inc.)

Zanoletti, Pietro, Via Monte Gugielpo, 4, I-25063 Gardone V.T., ITALY (Mandall Shooting Supplies, Inc.)

Zoli, Antonio, Via Zanardelli 39, Casier Postal 21, I-25063 Gardone V.T., ITALY

GUNS, U.S.-MADE

Beretta U.S.A. Corp., 17601 Beretta Drive, Accokeek, MD 20607/301-283-2191

Browning Arms Co. (Parts & Service), 3005 Arnold Tenbrook Rd., Arnold, MO 63010-9406/314-287-6800; FAX: 314-287-9751

Connecticut Valley Classics, P.O. Box 2068, 12 Taylor Lane, Westport, CT 06880/203-435-4600

Galazan, Div. of Connecticut Shotgun Mfg. Co., P.O. Box 622, 35 Woodland St., New Britain, CT 06051-0622/203-225-6581; FAX: 203-832-8707

H&R 1871, Inc., 60 Industrial Rowe, Gardner, MA 01440/508-632-9393; FAX: 508-632-2300

Ithaca Aquisition Corp., Ithaca Gun Co., 891 Route 34B, King Ferry, NY 13081/315-364-7171; FAX: 315-364-5134

Ljutic Industries, Inc., 732 N. 16th Ave., Yakima, WA 98902/509-248-0476; FAX: 509-457-5141

Maverick Arms, Inc., 7 Grasso Ave., P.O. Box 497, North Haven, CT 06473/203-230-5300; FAX: 203-230-5420

Mossberg & Sons, Inc., O.F, 7 Grasso Ave., North Haven, CT 06473/203-288-6491; FAX: 203-288-2404

New England Firearms, 60 Industrial Rowe, Gardner, MA 01440/508-632-9393; FAX: 508-632-2300

Remington Arms Co., Inc., 1007 Market St., Wilmington, DE 19898/302-773-5291

Savage Arms, Inc., Springdale Rd., Westfield, MA 01085/413-568-7001; FAX: 413-562-7764

Sporting Arms Mfg., Inc., 801 Hall Ave., Littlefield, TX 79339/806-385-5665; FAX: 806-385-3394

Sturm, Ruger & Co., Inc., Lacey Place, Southport, CT 06490/203-259-7843

Tar-Hunt Custom Rifles, Inc., RR3, Box 572, Bloomsburg, PA 17815/717-784-6368; FAX: 717-784-6368

U.S. Repeating Arms Co., Inc., 275 Winchester Ave., New Haven, CT 06511/203-789-5000; FAX: 203-789-5071

HUNTING AND CAMP GEAR, CLOTHING, ETC.

Ace Sportswear, Inc., 700 Quality Rd., Fayetteville, NC 28306/919-323-1223

Action Products, Inc., 22 N. Mulberry St., Hagerstown, MD 21740/301-797-1414

Adventure 16, Inc., 4620 Alvarado Canyon Rd., San Diego, CA 92120/619-283-6314

All Weather Outerwear, 1270 Broadway, Rm 1005, New York, NY 10001/212-244-2690

Bob Allen Co., 214 SW Jackson, Des Moines, IA 50315/515-283-2191; 800-685-7020

American Import Co., The, 1453 Mission St., San Francisco, CA 94103/415-863-1506; FAX: 415-863-0939

Aristocrat Knives, 1800 N. Highland Ave. No. 600, Los Angeles, CA 90028/213-461-1065; FAX: 213-461-3598

Armor Metal Products, P.O. Box 4609, Helena, MT 59604/406-442-5560

Atlanta Cutlery Corp., 2143 Gees Mill Rd., Box 839 CIS, Conyers, GA 30207/800-883-0300; FAX: 404-388-0246

Atsko/Sno-Seal, Inc., 2530 Russell SE, Orangeburg, SC 29115/803-531-1820; FAX: 803-531-2139

Bagmaster Mfg., Inc., 2731 Sutton Ave., St. Louis, MO 63143/314-781-8002

Barbour, Inc., 55 Meadowbrook Dr., Milford, NH 03055/603-673-1313; FAX: 603-673-6510

Barteaux Machete, 1916 SE 50th Ave., Portland, OR 97215-3238/503-233-5880

Eddie Bauer, 15010 NE 36th St., Redmond, WA 98052

Bausch & Lomb, Inc., 42 East Ave., Rochester, NY 14603/800-828-5423

Bear Archery, RR 4, 4600 Southwest 41st Blvd., Gainesville, FL 32601/904-376-2327

Beaver Park Products, Inc., 840 J St., Penrose, CO 81240/719-372-6744

Better Concepts Co., 663 New Castle Rd., Butler, PA 16001/412-285-9000

Bilsom Int., Inc., 109 Carpenter Dr., Sterling, VA 20164/703-834-1070

Boss Manufacturing Co., 221 W. First St., Kewanee, IL 61443/309-852-2131

Brell Mar Products, Inc., 5701 Hwy. 80 West, Jackson, MS 39209

Brown Manufacturing, P.O. Box 9219, Akron, OH 44305/800-837-GUNS

Browning Arms Co. (Parts & Service), 3005 Arnold Tenbrook Rd., Arnold, MO 63010-9406/314-287-6800; FAX: 314-287-9751

Brunton U.S.A., 620 E. Monroe Ave., Riverton, WY 82501/307-856-6559; FAX: 307-856-1840

Buck Stop Lure Co., Inc., 3600 Grow Rd. NW, P.O. Box 636, Stanton, MI 48888/517-762-5091; FAX: 517-762-5124

Bullet Master Bullets (See Gander Mountain)

Bushmaster Hunting & Fishing, 451 Alliance Ave., Toronto, Ont. M6N 2J1 CANADA/416-763-4040; FAX: 416-763-0623

Cabela's, 812-13th Ave., Sidney, NE 69160/308-254-5505; FAX: 308-254-7809

Camofare Co., 712 Main St. 2800, Houston, TX 77002/713-229-9253

Camp-Cap Products, P.O. Box 173, Chesterfield, MO 63006/314-532-4340

Carhartt, Inc., P.O. Box 600, Dearborn, MI 48121/800-358-3825; FAX: 313-271-3455

Chameleon Camouflage Systems, 15199 S. Maplelane Rd., Oregon City, OR 97045/503-657-2266

Chippewa Shoe Co., P.O. Box 2521, Ft. Worth, TX 76113/817-332-4385

James Churchill Glove Co., P.O. Box 298, Centralia, WA 98531

Clarkfield Enterprises, Inc., 1032 10th Ave., Clarkfield, MN 56223/612-669-7140

Cobra Gunskin, 133-30 32nd Ave., Flushing, NY 11354/718-762-8181; FAX: 718-762-0890

Coghlan's Ltd., 121 Irene St., Winnipeg, Man., CANADA R3T 4C7/204-284-9550

Coleman Co., Inc., 250 N. St. Francis, Wichita, KS 67201

Coulston Products, Inc., P.O. Box 30, Easton, PA 18044-0030/215-253-0167; FAX: 215-252-1511

Crane & Crane Ltd., 105 N. Edison Way #6, Reno, NV 89502-2355/702-856-1516; FAX: 702-856-1616

R.M. Crawford Co., Inc., P.O. Box 277, Everett, PA 15537/814-652-6536; FAX: 814-652-9526

Creedmoor Sports, Inc., P.O. Box 1040, Oceanside, CA 92051/619-757-5529

Dakota Corp., P.O. Box 543, Rutland, VT 05702/800-451-4167; FAX: 802-773-3919

Danner Shoe Mfg. Co., 12722 NE Airport Way, Portland, OR 97230/503-251-1100; FAX: 503-251-1119

DeckSlider of Florida, 27641-2 Reahard Ct., Bonita Springs, FL 33923/800-782-1474

Deer Me Products Co., Box 34, 1208 Park St., Anoka, MN 55303/612-421-8971; FAX: 612-422-0356

Degen Knives, 1800 N. Highland Ave. No. 600, Los Angeles, CA 90028/213-461-1065; FAX: 213-461-3598

Dr. O's Products Ltd., P.O. Box 111, Niverville, NY 12130/518-784-3333; FAX: 518-784-2800

Dunham Co., P.O. Box 813, Brattleboro, VT 05301/802-254-2316

Duofold, Inc., 120 W. 45th St., 15th Floor, New York, NY 10036

Duxbak, Inc., 903 Woods Rd., Cambridge, MD 21613/301-228-2990, 800-334-1845

Dynalite Products, Inc., 215 S. Washington St., Greenfield, OH 45123/513-981-2124

E-A-R, Inc., Div. of Cabot Safety Corp., 5457 W. 79th St., Indianapolis, IN 46268/800-327-3431; FAX: 800-488-8007

Ekol Leather Care, P.O. Box 2652, West Lafayette, IN 47906/317-463-2250; FAX: 317-463-7004

C.W. Erickson's Mfg., Inc., 530 Garrison Ave. N.E., Buffalo, MN 55313/612-682-3665; FAX: 612-682-4328

Fish-N-Hunt, Inc., 5651 Beechnut St., Houston, TX 77096/713-777-3285; FAX: 713-777-9884

Flow-Rite of Tennessee, Inc., 107 Allen St., Bruceton, TN 38317/901-586-2271; FAX: 901-586-2300

Forrest Tool Co., P.O. Box 768, 44380 Gordon Lane, Mendocino, CA 95460/707-937-2141; FAX: 717-937-1817

Fox River Mills, Inc., P.O. Box 298, 227 Poplar St., Osage, IA 50461/515-732-3798; FAX: 515-732-5128

Frankonia Jagd, Hofmann & Co., D-97064 Wurzburg, GERMANY/09302-200; FAX: 09302-20200

Fury Cutlery, 801 Broad Ave., Ridgefield, NJ 07657/201-943-5920; FAX: 201-943-1579

G&H Decoys, Inc., P.O. Box 1208, Hwy. 75 North, Henryetta, OK 74437/918-652-3314

Game Winner, Inc., 2625 Cumberland Parkway, Suite 220, Atlanta, GA 30339/404-434-9210; FAX: 404-434-9215

Gander Mountain, Inc., P.O. Box 128, Hwy. "W.," Wilmot, WI 53192/414-862-2331,Ext. 6425

Gerber Legendary Blades, 14200 SW 72nd Ave., Portland, OR 97223/503-639-6161; FAX: 503-684-7008

Glacier Glove, 4890 Aircenter Circle #206, Reno, NV 89502/702-825-8225; FAX: 702-825-6544

Hawken Shop, The (See Dayton Traister)

Bob Hinman Outfitters, 1217 W. Glen, Peoria, IL 61614/309-691-8132

Hodgman, Inc., 1750 Orchard Rd., Montgomery, IL 60538/708-897-7555; FAX: 708-897-7558

Houtz & Barwick, P.O. Box 435, W. Church St., Elizabeth City, NC 27909/800-775-0337, 919-335-4191; FAX: 919-335-1152

Hunter's Specialties, Inc., 6000 Huntington Ct. NE, Cedar Rapids, IA 52402-1268/319-395-0321

Innovision Enterprises, 728 Skinner Dr., Kalamazoo, MI 49001/616-382-1681; FAX: 616-382-1830

Joy Enterprises (See Fury Cutlery)

Just Brass, Inc., 121 Henry St., P.O. Box 112, Freeport, NY 11520/516-378-8588

K&M Industries, Inc., Box 66, 510 S. Main, Troy, ID 83871/208-835-2281; FAX: 208-835-5211

Kamik Outdoor Footwear, 554 Montee de Liesse, Montreal, Quebec, H4T 1P1 CANADA/514-341-3950; FAX: 514-341-1861

LaCrosse Footwear, Inc., P.O. Box 1328, La Crosse, WI 54602/608-782-3020

Langenberg Hat Co., P.O. Box 1860, Washington, MO 63090/800-428-1860; FAX: 314-239-3151

Leatherman Tool Group, Inc., P.O. Box 20595, Portland, OR 97220/503-253-7826; FAX: 503-253-7830

Liberty Trouser Co., 3500 6 Ave S., Birmingham, AL 35222-2406/205-251-9143

L.L. Bean, 386 Main St., Freeport, ME 04032/207-865-3111

MAG Instrument, Inc., 1635 S. Sacramento Ave., Ontario, CA 91761/714-947-1006; FAX: 714-947-3116

Marathon Rubber Prods. Co., Inc., 510 Sherman St., Wausau, WI 54401/715-845-6255

Melton Shirt Co., Inc., 56 Harvester Ave., Batavia, NY 14020/716-343-8750

Millenium Safety Products, P.O. Box 9802-916, Austin, TX 78766/512-346-3876

Molin Industries, Tru-Nord Division, P.O. Box 365, 204 North 9th St., Brainerd, MN 56401/218-829-2870

Nelson/Weather-Rite, 14760 Santa Fe Trail Dr., Lenexa, KS 66215/913-492-3200

Jim Noble Co., 1305 Columbia St., Vancouver, WA 98660/206-695-1309

North Specialty Products, 2664-B Saturn St., Brea, CA 92621/714-524-1665

Northlake Outdoor Footwear, P.O. Box 10, Franklin, TN 37065-0010/615-794-1556; FAX: 615-790-8005

Philip S. Olt Co., P.O. Box 550, 12662 Fifth St., Pekin, IL 61554/309-348-3633; FAX: 309-348-3300

Original Mink Oil, Inc., P.O. Box 20191, 11021 NE Beach St., Portland, OR 97220/503-255-2814, 800-547-5895; FAX: 503-255-2487

Orvis Co., The, Rt. 7, Manchester, VT 05254/802-362-3622 ext. 283; FAX: 802-362-3525

Palsa Outdoor Products, P.O. Box 81336, Lincoln, NE 68501/402-456-9281, 800-456-9281; FAX: 402-488-2321

John Partridge Sales Ltd., Trent Meadows, Rugeley, Staffordshire, WS15 2HS ENGLAND/0889-584438

PAST Sporting Goods, Inc., P.O. Box 1035, Columbia, MO 65205/314-445-9200

Pendleton Woolen Mills, P.O. Box 3030, 220 N.W. Broadway, Portland, OR 97208/503-226-4801

Pointing Dog Journal, Village Press Publications, P.O. Box 968, Dept. PGD, Traverse City, MI 49685/800-272-3246; FAX: 616-946-3289

Porta Blind, Inc., 2700 Speedway, Wichita Falls, TX 76308/800-842-5545

Pro-Mark, Div. of Wells Lamont, 6640 W. Touhy, Chicago, IL 60648/312-647-8200

Pyromid, Inc., 3292 S. Highway 97, Redmond, OR 97786

Randolph Engineering, Inc., 26 Thomas Patten Dr., Randolph, MA 02368/800-541-1405; FAX: 617-986-0337

Ranger Mfg. Co., Inc., 1536 Crescent Dr., Augusta, GA 30919/404-738-3469

Ranging, Inc., Routes 5 & 20, East Bloomfield, NY 14443/716-657-6161

Rattlers Brand, P.O. Box 311, Thomaston, GA 30286/800-652-1341; FAX: 404-647-2742

Red Ball, 100 Factory St., Nashua, NH 03060/603-881-4420

Red River Frontier Outfitters, P.O. Box 241, Dept. GD, Tujunga, CA 91043/818-821-3167

Refrigiwear, Inc., 71 Inip Dr., Inwood, Long Island, NY 11696

Re-Heater, Inc., 15828 S. Broadway, C, Gardena, CA 90248

Rocky Shoes & Boots, 294 Harper St., Nelsonville, OH 45764/800-421-5151, 614-753-1951; FAX: 614-753-4042

Rocky Mountain High Sports Glasses, 8121 N. Central Park Ave., Skokie, IL 60076/708-679-1012; FAX: 708-679-0184

Ruko Products, Inc., P.O. Box 1181, Buffalo, NY 14240-1181/905-874-2707; FAX: 905-826-1353

Rutgers Gun & Boat Center, 127 Raritan Ave., Highland Park, NJ 08904/908-545-4344; FAX: 908-545-6686

Ruvel & Co., Inc., 4128-30 W. Belmont Ave., Chicago, IL 60641/312-286-9494

Safesport Manufacturing Co., 1100 W. 45th Ave., Denver, CO 80211/303-433-6506; FAX: 303-433-4112

San Angelo Sports Products, Inc., 909 W. 14th St., San Angelo, TX 76903/915-655-7126; FAX: 915-653-6720

Savana Sports, Inc., 5763 Ferrier St., Montreal, Quebec, CANADA/514-739-1753; FAX: 514-739-1755

Scansport, Inc., P.O. Box 700, Enfield, NH 03748/603-632-7654

Scotch Hunting Products Co., Inc., 6619 Oak Orchard Rd., Elba, NY 14058/716-757-9958; FAX: 716-757-9066

Servus Footwear Co., 1136 2nd St., Rock Island, IL 61204-3610/309-786-7741; FAX: 309-786-9808

Silencio/Safety Direct, 56 Coney Island Dr., Sparks, NV 89431/800-648-1812, 702-354-4451; FAX: 702-359-1074

Slings 'N Things, Inc., 8909 Bedford Circle, Suite 11, Omaha, NE 68134/402-571-6954; FAX: 402-571-7082

Smith Whetstone Co., Inc., 1700 Sleepy Valley Rd., P.O. Box 5095, Hot Springs, AR 71902-5095/501-321-2244; FAX: 501-321-9232

Sno-Seal (See Atsko, Sno-Seal)

Streamlight, Inc., 1030 W. Germantown Pike, Norristown, PA 19403/215-631-0600

Swanndri New Zealand, 152 Elm Ave., Burlingame, CA 94010/415-347-6158

Teledyne Co., 290 E. Prairie St., Crystal Lake, IL 60014

10-X Products Group, 2915 Lyndon B. Johnson Freeway, Suite 133, Dallas, TX 75234/214-243-4016

Norm Thompson, 18905 NW Thurman St., Portland, OR 97209

T.H.U. Enterprises, Inc., P.O. Box 418, Lederach, PA 19450/215-256-1665; FAX: 215-256-9718

Tink's Safariland Hunting Corp., P.O. Box 244, Madison, GA 30650/404-342-4915

Torel, Inc., 1053 N. South St., P.O. Box 592, Yoakum, TX 77995/512-293-2341; FAX: 512-293-3413

TrailTimer Co., 1992-A Suburban Ave., P.O. Box 19722, St. Paul, MN 55119/612-738-0925

Venus Industries, P.O. Box 246, Sialkot-1, PAKISTAN/FAX: 92 432 85579

Wakina by Pic, 24813 Alderbrook Dr., Santa Clarita, CA 91321/805-295-8194

Walker Shoe Co., P.O. Box 1167, Asheboro, NC 27203-1167/919-625-1380

Walls Industries, P.O. Box 98, Cleburne, TX 76031/817-645-4366

Wideview Scope Mount Corp., 26110 Michigan Ave., Inkster, MI 48141/313-274-1238; FAX: 313-274-2814

Willson Safety Prods. Div., P.O. Box 622, Reading, PA 19603-0622/610-376-6161; FAX: 610-371-7725

Wolverine Boots & Outdoor Footwear Div., Wolverine World Wide, 9341 Courtland Dr., Rockford, MI 49351/616-866-5500

Woolrich Woolen Mills, Mill St., Woolrich, PA 17779/717-769-6464

Wyoming Knife Corp., 101 Commerce Dr., Ft. Collins, CO 80524/303-224-3454

Yellowstone Wilderness Supply, P.O. Box 129, W. Yellowstone, MT 59758/406-646-7613

KNIVES AND KNIFEMAKER'S SUPPLIES— FACTORY AND MAIL ORDER

Adventure 16, Inc., 4620 Alvarado Canyon Rd., San Diego, CA 92120/619-283-6314

African Import Co., 20 Braunecker Rd., Plymouth, MA 02360/508-746-8552

Aitor-Cuchilleria Del Norte, S.A., Izelaieta, 17, 48260 Ermua (Vizcaya), SPAIN/43-17-08-50; FAX: 43-17-00-01

American Import Co., The, 1453 Mission St., San Francisco, CA 94103/415-863-1506; FAX: 415-863-0939

American Target Knives, 1030 Brownwood NW, Grand Rapids, MI 49504/616-453-1998

Aristocrat Knives, 1800 N. Highland Ave. No. 600, Los Angeles, CA 90028/213-461-1065; FAX: 213-461-3598

Art Jewel Enterprises Ltd., Eagle Business Ctr., 460 Randy Rd., Carol Stream, IL 60188/708-260-0400

Atlanta Cutlery Corp., 2143 Gees Mill Rd., Box 839 CIS, Conyers, GA 30207/800-883-0300; FAX: 404-388-0246

B&D Trading Co., Inc., 3935 Fair Hill Rd., Fair Oaks, CA 95628/916-967-9366

Barteaux Machete, 1916 SE 50th Ave., Portland, OR 97215-3238/503-233-5880

Benchmark Knives (See Gerber Legendary Blades)

Beretta U.S.A. Corp., 17601 Beretta Drive, Accokeek, MD 20607/301-283-2191

Blackjack Knives, 1307 W. Wabash, Effingham, IL 62401/217-347-7700; FAX: 217-347-7737

Blue Ridge Knives, Rt. 6, Box 185, Marion, VA 24354/703-783-6143; FAX: 703-783-9298

Boker USA, Inc., 14818 West 6th Ave., Suite #10A, Golden, CO 80401-5045/303-279-5997; FAX: 303-279-5919

Bowen Knife Co., Inc., P.O. Box 590, Blackshear, GA 31516/912-449-4794

Browning Arms Co. (Parts & Service), 3005 Arnold Tenbrook Rd., Arnold, MO 63010-9406/314-287-6800; FAX: 314-287-9751

Brunton U.S.A., 620 E. Monroe Ave., Riverton, WY 82501/307-856-6559; FAX: 307-856-1840

Buck Knives, Inc., 1900 Weld Blvd., El Cajon, CA 92020/619-449-1100; FAX: 619-562-5774

Buster's Custom Knives, P.O. Box 214, Richfield, UT 84701/801-896-5319

CAM Enterprises, 5090 Iron Springs Rd., Box 2, Prescott, AZ 86301/602-776-9640

Camillus Cutlery Co./Western Cutlery Co., 54 Main St., Camillus, NY 13031/315-672-8111; FAX: 315-672-8832

W.R. Case & Sons Cutlery Co., Owens Way, Bradford, PA 16701/814-368-4123; FAX: 814-362-4877

Catoctin Cutlery, P.O. Box 188, Smithsburg, MD 21783/301-824-7416; FAX: 301-824-6138

Chicago Cutlery Co., 1536 Beech St., Terre Haute, IN 47804/800-457-2665

E. Christopher Firearms Co., Inc., Route 128 & Ferry St., Miamitown, OH 45041/513-353-1321

Chas Clements' Custom Leathercraft, 1741 Dallas St., Aurora, CO 80010-2018/303-364-0403

Coast Cutlery Co., 609 SE Ankeny, Portland, OR 97214/503-234-4545

Cold Steel, Inc., 2128 Knoll Dr., Unit D, Ventura, CA 93003/800-255-4716

Coleman Co., Inc., 250 N. St. Francis, Wichita, KS 67201

Colonial Knife Co., P.O. Box 3327, Providence, RI 02909/401-421-1600; FAX: 401-421-2047

Compass Industries, Inc., 104 East 25th St., New York, NY 10010/212-473-2614

R.M. Crawford Co., P.O. Box 277, Everett, PA 15537/814-652-6536; FAX: 814-652-9526

Creative Craftsman, Inc., The, 95 Highway 29 North, P.O. Box 331, Lawrenceville, GA 30246/404-963-2112

Crosman Blades (See Coleman Co., Inc.)

Cutco Cutlery, P.O. Box 810, Olean, NY 14760/716-372-3111

Cutlery Shoppe, 5461 Kendall St., Boise, ID 83706-1248/800-231-1272

Damascus-U.S.A., RR 1, Box 206-A, Tyner, NC 27980/919-221-2010; FAX: 919-221-2009

Dan's Whetstone Co., Inc., 130 Timbs Place, Hot Springs, AR 71913/501-767-1616; FAX: 501-767-9598

Degen Knives, 1800 N. Highland Ave. No. 600, Los Angeles, CA 90028/213-461-1065; FAX: 213-461-3598

Delhi Gun House, 1374 Kashmere Gate, Delhi, INDIA 110 006/(011)237375+239116; FAX: 91-11-2917344

DMT—Diamond Machining Technology, Inc., 85 Hayes Memorial Dr., Marlborough, MA 01752/508-481-5944; FAX: 508-485-3924

EdgeCraft Corp., P.O. Box 3000, Avondale, PA 19311/215-268-0500, 800-342-3255; FAX: 215-268-3545

EK Knife Co., 601 N. Lombardy St., Richmond, VA 23220/804-257-7272

Empire Cutlery Corp., 12 Kruger Ct., Clifton, NJ 07013/201-472-5155; FAX: 201-779-0759

Eze-Lap Diamond Prods., P.O. Box 2229, 15164 Weststate St., Westminster, CA 92683/714-847-1555

Fitz Pistol Grip Co., P.O. Box 610, Douglas City, CA 96024/916-623-4019

Flintlock Muzzle Loading Gun Shop, The, 1238 "G" S. Beach Blvd., Anaheim, CA 92804/714-821-6655

Forrest Tool Co., P.O. Box 768, 44380 Gordon Lane, Mendocino, CA 95460/707-937-2141; FAX: 717-937-1817

Forthofer's Gunsmithing & Knifemaking, 5535 U.S. Hwy 93S, Whitefish, MT 59937-8411/406-862-2674

Fortune Products, Inc., HC04, Box 303, Marble Falls, TX 78654/210-693-6111; FAX: 210-693-6394

Frank Knives, Box 984, Whitefish, MT 59937/406-862-2681; FAX: 406-862-2681

Frost Cutlery Co., P.O. Box 22636, Chattanooga, TN 37422/615-894-6079; FAX: 615-894-9576

Fury Cutlery, 801 Broad Ave., Ridgefield, NJ 07657/201-943-5920; FAX: 201-943-1579

Gerber Legendary Blades, 14200 SW 72nd Ave., Portland, OR 97223/503-639-6161; FAX: 503-684-7008

Golden Age Arms Co., 115 E. High St., Ashley, OH 43003/614-747-2488

Gutmann Cutlery Co., Inc., 120 S. Columbus Ave., Mt. Vernon, NY 10553/914-699-4044

H&B Forge Co., Rt. 2 Geisinger Rd., Shiloh, OH 44878/419-895-1856

Russell Harrington Cutlery, Inc., Subs. of Hyde Mfg. Co., 44 River St., Southbridge, MA 01550/617-765-0201

Hawken Shop, The (See Dayton Traister)

J.A. Henckels Zwillingswerk, Inc., 9 Skyline Dr., Hawthorne, NY 10532/914-592-7370

Hubertus Schneidwarenfabrik, P.O. Box 180 106, D-42626 Solingen, GERMANY/01149-212-59-19-94: FAX: 01149-212-59-19-92

Hunting Classics Ltd., P.O. Box 2089, Gastonia, NC 28053/704-867-1307; FAX: 704-867-0491

George Ibberson (Sheffield) Ltd., 25-31 Allen St., Sheffield, S3 7AW ENGLAND/0742-766123; FAX: 0742-738465

Imperial Schrade Corp., 7 Schrade Ct., Box 7000, Ellenville, NY 12428/914-647-7600

Iron Mountain Knife Co., P.O. Box 2146, Sparks, NY 89432-2146/702-356-3632; FAX: 702-359-2785

J.A. Blades, Inc. (See Christopher Firearms Co., Inc., E.)

Jantz Supply, P.O. Box 584, Davis, OK 73030/405-369-2316; FAX: 405-369-3082

Jenco Sales, Inc., P.O. Box 1000, Manchaca, TX 78652/512-282-2800; FAX: 512-282-7504

Johnson Wood Products, RR #1, Strawberry Point, IA 52076/319-933-4930

Joy Enterprises (See Fury Cutlery)

KA-BAR Knives, 31100 Solon Rd., Solon, OH 44139/216-248-7000; 800-321-9316, ext. 329; FAX: 216-248-8651

Kasenit Co., Inc., 13 Park Ave., Highland Mills, NY 10930/914-928-9595; FAX: 914-928-7292

Kellogg's Professional Products, 325 Pearl St., Sandusky, OH 44870/419-625-6551; FAX: 419-625-6167

Ken's Finn Knives, Rt. 1, Box 338, Republic, MI 49879/906-376-2132

Kershaw Knives, 25300 SW Parkway Ave., Wilsonville, OR 97070/503-682-1966; FAX: 503-682-7168

Knife Importers, Inc., P.O. Box 1000, Manchaca, TX 78652/512-282-6860

Koppco Industries, 1301 Franklin, Lexington, MO 64067/816-259-3239

Koval Knives, 460 D Schrock Rd., Columbus, OH 43229/614-888-6486; FAX: 614-888-8218

Lamson & Goodnow Mfg. Co., 45 Conway St., Shelburne Falls, MA 03170/413-625-6331

Lansky Sharpeners & Crock Stick, P.O. Box 800, Buffalo, NY 14231/716-877-7511; FAX: 716-877-6955

Leatherman Tool Group, Inc., P.O. Box 20595, Portland, OR 97220/503-253-7826; FAX: 503-253-7830

Linder Solingen Knives, 4401 Sentry Dr., Tucker, GA 30084/404-939-6915

L.L. Bean, 386 Main St., Freeport, ME 04032/207-865-3111

Al Mar Knives, Inc., 5755 SW Jean Rd., Suite 101, Lake Oswego, OR 97035/503-635-9229

Matthews Cutlery, 4401 Sentry Dr., Tucker, GA 30084

Molin Industries, Tru-Nord Division, P.O. Box 365, 204 North 9th St., Brainerd, MN 56401/218-829-2870

Mountain State Muzzleloading Supplies, Box 154-1, Rt. 2, Williamstown, WV 26187/304-375-3737; FAX: 304-375-3737

R. Murphy Co., Inc., 13 Groton-Harvard Rd., P.O. Box 376, Ayer, MA 01432/617-772-3481

Normark Corp., 1710 E. 78th St., Minneapolis, MN 55423/612-869-3291

North American Specialties, 25442 Trabuco Rd., 105-328, Lake Forest, CA 92630/714-837-4867

Outdoor Edge Cutlery Corp., 2888 Bluff St., Suite 130, Boulder, CO 80301/303-530-3855; FAX: 303-530-3855

Plaza Cutlery, Inc., 3333 Bristol, #161, South Coast Plaza, Costa Mesa, CA 92626/714-549-3932

Precise International, 15 Corporate Dr., Orangeburg, NY 10962/914-365-3500

Queen Cutlery Co., 507 Chestnut St., Titusville, PA 16354/800-222-5233

R&C Knives & Such, P.O. Box 1047, Manteca, CA 95336/209-239-3722

Randall-Made Knives, P.O. Box 1988, Orlando, FL 32802/407-855-8075

Ravell Ltd., 289 Diputacion St., 08009, Barcelona SPAIN

Wayne Reno, 2808 Stagestop Rd., Jefferson, CO 80456/719-836-3452

Ruko Products, Inc., P.O. Box 1181, Buffalo, NY 14240-1181/905-874-2707; FAX: 905-826-1353

A.G. Russell Knives, Inc., 1705 Hwy. 71B North, Springdale, AR 72764/501-751-7341

Safesport Manufacturing Co., 1100 W. 45th Ave., Denver, CO 80211/303-433-6506; FAX: 303-433-4112

Scansport, Inc., P.O. Box 700, Enfield, NH 03748/603-632-7654

Mike Schiffman, 8233 S. Crystal Springs, McCammon, ID 83250/208-254-9114

Bob Schrimsher's Custom Knifemaker's Supply, P.O. Box 308, Emory, TX 75440/903-473-3330; FAX: 903-473-2235

Sheffield Knifemakers Supply, P.O. Box 141, Deland, FL 32721/904-775-6453; FAX: 904-774-5754

Austin Sheridan USA, Inc., P.O. Box 577, Durham, CT 06422

Smith & Wesson, 2100 Roosevelt Ave., Springfield, MA 01102/413-781-8300

Jesse W. Smith Saddlery, 3601 E. Boone Ave., Spokane, WA 99202-4501/509-325-0622

Smith Whetstone Co., Inc., 1700 Sleepy Valley Rd., P.O. Box 5095, Hot Springs, AR 71902-5095/501-321-2244; FAX: 501-321-9232

Soque River Knives, P.O. Box 880, Clarkesville, GA 30523/706-754-8500; FAX: 706-754-7263

Spyderco, Inc., P.O. Box 800, Golden, CO 80402/800-525-7770

Stone Enterprises Ltd., Rt. 609, P.O. Box 335, Wicomico Church, VA 22579/804-580-5114; FAX: 804-580-8421

Swiss Army Knives, Inc., 151 Long Hill Crossroads, 37 Canal St., Shelton, CT 06484/800-243-4032

T.F.C. S.p.A., Via G. Marconi 118, B, Villa Carcina, Brescia 25069, ITALY/030-881271; FAX: 030-881826

Traditions, P.O. Box 235, Deep River, CT 06417/203-526-9555; FAX: 203-526-4564

Tru-Balance Knife Co., 2155 Tremont Blvd. NW, Grand Rapids, MI 49504/616-453-3679

United Cutlery Corp., 1425 United Blvd., Sevierville, TN 37862/615-428-2532

Utica Cutlery Co., 820 Noyes St., Utica, NY 13503/315-733-4663

Valor Corp., 5555 NW 36th Ave., Miami, FL 33142/305-633-0127

Venus Industries, P.O. Box 246, Sialkot-1, PAKISTAN/FAX: 92 432 85579

Walt's Custom Leather, Walt Whinnery, 1947 Meadow Creek Dr., Louisville, KY 40218/502-458-4361

Washita Mountain Whetstone Co., P.O. Box 378, Lake Hamilton, AR 71951/501-525-3914

Rudolf Weber Jr., P.O. Box 160106, D-5650 Solingen, GERMANY/0212-592136

Wenoka/Seastyle, P.O. Box 10969, Riviera Beach, FL 33419/407-845-6155; FAX: 407-842-4247

Whinnery, Walt (See Walt's Custom Leather)

Wostenholm (See Ibberson [Sheffield] Ltd., George)

Wyoming Knife Corp., 101 Commerce Dr., Ft. Collins, CO 80524/303-224-3454

MUZZLE-LOADING GUNS, BARRELS AND EQUIPMENT

Accuracy Unlimited, 7479 S. DePew St., Littleton, CO 80123

Ackerman & Co., 16 Cortez St., Westfield, MA 01085/413-568-8008

Luther Adkins, 1292 E. McKay Rd., Shelbyville, IN 46176-9353/317-392-3795

All American Bullets, 889 Beatty St., Medford, OR 97501/503-770-5649

Allen Mfg., 6449 Hodgson Rd., Circle Pines, MN 55014/612-429-8231

American Pioneer Video, P.O. Box 50049, owling Green, KY 42102-2649/800-743-4675

Anderson Manufacturing Co., Inc., P.O. Box 2640, 2741 N. Crosby Rd., Oak Harbor, WA 98277/206-675-7300; FAX: 206-675-3939

Armi San Paolo, via Europa 172-A, I-25062 Concesio, 030-2751725 (BS) ITALY

Armoury, Inc., The, Rt. 202, Box 2340, New Preston, CT 06777/203-868-0001

Armsport, Inc., 3950 NW 49th St., Miami, FL 33142/305-635-7850; FAX: 305-633-2877

Barton, Michael D. (See Tiger-Hunt)

Bauska Barrels, 105 9th Ave. W., Kalispell, MT 59901/406-752-7706

Beauchamp & Son, Inc., 160 Rossiter Rd., Richmond, MA 01254/413-698-3822; FAX: 413-698-3866

Beaver Lodge, 9245 16th Ave. SW, Seattle, WA 98106, 06-763-1698

John Bentley, 128-D Watson Dr., Turtle Creek, PA 15145

W.E. Birdsong & Assoc., 4832 Windermere, Jackson, MS 39206/601-366-8270

Blackhawk East, Box 2274, Loves Park, IL 61131

Blackhawk Mountain, Box 210, Conifer, CO 80433

Blackhawk West, Box 285, Hiawatha, KS 66434

Blake Affiliates, Box 133, Roscoe, IL 61073

Blount, Inc., Sporting Equipment Div., 2299 Snake River Ave., P.O. Box 856, Lewiston, ID 83501/800-627-3640, 208-746-2351

Blue and Gray Products, Inc. (See Ox-Yoke Originals, Inc.)

Bridgers Best, P.O. Box 1410, Berthoud, CO 80513

Buckskin Machine Works, A. Hunkeler, 3235 S. 358th St., Auburn, WA 98001/206-927-5412

Buffalo Bullet Co., Inc., 12637 Los Nietos Rd. Unit A, Santa Fe Springs, CA 90670/310-944-0322; FAX: 310-944-5054

R.W. Burgess & Son Gunsmiths, P.O. Box 3364, Warner Robins, GA 31099/912-328-7487

Butler Creek Corp., 290 Arden Dr., Belgrade, MT 59714/800-423-8327, 406-388-1356; FAX: 406-388-7204

Cache La Poudre Rifleworks, 140 N. College, Ft. Collins, CO 80524/303-482-6913

Camas Hot Springs Mfg., P.O. Box 639, Hot Springs, MT 59845/406-741-3756

Cape Outfitters, Rt. 2, Box 437C, Cape Girardeau, MO 63701/314-335-4103; FAX: 314-335-1555

Cash Mfg. Co., Inc., P.O. Box 130, 201 S. Klein Dr., Waunakee, WI 53597-0130/608-849-5664

CenterMark, P.O. Box 4066, Parnassus Station, New Kensington, PA 15068/412-335-1319

Jim Chambers Flintlocks Ltd., Rt. 1, Box 513-A, Candler, NC 28715/704-667-8361

Chopie Mfg., Inc., 700 Copeland Ave., LaCrosse, WI 54603/608-784-0926

Cimarron Arms, P.O. Box 906, Fredericksburg, TX 78624-0906/210-997-9090; FAX: 210-997-0802

Cogar's Gunsmithing, P.O. Box 755, Houghton Lake, MI 48629/517-422-4591

Colt Blackpowder Arms Co., 5 Centre Market Place, New York, NY 10013/212-925-2159; FAX: 212-966-4986

Cousin Bob's Mountain Products, 7119 Ohio River Blvd., Ben Avon, PA 15202/412-766-5114; FAX: 412-766-5114

Cumberland Arms, Rt. I, Box 1150 Shafer Rd., Blantons Chapel, Manchester, TN 37355

Cumberland Knife & Gun Works, 5661 Bragg Blvd., Fayetteville, NC 28303/919-867-0009

CVA, 5988 Peachtree Corners East, Norcross, GA 30071/404-449-4687; FAX: 404-242-8546

Homer L. Dangler, Box 254, Addison, MI 49220/517-547-6745

Leonard Day & Sons, Inc., P.O. Box 122, Flagg Hill Rd., Heath, MA 01346/413-337-8369

Dayton Traister, P.O. Box 593, Oak Harbor, WA 98277/206-679-4657; FAX:206-675-1114

deHaas Barrels, RR #3, Box 77, Ridgeway, MO 64481/816-872-6308

Delhi Gun House, 1374 Kashmere Gate, Delhi, INDIA 110 006/(011)237375+239116; FAX: 91-11-2917344

Denver Arms, Ltd., P.O. Box 4640, Pagosa Springs, CO 81157/303-731-2295

Dixie Gun Works, Hwy. 51 South, Union City, TN 38261/901-885-0700, order 800-238-6785; FAX: 901-885-0440

Dixon Muzzleloading Shop, Inc., RD 1, Box 175, Kempton, PA 19529/215-756-6271

Don Eades' Muzzleloader Builders' Supply, 201-J Beasley Dr., Franklin, TN 37064/615-791-1731

Ed's Gun House, Rt. 1, Box 62, Minnesota City, MN 55959/507-689-2925

EMF Co., Inc., 1900 E. Warner Ave. Suite 1-D, Santa Ana, CA 92705/714-261-6611; FAX: 714-956-0133

Euroarms of America, Inc., 208 E. Piccadilly St., Winchester, VA 22601/703-662-1863; FAX: 703-662-4464

Eutaw Co., Inc., The, P.O. Box 608, U.S. Hwy. 176 West, Holly Hill, SC 29059/803-496-3341

Andy Fautheree, P.O. Box 4607, Pagosa Springs, CO 81157/303-731-5003